ORACLE SQL

Bijoy Bordoloi

*Southern Illinois University
Edwardsville*

Douglas Bock

*Southern Illinois University
Edwardsville*

Prentice
Hall

UPPER SADDLE RIVER, NEW JERSEY 07458

Library of Congress Cataloging-in-Publication Data

Bordoloi, Bijoy
   Oracle SQL / Bijoy Bordoloi, Douglas Bock.
     p. cm.
    ISBN 0-13-101138-3 (pbk.)
     1. SQL (Computer program language) 2. Oracle (Computer file) I. Bock, Douglas
Brian II. Title.

    QA76.73.S67 B57 2003
    005.75′85—dc21   200204566

AVP/Executive Editor: Bob Horan
Project Manager (Editorial): Lori Cerreto
Editorial Assistant: Maat Van Uitert
VP/Publisher: Natalie Anderson
Media Project Manager: Joan Waxman
Senior Marketing Manager: Sharon K. Turkovich
Marketing Assistant: Danielle Torio
Managing Editor (Production): John Roberts
Production Editor: Maureen Wilson
Production Assistant: Joe DeProspero
Permissions Coordinator: Suzanne Grappi
Associate Director, Manufacturing: Vincent Scelta
Production Manager: Arnold Vila
Manufacturing Buyer: Michelle Klein
Cover Design: Bruce Kenselaar
Cover Illustration/Photo: Gettyimages/PhotoDisc
Composition and Full-Service Project Management: Rainbow Graphics
Project Manager: Rhonda Peters
Printer/Binder: Maple Vail

Credits and acknowledgments borrowed from other sources and reproduced, with permission, in this textbook appear on appropriate page within text.

Pearson Education LTD.
Pearson Education Australia PTY, Limited
Pearson Education Singapore, Pte. Ltd
Pearson Education North Asia Ltd.
Pearson Education, Canada, Ltd.
Pearson Educación de Mexico, S.A. de C.V.
Pearson Education–Japan
Pearson Education Malaysia, Pte. Ltd.

10 9 8 7 6 5 4 3 2 1
ISBN 0-13-101138-3

BRIEF CONTENTS

CONTENTS

PREFACE

The Structured Query Language (SQL) is one of the foundation building blocks of relational database technology. SQL is taught within schools of business and computer science departments in two-year, four-year, and graduate degree programs. Regardless of the level of instruction, students studying in the computing field need to acquire SQL skills. Our book provides fundamental skills in SQL with additional coverage of Oracle's implementation of SQL. While we use Oracle as a database management systems (DBMS) platform for teaching the material, each chapter's concept questions and coding exercises, specifically in Chapters 3 through 8, that cover the core commands for data retrieval, are applicable to any standard SQL implementation.

THE COURSE

SQL is taught using many different approaches, depending on the collegiate level of the students. This book can serve as a main text for a stand-alone course on SQL or as a supplemental text for either an introductory DBMS course or an advanced course on information systems (IS) implementation.

USING OUR BOOK AS A MAIN TEXT

At the junior college level, SQL is often taught as a single course separate from the normal course in DBMS. Our book meets the needs of this type of course and can serve as the primary instructional text for the course. Instructors will find that the book fits easily into a single term. We suggest covering the chapters in the order in which they are presented, especially Chapters 1 through 9, which comprise the core subject matter. You may alternatively reverse the order of Chapters 6 and 7. Chapters 10, 11, and 12 are *overview* chapters and vary in terms of the technical background required of students. Hence, these chapters can be optionally covered.

USING OUR BOOK AS A SUPPLEMENTAL TEXT

Many baccalaureate (BA, BS) and masters programs (MS, MBA) within business schools (management information systems) and science/engineering schools (computer science degrees) offer a single introductory course in DBMS and include coverage of SQL as a topic within the course. The database textbooks used most often for these courses provide limited coverage of SQL. Instructors seeking more depth of coverage for SQL will find that this text provides the supplementary instruction that students will need in order to learn SQL well. Depending on the desired technical orientation of the course, you may wish to allocate considerable time to SQL, ranging from one-fifth to even one-third of the course duration. When the instructional focus is on *data retrieval,* Chapters 3 through 8 provide a focus on writing SQL queries. The database creation process described in Chapter 2 can be accomplished by having students download the SQL scripts necessary to create the databases used in the end-of-chapter and end-of-book exercises.

This text can also meet the needs of instructors seeking a supplementary SQL book that supports "self-study" for IS implementation and "capstone" IS project courses. Our book provides an approach that facilitates self-study complete with exercises and solutions to the exercises, while requiring minimal student assistance from instructors.

PEDAGOGY

This book focuses on teaching standard ANSI SQL; however, the textbook is "flavored" with additional examples of the supplemental commands provided in the Oracle implementation of SQL. Hence, most of the SQL concepts and commands covered in the book, with the exception of Chapters 9 through 12, which are primarily specific to Oracle, are applicable to DBMS software that follow the ANSI SQL standard, including DB2, SQL Server, and SYBASE, among others. We believe that an approach that also covers Oracle extensions to SQL is important because of the wide adoption of the Oracle relational DBMS product in industry and academic institutions.

SHORT CHAPTERS

Pedagogically, students often learn complex technical materials better when the material is taught in "bite-size" chunks. This enables students to assimilate the material better. Consequently, we have divided the various topics into short chapters. The typical chapter can be completed in one or two settings, depending on the length of a class period.

FEATURES AND USAGE ("PROBLEM SOLVING") APPROACH

Students learn more by *doing* than by *listening*. This book emphasizes a *doing* approach. At first, the text focuses on teaching students the *features* of SQL commands. This approach is necessary for students who are new to the topic in order to build their basic SQL knowledge. Following this, the text emphasizes *usage* of SQL commands. The *usage* focus is based on management questions that typically arise as part of the management decision-making process. This puts students in situations similar to those posed to computer technical support staff members in operational companies and organizations. The text presents management questions and gives examples of how

SQL can be used to provide the data needed to support the decision-making task. This pedagogical approach enables students to learn to match SQL coding techniques to different types of management questions. Hence, relevant management questions precede most query examples in the text.

EXAMPLES AND EXERCISES

Each chapter provides numerous examples that initially present and then reinforce the concepts through the use of repetition. As mentioned above, we focus on the *features* and *usage* approach in presenting the material. The book provides numerous end-of-chapter exercises. Additionally, there are corresponding end-of-book exercises to supplement each chapter and to provide additional opportunities for instructors to reinforce the concepts presented in a comprehensive manner. As you proceed through the book, you will find that many of the end-of-chapter exercises reinforce concepts taught in earlier chapters. This requires students to integrate material learned earlier in the course with new material as they progress through the book.

Solutions to the odd-numbered end-of-chapter and end-of-book exercises are provided to facilitate a student self-study and self-assessment of their learning. The solutions to the remaining exercises are available through the book's Web site for instructors only.

SAMPLE DATABASES

Chapter examples and exercises are based on two separate sample databases. The "Company" database provides the majority of the coding examples within the body of the text of each chapter. This database is also used for the end-of-chapter exercises. The database consists of six entities and eight relationships. The Oracle script to generate the Company database is included in the text. The script can also be downloaded from the book's Web site.

The "Riverbend Hospital" database is somewhat more complex. This database has 14 tables and 14 relationships and is used to provide end-of-book exercises. This enables students to complete additional work in a self-taught mode. Additionally, instructors may use the end-of-book exercises to assess student learning of topics covered in the chapters as material for quizzes and examinations. The Oracle script for this database is not included in the text. It can be downloaded by instructors only from the book's Web site.

CHAPTER OVERVIEW

In Chapter 1, students are introduced to some basic relational database concepts. This serves two purposes. First, it ensures that all students are familiar with the fundamental relational database concepts, the knowledge of which is essential to learn SQL well. Second, it provides an opportunity to introduce the primary database used for end-of-chapter exercises throughout the book. For students who have already studied the fundamentals of relational technology, this chapter serves as a brief review.

Chapter 2 teaches students to define and create their own tables as part of the example database. The students are provided step-by-step instructions to follow. By defining and creating their own critical elements of a database such as tables, fields within tables, datatypes, primary keys, foreign keys, integrity constraints, and indexes, the relational database principles covered in Chapter 1 are practiced and reinforced.

Chapters 3 through 8 cover all of the primary components of SQL. The topics covered include querying single tables, multiple tables ("joins"), nested subqueries, correlated subqueries, common functions, views, synonyms, sequences, and other topics.

The last four chapters are chapters that we believe are important in teaching students how SQL may be used in an operational environment. Chapter 9 provides comprehensive, yet succinct coverage of SQL*Plus. The topics covered in this chapter teach students to write interactive queries and format the results of their queries in a business-like report. Chapter 10 introduces additional Oracle *functions* that can add power to queries. Chapter 11 is an overview of embedded SQL. The chapter gives examples of SQL code embedded in different languages including Visual Basic (6.0), Visual Basic.NET, and COBOL. This chapter does not teach embedded SQL coding; rather, it provides students with familiarity about how SQL is incorporated within procedural logic in database applications. Finally, Chapter 12 introduces students to database administration (DBA) concepts and activities for maintaining an Oracle database.

SUPPLEMENTS

The book is supplemented by a Web site that provides the Oracle script to accompany the "Company" database for students, as well as the following password-protected supplementary materials to facilitate instruction:

1. Suggested syllabi for 2-year, 4-year, and graduate level programs
2. PowerPoint slides for all chapters
3. Complete Oracle scripts for generating both sample databases (Riverbend Hospital Case script for instructors only)
4. Solutions to all end-of-chapter and end-of-book exercises to facilitate easy development of examinations and quizzes.

ACKNOWLEDGMENTS

The origin of this book is our SQL class notes that we have modified over many years based on student feedback. It is their feedback that shaped the contents, structure, and pedagogy of this book. While we are thankful to all our students, we are specifically thankful to Nathan Boehler, Osman Hyder, and Susan Briner. Next, we are grateful to our reviewers for their insights and detailed comments and suggestions. Our reviewers include the following:

Betty Glenn, Roane State Community College
Connie Hagmann, Kansas State University
Sarah Jones, Santa Fe Community College, Gainesville, Florida

Edd Joyner, University of Tennessee at Martin
David Kamper, Northeastern Illinois University
Dan McCuaig, Lower Columbia College
David Olsen, Utah State University
Michael Riha, Thomas Nelson Community College
Terry Ryan, Claremont Graduate University
Randall Sexton, Southwestern Missouri State University
Craig Shaw, Central Community College
Cherie Sherman, Ramapo College of New Jersey
Amy Wilson, Devry Atlanta

We extend our special thanks to the staff and associates of Prentice Hall for their support and guidance throughout this project. In particular, we would like to thank Robert F. Horan, Executive Editor of Prentice Hall, who guided us through this project. We also extend special thanks to Mary Ellen Bock, R.N., for her support and guidance in creating the Riverbend Hospital database used for end-of-book exercises.

This book is dedicated to our wives and children for their support.

INTRODUCTION

Welcome to the study of the *Structured Query Language,* or simply SQL as it is more commonly known. SQL, pronounced Sequel or simply S-Q-L, is a computer programming language used for *querying* relational databases following a *nonprocedural* approach. When you extract information from a database using SQL, this is termed *querying* the database. The term *nonprocedural* means that you can extract information by simply telling the system what information you need without telling the system how to perform the data retrieval. At this point in your computing career, you may not have a complete understanding of what a relational database is. This chapter will teach you some fundamental relational database concepts. Our main objective is to aid you in learning the fundamentals of SQL—one of the primary languages for interacting with databases. SQL is an easy language to learn in terms of writing queries, but it has considerable complexity because it is a very powerful language with a simple vocabulary of commands. You will master the fundamentals of SQL and build your skill set one chapter at a time.

OBJECTIVES

In this chapter, you will study basic concepts about SQL with a focus on how SQL is used with Oracle Corporation's relational database management system. This chapter has the following learning objectives:

- Develop a basic understanding of what a relational database is.
- Learn the general capabilities of a relational database management system.
- Familiarize with the features of the Oracle relational database management system.
- Learn to use SQL*Plus.
- Learn the basic relational operations including the selection, projection, and join operations.
- Familiarize with the basic syntax of the SELECT statement.
- Learn the SQL naming conventions.

DATA AND INFORMATION

Companies and organizations, both large and small, create and manage large quantities of information. Information is derived from raw facts known as *data*. Data has little meaning or usefulness to managers unless it is organized in some logical manner. One of the most efficient ways to organize and manage data is through use of a database management system (DBMS). A DBMS is a very complex software package. Several software vendors produce and sell competing DBMS products including Oracle Corporation, IBM, and Microsoft. Some of the more common DBMS products are the Oracle RDBMS, IBM's DB2, Microsoft's SQL Server, and Microsoft's desktop single-user DBMS named Microsoft Access.

A DBMS provides both systems development professionals and information system users with an easy-to-use interface to their organization's database. Two types of data are stored within a database:

- *User data:* Business-related data stored by an organization. User data includes all information relevant to an organization's computer software applications that aid in running and managing the organization's various business operations.
- *System data:* Data the database system needs to manage user data and to manage itself. This is also termed *metadata,* or data about data. System data includes information such as the maximum allowable characters that can be entered when storing an employee's name.

RELATIONAL DATABASE

A database is an integrated unit of collected data. A database is typically stored to an online permanent storage device such as a disk drive unit. The DBMS interfaces with a computer operating system in order to store and retrieve data to and from a database. In order for data to be manipulated and converted into useful information, the data must be retrieved from disk storage and moved into computer memory. In a typical client–server computing environment, this means that data stored on one or more *server* computers is moved across a computer network to *client* computers that are used by employees of the organization. The network may be either a local or wide area network.

The most common type of DBMS software in use today is termed a *relational* DBMS or RDBMS. Conceptually, a relational database stores data in the form of tables, such as that shown in Figure 1.1. A *table* is defined as a collection of *rows* and *columns*. The tables are formally known as *relations;* this is where the relational database gets its name. However, it is actually fairly rare to hear someone refer to tables as relations. Usually, the term *tables* is used.

As you can see in Figure 1.1, rows represent records and columns represent fields in a file-processing sense. The DBMS enables you to access any combination of rows and columns through use of a special data manipulation language or data querying language such as SQL.

A relational database provides the ability to store and access data in a manner consistent with a defined data model known as the *relational model*. E. F. Codd developed the relational model in 1970. This model consists of a number of guidelines for

TABLE NAME   COLUMN NAME   COLUMN ALIAS NAME

| EMPLOYEE | | | | | |
EMP_SSN	EMP_LAST_NAME	EMP_DATE_	EMP_SALARY	Gender	Department
999666666	Bordoloi	10-NOV-67	55000	M	1
999555555	Joyner	20-JUN-71	43000	F	3
999444444	Zhu	08-DEC-75	43000	M	7
999887777	Markis	19-JUL-78	25000	F	3
999222222	Amin	29-MAR-69	25000	M	3
999111111	Bock	01-SEP-55	30000	M	7
999333333	Joshi	15-SEP-72	38000	M	7
999888888	Prescott	31-JUL-72	25000	F	7

ROW

PRIMARY KEY   COLUMN   SECONDARY KEY

FIGURE 1.1

recording data in a relational database, together with a number of operators that are used to manipulate the information. The characteristics of a relational database are:

- *It is data driven, not design driven.* This means that the design of a database will tend to be stable over a long time period because the types of data that an organization stores over time are very stable. Also, a database designed with a data-driven approach will not have duplicate data stored—older, design-driven approaches often caused organizations to build information systems that could not communicate among themselves well because of data definition inconsistencies.
- *The data are self-describing.* This means that names for tables and columns in tables are meaningful.
- *Consistency of data values is maintained among all applications.* With older technologies, a customer's address might be stored by an organization in two different data files. If the customer address is changed in one file but not the other, the data values become inconsistent. Relational databases minimize the duplicate storage of data.
- *Rules are defined and enforced regarding how data values are stored.* This means that the data stored in the database will be valid (termed *data integrity*). As an example, an organization may have a rule that no hourly wage can exceed $75/hour. Another example of data integrity is the enforcement of a restriction that states that no customer sales order can exist in the database without a corresponding customer record.

The advantage of a relational database is that it is generally easier to use and has a higher degree of data independence than older database technologies. Data independence is the ability to make changes in a database structure without having to make changes in the computer application programs that access a database. Examples of computer application programs include programs that enable a system user to store new sales order information or information about new customer accounts.

DATABASE MANAGEMENT SYSTEMS (DBMS)

A database management system (DBMS) manages the data in a database. It acts as a layer between the user and the database and enables users to interact with the database. A DBMS is a collection of programs that enables users to create and maintain a database. A DBMS is a general-purpose software system that facilitates the processes of defining, constructing, and maintaining databases for various applications. Without a DBMS, it is impossible to retrieve or look at data, update data, or delete obsolete data in a database. It is the DBMS alone that knows how and where the data are stored on an organization's permanent storage devices. A DBMS also enables data to be shared; information system users and managers can get more *information value* from the same amount of data when data sharing occurs.

A DBMS is complete software for the management of a database. It provides the following services:

- Data definition for defining and storing all of the objects that comprise a database such as tables and indexes.
- Data maintenance for maintaining rows (records) for each table in a database.
- Data manipulation for inserting, updating, and sorting data in a database.
- Data display for optionally providing some method of displaying the data for the user.
- Data integrity for ensuring the accuracy of the data.
- Data security for ensuring that only authorized information system users can access specific pieces of data.
- Database backup and recovery to automate the backup of important organizational data and to support recovery operations in the event of some type of systems failure.

ORACLE'S RELATIONAL DBMS

A relational database is implemented through the use of a Relational Database Management System (RDBMS). An RDBMS performs all the basic functions of the DBMS software mentioned above along with a multitude of other functions that make the relational model easier to understand and to implement. One of the most important features of an RDBMS is that it provides services that allow information systems professionals to change the structure of a database easily.

Oracle Corporation's RDBMS is one of the most widely used RDBMS products. It is widely used because it is a powerful data management product, and because Oracle Corporation provides versions of the Oracle RDBMS for virtually every kind of computer—from PCs and Macintoshes to minicomputers and giant mainframes. We will simply refer to the Oracle RDBMS as *Oracle*. Oracle software functions almost identically on all computer platforms, large or small. Therefore, an information system professional or system user who learns skills using one type of computer can easily transfer these skills to the use of Oracle on another computer. This fact makes knowledgeable Oracle users and developers very much in demand, and makes Oracle knowledge and skills very portable. The significant features of Oracle are:

- *Security mechanisms.* Oracle's sophisticated security mechanisms control access to sensitive data through an assortment of privileges, for example, the privilege to read or write specific information within a database.
- *Backup and recovery.* Oracle's sophisticated backup and recovery programs minimize data loss and downtime if problems arise.
- *Space management.* Oracle's flexible space management capabilities allow allocation of disk space for storage. These capabilities also control subsequent allocations by instructing Oracle on how much space to set aside for future requirements.
- *Open connectivity.* Oracle's open connectivity functionality provides uninterrupted access to the database throughout the day. It also provides open connectivity to and from other vendors' software.
- *Tools and applications.* Oracle supports a wide range of development tools, end-user query tools, and off-the-shelf applications that are used to model business processes and data and to generate program language code automatically.

SQL AND ORACLE'S SQL*PLUS

RDBMS users manipulate data through the use of a special *data manipulation language.* Database structures are defined through the use of a *data definition language.* The commands that system users execute in order to store and retrieve data can be entered at a terminal with an RDBMS interface by typing the commands, or entered through use of some type of graphical interface. The DBMS then processes the commands.

SQL is the most popular database language and has commands that enable it to be used for both the manipulation and definition of relational databases because of its English-based syntax. Oracle was one of the first companies to release RDBMS software that used an English-based structured query language. All of Oracle's data access and manipulation tools are firmly based on the current American National Standards Institute (ANSI) version of SQL.

SQL is a comprehensive database language. Prior to SQL, there were no standard data access languages. IBM developed an SQL relational database interface in the late 1970s. The ANSI and the International Standards Organization (ISO) both adopted SQL as the standard language for relational database management access. SQL has increased in popularity because programming knowledge is not a necessity for SQL users.

SQL is used by Oracle for all interaction with the database. SQL statements fall into the two major categories noted below:

- *Data Definition Language (DDL):* A set of SQL commands that create and define objects in a database, storing their definitions in a data dictionary. An example DDL command is the CREATE TABLE command. DDL allows the user to create, drop, and alter a database object, and to grant and revoke privileges on a database object.

- *Data Manipulation Language (DML):* A set of SQL commands that allow users to manipulate the data in a database. An example DML command is the INSERT command. DML allows the user to insert, update, delete, and select data in a database.

SQL is basically a free format language. This means that there are no particular spacing rules that must be used when typing an SQL command. In addition, SQL's vocabulary is rather limited. Because of the limited vocabulary, SQL is relatively easy to learn.

Earlier, we mentioned that SQL is a *nonprocedural language.* Procedural languages such as COBOL or C++ require a computer programmer to specify in detail the steps that are required to complete a programming task. A typical procedural program may consist of hundreds of lines of coding instructions. A nonprocedural language requires you to specify only the task for the DBMS to complete—you do not have to write detailed programming instructions. Nonprocedural programs tend to be very short. You also do not need to know how data are physically stored in terms of the storage format in order to use SQL. The DBMS converts or *parses* SQL commands that you write and completes the task of retrieving or storing data. However, you do need to understand the logical database structure. For example, you need to know the table and column names that store and refer to organizational data. You will learn to create tables including the specification of table and column names in Chapter 2.

SQL*Plus provides the primary interface used by database administrators, application programmers and analysts, and other information technology professionals who want to use the Oracle DBMS. SQL*Plus provides a full implementation of ANSI standard SQL. Additionally, it provides numerous extensions that you can use to complete special tasks such as describing the logical structure of a table. You can use SQL*Plus to query a table, define table and column structures, and manipulate data by inserting, updating, and deleting rows of data. Extensive online help is also available. SQL*Plus also includes various Oracle-specific features that can help you create both monitor screen and printed reports. These features enable you to format the way that output is presented to a monitor screen or printed report. These features extend the capabilities of standard SQL. Through SQL*Plus users can:

- Enter, edit, store, retrieve, and run SQL commands and PL/SQL blocks. PL/SQL blocks are small programs written in the procedural language version of SQL. PL/SQL is an advanced programming language that includes the ability to write programs that process data procedurally as do languages such as C++ and Visual Basic.NET.
- Format, perform calculations on, store, and print query results in the form of reports.
- List column definitions for any table.
- Access and copy data between SQL databases.
- Send messages to and accept responses from an information system user.

RELATIONAL OPERATIONS

SQL operations can create new tables, insert data rows into tables, update table rows, delete table rows, and query tables to display data stored therein. The remainder of this chapter focuses on the concept of querying tables and begins an exploration of the use of SQL*Plus to write simple SQL queries.

The SELECT statement is used primarily to write queries that extract information from database tables. Remember that a database is a collection of related tables, with each table being comprised of rows and columns. The power of the SELECT statement comes from its ability to combine data from many tables to produce output in the form of a *result table.* Consider the SELECT statement shown in SQL Example 1.1 and the result table that is produced. Here, the SELECT statement queries the *employee* table and *selects* values from two columns named *emp_ssn* and *emp_last_name.*

```
/* SQL Example 1.1 */
SELECT emp_ssn, emp_last_name
FROM employee;

EMP_SSN         EMP_LAST_NAME
--------        ------------
999666666       Bordoloi
999555555       Joyner
999444444       Zhu
more rows will be displayed . . .
```

For now, you do not need to worry about the syntax or format for the SELECT statement. Note that the *result table* is in tabular format with columns and rows. Each column has the column name as the heading. Oracle will dutifully display each row in the table. Later, you will learn how to limit the display to a subset of the rows from a table. You will also learn to write SELECT statements that can include columns from more than one table. The ability to select specific rows and columns from one or more tables is referred to as the fundamental relational operations, and there are three of these operations: ***select, project,*** and ***join.***

Select Operation

A select operation selects a subset of rows (records) in a table (relation) that satisfy a selection condition. The subset can range from no rows, if none of the rows satisfy the selection condition, to all rows in a table. The SELECT statement in SQL Example 1.2 selects a subset of rows through use of a WHERE clause. The result table displays only rows that satisfy the condition of the WHERE clause. Chapter 3 covers the WHERE clause in detail.

```
/* SQL Example 1.2 */
SELECT emp_ssn, emp_first_name
FROM employee
WHERE emp_ssn = '999111111';

EMP_SSN         EMP_FIRST_NAME
--------        ------------
999111111       Douglas
```

Since each employee has a unique Social Security number (*emp_ssn*), SQL Example 1.2 selects a subset of exactly one row. Of course, if none of the employees has a Social Security number matching that specified in the WHERE clause, then the result table will not display any rows.

PROJECT OPERATION

A project operation selects only certain columns (fields) from a table. The result table has a subset of the available columns and can include anything from a single column to all available columns. SQL Example 1.3 selects a subset of columns from the *employee* table, specifically each employee's Social Security number, first name, and last name. Chapter 3 covers project operations in detail.

```
/* SQL Example 1.3 */
SELECT emp_ssn, emp_first_name, emp_last_name
FROM employee;

EMP_SSN         EMP_FIRST_NAME       EMP_LAST_NAME
---------       -------------        -----------
999666666       Bijoy                Bordoloi
999555555       Suzanne              Joyner
999444444       Waiman               Zhu
more rows will be displayed . . .
```

JOIN OPERATION

A join operation combines data from two or more tables based on one or more ***common column values.*** Consider the *employee* and *department* tables depicted in Figure 1.2. We know that a typical company may be organized into departments. Employees are assigned to work in a single department, and each department may have more than one employee.

FIGURE 1.2

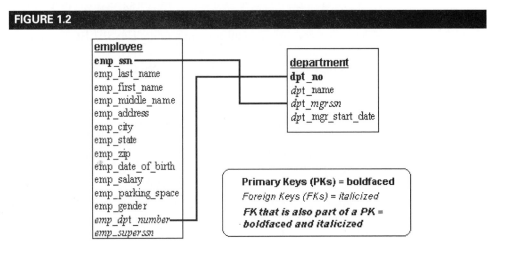

The *employee* table has the *emp_ssn* column as the primary key column. A primary key column uniquely identifies rows in a table. The *department* table has the *dpt_no* column as the primary key column. Follow the line that links the *department* table's *dpt_no* column to the *employee* table's *emp_dpt_number* column. The *dpt_no* and *emp_dep_number* columns share common values, and rows from the two tables can be joined based on the values stored in these columns. The *emp_dpt_number* column in the employee table is termed a foreign key column. Chapter 2 covers primary and foreign keys in detail.

A join operation enables an information system user to process the relationships that exist between tables. The SELECT statement in SQL Example 1.4 will display column information from both the *employee* and *department* tables. Note that this SELECT statement also completes both select and project operations. The tables are joined based on values stored in the department number columns named *emp_dpt_number* in the *employee* table and *dpt_no* in the *department* table. The result table enables a system user to determine the name of the department to which each employee is assigned. The join operation is very powerful because it allows system users to investigate relationships among data elements that might not be anticipated at the time that a database is designed. Chapter 6 covers join operations in detail.

```
/* SQL Example 1.4 */
SELECT emp_ssn, emp_first_name, emp_last_name, dpt_name
FROM employee, department
WHERE emp_dpt_number = dpt_no;

EMP_SSN        EMP_FIRST_NAME    EMP_LAST_NAME     DPT_NAME
---------      --------------    -------------     ----------------
999666666      Bijoy             Bordoloi          Headquarters
999555555      Suzanne           Joyner            Admin and Records
999444444      Waiman            Zhu               Production
more rows will be displayed . . .
```

USING SQL*PLUS

STARTING SQL*PLUS

Because Oracle can be used on many different types of computers, it is difficult to predict what type of interface you will use in your class. Your instructor will assist you in learning to use SQL*Plus on the computers available in your laboratory. However, at some point in your computing career, you will undoubtedly use either the standard Oracle SQL*Plus that is available for a Windows-type interface or by connecting to an Oracle database via a telnet session. A telnet session is opened by running a program named *telnet.exe* that is available on all Microsoft Windows–based computers. Telnet enables you to connect from your desktop computer to other computers such as database servers. Telnet sessions are described later in this chapter.

Figure 1.3 shows a standard Oracle SQL*Plus program for Microsoft Windows. This displays a Log On screen where a user named *dbock* has entered account (User Name) and password information along with the name of the database (Host String) to which a connection is to be made. Here the database is named *oracle*. If you use this

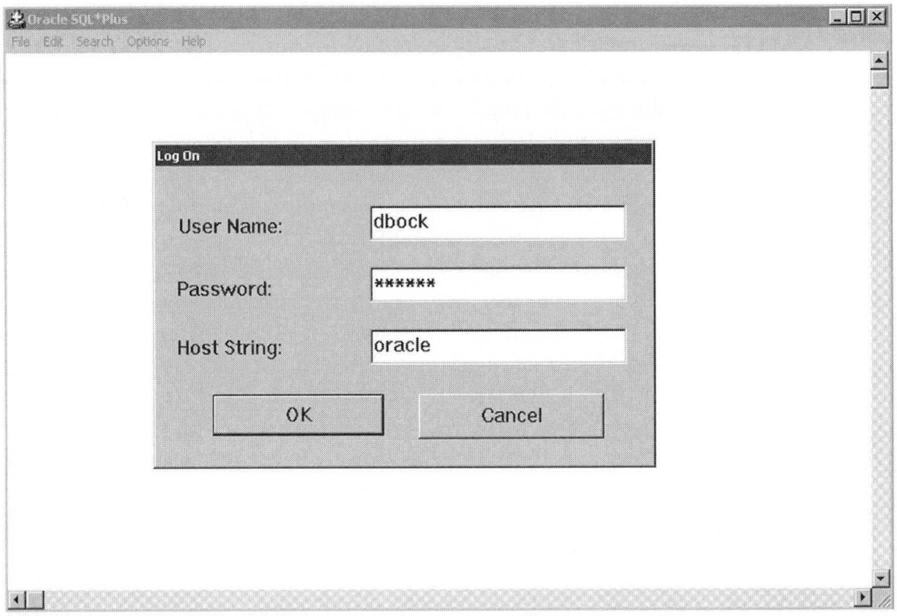

FIGURE 1.3

type of Log On connection to a database, your instructor will provide you with a User Name and Password for your class.

Figure 1.4 shows the Oracle SQL*Plus program after the logon connection has been completed. The screen gives information about the version of Oracle that is being used. Following this, you will be presented with an SQL prompt in the following form:

SQL>

This means that SQL*Plus is ready for you to type a command such as a SELECT statement. Figure 1.4 displays such a SELECT statement along with the result table that Oracle produced. The rows displayed in Figure 1.4 are from the *department* table. The asterisk (*) in the SELECT statement simply means to display all columns in the *department* table.

You may find that your particular computer does not have the Microsoft Windows version of the Oracle SQL*Plus product installed. You can still connect to a database by using the standard *telnet* client software that is part of your operating system installation. Figure 1.5 shows a sample telnet session screen. This particular Log On session shows a connection to an Oracle database located on a Sun Microsystems server running the UNIX operating system. The UNIX operating system prompt is the dollar sign ($) shown in Figure 1.5.

A SQL*Plus session is begun by typing the command *sqlplus* and entering the User Name and Password information for your account on the database. Again you will see the SQL> prompt that means Oracle is prepared to respond to SQL commands. At this point you may wish to connect to a database and, if your instructor has provided you a Log On user name and password, practice using SQL*Plus.

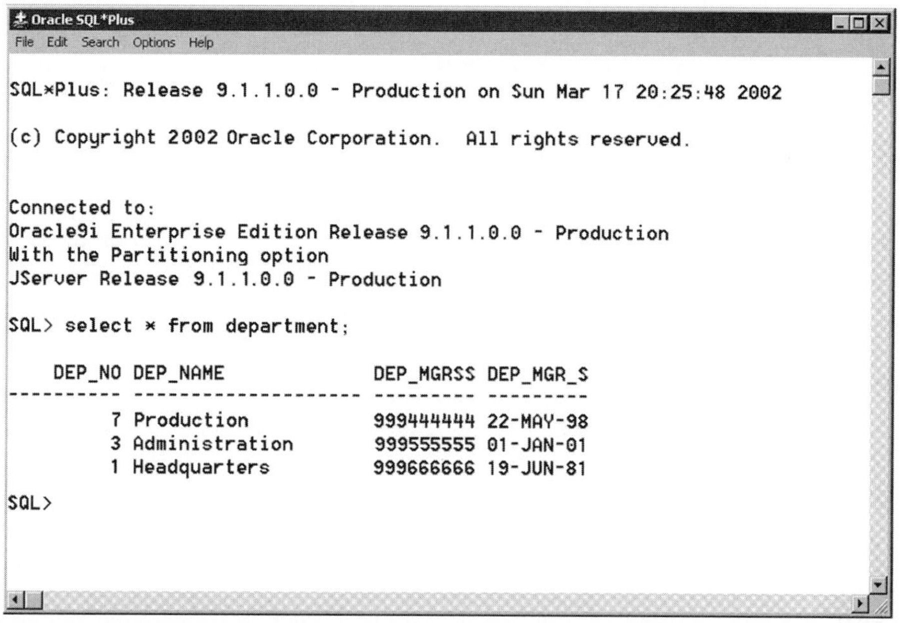

FIGURE 1.4

FIGURE 1.5

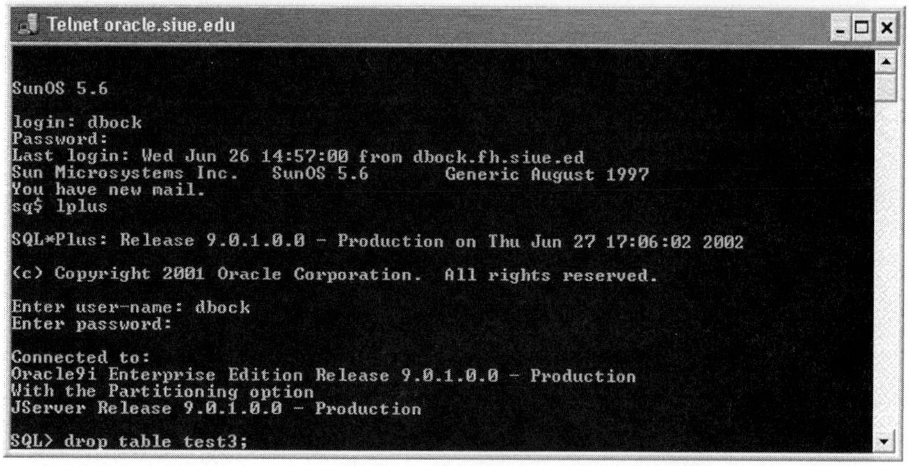

EXITING SQL*PLUS

You end an SQL*Plus session by typing either the *exit* or *quit* command at the SQL prompt. Both of these commands work identically and will terminate the session.

RUNNING (EXECUTING) A COMMAND FILE

Throughout this textbook you will study example SQL commands that use the Company database described in Appendix A. You may wish to familiarize yourself with Appendix A at this time. You may not understand everything you read in Appendix A, but that is not a problem since you are familiarizing with the Company database. By the time you finish this textbook, you will understand all of the material in Appendix A.

The Company database consists of six tables: *employee, dependent, assignment, project, department,* and *dept_locations.* You've already seen SELECT statements for the *employee* and *department* tables. Appendix A lists the sample data rows stored in each of these six tables. The number of data rows for each table is kept small intentionally. This will aid you in determining whether or not a query that you are writing works properly.

You can create your own set of tables for the Company database by running a command file named **CreateCompanyDatabase.sql.** The **"sql"** filename extension means that the command file stores SQL commands. Execute (run) the command file by typing the START CreateCompanyDatabase.sql command shown in SQL Example 1.5. Note that on computers connected to servers with the UNIX operating system, you must type the filename exactly as it appears on your system because UNIX is case sensitive. You may also use a form of shorthand when executing a command file by replacing the word START with the @ ("at" symbol).

```
/* SQL Example 1-5 */
SQL> START CreateCompanyDatabase.sql
SQL> @ CreateCompanyDatabase.sql
```

From this point on, we will assume that all SQL statements and commands are typed at the **SQL>** prompt; thus, we will not display the SQL> prompt unless it is necessary in order to clarify the programming procedure. As the **CreateCompanyDatabase.sql** command file executes a series of messages will flash across your computer screen. The first set of SQL statements that will execute are shown in SQL Example 1.6.

```
/* SQL Example 1.6 */
REM First drop necessary constraints and tables that
REM might already exist in order to create a clean database.

ALTER TABLE department
    DROP CONSTRAINT fk_dept_emp;
DROP TABLE dependent;
DROP TABLE assignment;
DROP TABLE employee;
. . . more commands follow
```

If you previously created the Company database and wish to recreate it, the commands shown in SQL Example 1.6 will delete the tables. If this is the first time you've created the Company database, these commands will generate the error message ***ORA-00942: table or view does not exist*** or some similar message. You can ignore these error messages. They simply indicate that the tables to be deleted do not exist. You will also see messages such as "Table Created" and "1 row updated" as the database tables are created and data rows are inserted into the tables. When the **CreateCompanyDatabase.sql** program file completes execution, you will again see the **SQL>** prompt.

STORING COMMANDS TO A COMMAND FILE

At some point, you may wish to create a command file that contains SQL commands. This is useful if you execute the same query regularly or if you wish to store several SQL commands in a file to be executed together. There are a number of approaches that you can take. One approach is to type the commands into a plain ASCII file by using a software text editor such as Microsoft's Notepad. You can then use FTP software to transfer the file to your Oracle account or execute it using the Oracle SQL*Plus for Microsoft Windows program described earlier in this chapter.

You can also create a command file by using the INPUT and SAVE commands at the **SQL>** prompt. In order to save the SQL command that you compose, you first need to clear the SQL buffer. The SQL buffer is a memory location that is used to store the most recently executed SQL command. This is done with the CLEAR BUFFER command. Simply type this command at the **SQL>** prompt and the system will respond.

```
/* SQL Example 1.7 */
CLEAR BUFFER
buffer cleared
```

Now, use the INPUT command to begin entering an SQL command. Let's use the SELECT statement that we saw earlier to display each employee's Social Security number and last name.

```
/* SQL Example 1.8 */
SQL> INPUT
  1 SELECT emp_ssn, emp_last_name
  2 FROM employee
  3
SQL> SAVE EmployeeInfo.sql
Created file EmployeeInfo.sql
```

Notice that after the INPUT command is typed, Oracle begins to number each line. You type the SELECT statement and when you've finished, simply press the ENTER key one additional time. This is shown above in SQL Example 1.8 by line #3 that is blank.

Following this, type the SAVE filename command to save the file. The filename entered in SQL Example 1.8 was **EmployeeInfo.sql,** and the system responded that the file was created.

You can test your command file by using the START command to execute the file as is shown in SQL Example 1.9. The output produced by the SQL commands stored in the **EmployeeInfo.sql** command file lists employee Social Security numbers and associated last names.

```
/* SQL Example 1.9 */
START EmployeeInfo.sql

More . . .
EMP_SSN        EMP_LAST_NAME
--------       ------------
999666666      Bordoloi
999555555      Joyner
999444444      Zhu
999887777      Markis
999222222      Amin
999111111      Bock
999333333      Joshi
999888888      Prescott
8 rows selected.
```

Although you won't see it appear on the screen when you create a command file, Oracle will append a slash (/) to the end of the command file. This slash tells SQL*Plus to run the commands stored in the file when you execute it with the START command. Additionally, if you wish to overwrite an existing command file with a new version, you must use the REPLACE optional keyword with the SAVE command as is shown in SQL Example 1.10.

```
/* SQL Example 1.10 */
SAVE EmployeeInfo.sql REPLACE
```

COPYING AND PASTING COMMANDS

You can also execute SQL commands to a file by using a text editor such as Microsoft's Notepad. You can use Microsoft Windows *copy and paste* techniques to paste the commands to your SQL*Plus or telnet session window.

INSERTING REMARKS IN A FILE

You may wish to include remarks within your command files in order to provide programming documentation. These remarks will help you remember what task the SQL statements in a command file perform at some later date. There are three different ways to enter remarks. One way is to use the SQL*Plus REMARK command shown in *SQL* Example 1.11. This can be abbreviated REM.

```
/* SQL Example 1.11 */
SQL> CLEAR BUFFER
SQL> INPUT
```

```
  1 REM Employee Info Report lists SSN and last name.
  2 SELECT emp_ssn, emp_last_name
  3 FROM employee
  4
SQL> SAVE EmployeeInfo.sql
```

A second method to embed remarks for documentation is to use the SQL comment delimiters, /* ....comments go here....*/, as is shown in SQL Example 1.12.

```
/* SQL Example 1.12 */
SQL> CLEAR BUFFER
SQL> INPUT
  1 /* Employee Info Report lists SSN and last name. */
  2 SELECT emp_ssn, emp_last_name
  3 FROM employee
  4
SQL> SAVE EmployeeInfo.sql
```

Still a third method is to use the ANSI/ISO comment notation of two dash marks as is shown in SQL Example 1.13.

```
/* SQL Example 1.13 */
SQL> CLEAR BUFFER
SQL> INPUT
  1 -- Employee Info Report lists SSN and last name.
  2 SELECT emp_ssn, emp_last_name
  3 FROM employee
  4
SQL> SAVE EmployeeInfo.sql
```

SYNTAX CONVENTIONS

Now that you've learned to use SQL*Plus, you may have noticed that SQL requires you to follow certain syntax rules; otherwise, an error message is returned by the system and your statements fail to execute. This section formally defines the syntax conventions that you must follow in writing SQL commands. These rules will be expanded on throughout the remaining chapters of the text. We begin with the SELECT statement.

Each SELECT statement must follow precise syntactical and structural rules. The following is the minimum structure and syntax required for an SQL SELECT statement.

```
SELECT [DISTINCT | ALL] {* | select_list}
FROM {table_name [alias] | view_name}
    [{table_name [alias] | view_name}]. . .
```

You may find syntax and structure examples such as the one above confusing. In the following paragraphs you will learn how to interpret the brackets ([]), braces ({}), vertical bars (|), and ellipses (. . .) used to define syntax and structure for commands. With a little bit of reading and work, the conventions will become second nature.

BRACES ({}) surround mandatory options. In the example above, braces surround the second row. This indicates that either a table name or a view name *must be* specified.

```
{table_name [alias] | view_name}
```

A VERTICAL BAR (|) indicates that one and only one option must be chosen. Refer again to the second row.

```
{table_name [alias] | view_name}
```

The ({}) indicate that a table_name or view_name *must be* chosen. The (|) specifies that *either* a table_name or a view_name must be chosen—not both.

When options are separated by a comma (,), both a table name and a view name can be chosen. See the command line below. If more than one option is chosen, the options must be separated by commas in the SELECT statement.

```
{table_name [alias], view_name}
```

BRACKETS ([]) surround optional keywords or identifiers. When more than one option is presented it will be separated by either a vertical bar (|) or a comma (,). In the following example, DISTINCT and ALL are optional keywords. You may use either DISTINCT or ALL, but not both.

```
[DISTINCT | ALL]
```

The square brackets ([ ]) indicate that a keyword can be chosen. The vertical bar specifies that one and only one option should be chosen. If a comma had separated the optional items, you could choose none, one, or more than one of the items enclosed in brackets ([ ]).

ELLIPSES (. . .) mean that you can repeat the last unit as many times as you like.

```
[{table_name [alias] | view_name}]. . . ]
```

PARENTHESES (( )), when encountered, are to be included in your SQL statements when indicated.

> NOTE: Brackets, braces, vertical bars, and ellipses are never included in a SQL statement. They are guides to usage and are not part of the SQL language.

SQL KEYWORDS

Keywords are words that have a predefined meaning in SQL. Keywords must be spelled as shown. Uppercase letters are used above to depict keywords. However, in practice, keywords may be entered in upper- or lowercase letters; however, most information technology professionals follow the practice of always entering keywords in uppercase. Since this is an accepted naming convention, you should follow it. You should understand, though, that SQL statements entered in both upper- and lowercase letters are exactly the same as would be the case for the SELECT statements shown as SQL Examples 1.14 and 1.15.

```
/* SQL Example 1.14 */
SELECT *
FROM employee;
```

```
/* SQL Example 1.15 */
select *
from employee;
```

In some cases, keywords can be abbreviated. The allowed abbreviation is shown in uppercase letters with the remainder shown in lowercase, which means you can use either the full word or only the uppercase part.

DESCribe: can be entered as either DESC or DESCRIBE.

Lowercase letters denote user-supplied identifiers, expressions, constants, etc. The use of expressions and constants are covered in later chapters. For now, we will focus on creating identifiers.

SQL NAMING CONVENTIONS

Identifiers are the names given by information system developers and system users to database objects such as tables, columns, indexes, and other objects as well as the database itself. There are several rules for naming database objects that must be followed:

- Identifiers should contain between 1 and 30 characters.
- The first character must be either alphabetic (a-z, A-Z) or the @ symbol or _ (underscore).
- After the first character, you may use digits, letters, or the symbols $, #, or _ (underscore).
- No embedded spaces are allowed in identifiers.
- SQL keywords cannot be used as an identifier. (Appendix E contains a listing of keywords.)

OVERVIEW OF SELECT STATEMENT SYNTAX

The basic syntax for a SELECT statement is presented below. We have intentionally limited the discussion to a description of the main clauses of the SELECT statement because you will learn the various clauses throughout your study of this text. Some of the clauses are optional as is indicated by the square brackets. However, you need to understand that when optional clauses are included, they must be placed in the order as shown below:

```
SELECT [DISTINCT | ALL] {* | select_list}
FROM {table_name [alias] | view_name}
    [{table_name [alias] | view_name}]. . .
```

```
[WHERE condition]
[GROUP BY condition_list]
[HAVING condition]
[ORDER BY {column_name | column_# [ ASC | DESC ] } . . .
```

As you've already seen, the SELECT clause is mandatory and carries out the relational project operation. It "selects" the *columns* to be included in the result table.

The FROM clause is also mandatory. It identifies one or more tables and/or views from which to retrieve the column data displayed in a result table.

The WHERE clause is optional and carries out the relational select operation. It specifies which *rows* are to be selected.

The GROUP BY clause is optional. It organizes data into groups by one or more column names listed in the SELECT clause.

The optional HAVING clause sets conditions regarding which groups to include in a result table. The groups are specified by the GROUP BY clause. As you will see, the HAVING and GROUP BY clauses tend to go hand in hand.

The ORDER BY clause is optional. It sorts query results by one or more columns in ascending or descending order. The maximum number of columns allowed in ORDER BY is 16 columns, which is a very large number of columns by which to sort any type of data!

SUMMARY

As you can see, a SELECT statement can be very complex. This is reasonable considering that the SELECT statement is the primary tool used to query a database. You will be able to reduce this complexity by studying the SELECT statement a clause at a time. In the chapters that follow, you will learn about the different clauses of the SELECT statement. In each chapter, the minimum SELECT syntax to query a database will be explained and demonstrated.

REVIEW EXERCISES

LEARN THESE TERMS

Column. A term used to refer to a "column" of data in a relational database table. This term is analogous to "field" in a file-processing sense.

Data. Raw facts.

Data Definition Language (DDL). A set of SQL commands used to create and define objects in a database.

Data Manipulation Language (DML). A set of SQL commands that allow users to manipulate the data in a database.

Data Independence. The ability to make changes in the database structure without having to make changes in the programs that access the database.

Database. An integrated unit of collected data.

Database Management System (DBMS). Manages the data in a database.

Information. Data organized in a logical/meaningful way.

Join. An operation that combines data from two or more tables.

Project. An operation that selects only certain columns of a table or a subset of all available columns.

Query. An SQL command that retrieves information (data rows) from database tables.

Relational Database. A collection of tables (relations).

Relational Database Management System (RDBMS). A DBMS based on the relational model.

Row.   A term that refers to a "row" of data in a relational database table. This term is analogous to a "record" in a file-processing sense.

Select.   An operation that selects a subset of rows in a relation that satisfy a selection condition.

Structured Query Language (SQL).   The most popularly used database language for the manipulation of relational databases.

Table.   A database object that stores organizational information. Conceptually, a table stores information in rows, one row per record, and columns, one column per data field.

CONCEPTS QUIZ

1. Differentiate between User data and System data.
2. What is another term for System data?
3. Conceptually, how are data stored in a relational DBMS?
4. What are some of the characteristics of a relational DBMS?
5. List and describe four of the seven services provided by a DBMS for the management of a database.
6. List and describe three of the significant features of Oracle as a DBMS.
7. One of your colleagues has proposed using the names listed below as column names for an Oracle database table. Explain whether or not the names proposed are suitable for column names.
   - First Name
   - &Salary
   - Weekly_4
   - Select
8. What type of activities can be accomplished with a data definition language?
9. What type of activities can be accomplished with a data manipulation language?
10. SQL is described as a nonprocedural language. What does this mean?

SQL CODING EXERCISES AND QUESTIONS

1. What is the purpose of the SQL SELECT statement?
2. What is the purpose of the WHERE clause in a SELECT statement?
3. How do you specify which columns from a table are displayed by a SELECT statement? How do you specify the order in which columns are displayed by a SELECT statement?
4. What type of operation is used to combine data from two or more tables based on common table column values?
5. What syntactical operator is used to separate column names and table names in a SELECT statement?
6. Complete the following paragraph by filling in all spaces: It is important to learn how to interpret syntax and structure examples. It is essential to understand that _____ surround mandatory options. In addition, a _____ indicates that only one option must be chosen. Whereas, a _____ indicates that one or both options can be chosen. _____ surround optional keywords or identifiers.
7. What effect does typing a command in either uppercase or lowercase letters have on execution by Oracle?
8. What are the rules for naming a database object?
9. Which clause in a SELECT command is used to sort query results?

CREATING TABLES AND INDEXES

Databases vary in complexity. To a great extent, this complexity depends on the organizational environment. Some databases, like those used by government agencies or large corporations are very large and are distributed across wide-area networks. Distributed databases provide database access for thousands of system users and enable the storage of millions and millions of rows of data in hundreds of tables. At the other extreme are small, personal databases that run on desktop computers. Most databases fall somewhere between these extremes.

Database design involves identifying system user requirements for various organizational systems such as order entry, inventory management, and accounts receivable. Databases grow and evolve over time. A single information system, such as that associated with processing customer orders, will interface with a number of tables, and often these tables will be accessed by many different, yet related information systems. A typical corporate organization will have several hundred tables within the enterprise-wide database.

OBJECTIVES

Regardless of database size and complexity, each database is comprised of *tables*. One of the first steps in creating a database is to create the tables that will store an organization's data. In this chapter, you will learn to create tables and store data in tables. You will also learn how to define a relationship between rows in one table to rows in another table by using the concept of *Foreign Keys*. Additionally, you will learn to define different types of *integrity constraints* for database tables in order to maintain the correctness of the data that are stored. The latter part of this chapter will teach you how to modify tables and how to create indexes that enable the rapid retrieval of data based on data characteristics. In later chapters, we will study the creation of other physical components of a database. Your learning objectives for this chapter are:

- Learn how to name tables, columns, and constraints.
- Select appropriate datatypes for data storage (includes understanding the different characteristics of Oracle's datatypes).

- Create and drop tables (includes understanding data integrity and table constraints).
- Use the DESC command to describe table structures.
- Rename and modify tables.
- Specify and maintain referential integrity among tables.
- Specify primary and foreign keys.
- Insert rows into and update rows in tables.
- Delete rows from tables.
- Create and drop indexes.

TABLE CREATION

In order to create a table, four pieces of information must be determined: (1) the table name, (2) the column (field) names, (3) column datatypes, and (4) column sizes.

NAMING TABLES AND COLUMNS

Naming tables and columns is a type of physical design task. You may work as a database designer or systems analyst or may, in fact, fill both roles by developing and/or following written system specifications for the logical design of an information system. The logical design documentation usually specifies table names, column names, and the type of data to be stored in each column. As a database designer, you will translate the logical system specifications into physical specifications.

When you build a new information system, you don't build it in a vacuum. The typical firm that exists in today's business environment will already have existing databases with defined tables storing data that are already used for automated systems. In fact, it is very likely that a new information system will access some database tables that already exist. Additionally, a new information system may require the creation of new tables or the modification of existing tables. For example, if a firm has an existing automated inventory system that stores product information to a database, the *product* table will already exist. If you are building a new, automated order entry system that needs to access product information, then the existing product table used by the inventory system will also be accessed by the order entry system. You would not build two separate product tables because the duplicate storage of product data would be costly and could result in data inconsistencies, that is, data values such as product descriptions that are different in two separate tables. In larger firms, an experienced database administrator (DBA) will assist you with the table creation task. In smaller firms, you may be responsible for completing both logical and physical design tasks.

Table and column names should be meaningful and reflect the nature of the data that is to be stored. If you are storing data about products that a firm sells, then the table should probably be named *product!* Similarly, if products are identified by a string of eight characters, then the column that stores product identification data should be named *product_number,* or *product_code,* or a similar meaningful name.

PICKING A DATATYPE

The datatype you choose for a column determines the nature of the data that can be stored in the column. This is termed the *domain* of valid column values. For example, if you declare a column to be DATE type data, then any date value stored to the column will only be accepted by the DBMS if the date is valid. Attempting to store March 32 will not work because there is no 32 day in March! Likewise, attempting to store the value 182 or the value "Tom" to a DATE column will not work because datatypes provide rudimentary error checking. This reduces the probability that incorrect values are assigned to a column. Datatypes also allow disk storage space to be used efficiently.

Oracle provides a number of predefined datatypes as well as the ability to declare your own datatypes. We will focus on a limited number of the predefined datatypes. Most tables are comprised of columns that store data that can be classified into the datatypes shown in Table 2.1.

Character Data

Oracle supports three predefined character datatypes including CHAR, VARCHAR/VARCHAR2, and LONG. VARCHAR and VARCHAR2 are actually synonymous, and Oracle recommends using VARCHAR2 instead of VARCHAR. You should choose either CHAR or VARCHAR2 when you need a table column to store alphanumeric or character data. Alphanumeric data include letters in the alphabet and numbers that will not be used for calculations, as well as special characters. Examples of alphanumeric data include: customer name, customer address, customer zip code, customer telephone number, product number, and product description. Have you noticed that some alphanumeric data consist strictly of numbers such as a zip code or

TABLE 2.1

Datatype	Description
CHAR	Stores fixed-length alphanumeric data up to 2,000 characters. Default size is one character. Data values smaller than the specified size are blank-padded. Example declarations: CHAR(5), CHAR, CHAR(400).
VARCHAR2	Stores variable-length alphanumeric data up to 4,000 characters. You must specify the maximum size of a column. A column is NOT blank padded to fill up the declared space. Example declarations: VARCHAR2(15), VARCHAR2(50), VARCHAR2(1525).
LONG	Stores variable-length alphanumeric data up to two gigabytes in length.
NUMBER	Stores integer, fixed-point, and floating-point numeric values. The range of numeric values stored is 1.0 x 10 to the −130th and 1.0 x 10 to the 126th − 1. Example integer declarations: NUMBER(4), NUMBER(8), NUMBER(22). Example fixed-point declaration: NUMBER. Example floating-point declarations: NUMBER(9,2), NUMBER(15,4), NUMBER(35,16).
DATE	Stores valid date values. The default format for expressing a date is the *date mask* 'DD-MON-YY'; thus, the 4th of April, 2002, would be expressed as '4-APR-02'.
LOB	A large object. Includes CLOB, BLOB, and other LOB types. Used to store unstructured data including text, image, video, and spatial data. Maximum size is four gigabytes.

telephone number? In general, strings of numbers are stored as character data as opposed to numeric data if they will not be used in mathematical calculations.

CHAR DATATYPE

Use the CHAR datatype when the column will store character values that are *fixed-length*. For example, a Social Security number (SSN) in the United States is assigned to every citizen and is always 9 characters in size (even though an SSN is strictly composed of digits, the digits are treated as characters), and would be specified as CHAR(9). If the value to be stored in a CHAR column does not fill up the space allocated, Oracle adds "blank characters" to the end of the value because a CHAR column is always fixed in length. If you do not specify a column size, the default size is one character. The maximum size of a CHAR column is 2,000 characters, for example, CHAR(2000).

VARCHAR2 DATATYPE

Use the VARCHAR2 datatype to store alphanumeric data that is *variable-length*. For example, a customer name or address will vary considerably in terms of the number of characters to be stored. The name *Tom Jones* is a much shorter name than the name *Christina Aguilera*. You must specify the maximum number of characters that will be stored in a VARCHAR2 column. If you attempt to store a string of characters larger than the specified maximum size, Oracle will return an error code.

The maximum size of a VARCHAR2 column is 4,000 characters, for example, VARCHAR2(4000), but you will rarely use a VARCHAR2 column that is this large. You should set the maximum value large enough to store the largest value that will ever be stored in a column. Because a database allocates only enough space to store the actual data (no blank-padding), storage space will not be wasted because the columns vary in length. For example, you might declare a customer first name column to be VARCHAR2(100) even though most customer first names will be considerably shorter than 100 characters!

LONG DATATYPE

The LONG datatype can store very long strings of variable-length alphanumeric data—up to two gigabytes of text. The LONG datatype is primarily used to store database object definitions in the data dictionary, and is provided for backward compatibility to earlier versions of Oracle for existing computer applications. You should avoid using this datatype to create new tables, but you may encounter its use in existing databases.

There are some restrictions on the use of LONG columns. A table can have only one LONG column, and you cannot index a LONG column. Since a LONG column can be quite large, application processing may be limited by the amount of memory available on the server platform. Additional LONG column restrictions are explained in Oracle documentation available through Oracle's Web site.

NUMERIC DATA

The NUMBER datatype encompasses both integer, fixed-point, and floating-point numeric values. Early versions of Oracle defined different datatypes for each of these different types of numbers, but now the NUMBER datatype serves all of these purposes. Choose the NUMBER datatype when a column must store numerical data that can be used in mathematical calculations. Occasionally, the NUMBER datatype is used to store identification numbers where those numbers are generated by the DBMS as sequential numbers.

You may be surprised to discover that the NUMBER datatype is also stored as *variable-length* data. In fact, the NUMBER datatype can store both positive and negative fixed-point and floating-point numbers. Stored value lower/upper limits are 1.0 times 10 to the −130th power and 1.0 times 10 to the 126th power −1, respectively. Stated another way, the upper limit is 9.9 . . . 9 times 10 to the 125th power, wherein you can have 38 nines or digits of precision! The key point is that Oracle allocates more storage space to large numbers than small numbers, and in this fashion optimizes the use of storage space. However, the storage space allocated does not directly map to the number of digits expressed when you write out a number. We will not worry about how much physical space is allocated to the storage of any given number, but we will be concerned with specifying the precision and scale of a NUMBER column as you will see below.

NUMBER FOR INTEGER VALUES

Consider a column declaration of NUMBER(8). This specifies that an integer value with a precision of up to eight digits can be stored in a column. If the number stored is greater than eight digits, Oracle returns an error message. Use this type of declaration when a column does not need a decimal point as is the case for counting or whole numbers.

NUMBER FOR FLOATING-POINT VALUES

Here the column declaration is simply the word NUMBER with no digits specified. Oracle will "float" the decimal point in order to store the number specified as precisely as is possible. Oracle will allow storage of a number with up to 38 digits of precision. If the value stored is greater than 38 digits of precision, Oracle returns an error message. There is no restriction on the number of digits that can appear to the right of the decimal point.

NUMBER FOR FIXED-POINT VALUES

When you store fixed-point values, you need to specify both the *precision* (total number of digits) and scale (number of digits to the right of the decimal point) of the numeric value. For example, NUMBER(15,2) specifies that a total of 15 digits (precision) can be stored with two digits to the right of the decimal (scale). The limit on precision is 38 digits. The limit on scale is 127 digits to the right of the decimal point. Yes, you can actually have more digits to the right of the decimal than is specified in precision, and the possible scale level is very large!

If the value stored exceeds the specified level of precision, Oracle returns an error message. If the value stored exceeds the specified level of scale, Oracle rounds the value stored. This means that Oracle rounds values stored to the right of the decimal point. But Oracle can also round to the left of the decimal point. A specification of NUMBER(10, −3) would mean to round to the nearest thousandth. Table 2.2 reflects how different values would be stored by Oracle based on the NUMBER column declaration.

TABLE 2.2

Value to Be Stored	NUMBER Declaration	Data Value Stored
7890.453	NUMBER	7890.453
7890.453	NUMBER(8)	7890
7890.453	NUMBER(5,2)	Error—Exceeds Precision
7890.453	NUMBER(6,2)	7890.45
7890.453	NUMBER(7,2)	7890.45
7890.453	NUMBER(7,3)	7890.453
7890.453	NUMBER(7,1)	7890.5
7890.453	NUMBER(4,−2)	7900

DATE DATA

Quite simply, a DATE column is used to store valid date information. For example, organizations may store the date on which a customer order is processed, or the date of birth of a newborn child in a hospital database, or even the date on which you complete your college degree.

You may be surprised to discover that a DATE column also stores *time* information. A column specified as DATE actually stores the century, year, month, day, hour, minute, and second on which an event occurs. If a date is stored without specifying the time value, then the default time of 12:00 A.M. is stored. Similarly, if you store a time value without specifying a date, the default date stored is the first day of the current month according to the system clock. You can generate the current system date and time by using the Oracle function named SYSDATE. We will study this function in Chapter 10.

The default format for expressing a date is the *date mask* 'DD-MON-YY'; thus, the 4th of April, 2002, would be expressed as '4-APR-02,' and the 15th of March, 1998, would be expressed as '15-MAR-98'. In order to declare a DATE column, you simply use the declaration: DATE.

Oracle has rules for storing the century when it is not expressed. If the current year's last two digits are less than 50, for example, the year 2003, and if the YY year values expressed are greater than 50, for example, 75, then the two digits stored and returned for the year in the DATE column are the same as the first two digits of the current year. The year stored/returned would be 2075.

But what will be displayed if you retrieve data from older records that were stored in the latter part of the 20th century, say 1990. If the last two digits of the year stored are greater than 50, as would be the case for 1990, but the current calendar year is still less than 50, as would be the case for 2003 as well as for most of your entire work life, then the century returned by Oracle is one less than the current calendar century. In other words, if a value stored in a DATE column is '12-APR-99', Oracle will return a century value of 19.

The real issue for you is to understand what century value is stored if you insert the date '15-MAR-90' into a DATE column? Oracle will store the year 2090. If you need to store a date value from the past century in order to modify or update older records, you must explicitly specify the century value, for example, '15-MAR-1990'.

LARGE OBJECT (LOB) DATA

Oracle provides several different LOB datatypes, including CLOB (character large object) and BLOB (binary large object). Columns of these datatypes can store unstructured data including text, image, video, and spatial data. The CLOB datatype can store up to four gigabytes of character data using the CHAR database character set. The BLOB datatype is used to store unstructured binary large objects such as those associated with image and video data where the data is simply a stream of *"bit"* values. A BLOB datatype can store up to four gigabytes of binary data.

CREATING A TABLE

Now that you understand how to choose appropriate datatypes, we can begin creating a table. Let's create a very simple table that will store five items of information about employees for an organization. We will name the table *employee* and store information about each employee's Social Security number, last name, first name, date hired, and annual salary. The CREATE TABLE statement shown in SQL Example 2.1 will create this simple table:

```
/* SQL Example 2.1 */
CREATE TABLE employee (
  emp_ssn                CHAR(9),
  emp_last_name          VARCHAR2(25),
  emp_first_name         VARCHAR2(25),
  emp_date_of_birth      DATE,
  emp_salary             NUMBER(7,2)
);
```

Examine the syntax of the CREATE TABLE command. The table name *employee* is specified along with five data columns. Each column has a name that is unique within the table. Some information systems departments require system developers to follow specific naming conventions when naming columns. Here the convention is to use a prefix abbreviation of the table name (our abbreviation is *emp*) as part of the column name. This is optional and is not always followed although the practice may make it simpler to work with tables and column names.

Each column is specified to store a specific type of data. The specification of column names begins with a left parenthesis before the first column name, and ends with a closing right parenthesis after the last column name. Each column name specification is separated from the previous column specification by a comma. For clarity, each column name and associated datatype specification is typed on a separate command line. If you type this command at the SQL*PLUS command prompt, Oracle will automatically number each line beginning with line 2 as soon as you press the ENTER key on your keyboard. Also, the CREATE TABLE command must end with a semicolon. There are numerous additional options for the CREATE TABLE command. We will cover some of those options later in this chapter. Other options are beyond the scope of this book.

The first column is *emp_ssn* (Social Security number). Later in this chapter, we will designate this column as the primary key for the table. This column will store a unique, nine-digit Social Security number for each employee in the database; however, we have specified that the column is CHAR because we do not intend to perform any mathematical operations with social security numbers.

When the CREATE TABLE command executes, SQL*PLUS will process the command. If there are no syntactical errors, the message *Table Created* will display to confirm that the table definition was successfully stored to the database.

DATA INTEGRITY AND TABLE CONSTRAINTS

The simple *employee* table shown above has some very severe limitations. It lacks the specifications needed to aid in maintaining the integrity of data that are stored in the table. The term *data integrity* simply means that the data stored in the table is valid. There are different types of data integrity, and we often refer to these as *constraints*. In fact, the specification of different datatypes aids in maintaining certain aspects of the data stored for employees. For example, specifying the *emp_date_of_birth* column as DATE will prevent the storage of invalid dates and nondate data. But, there are additional integrity constraints that can be used to aid in maintaining data integrity.

NOT NULL CONSTRAINT

A NOT NULL constraint means that a data row must have a value for the column specified as NOT NULL. The code in SQL Example 2.2 specifies that every employee must have a first and last name. If a column is specified as NOT NULL, the Oracle RDBMS will not allow rows to be stored to the *employee* table that violate this constraint. In order to allow a column to store a NULL value (really, the absence of a value), you simply do not specify an integrity constraint for that column. For example, this means that the *emp_date_of_birth* column is allowed to be NULL.

```
/* SQL Example 2.2 */
emp_last_name              VARCHAR2(25)
    CONSTRAINT nn_emp_last_name NOT NULL,
emp_first_name             VARCHAR2(25)
    CONSTRAINT nn_emp_first_name NOT NULL,
```

A fairly standard practice is to assign each constraint a *unique constraint name*. In selecting a constraint name, it is common to use a prefix to denote the type of constraint. The prefix for a NOT NULL constraint is *'nn,'* and it is common to combine this prefix with the table name and/or column name to make it easy to determine the nature of an error whenever a constraint violation is reported by Oracle. If you do not name constraints, then Oracle assigns fairly meaningless system-generated names to each constraint.

PRIMARY KEY CONSTRAINT

Each table must normally contain a column or set of columns that uniquely identifies rows of data that are stored in the table. This column or set of columns is referred to as the *primary key*. Most tables have a single column as the primary key. This is the case for the *employee* table where the *emp_ssn* column is unique and, thus, qualifies to serve as the primary key. If a table requires two or more columns in order to identify each row uniquely, the primary key is termed a *composite* primary key. We will study examples of composite primary keys later in the chapter.

By assigning a PRIMARY KEY constraint to the *emp_ssn* column, we will automatically give the column two properties. First, the *emp_ssn* column must be NOT NULL for each row by default—this constraint is built into the PRIMARY KEY constraint specification. Second, an *emp_ssn* value may not occur twice within the *employee* table—that is, each *emp_ssn* value must be unique within the table. If you attempt to enter the same value for the *emp_ssn* for two employees, Oracle will store the first row of data; however, Oracle will generate an error message and refuse to store the second data row. The PRIMARY KEY constraint shown in SQL Example 2.3 is essential to maintaining the integrity of a database. Imagine the tax reporting and pay problems that would result if two employees were accidentally assigned identical Social Security numbers.

```
/* SQL Example 2.3 */
emp_ssn            CHAR(9)
    CONSTRAINT pk_employee PRIMARY KEY,
```

Note that the PRIMARY KEY constraint is assigned a constraint name of *pk_employee*. In naming a primary key constraint, the standard practice is to use a two-character prefix of '*pk*' combined with an underscore and the name of the table. Later in this chapter, you will learn how to specify a PRIMARY KEY constraint for a composite primary key.

CHECK Constraint

Sometimes the data values stored in a specific column must fall within some acceptable range of values. For example, the organization owning our *employee* table may specify that employee salary figures stored to the database represent the annual salary of each employee, and that annual salary cannot exceed $85,000. SQL Example 2.4 shows how to write a CHECK constraint to enforce this data limit.

```
/* SQL Example 2.4 */
emp_salary              NUMBER(7,2)
    CONSTRAINT ck_emp_salary
        CHECK (emp_salary <= 85000),
```

The CHECK constraint is named *ck_emp_salary,* and uses a two-character prefix of '*ck*' to denote that it is a CHECK constraint. A CHECK constraint requires that the specified check condition is either true or unknown for each row stored in the table. The condition is classified as unknown if the *emp_salary* value for a given row is NULL. If it is desirable to require that the monthly salary value be stored for every row in the table, then both CHECK and NOT NULL constraints could be specified as shown in SQL Example 2.5.

```
/* SQL Example 2.5 */
emp_salary                  NUMBER(7,2)
    CONSTRAINT ck_emp_salary
        CHECK emp_salary <= 85000
    CONSTRAINT nn_emp_salary NOT NULL,
```

If a computer application or an information system user attempts to store a row to the *employee* table that violates either constraint, Oracle will return an error message and the row will not be stored to the table. The error message will use the constraint name to reference the specific constraint that is violated. Also, Oracle allows a single column to have more than one CHECK constraint. In fact, there is no practical limit to the number of CHECK constraints that can be defined for a column.

UNIQUE Constraint

Sometimes it is necessary to enforce uniqueness for a column value that is not a primary key column. Let's add another column to the employee table that will store information about the parking space that is assigned to each employee. Assume that each parking space for the organization is numbered a unique, integer number, and that no two employees can be assigned the same parking space. The UNIQUE constraint can be used to enforce this rule and Oracle will reject any rows that violate the constraint. The SQL code is shown in SQL Example 2.6.

```
/* SQL Example 2.6 */
emp_parking_space          NUMBER(4)
    CONSTRAINT un_emp_parking_space UNIQUE,
```

The *un_emp_parking_space* constraint has a two-character prefix of *'un'* to denote that it is a UNIQUE constraint. The updated CREATE TABLE command for the *employee* table is shown in SQL Example 2.7.

```
/* SQL Example 2.7 */
CREATE TABLE employee (
  emp_ssn                   CHAR(9)
     CONSTRAINT pk_employee PRIMARY KEY,
  emp_last_name             VARCHAR2(25)
     CONSTRAINT nn_emp_last_name NOT NULL,
  emp_first_name            VARCHAR2(25)
     CONSTRAINT nn_emp_first_name NOT NULL,
  emp_date_of_birth         DATE,
  emp_salary                NUMBER(7,2)
     CONSTRAINT ck_emp_salary
        CHECK (emp_salary <= 85000),
  emp_parking_space         NUMBER(4)
     CONSTRAINT un_emp_parking_space UNIQUE
);
```

Additional constraints that enforce data integrity for rows that are stored in related tables are discussed later in this chapter.

COMMANDS TO MANAGE, DROP, AND ALTER TABLES

In addition to creating tables, database administrators and programmers must be able to view table descriptions as part of the system development process. Sometimes tables must be dropped or altered. This section will cover the commands used to manage, drop, and alter tables.

VIEWING A TABLE DESCRIPTION

The SQL*Plus DESCRIBE (DESC) command can display the column names and datatypes for any table. The DESCRIBE command is not part of the ANSI standard specification for SQL. Rather, it is an extension command added to the Oracle RDBMS to assist you in your data management tasks. This command can be used when exact datatypes and column sizes for a table are unknown. SQL Example 2.8 shows the DESCRIBE command for the *employee* table. Note that while the *emp_ssn* column was specified to have a PRIMARY KEY constraint, the *Null?* column displayed in the table description indicates whether or not a column is constrained as NOT NULL.

```
/* SQL Example 2.8 */
DESC employee;

Name                     Null?          Type
----------------         -------        -----------
EMP_SSN                  NOT NULL       CHAR(9)
EMP_LAST_NAME            NOT NULL       VARCHAR2(25)
EMP_FIRST_NAME           NOT NULL       VARCHAR2(25)
EMP_DATE_OF_BIRTH                       DATE
EMP_SALARY              NOT NULL        NUMBER(7,2)
EMP_PARKING_SPACE                       NUMBER(4)
```

DROPPING A TABLE

You can delete the *employee* table with the DROP TABLE command shown in SQL Example 2.9. This command deletes both the table structure, its data, related constraints, and indexes.

```
/* SQL Example 2.9 */
DROP TABLE employee;
```

RENAMING A TABLE

Although it is rare to do so, you may choose to rename a table with the RENAME command as shown in SQL Example 2.10. This command does not affect table structure or data; it simply gives the current table a new name

```
/* SQL Example 2.10 */
RENAME employee TO worker;
```

ADDING AND ALTERING A COLUMN FOR AN EXISTING TABLE

Over time it is fairly common to modify existing tables to either add new columns or alter existing columns. This is accomplished with the ALTER TABLE MODIFY and ALTER TABLE ADD commands. For example, as an organization grows, it may be necessary to add employee parking spaces. The current datatype of the *emp_parking_space* column is NUMBER(4). A very large organization may have in excess of 9,999 employees such as may be the case at the Pentagon in Washington, D.C. The ALTER TABLE command shown in SQL Example 2.11 modifies the *emp_parking_space* column to enable the allocation of up to 99,999 parking spaces.

```
/* SQL Example 2.11 */
ALTER TABLE employee MODIFY (emp_parking_space NUMBER(5));
```

If a column modification will result in a column that is smaller than was originally specified, Oracle will return an error message if data rows exist such that their data will not fit into the new specified column size, and the ALTER TABLE MODIFY command will fail to execute.

Suppose that an organization recognizes the need to track the gender of employees in order to meet a governmental reporting requirement. An *emp_gender* column can be added to the *employee* table as shown in SQL Example 2.12. The *emp_gender* column is a single character column used to store a coded value, where M = male and F = female.

```
/* SQL Example 2.12 */
ALTER TABLE employee ADD (emp_gender CHAR(1));
```

The ALTER TABLE command has many additional capabilities including the ability to move a table, drop a column in a table, and set a column as temporarily unusable. You may wish to explore these capabilities by visiting the Oracle Technology Network Web site at: *http://otn.oracle.com*.

RELATING TABLES–IDENTIFYING FOREIGN KEYS

Tables in a database rarely exist by themselves. Normally, data rows in one table are related to data rows in other tables. Let's build a second table named *department*. The *department* table will store information about departments within our organization. Each department has a unique, two-digit, department number. Each department also has a department name, location, and primary telephone number for contacting the department manager (you're more likely to reach an administrative assistant). The CREATE TABLE command is shown in SQL Example 2.13.

```
/* SQL Example 2.13 */
CREATE TABLE department (
    dpt_no                NUMBER(2)
        CONSTRAINT pk_department PRIMARY KEY,
    dpt_name              VARCHAR2(20)
        CONSTRAINT nn_dpt_name NOT NULL
);
```

Employees are generally assigned to work in departments. In our organization, an employee is usually hired into a department and at any given time is only assigned to a single department, although an employee can be reassigned to another department depending upon departmental workloads. Of course, a department may have many different employees assigned to it. In order to link rows in the *employee* table to rows in the *department* table we need to introduce a new type of constraint, the FOREIGN KEY constraint.

Figure 2.1 depicts the *employee* and *department* tables. The primary key column *dpt_no* of the *department* table is shown in bold face. Note the line leading from *dpt_no* column to the *emp_dpt_number* column of the *employee* table. The *emp_dpt_number* column is a foreign key.

Foreign keys (FKs) are columns in one table that reference primary key values in another table or in the same table. In this situation we will relate *employee* rows to the primary key column named *dpt_no* in the *department* table. We will do this by specifying a FOREIGN KEY constraint as part of the CREATE TABLE command. If this was a new database, we would most likely first create the *department* table, then create the *employee* table. This would facilitate creating the FOREIGN KEY constraint since it would be impossible to reference a column in the *department* table if the table has not yet been created! The new *employee* table CREATE TABLE command shown in SQL Example 2.14 includes a column to store the department number to which each employee is assigned. The new *emp_dpt_number* column and FOREIGN KEY constraint are shown here:

FIGURE 2.1

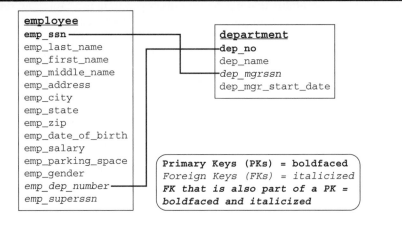

```
/* SQL Example 2.14 */
CREATE TABLE employee (
    emp_ssn                  CHAR(9)
        CONSTRAINT pk_employee PRIMARY KEY,
    emp_last_name            VARCHAR2(25)
        CONSTRAINT nn_emp_last_name NOT NULL,
    emp_first_name           VARCHAR2(25)
        CONSTRAINT nn_emp_first_name NOT NULL,
    emp_date_of_birth        DATE,
    emp_salary               NUMBER(7,2)
        CONSTRAINT ck_emp_salary
            CHECK (emp_salary <= 85000),
    emp_parking_space        NUMBER(4)
        CONSTRAINT un_emp_parking_space UNIQUE,
    emp_gender               CHAR(1),
    emp_dpt_number           NUMBER(2),
CONSTRAINT fk_emp_dpt FOREIGN KEY (emp_dpt_number)
    REFERENCES department ON DELETE SET NULL
);
```

The value stored to the *emp_dpt_number* column for any given *employee* row must match a value stored in the *dpt_no* column of one of the rows of the *department* table. Note that we did not specify a NOT NULL constraint for the *emp_dpt_number* column. This will enable the organization to hire a new employee who has not yet been assigned to a specific department. In this case, the value of the *emp_dpt_number* column would be NULL for the new employee.

If the *employee* table already exists and the department table is subsequently added to the database, then we must use the ALTER TABLE command to modify the *employee* table. In this situation, we would be adding the *emp_dpt_number* column and the associated FOREIGN KEY constraint shown in SQL Example 2.15.

```
/* SQL Example 2.15 */
ALTER TABLE employee ADD (emp_dpt_number NUMBER(2));

ALTER TABLE employee ADD CONSTRAINT fk_emp_dpt
    FOREIGN KEY (emp_dpt_number) REFERENCES department
        ON DELETE SET NULL;
```

Did you notice the ON DELETE SET NULL clause? This is a referential integrity clause, and is explained in the next section of this chapter.

MAINTAINING REFERENTIAL INTEGRITY

FOREIGN KEY constraints are also referred to as *referential integrity* constraints, and assist in maintaining database integrity. Referential integrity stipulates that values of a foreign key must correspond to values of a primary key in the table that it references. For example, you cannot enter a row in the *employee* table with a department number unless that department number already exists within one of the *department* table rows.

TABLE 2.3	
On Update (Delete) Restrict	Any update/delete made to the *department* table that would delete or change a primary key value will be rejected unless no foreign key references that value in the *employee* table.
On Update (Delete) Cascade	Any update/delete made to the *department* table should be cascaded through to the *employee* table.
On Update (Delete) Set Null	Any values that are updated/deleted in the *department* table cause affected columns in the *employee* table to be set to null.

But what happens if the primary key values change or the row that is referenced is deleted? That is, what happens if the department to which an employee is assigned is deleted?

Several methods exist to ensure that referential integrity is maintained. For example, we can specify what to do if our organization decides to reorganize and eliminate a specific department. In this situation, one or more *employee* table rows will reference a nonexistent *department* table row. Recall that we allow the *emp_dpt_number* column in *employee* to be NULL for employees not currently assigned to a department. As part of the reorganization, there could be employees that fall into this exact situation, and it could take time for management to decide where to assign these employees. We can use the ON DELETE SET NULL clause of a FOREIGN KEY constraint shown in SQL Example 2.16 to specify that the value of *emp_dpt_number* should be set to NULL if the referenced *department* row is deleted. The deletion of any PK value in the *department* table will be propagated to the *employee* table as well.

```
/* SQL Example 2.16 */
CONSTRAINT fk_emp_dpt FOREIGN KEY (emp_dpt_number)
    REFERENCES department ON DELETE SET NULL
```

Table 2.3 lists additional referential integrity constraints that can be used to enforce database integrity. These constraints are automatically enforced when a row in a table is updated or deleted according to the specification in the CREATE TABLE command. The RESTRICT constraint disallows the update or deletion of referenced data. Cascade causes effects to cascade to related row/columns in other tables. The SET NULL option stores NULL values to related rows and columns in other tables.

COMPOSITE PRIMARY KEYS AND MULTIPLE FOREIGN KEYS

You will often encounter situations where you need to create an association table that represents a many-to-many relationship between two base tables or entities. A many-to-many relationship is one in which a row in table 1 may be related to many rows in table 2, and similarly, a row in table 2 may be related to many rows in table 1. As an example, consider the relationship between rows in the *employee* table and rows in the *project* table. Each employee can be assigned to work on more than one project. Further, each project can have many employees assigned to work on the project. We will extend our database by creating a table to store information about projects. The command to create the *project* table is shown in SQL Example 2.17.

```
/* SQL Example 2.17 */
CREATE TABLE project (
    pro_number              NUMBER(2)
        CONSTRAINT pk_project PRIMARY KEY,
    pro_name                VARCHAR2(25)
        CONSTRAINT nn_pro_name NOT NULL,
    pro_location            VARCHAR2(25),
    pro_dept_number         NUMBER(2),
CONSTRAINT fk_pro_dept_number FOREIGN KEY (pro_dept_number)
    REFERENCES department ON DELETE SET NULL
);
```

The column *pro_number* will store the project number for each project. It will also serve as the primary key. Each project also has a project name and location. A specific department will control each project. This relationship is enforced through the *pro_dept_number* column and associated FOREIGN KEY constraint that references back to the *department* table.

Employees can be assigned to work on many different projects at the same time, and a project can have many different employees assigned to complete various project tasks. This *Works-On* relationship between employees and projects is implemented by creating an association table named *assignment* as shown in Figure 2.2.

The CREATE TABLE command for the *assignment* table is shown in SQL Example 2.18.

```
/* SQL Example 2.18 */
CREATE TABLE assignment (
    work_emp_ssn            CHAR(9),
    work_pro_number         NUMBER(2),
    work_hours              NUMBER(5,1),
CONSTRAINT pk_assignment
    PRIMARY KEY (work_emp_ssn, work_pro_number),
CONSTRAINT fk_work_emp
    FOREIGN KEY (work_emp_ssn) REFERENCES employee
        ON DELETE CASCADE,
CONSTRAINT fk_work_pro_number
    FOREIGN KEY (work_pro_number) REFERENCES project
        ON DELETE CASCADE
);
```

The primary key for the *assignment* table is a composite key consisting of both the *work_emp_ssn* and *work_pro_number* columns. Study the syntax of the PRIMARY KEY constraint declaration.

It is also necessary to enforce FOREIGN KEY constraints between the *assignment* table and the *employee* and *project* tables. Values stored in the *assignment* table's

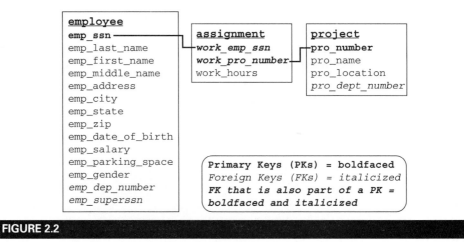

FIGURE 2.2

work_emp_ssn column will reference values in the *emp_ssn* column of the *employee* table, while values stored in the *assignment* table's *work_pro_number* column will reference values in the *pro_number* column of the *project* table. Thus, there are two FOREIGN KEY constraints specified. This enforces the following rule: We cannot have a row in the *assignment* table for a nonexistent employee or nonexistent project. The total hours an employee works on a project are accumulated in the *work_hours* column. The placement of commas after each column and constraint specification is important in order to avoid syntax errors.

POPULATING TABLES WITH DATA

The task of populating tables with data for systems that are converted from one type of database to another will generally be handled by using special utility programs. However, application programs will use the commands described in this section to manage table data, including row insertions, row updates, and row deletions.

THE INSERT COMMAND

We have created several tables, but have yet to store data in any of them. The INSERT command is used to store data in tables. The INSERT command is often used in higher-level programming languages such as Visual Basic.NET or C++ as an embedded SQL command; however, this command can also be executed at the SQL*PLUS prompt in command mode. There are two different forms of the INSERT command. The first form is used if a new row will have a value inserted into each column of the row. SQL Example 2.19 gives the general form of the INSERT command.

```
/* SQL Example 2.19 */
INSERT INTO table
    VALUES (column1 value, column2 value, ...);
```

For example, the INSERT commands in SQL Example 2.20 will insert a complete row of data into the *department* table, and three rows of data into the *employee* table.

```
/* SQL Example 2.20 */
INSERT INTO department
    VALUES ( 7, 'Production' );
INSERT INTO employee VALUES( '999666666', 'Bordoloi', 'Bijoy',
    TO_DATE('11-10-67', 'MM-DD-YY'), 55000, 1, 'M', 1 );
INSERT INTO employee VALUES( '999555555', 'Joyner', 'Suzanne',
    TO_DATE('06-20-71', 'MM-DD-YY'), 43000, 3, 'F', 3 );
INSERT INTO employee VALUES( '999444444', 'Zhu', 'Waiman',
    TO_DATE('12-08-75', 'MM-DD-YY'), 43000, 32, 'M', 7 );
```

As each row is successfully stored to a table, the message *1 row created* displays on the computer monitor screen. Character data values are enclosed in single quotes, whereas numeric data are not. You can use the SQL*Plus TO_DATE function to store date values in the *emp_date_of_birth* column. The TO_DATE function converts the character string representation of a date value to an internal date form used by Oracle and is covered in more detail in Chapter 10.

The second form of the INSERT command shown in SQL Example 2.21 is used to insert rows where some of the column data is unknown (NULL). This form of the INSERT command requires that you specify column names for which data are being stored.

```
/* SQL Example 2.21 */
INSERT INTO table (column1 name, column2 name, . . .)
    VALUES (column1 value, column2 value, . . .);
```

The INSERT command in SQL Example 2.22 stores information to the columns listed for a new data row in the *employee* table.

```
/* SQL Example 2.22 */
INSERT INTO employee (emp_ssn, emp_last_name, emp_first_name)
    VALUES ('999111111', 'Bock', 'Douglas');
```

THE DELETE COMMAND

The DELETE command is one of the simplest of the SQL statements. It removes one or more rows from a table. Multiple table delete operations are not allowed in SQL. The syntax of the DELETE command is given in SQL Example 2.23.

```
/* SQL Example 2.23 */
DELETE FROM table_name
    [WHERE condition];
```

The DELETE command deletes all rows in the table that satisfy the *condition* in the optional WHERE clause. BE CAREFUL!! Since the WHERE clause is optional, you can easily delete all rows from a table by omitting a WHERE clause since the WHERE clause limits the scope of the DELETE operation. For example, the DELETE FROM command in SQL Example 2.24 removes all rows in the *assignment* table.

```
/* SQL Example 2.24 */
DELETE FROM assignment;
```

The COMMIT and ROLLBACK Commands

If you inadvertently delete all rows from a table, all is not lost. INSERT, UPDATE, and DELETE commands are not committed to the database until the COMMIT statement is executed. COMMIT is a transaction managing command that confirms operations to the database on the server. Closing Oracle also acts as a confirmation of the commands entered. You can immediately issue the SQL command ROLLBACK (ROLL) to cancel any database operations since the most recent COMMIT. Like COMMIT, ROLLBACK is also a transaction managing command; however, it cancels operations instead of confirming them.

Let's delete a record using a proper WHERE clause to limit the scope of the delete operation. For this delete operation we will use the *employee* table. The DELETE command in SQL Example 2.25 will delete employee Douglas Bock from the *employee* table:

```
/* SQL Example 2.25 */
DELETE FROM employee
    WHERE emp_ssn = '9991111111';
```

To make the deletion irrevocable, you execute a COMMIT command. Alternatively, you execute a ROLLBACK command to reverse the DELETE command. In fact, ROLLBACK can reverse the effect of any data manipulation command.

The UPDATE Command

You can modify (update) values stored in individual columns of selected rows with the UPDATE command. *Updating* columns is different from *altering* columns. Earlier in this chapter, you studied the ALTER command. The ALTER command changes the table structure, but leaves the table data unaffected. The UPDATE command changes data in the table, not the table structure. The general syntax of the UPDATE command is given in SQL Example 2.26.

```
/* SQL Example 2.26 */
UPDATE table
    SET column = expression [,column = expression] . . .
    [WHERE condition];
```

The SET column = *expression* can be any combination of characters, formulas, or functions that will update data in the specified column name. The WHERE clause is optional, but if it is included, it specifies which rows will be updated. Only one table can be updated at a time with an UPDATE command.

Suppose you wish to update the salary of Waiman Zhu who is presently paid $43,000 annually. He has been given a raise of $2,000, which results in a new salary of $45,000 annually. SQL Example 2.27 gives the command to update Zhu's row in the *employee* table.

```
/* SQL Example 2.27 */
UPDATE employee
   SET emp_salary = 45000
   WHERE emp_ssn = '999444444';
```

INDEXES

Indexes are optional structures associated with tables. Indexes facilitate the rapid retrieval of information from tables. There are different types of indexes including those used to enforce primary key constraints, unique indexes, nonunique indexes, and concatenated indexes, among others. Without indexes, queries would require Oracle to scan all rows in a table in order to return the required rows for the result table.

PRIMARY KEY Indexes

When you specify a PRIMARY KEY constraint, Oracle will automatically create a unique index to support rapid data retrieval for the specified table. Without an index, a command that retrieves data will cause Oracle to completely scan a table for rows that satisfy the retrieval condition. For example, consider the SELECT statement in SQL Example 2.28 that displays a list of employees assigned to a specific department:

```
/* SQL Example 2.28 */
SELECT emp_last_name, emp_first_name, emp_dpt_number
FROM employee
WHERE emp_dpt_number = 7;
```

If the *employee* table is not indexed on the *emp_dpt_number* column, Oracle will have to scan the entire table in order to satisfy the query.

A DBA will usually supervise the creation of indexes. This is necessary because, while indexes can speed the retrieval of data, they also slow down data storage because when new rows are added to a table, the index object must also be updated.

Indexes are logically and physically independent of the data in the associated table. We can create or drop an index at anytime without affecting the base tables or other indexes. If we drop an index, all applications that access the associated table will continue to work; however, access to previously indexed data will probably slow down considerably. You also need to understand that indexes are database objects and, as such, require storage space.

CREATING AN INDEX

The general form of the CREATE INDEX command is given in SQL Example 2.29.

```
/* SQL Example 2.29 */
CREATE INDEX <index name>
    ON <table name> (column1, column2...);
```

Let's create an index on the *emp_dpt_number* column of the *employee* table. The command is shown in SQL Example 2.30. This is an example of a *nonunique* index since many different employees can be assigned to each department.

```
/* SQL Example 2.30 */
CREATE INDEX employee_emp_dpt_number
    ON employee (emp_dpt_number);
Index created.
```

CREATING A UNIQUE INDEX

The Riverbend Hospital Case described in Appendix B stores data in numerous tables. One of the most important tables is the *patient* table that stores information about hospital patients. The Riverbend Hospital assigns each patient a patient identification number (*patient_id*), and this serves as the primary key for the *patient* table. Additionally, each patient has an assigned social security number (*pat_ssn*). Management at the hospital has identified the need to retrieve patient records by the social security number. In order to facilitate efficient row retrieval, you need to create a unique index based on the *pat_ssn* column. The general form of the CREATE UNIQUE INDEX command is given in SQL Example 2.31.

```
/* SQL Example 2.31 */
CREATE UNIQUE INDEX <index name>
    ON <table name> (column1, column2...);
```

SQL Example 2.32 shows the command to create the *patient_pat_ssn* unique index.

```
/* SQL Example 2.32 */
CREATE UNIQUE INDEX patient_pat_ssn
    ON patient (pat_ssn);
Index created.
```

CREATING A COMPOSITE INDEX

A *composite index* (also called a *concatenated index*) is an index created on multiple columns of a table. Columns in a composite index can appear in any order and need not be adjacent columns in the table. Composite indexes enhance row retrieval speed for queries in which the WHERE clause references all or the leading portion of the columns in the composite index. Generally, the most commonly accessed or most selective columns are listed first when creating the index. An index can contain a maximum of 32 columns.

The *treatment* table in the Riverbend Hospital database stores data about treatment services. These services are provided by various staff members to hospital patients. It may be desirable to create a composite index on this table based on the staff identification (*staff_id*) and patient identification (*pat_id*) columns in order to support the preparation of a weekly staff-to-patient load report. The CREATE INDEX command shown in SQL Example 2.32 is appropriate because this index will not be unique.

```
/* SQL Example 2.32 */
CREATE INDEX treatment_staff_id_pat_id
    ON treatment (staff_id, pat_id);
Index created.
```

DROPPING INDEXES

An index should not be retained unless it improves system processing in some fashion. All indexes on a table must be updated whenever row data is changed that is referenced by an index. Useless indexes burden the system by adding unnecessary maintenance and by needlessly occupying disk space. These indexes should be dropped. You also need to understand that you cannot modify indexes. In order to change an index, you must drop it, and then create a replacement index. The syntax of the DROP INDEX command is simple.

```
/* SQL Example 2.33 */
DROP INDEX index_name;
```

The DROP INDEX command in SQL Example 2.34 drops the index named *treatment_staff_id_pat_id*.

```
/* SQL Example 2.34 */
DROP INDEX treatment_staff_id_pat_id;
Index dropped.
```

Oracle provides for additional types of indexes and index usage. For a complete treatment of indexes, refer to the Oracle online documentation at their Web TechNet site.

SUMMARY

In this chapter you have learned the basics of table creation including table modification. You have also learned how to modify individual columns of a table and to insert data into tables. The most common datatypes have been covered and examples of the use of these datatypes have been provided. You have also learned how to link various tables (as per the Entity-Relationship definitions) using the concept of *foreign keys* and define various types of *integrity constraints* for each of the tables in the database. In addition, you have also learned some basic concepts about creating and dropping indexes, including both unique and non-unique indexes as well as composite indexes. After completing the review exercises provided in the next section, you will have the skills needed to work with tables and to understand the material that follows in later chapters.

REVIEW EXERCISES

LEARN THESE TERMS

ALTER. A command used to alter the structure of a database object such as a table.

BLOB. A type of LOB column specification that is short for binary large object, and used to store unstructured data including text, image, video, and spatial data.

CHAR. A type of column data used to store fixed-length character data.

Check constraint. A constraint that forces data values stored in a specific column to fall within some acceptable range of values.

COMMIT. A command used to irrevocably commit data manipulation transactions to a database.

Composite index. An index created on multiple columns of a table.

Composite primary key. When a primary key consists of two or more columns in order to identify each row uniquely.

CREATE INDEX. A command used to create an index for a table.

CREATE TABLE. A statement used to create a table in a database.

Data integrity. Simply means that the data stored in a column is valid.

DATE. A type of column data that can only store valid dates.

Date mask. The default format for expressing a date is the *date mask*—'DD-MON-YY'.

DELETE. A command used to delete rows from a table.

DESCRIBE. A command used to display column names and datatypes for a table.

Domain. Describes the nature of the data that can be stored in a column; a *domain* of valid column values.

DROP. A command used to drop a database object such as tables.

DROP INDEX. A command used to drop or delete an index.

Foreign keys (FKs). Columns in one table that reference primary key (PK) values in another table or in the same table.

INSERT. A command used to insert values into a table.

LOB. A type of column data used to store large object data of either character or binary type that is up to four gigabytes in size.

LONG. A type of column data used to store variable-length, character data that is up to two gigabytes in size.

Not NULL. A constraint meaning every data row must have a value for the column.

NUMBER. A type of column data used to store numeric data values.

PRECISION. The total number of digits specified for a NUMBER column specification.

Primary key. A column or set of columns that uniquely identifies rows of data that are stored in the table.

Referential integrity. The enforcement of FOREIGN KEY constraints to ensure that values of a foreign key correspond to values of a primary key in the table that is referenced.

RENAME. A command used to rename a database object such as a table.

ROLLBACK. A command used to reverse the effect of any data manipulation command.

SCALE. The number of digits to be stored to the right of the decimal point for a fixed-point NUMBER specification.

Table. An object that stores organizational data.

Unique constraint. A constraint used to enforce uniqueness for a column value that is not a primary key column.

UPDATE. A command used to alter data values for rows that already exist within a table.

VARCHAR2. A type of column data used to store variable-length, character data up to 2,000 characters per column entry.

CONCEPTS QUIZ

1. One of your colleagues is building a new information system that would normally access data from the organization's *product* table in the database. However, the system must store data about the quantity of each product that is on order and the current product table does not have a column that can be used to store this data. Your colleague insists that a new product table will be needed to support the new application. What is your response and recommendation?

2. Briefly describe the use of each of the following datatypes:
   a. CHAR
   b. VARCHAR2
   c. LOB
   d. LONG
   e. NUMBER
   f. DATE

3. With regard to the NUMBER datatype, describe how columns are specified for each of the following different types of numeric data:
   a. Integer
   b. Fixed-point
   c. Floating-point

4. Would you specify a table column that will store telephone numbers as NUMBER, CHAR, or VARCHAR2? Justify your selection.

5. Exactly what type of information is stored in a column that is specified as the DATE datatype?

6. Complete this statement: Table and column names should be _____ and reflect the _____ of the data that is to be stored.

7. What are some of the limitations with respect to LONG columns?

8. A column is specified as NUMBER(4). An application program attempts to store the value 56728 to this column. How does Oracle respond, and why?

9. If a date value is stored to a DATE column without specifying a time value, what value for time is stored?

10. Explain the rules that Oracle uses for storing a century value to a date column when the system user or application program does not specify a century.

11. If you want to be able to store a NULL value for a column in a table, what must you do in specifying this capability with the CREATE TABLE command?

12. What constraint type is built into the PRIMARY KEY constraint specification?

13. You are creating a table to store information about products. You want to require each product row to store a value for the *quantity_on_hand* column, and this value cannot be less than zero. What two constraints would you use?

14. You plan to use the ALTER TABLE command to modify a column that already exists within a table. The table already has data rows stored to it. If the column will have a size that is smaller than was originally specified, how will Oracle respond to the ALTER TABLE command?

15. In creating a *department* table for a university database, you wish to specify that each faculty member must be assigned to a department. What type of constraint is this?

16. You plan to insert some new data rows into a table, but do not have complete data row values to insert. Some of the fields will remain blank. How do you accomplish this task?

17. When you specify a PRIMARY KEY constraint, what action does Oracle take with regard to indexes?

18. You need to improve system response time performance for a program application that accesses employee record by a department code column. How can you accomplish this performance improvement?

19. You need to improve system response time for queries that access rows from tables based on several columns as part of the query. What type of index might improve system performance?

SQL CODING EXERCISES AND QUESTIONS

In answering the SQL exercises and questions, submit a copy of each command that you execute and any messages that Oracle generates while executing your SQL commands. Also list the output for any result table that is generated by your SQL statements.

1. Create a table named *test_table*. This table should have two columns named *test_id* and *test_description*. These columns should be defined to store the following type of data, respectively: *test_id* stores numeric data that is a maximum of three characters in size; *test_description* stores variable character data that is a maximum of 25 characters in size. Insert two rows into the *test_table*. You should create your own data.

2. Use the DESCRIBE command to describe the *test_table*.

3. Use the following SELECT command to display the rows in the *test_table*.

```
SELECT * FROM test_table;
```

4. Use the DROP command to drop the *test_table*.

5. Create the *department* table described in Appendix A. Include all constraint specifications required to ensure data integrity.

6. Add the data shown here to the *department* table. Leave the `dpt_mgrssn` and `dpt_mgr_start_date` column values as NULL. Commit your row insertions in the *department* table.

dpt_no	dpt_name	dpt_mgrssn	Dpt_mgr_start_date
7	Production	NULL	NULL
3	Admin and Records	NULL	NULL
1	Headquarters	NULL	NULL

7. Use the DESCRIBE command to describe the *department* table.

8. Use the following SELECT command to display the rows in the *department* table.

```
SELECT *
FROM department;
```

9. Create the *employee* table described in Appendix A. Include all constraint specifications required to ensure data integrity. Create the referential integrity constraints needed to ensure that the department to which employees are assigned for

work exists within the *department* table. Your integrity constraints should also allow employees to NOT be assigned to a department.

10. Add the data shown in Appendix A to the *employee* table. Add an additional row to the employee data consisting of data that describes yourself (your own employee row). Assign yourself a salary of 50,000, parking space 999, department 7, and supervisor SSN of '333445555'. Commit your row insertions in the *employee* table.

11. Use the following SELECT statement to display the rows in the *employee* table.

```
SELECT emp_ssn, emp_last_name
FROM employee;
```

12. Delete your row from the *employee* table. Use the SELECT statement given in question 11 to display the employee rows. Verify your record has been deleted. Assume that the deletion of your row was an error. Execute the command that will undelete your row (*Note:* Do not simply reinsert the row to the table). Use the SELECT statement again to verify that your row has been restored to the table.

13. Employee Zhu has reported that his address is incorrect. The correct street address is: 6 Main St. Update the *emp_address* column of his data row accordingly.

14. Download the script needed to create the remaining tables of the Company Database schema shown in Appendix A. Run the script to create the entire database. Prior to running the script, you will need to delete the *employee* and then the *department* tables that you created for earlier exercises.

15. Alter the *employee* table to add a column that will be used to store the salary earned year-to-date. Name this column *salary_year_to_date* and use an appropriate NUMBER datatype specification. You do not need to store any data to this column.

16. Create a nonunique index on the *employee* table for the employee zip code (*emp_zip*) column. Give the index an appropriate name.

17. Create a composite, nonunique index on the *employee* table for the employee zip code (*emp_zip*) and employee last name (*emp_last_name*) columns.

CHAPTER 3

SINGLE TABLE QUERY BASICS

This chapter focuses on learning to write SELECT statements to retrieve information from tables. This is termed *querying a table,* and this chapter covers single-table queries, meaning that the information retrieved will come from a single database table. As you have probably determined by this point in your studies, a database can be queried to produce both small and large quantities of information. Simple queries often tend to produce large quantities of information in terms of row output, while more complex queries are capable of extracting specific information from a database. If a query produces a large quantity of information, managers who seek to use the information to aid them in decision making may be overwhelmed by the sheer volume of information. Usually, managers need specific pieces of information to help them make decisions. In this chapter, we will initially learn to write simple queries, and will progress to increasingly complex queries.

OBJECTIVES

You query relational databases through use of the SELECT statement. Chapter 1 introduced the SELECT statement. In this chapter, you will master the basics of the SELECT statement. You will learn to write queries to select both specific rows and specific columns from a table. You will also learn to sort the output in various ways. Additionally, you will learn to avoid some of the common errors that can be made when writing a SELECT statement. The learning objectives for this chapter are:

- Write simple SELECT statements.
- Learn to use the COLUMN command to format output.
- Eliminate duplicate rows with the DISTINCT clause.
- Use the WHERE clause to specify selection criteria and conditions.
- Order rows with the ORDER BY clause.

SIMPLE SELECT STATEMENTS

The main element in a SQL query is the SELECT statement. A properly written SELECT statement will always produce a result in the form of one or more rows of output. The SELECT statement chooses (selects) rows from one or more tables according to specific criteria. In this chapter we focus on selecting rows from a single table. SQL Example 3.1 shows the simplest form of a query.

```
/* SQL Example 3.1 */
SELECT *
FROM employee;

EMP_SSN        EMP_LAST_NAME      EMP_FIRST_NAME      EMP_MIDDLE_NAME
--------       -------------      -------------       -------------
999666666      Bordoloi           Bijoy
999555555      Joyner             Suzanne             A
999444444      Zhu                Waiman              Z
more rows and columns will be displayed...
```

This query selects rows from the *employee* table. The asterisk (*) tells Oracle to select (display) *all* columns contained in the table *employee*. The resulting output is termed a *result* table. The result table displayed in SQL Example 3.1 only lists the first three rows and first four columns of the result table. The full *employee* table is described in Appendix A and is part of the Company database. The full result table output will wrap around your computer screen because the rows of data are too large to display to a single line. Additionally, you will notice that the *emp_last_name*, *emp_first_name*, and *emp_middle_name* columns are quite wide when they display to your computer monitor because when the *employee* table was created, these columns were defined to be large enough to store the largest last, first, or middle name data values that might ever occur for an employee. Later in this chapter, you will learn to format the width of result table columns.

This particular type of query uses an asterisk (*) symbol to tell Oracle: "Give me everything you have on employees. Don't hold anything back." All rows and all columns are selected. The SELECT statement in SQL Example 3.2 produces an identical result table by listing all column names in the *employee* table.

```
/* SQL Example 3.2 */
SELECT emp_ssn, emp_last_name, emp_first_name, emp_middle_name,
    emp_address, emp_city, emp_state, emp_zip, emp_date_of_birth,
    emp_salary, emp_parking_space, emp_gender,
    emp_dpt_number, emp_superssn
FROM employee;
```

Clearly, it is simpler to type the first query as opposed to the one given above that lists each column name individually, but you would only use the asterisk (*) in a SELECT statement if you wished to display all columns in the result table. Normally, this is not the case.

Note that a comma separates each column name. This syntax is required. The SELECT statement also specifies the table name in a FROM clause. Finally, the semicolon at the end of the query tells Oracle that this is the end of the query. You may wonder about the ordering of the column names. It happens that the ordering of column names is immaterial except that the result table will display the columns in the order specified in the SELECT statement. Let's examine the data stored in the *department* table. We'll begin by first describing the *department* table.

```
/* SQL Example 3.3 */
DESC department;
Name                        Null?        Type
---------------             -------      -----------
DPT_NO                      NOT NULL     NUMBER(2)
DPT_NAME                    NOT NULL     VARCHAR2(20)
DPT_MGRSSN                                CHAR(9)
DPT_MGR_START_DATE                        DATE
```

There are only four columns in the *department* table. These columns store the department number, department name, department manager's Social Security Number (SSN), and the date that each department manager was assigned to the job of department manager. The two queries in SQL Examples 3.4 and 3.5 produce exactly the same result table.

```
/* SQL Example 3.4 */
SELECT *
FROM department;
```

```
/* SQL Example 3.5 */
SELECT dpt_no, dpt_name, dpt_mgrssn, dpt_mgr_start_date
FROM department;

DPT_NO    DPT_NAME           DPT_MGRSS    DPT_MGR_S
------    ---------------    --------     --------
7         Production         999444444    22-MAY-98
3         Admin and Records  999555555    01-JAN-01
1         Headquarters       999666666    19-JUN-81
```

SQL Example 3.6 is a revision of SQL Example 3.5 to reorder the columns. The output in terms of rows is identical, but the ordering of the columns changes to match the ordering in the SELECT statement.

```
/* SQL Example 3.6 */
SELECT dpt_name, dpt_no, dpt_mgr_start_date, dpt_mgrssn
FROM department;
```

DPT_NAME	DPT_NO	DPT_MGR_S	DPT_MGRSS
Production	7	22-MAY-98	999444444
Admin and Records	3	01-JAN-01	999555555
Headquarters	1	19-JUN-81	999666666

INDENTING SQL CODE

Have you noticed that we always start a new line for the FROM clause in a SELECT statement. We have also indented four characters in listing the columns to be displayed where the list of columns is too large to fit within a single line. It is fairly common to follow this type of indentation convention when writing a query because it makes a query easier to read. However, Oracle will process a query regardless of whether you type an entire query on one line or indent. Oracle simply looks for the semicolon marking the end of the query. This is because SQL is a free-form language. This means that there are no rules about how many words you can put on a line or where you break a line. For example, the SQL statements in SQL Examples 3.7 and 3.8 are considered exactly the same.

```
/* SQL Example 3.7 */
SELECT * FROM employee;
```

```
/* SQL Example 3.8 */
SELECT
*
FROM
employee;
```

Although Oracle does not require it, a new line should be started for each clause in a SQL statement. This will increase maintenance and readability. The following keywords are your signal to start a new line:

- SELECT
- FROM
- WHERE
- GROUP BY
- HAVING
- ORDER BY

SELECTING SPECIFIC COLUMNS

As you can see, using asterisk (*) is a quick and easy way to list all column names in a table. However, in day-to-day queries you will rarely need to specify all of the available column names in a table. If you provided your boss with all of the columns and rows from a table, the boss would likely tell you that you were providing too much detail! Let's suppose that your boss wants a listing of only employee SSNs, last names, and first names. The SELECT statement to produce this output is shown in SQL Example 3.9.

```
/* SQL Example 3.9 */
SELECT emp_ssn, emp_last_name, emp_first_name
FROM employee;

EMP_SSN          EMP_LAST_NAME       EMP_FIRST_NAME
--------         -------------       -------------
999666666        Bordoloi            Bijoy
999555555        Joyner              Suzanne
999444444        Zhu                 Waiman
more rows will be displayed...
```

NOTE: Throughout this manual, the rows of a result table produced by a query are limited to only the number of rows needed in order for you to understand the query. As you execute each query, you will sometimes see that we have omitted rows of data output for the purpose of brevity or clarity.

To review, the rules for writing a simple SELECT query are:

- Specify the column names you want displayed in the result set by typing the exact, complete column names.
- Separate each column name with a comma (,).
- Specify the name of the table after the FROM clause.
- Terminate the query with a semi-colon (;).

USING COLUMN COMMANDS TO FORMAT OUTPUT

At times you will write a query where the columnar output will not fit onto a single display line. When this happens, the result table will display lines that "wrap" around to the next line and the information will be difficult to read. SQL Example 3.10 produces output that wraps to the next line.

```
/* SQL Example 3.10 */
SELECT emp_ssn, emp_last_name, emp_first_name,
    emp_date_of_birth, emp_superssn
FROM employee;

EMP_SSN          EMP_LAST_NAME       EMP_FIRST_NAME       EMP_DATE_
--------         -------------       -------------        --------
EMP_SUPER
--------
999666666        Bordoloi            Bijoy                10-NOV-67
999555555        Joyner              Suzanne              20-JUN-71
more rows will be displayed...
```

You can clean up the result table of such a query by modifying the output display size of specific columns. This is termed formatting the result table. Column output is formatted with the COLUMN-FORMAT command. The example shown below formats the *emp_last_name* and *emp_first_name* columns to restrict their output to 15 characters each. This is significantly smaller than the 25-character column width specified for each of these columns in the *employee* table. This means that employees with first or last names larger than 15 characters will have all characters after 15 wrap to the next line. If you do not want the output to wrap to the next line, you can use the SET WRAP OFF command to cause any characters beyond 15 to simply truncate in the display of the result table. The advantage is that each single row of output is displayed on a single line, thereby improving the readability of the information as is done in SQL Example 3.11.

```
/* SQL Example 3.11 */
SET WRAP OFF;
COLUMN emp_last_name FORMAT A15;
COLUMN emp_first_name FORMAT A15;
SELECT emp_ssn, emp_last_name, emp_first_name, emp_date_of_birth,
    emp_superssn
FROM employee;

EMP_SSN      EMP_LAST_NAME   EMP_FIRST_NAME   EMP_DATE_   EMP_SUPER
---------    -------------   --------------   ---------   ---------
999666666    Bordoloi        Bijoy            10-NOV-67
999555555    Joyner          Suzanne          20-JUN-71   999666666
999444444    Zhu             Waiman           08-DEC-75   999666666
more rows will be displayed...
```

SQL Example 3.11 formatted character data. You can also format the output of numeric columns. By default, a numeric column displays with a width equal to the width of the heading. You can both increase or decrease the width of a numeric column displayed in a result table. Additionally, SQL*PLUS displays numbers with as many digits as necessary in order to ensure that the numeric value is accurately displayed. You can set the default width of numeric column displays with the SET command. SQL Example 3.12 sets the NUMWIDTH parameter to 8 characters of output display (the default value of NUMWIDTH is normally 10). You should understand that formatting commands such as NUMWIDTH do not affect the actual table's structure in any way—only the output displayed in a result table is affected.

```
/* SQL Example 3.12 */
SET NUMWIDTH 8;
```

Setting the NUMWIDTH parameter value overrides the width of numeric column displays to ensure that the columnar output is at least NUMWIDTH digits in width! When using the COLUMN command to format numeric data, the placeholders "9" and "0" are used to denote a position to display one digit of output. The placeholder "9" will format numeric output, but values are not required to be displayed. The placeholder "0" also formats numeric output, but requires output. SQL Example 3.13 shows the use of the "9" placeholder.

```
/* SQL Example 3.13 */
COLUMN emp_salary FORMAT 99999.99;
SELECT emp_salary
FROM employee;

EMP_SALARY
---------
  55000.00
  43000.00
  43000.00
more rows will be displayed...
```

If the *emp_salary* is formatted as 0099999.99, the output display changes to reflect that output is required in the first two-digit locations.

```
/* SQL Example 3.14 */
COLUMN emp_salary FORMAT 0099999.99;
SELECT emp_salary
FROM employee;

EMP_SALARY
----------
  0055000.00
  0043000.00
  0043000.00
more rows will be displayed...
```

The output display is fairly "plain" and may not satisfy managers simply because large numbers are difficult to interpret if they are not displayed in the manner in which managers are used to seeing them displayed. In this case, managers might prefer that salary figures be displayed with a dollar sign ($) and appropriate comma to separate the thousands and hundreds digits. This is demonstrated in SQL Example 3.15.

```
/* SQL Example 3.15 */
COLUMN emp_salary FORMAT $99,999.99;
SELECT emp_salary
FROM employee;

EMP_SALARY
----------
  $55,000.00
  $43,000.00
  $43,000.00
more rows will be displayed...
```

COMMON ERRORS

Although SQL is a free-form language, there are still syntactical rules that you must follow or you will receive an error message instead of the desired result table. The Oracle relational database management system communicates errors in SELECT statements by providing unique error numbers and accompanying error descriptions. Let's examine some example errors.

INVALID COLUMN NAME

The SELECT statement in SQL Example 3.16 has the employee SSN column name spelled incorrectly.

```
/* SQL Example 3.16 */
SELECT emp_socsecno
FROM employee;

ERROR at line 1:
ORA-00904: invalid column name
```

Oracle responds by specifying which line has the error. Here the error is in line 1 where the employee SSN column should be *emp_ssn,* not *emp_socsecno.* The Oracle error number is ORA-00904 and the accompany message is invalid column name. If you receive this error message, check the spelling of the column name for typographical errors.

FROM KEYWORD MISSING

SQL Example 3.17 shows a SELECT statement that is missing the FROM clause so that no table name is specified. Without a table name, the database management system does not know which table to query.

```
/* SQL Example 3.17 */
SELECT emp_ssn;

ERROR at line 1:
ORA-00923: FROM keyword not found where expected
```

UNKNOWN COMMAND—INVALID COMMAND STRUCTURE

In SQL Example 3.18, the order of the SELECT and FROM clauses is reversed. Oracle is very confused by this command and simply returns an unknown command error message.

```
/* SQL Example 3.18 */
FROM employee SELECT emp_ssn;
SP2-0734: unknown command beginning "FROM emplo . . ." - rest of line
ignored.
```

ERRORS IN PLACING COMMAS

Some types of syntax errors cause Oracle to return error messages that are not particularly helpful in debugging the error. In SQL Example 3.19, a comma is missing after the *emp_last_name* column specification. Instead of reporting back that there is a syntax error or that a comma is missing, Oracle produces a result set that is missing one column of data. At first glance, it appears that Oracle is listing only the SSN and first name for each employee, but a closer inspection of the output rows reveals that the last name of each employee is listed, but the column heading is wrong! Oracle did not treat this as an error. Instead, Oracle thought that you only wanted two columns of output, and that you wanted the second column to have a special column heading other than the default of EMP_LAST_NAME.

```
/* SQL Example 3.19 */
SELECT emp_ssn, emp_last_name emp_first_name
FROM employee;

EMP_SSN        EMP_FIRST_NAME
---------      --------------
999666666      Bordoloi
999555555      Joyner
999444444      Zhu
more rows will be displayed...
```

There is another possible type of comma placement error and that is placing a comma after the last column name specified in a SELECT statement as is done in SQL Example 3.20. In this situation, Oracle returns the ORA-00936: missing expression error. This means that Oracle expected you to provide an additional column specification after the *emp_first_name* column.

```
/* SQL Example 3.20 */
SELECT emp_ssn, emp_last_name, emp_first_name,
FROM employee;

ERROR at line 2:
ORA-00936: missing expression
```

THE DISTINCT CLAUSE: ELIMINATING DUPLICATE ROWS

As we learned in Chapter 2, tables are generally designed with a primary key that guarantees that each row in a table is unique. Thus, if you select all columns from a table, no two rows in the result table will be duplicates. However, if a SELECT statement does not select all columns, it is possible for the result table to contain duplicate rows. This can occur when the SELECT statement does not select the primary key column(s) as part of the output.

Oracle provides a means for eliminating duplicate rows in a result table through use of the DISTINCT keyword. The SELECT statement in SQL Example 3.21 produces a simple listing of salaries paid to employees. The result table contains rows with duplicate values—remember that the *emp_salary* column was formatted earlier.

```
/* SQL Example 3.21 */
SELECT emp_salary
FROM employee;

EMP_SALARY
----------
  $55,000.00
  $43,000.00
  $43,000.00
  $25,000.00
  $25,000.00
  $30,000.00
  $38,000.00
  $25,000.00
8 rows selected.
```

When row output is duplicated, it is possible for the duplicate values to obscure the relevant data that managers seek to use in making decisions. The query is rewritten in SQL Example 3.22 and uses the DISTINCT keyword to eliminate duplicate rows. When the DISTINCT keyword is used, the output ordering of rows usually change unless the rows are explicitly sorted with the ORDER BY clause. Do not worry about row order for now as you will learn to control row output ordering later in this chapter.

```
/* SQL Example 3.22 */
SELECT DISTINCT emp_salary
FROM employee;

EMP_SALARY
----------
  $25,000.00
  $30,000.00
  $38,000.00
  $43,000.00
  $55,000.00
```

The DISTINCT keyword must immediately follow the SELECT keyword and is not separated from the first column name with a comma. If you mistakenly place the DISTINCT keyword other than immediately following the SELECT statement, the query will generate the ORA-00923: FROM keyword not found where expected error message as is shown in SQL Example 3.23.

```
/* SQL Example 3.23 */
SELECT emp_salary DISTINCT
FROM employee;

ERROR at line 1:
ORA-00923: FROM keyword not found where expected
```

The DISTINCT keyword also eliminates duplicate rows where more than one column is displayed in the result table. SQL Example 3.24 shows a query of the *bed* table for the Riverbend Hospital database described in Appendix B. Note the duplicate rows highlighted in bold text.

```
/* SQL Example 3.24 */
COLUMN room_id FORMAT A7;
COLUMN bed_type_id FORMAT A11;
SELECT room_id, bed_type_id
FROM bed;

ROOM_ID   BED_TYPE_ID
-------   -----------
SW1001    R1
SW1002    R1
SW1003    R2
SW1004    R1
SW1005    R2
SW1006    R1
SW1010    R1
SW1010    R2
SW1011    R2
SW1011    R2
more rows will be displayed...
```

The DISTINCT clause eliminates duplicate row output as shown in SQL Example 3.25.

```
/* SQL Example 3.25 */
SELECT DISTINCT room_id, bed_type_id
FROM bed;

ROOM_ID   BED_TYPE_ID
-------   -----------
SW1001    R1
SW1002    R1
SW1003    R2
SW1004    R1
SW1005    R2
SW1006    R1
SW1010    R1
SW1010    R2
SW1011    R2
more rows will be displayed...
```

SELECTING ROWS: THE WHERE CLAUSE

You have learned how to display specific columns from a table, as well as how to reduce the number of rows displayed through use of the DISTINCT keyword. As you may recall from Chapter 1, displaying specific columns from a table is known as a *project* operation. We will now focus on displaying specific rows of output. This is known as a *select* operation.

Specific rows can be selected by adding a WHERE clause to a SELECT query. Suppose that your boss is working on the quarterly budget for your organization. As part of this activity, it is necessary to produce a listing of each employee's SSN, last name, first name, and salary, but only for employees that are paid at least $25,000 annually. SQL Example 3.26 accomplishes this task. Note the use of the WHERE clause shown in bold text.

```
/* SQL Example 3.26 */
COLUMN emp_last_name FORMAT A15;
COLUMN emp_first_name FORMAT A15;
SELECT emp_ssn, emp_last_name, emp_first_name, emp_salary
FROM employee
WHERE emp_salary >= 35000;

EMP_SSN      EMP_LAST_NAME    EMP_FIRST_NAME    EMP_SALARY
---------    -------------    --------------    ----------
999666666    Bordoloi         Bijoy             $55,000.00
999555555    Joyner           Suzanne           $43,000.00
999444444    Zhu              Waiman            $43,000.00
more rows will be displayed...
```

As you can see, the result table contains only rows where the *condition* (salary >= 35000) is met. Further, the dollar sign ($) and comma (,) are *not* used in specifying the numeric value for the employee salary in the WHERE clause. In this example, we used the greater-than-or-equal-to operator (>=) equal. You could just as easily request a list of employees that are paid less than or equal to $35,000 or any other value for employee salary as is done in SQL Example 3.27.

```
/* SQL Example 3.27 */
SELECT emp_ssn, emp_last_name, emp_first_name, emp_salary
FROM employee
WHERE emp_salary < 35000;

EMP_SSN      EMP_LAST_NAME    EMP_FIRST_NAME    EMP_SALARY
---------    -------------    --------------    ----------
999887777    Markis           Marcia            $25,000.00
999222222    Amin             Hyder             $25,000.00
999111111    Bock             Douglas           $30,000.00
more rows will be displayed...
```

COMPARISON OPERATORS

In all, Oracle has nine different *comparison operators*. These are listed in Table 3.1.

COMPARING CHARACTER DATA

The use of comparison operators is not limited to numeric data. They can also be used with columns containing character data. When comparing CHAR and VARCHAR2 data, the less than operator (<) means earlier in the alphabet (A comes before B), while the greater than operator (>) means later in the alphabet (Z comes after Y).

When you use comparison operators in a WHERE clause, the arguments (objects or values you are comparing) on both sides of the operator must be either a column name, or a specific value. If a specific value is specified, then the value must be either a numeric value or a literal string. If the value is a character string or date, you must surround the value (string of characters) with which a column is being compared with *single quotation marks* (' ').

Suppose your manager wants a listing of the social security number, last name, and first name for all male employees. The SELECT query requires a WHERE clause that selects rows based on the employee gender (*emp_gender*) column. The *emp_gender* column stores coded data wherein M = male and F = female employees. SQL Example 3.28 shows a SELECT statement with the correct WHERE clause.

```
/* SQL Example 3.28 */
SELECT emp_ssn, emp_last_name, emp_first_name
FROM employee
WHERE emp_gender = 'M';

EMP_SSN        EMP_LAST_NAME      EMP_FIRST_NAME
---------      -------------      --------------
999666666      Bordoloi           Bijoy
999444444      Zhu                Waiman
999222222      Amin               Hyder
more rows will be displayed...
```

TABLE 3.1

Operator	Meaning
=	equal to
<	less than
>	greater than
>=	greater than or equal to
<=	less than or equal to
!=	not equal to
<>	not equal to
!>	not greater than
!<	not less than

Note that the *emp_gender* column does not have to be specified in the listing of columns selected for display in the result table in order to use the column name in the WHERE clause. Now let's see what happens if you make a mistake and fail to enclose the employee gender code within single quotation marks.

```
/* SQL Example 3.29 */
SELECT emp_ssn, emp_last_name, emp_first_name
FROM employee
WHERE emp_gender = M;

ERROR at line 3:
ORA-00904: invalid column name
```

Oracle returns error ORA-00904: invalid column name. While this error message does not tell you exactly what you did wrong, it does identify the line that has the error (line 3 above). Recall our earlier rule about the arguments in a WHERE clause. Since the literal string value was not enclosed by single quote marks, Oracle assumed the letter M to be a column name. Of course, there is no column named M in the *employee* table so an error was returned. So, when you see this error with a reference to a line associated with a WHERE clause, you need to determine whether or not the column referenced by the WHERE clause stores character data.

You can also write SELECT statements that use operators other than the equal sign. For example, suppose your manager needs a listing of employees that have a first name that begins with the letter "J," or that begins with a letter that occurs later in the alphabet than the letter "J." SQL Example 3.30 shows the appropriate WHERE clause.

```
/* SQL Example 3.30 */
SELECT emp_last_name, emp_first_name
FROM employee
WHERE emp_last_name >= 'J';

EMP_LAST_NAME      EMP_FIRST_NAME
-------------      --------------
Joyner             Suzanne
Zhu                Waiman
Markis             Marcia
more rows will be displayed...
```

ORDERING ROWS: THE ORDER BY CLAUSE

Normally, when rows are added to a table they are appended to the end of the table. This produces a table containing unordered rows. This is clear when examining the result table for SQL Example 3.30; the rows are not in alphabetic order.

When you display only a few rows of data, it may be unnecessary to sort the output; however, when you display numerous rows, managers may be aided in decision making by having the information sorted. Output from a SELECT statement can be sorted by using the optional ORDER BY clause. When you use the ORDER BY clause, the column name on which you are ordering must also be a column name that is specified in the SELECT clause.

The query from SQL Example 3.30 is expanded in SQL Example 3.31 to add an ORDER BY clause that sorts the result table by the *emp_last_name* column in ascending order. Ascending order is the default sort order.

```
/* SQL Example 3.31 */
SELECT emp_last_name, emp_first_name
FROM employee
WHERE emp_last_name >= 'J'
ORDER BY emp_last_name;

EMP_LAST_NAME        EMP_FIRST_NAME
------------         --------------
Joshi                Dinesh
Joyner               Suzanne
Markis               Marcia
more rows will be displayed...
```

You can also sort data based on numeric column values. SQL Example 3.32 sorts employees based on their monthly salary.

```
/* SQL Example 3.32 */
SELECT emp_last_name, emp_first_name, emp_salary
FROM employee
WHERE emp_salary > 35000
ORDER BY emp_salary;

EMP_LAST_NAME        EMP_FIRST_NAME      EMP_SALARY
------------         --------------      ---------
Joshi                Dinesh              $38,000.00
Joyner               Suzanne             $43,000.00
Zhu                  Waiman              $43,000.00
Bordoloi             Bijoy               $55,000.00
```

SORT ORDER

It is fairly intuitive that *numeric* columns will sort by default from smallest to largest values. But what about sorts of *character* data? Character data sorts are language dependent. The parameter NLS_LANGUAGE is set to support a specific national language when a database is created, for example NLS_LANGUAGE = ENGLISH. The NLS_LANGUAGE can be explicitly modified for sort operations, but this is beyond the scope of this book.

Table 3.2 displays the sort order that Oracle uses when sorting English language and special characters. The sort order here is based on the ASCII character coding scheme. Lower case letters come *after* upper case letters in the sort order. Oracle converts the ASCII character codes to hexadecimal equivalents when sorting.

TABLE 3.2   Characters, in ASCII Order
! " # $ % & ' ( ) * + , - . / 0 1 2 3 4 5 6 7 8 9 : ; < = > ? @
A B C D E F G H I J K L M N O P Q R S T U V W X Y Z [\ ] ^ _ '
a b c d e f g h i j k l m n o p q r s t u v w x y z { | } ~

ORDER BY with ASC and DESC Options

By default, the ORDER BY clause will sort output rows in the result table in ascending order. However, there are situations when you will need to display the results in descending order. Let's rewrite SQL Example 3.32 to display the rows in reverse-salary order, that is, highest salaries first. We will use the keyword DESC (short for descending) to force this descending sort. The alternative default is ASC which sorts in ascending order, but the ASC keyword is rarely used since it is the default.

When the ASC or DESC optional keyword is used, it must follow the column name on which you are sorting in the WHERE clause. SQL Example 3.33 demonstrates the DESC keyword.

```
/* SQL Example 3.33 */
SELECT emp_last_name, emp_first_name, emp_salary
FROM employee
WHERE emp_salary > 35000
ORDER BY emp_salary DESC;

EMP_LAST_NAME        EMP_FIRST_NAME        EMP_SALARY
------------         --------------        ---------
Bordoloi             Bijoy                 $55,000.00
Joyner               Suzanne               $43,000.00
Zhu                  Waiman                $43,000.00
Joshi                Dinesh                $38,000.00
```

SQL Example 3.34 shows what happens when you misplace the DESC keyword. Here the DESC is placed before *emp_salary* and the resulting error message is ORA-00936: missing expression.

```
/* SQL Example 3.34 */
SELECT emp_last_name, emp_first_name, emp_salary
FROM employee
WHERE emp_salary > 35000
ORDER BY DESC emp_salary;

ERROR at line 4:
ORA-00936: missing expression
```

ORDER BY with More Than One Column

Thus far, you have learned how to sort output to a result table based upon a single column; however, there are occasions wherein it is necessary to sort data based on more than one column. Sorting by multiple columns can improve the look and usability of information. As your boss learns more about the information you can extract from the company database, the demands on your skills increase. The latest request is for a listing of employees sorted alphabetically within department. In order to meet this request for information, you may wish to study the *employee* table description provided in Appendix A or use the DESCRIBE command within SQL*PLUS to examine the structure of the *employee* table. In addition to storing employee names and social security numbers, you note that each row has a column named *emp_dpt_number*. The values stored in this column are the department number to which employees are assigned.

The type of output desired by your manager involves a sort within a sort. We will define the *emp_dpt_number* column as the major sort column. The *emp_last_name* column will serve as the minor sort column. We shall sort employees by name within department by listing the major sort column first in the ORDER BY clause, followed by the minor sort column.

Note that the result shown in SQL Example 3.35 lists employees sorted by department number first. Within each department, employees are sorted by last name.

```
/* SQL Example 3.35 */
SELECT emp_dpt_number, emp_last_name, emp_first_name
FROM employee
ORDER BY emp_dpt_number, emp_last_name;

EMP_DPT_NUMBER       EMP_LAST_NAME        EMP_FIRST_NAME
--------------       -------------        --------------
             1       Bordoloi             Bijoy
             3       Amin                 Hyder
             3       Joyner               Suzanne
             3       Markis               Marcia
             7       Bock                 Douglas
             7       Joshi                Dinesh
             7       Prescott             Sherri
             7       Zhu                  Waiman
```

You can combine both ascending and descending sort variables within a single ORDER BY clause. Suppose that you wish to display the data shown above, but sort the departments in descending order while maintaining the employee names in ascending order by last name. SQL Example 3.36 shows the correct query.

```
/* SQL Example 3.36 */
SELECT emp_dpt_number, emp_last_name, emp_first_name
FROM employee
ORDER BY emp_dpt_number DESC, emp_last_name;

EMP_DPT_NUMBER       EMP_LAST_NAME        EMP_FIRST_NAME
--------------       -------------        --------------
             7       Bock                 Douglas
             7       Joshi                Dinesh
             7       Prescott             Sherri
```

```
7        Zhu            Waiman
3        Amin           Hyder
3        Joyner         Suzanne
3        Markis         Marcia
1        Bordoloi       Bijoy
```

Note that the department numbers are now in descending order, but within each department, the employee names are still displayed in alphabetic order by last name. In summary, the ORDER BY clause is a powerful tool for improving the usability of any result table listing, and it is easy to use with very few rules.

- You can include a maximum of 16 column names in the ORDER BY clause.
- You must separate column names within the ORDER BY clause with a comma (,) in order to avoid syntax error messages.

SUMMARY

In this chapter, we explored the power of simple SELECT statements. You learned to select specific rows and columns from individual tables by specifying column names to be displayed, and by using the WHERE clause to specify conditions for displaying rows. Additionally, you learned to sort the information displayed by using the ORDER BY clause. After completing the exercises at the end of this chapter you should feel comfortable executing simple queries.

REVIEW EXERCISES

LEARN THESE TERMS

SELECT.   The SQL statement used to query a database.

FROM.   The SELECT statement clause used to specify the table(s) from which data are to be retrieved.

COLUMN-FORMAT.   A statement used to format columnar output in order to restrict the number of characters of output assigned to specific columns.

DISTINCT.   A keyword used as a means for eliminating duplicate rows in a result table.

WHERE.   A clause in a query used to specify conditions for selecting rows to be displayed in the result table.

Comparison operator.   Operators used in WHERE clauses that are used to specify conditions for selecting rows. There are nine operators with means such as "equal to, "less than," and "greater than," as well as others.

ORDER BY.   A clause used to sort the display of rows in a result table. The column name on which you are sorting must be specified in the SELECT clause.

ASC.   A keyword used to specify that the ORDER BY is in ascending order. This is the default.

DESC.   A keyword used to specify that the ORDER BY is in descending order.

CONCEPTS QUIZ

1. Explain what the asterisk (*) means when used in a SELECT statement.
2. Which clause is used to specify the name of a table from which data are to be retrieved?

3. What can you do to create a result table that has columns ordered in a specific sequence or ordering?
4. What special syntax is used to mark the end of a SELECT query?
5. Why is a new line started for each clause in a SQL statement?
6. What does the following statement do?

```
COLUMN emp_last_name FORMAT A12;
```

7. What does the SET WRAP OFF command do?
8. What is the default width of a numeric column in a result table?
9. Which command is used to set the width of numeric column displays?
10. What is the default value of NUMWIDTH?
11. If the FORMAT for a numeric column is FORMAT $99,990.00, what will be displayed if the value for the column for a specific table row is NULL?
12. What error message is returned by the Oracle relational DBMS when a SELECT statement specifies a column name that does not exist within the table that is being queried?
13. How does the Oracle relational DBMS respond if the order of the SELECT and FROM clauses in a query is reversed?
14. How does the Oracle relational DBMS respond if your query is missing a comma between two column names?
15. What is the purpose of the DISTINCT keyword in a query?
16. Where is the DISTINCT keyword placed in a query?
17. What is the purpose of the WHERE clause in a query?
18. List the nine comparison operators and their meaning.
19. When comparing column values that are character data, what does the less than operator (<) mean?
20. If you are comparing a column value that is character to a literal string, what syntax is used to specify the literal string of characters?
21. What is the purpose of the ORDER BY clause?
22. How is the sort order for an ORDER BY clause determined when sorting by a character column?
23. What is the optional keyword used to specify descending order for an ORDER BY clause?
24. A manager wants a result table sorted by two columns, department number (*emp_dpt_number*) and employee last name (*emp_last_name*) within the department number. Which column is the major sort column and which one is the minor sort column, and how is this denoted in the ORDER BY clause?

SQL CODING EXERCISES AND QUESTIONS

In answering the SQL exercises and questions, submit a copy of each command that you execute and any messages that Oracle generates while executing your SQL commands. Also list the output for any result table that is generated by your SQL statements.

1. Your manager wants a listing that will display all of the data from the *assignment* table. Write the query. You may wish to use the DESCRIBE command to examine the structure of the *assignment* table.

2. Write a query that will select all columns from the *assignment* table without using the (*) in your query.

3. Your manager wants the listing that you created for question 2 modified. The query should list only the employee SSN (*work_emp_ssn*) and number of hours an employee has worked on a project (*work_hours*) in the result table.

4. Rewrite the query from question 3, but reverse the order in which the two columns are displayed. Display *work_hours* first and *work_emp_ssn* second.

5. Your manager requires a listing of employees from the organization's *employee* table in order to meet the reporting requirements for a government agency. The listing must include each employee's last name (*emp_last_name*), first name (*emp_first_name*), date of birth (*emp_date_of_birth*) and gender code (*emp_gender*). Write the query to display the output sorted by *emp_last_name*.

6. The last query caused the result table to display with rows wrapped because each line was too long to fit onto a single line of output. Use the appropriate command to limit the output column width for the employee last and first names to 15 characters. Limit the output column width for the employee middle name to 1 character. Execute the query to display the new result table.

7. Management has determined that the listing has the appropriate information; however, they wish for the data to be sorted first by employee gender (major sort column is *emp_gender*) and then by employee last name within gender (minor sort column is *emp_last_name*). As such, they want the *emp_gender* column to be displayed first, followed by the remainder of the columns used in question 6. Rewrite the query keeping the column width settings specified in question 6.

8. Your boss's boss is concerned about employee dependents. Your manager directs you to prepare a listing of dependent names (*dep_name*), dates of birth (*dep_date_of_birth*), and the relationship to employees (*dep_relationship*) from the dependant table. The first column displayed should be the employee's SSN (*dep_emp_ssn*). All of the data for this query is stored in the *dependent* table. Sort the output by *dep_emp_ssn* (major sort column) and by *dep_name* (minor sort column). The *dep_name* column should display no more than 20 characters of output.

9. Produce a second listing that will display only those employee dependents who are children (i.e., (*dep_relationship*) is either SON or DAUGHTER, but not SPOUSE). The result table should display the *dep_emp_ssn, dep_name,* and *dep_relationship* columns, and be sorted by *dep_emp_ssn* in descending order.

10. Your manager wonders what types of dependent relationships are tracked within the *dependent* table. Produce a simple listing of the *dep_relationship* column that does not contain duplicate output rows.

11. Your manager desires a listing of departments and the cities where they are located. Examine the *dept_locations* table. Write a query to display the department number and department location. Sort the output in descending order by department number.

ADDING POWER TO QUERIES

In Chapter 3, you learned the basic SELECT statement including the FROM, WHERE, and ORDER BY clauses. As you are beginning to see, the SELECT statement is a very powerful tool for retrieving information from databases. This chapter focuses on teaching you how to add power to your queries by building on the capabilities of the WHERE clause.

OBJECTIVES

The SELECT statement's WHERE clause is one of the most important clauses because it has the ability to retrieve data through the use of many different operators. These special operators make it easy to retrieve data non-procedurally. We will examine the power of logical operators named AND, OR, and NOT that can be used to link multiple WHERE conditions together. We will also examine the LIST operators that are used to retrieve rows where the data falls within a specified list of data values. We will also examine the power of the BETWEEN and LIKE operators that can greatly simplify how you write WHERE clauses. As you will see, these and more operators can add power to the WHERE clause. Your learning objectives for this chapter are:

- Use logical operators (AND, OR, NOT) to write complex query conditions.
- Use the IN and BETWEEN operators to write query conditions for lists of values and value ranges.
- Use the LIKE operator for character matching.
- Use the IS NULL operator when querying for unknown values.
- Use expressions in WHERE clauses.

LOGICAL OPERATORS (AND, OR, AND NOT)

In Chapter 3, you learned to write SELECT statements with a WHERE clause that had a single condition to be used to retrieve data rows. We will now learn to use the logical operators, AND and OR, to add power to our queries. This additional power comes from combining more than one condition in the WHERE clause. The NOT operator permits the creation of simple queries that otherwise would be unnecessarily bulky or complex.

AND:	joins two or more conditions, and returns results only when ***all*** of the conditions are true.
OR:	joins two or more conditions, and it returns results when ***any*** of the conditions are true.
NOT:	negates the expression that follows it.

USING THE **AND** OPERATOR

As we learned in the previous section, the AND operator links two or more conditions in a WHERE clause. Suppose that one of our organizational managers needs a list of female employees. Further, the list should only contain employees with last names that begin with the letter "E" or that come later in the alphabet. Additionally, the result table should be sorted by employee last name. There are two conditions to be met. The WHERE clause may be written as: **WHERE emp_gender = 'F' AND emp_last_name > 'E'**

Note that both conditions must be met in order for the entire WHERE clause to be evaluated as true. SQL Example 4.1 shows the complete SELECT statement and result table.

```
/* SQL Example 4.1 */
COLUMN "Last Name" FORMAT A15;
COLUMN "First Name" FORMAT A15;
COLUMN "Gender" FORMAT A6;
SELECT emp_last_name "Last Name", emp_first_name "First Name",
    emp_gender "Gender"
FROM employee
WHERE emp_gender = 'F' AND emp_last_name > 'E'
ORDER BY emp_last_name;

Last Name       First Name      Gender
---------       ----------      ------
Joyner          Suzanne         F
Markis          Marcia          F
Prescott        Sherri          F
```

SQL Example 4.1 can be expanded to test additional conditions. SQL Example 4.2 retrieves *employee* table data rows based on four different conditions. You may wish to review the *employee* table description provided in Appendix A in order to aid your understanding of the WHERE clause.

```
/* SQL Example 4.2 */
COLUMN "Last Name" FORMAT A15;
COLUMN "First Name" FORMAT A15;
COLUMN "Gender" FORMAT A6;
COLUMN "Salary" FORMAT $99,999.99
SELECT emp_last_name "Last Name", emp_first_name "First Name",
    emp_date_of_birth "Birth Day",
    emp_gender "Gender", emp_salary "Salary"
FROM employee
WHERE emp_last_name > 'E' AND
    emp_date_of_birth > '20-Jun-71' AND
    emp_gender = 'M' AND
    emp_salary > 20000
ORDER BY emp_last_name;

Last Name       First Name      Birth Day      Gender    Salary
--------        ---------       ---------      ------    ---------
Joshi           Dinesh          15-SEP-72      M         $38,000.00
Zhu             Waiman          08-DEC-75      M         $43,000.00
```

The query in SQL Example 4.2 is a bit contrived to say the least, but it is a legal query and will execute. It also shows the power of the AND logical operator. Each employee listed in the result table satisfies all of the query conditions. Imagine how long it would take for you to scan an employee table to create such a listing manually based on these four quite different conditions!

It is possible to write a WHERE clause using the AND operator that yields a result table that is empty. This is exactly what the query in SQL Example 4.3 does for the employees in the Company database.

```
/* SQL Example 4.3 */
SELECT emp_last_name, emp_first_name
FROM employee
WHERE emp_ssn = '999666666' AND emp_gender = 'F';
no rows selected
```

Oracle returned an empty result table because none of the rows in the *employee* table meet both of the conditions specified in the WHERE clause. Employee 999-66-6666 is Bijoy Bordoloi, a male employee.

USING THE OR OPERATOR

Suppose that your organizational manager's requirements change a bit. Another an employee listing is needed, but in this listing the employees should: (1) be female or, (2) have a last name that begins with the letter "M" or a letter that comes later in the alphabet. The result table should be sorted by employee last name. In this situation either of the two conditions can be met in order to satisfy the query. Female employees should be listed along with employees having a name that satisfies the second condition. The query can be written with the OR logical operator as is shown in SQL Example 4.4.

```
/* SQL Example 4.4 */
SELECT emp_last_name "Last Name", emp_first_name "First Name",
    emp_gender "Gender"
FROM employee
WHERE emp_gender = 'F' OR emp_last_name > 'M'
ORDER BY emp_last_name;

Last Name       First Name      Gender
--------        ---------       ------
Joyner          Suzanne         F
Markis          Marcia          F
Prescott        Sherri          F
Zhu             Waiman          M
```

The query produces a result table with four rows. Three of the rows are listed because the employee gender is female. The other row is listed because the employee's last name begins with the letter "M" or later in the alphabet (Zhu). Additionally, two of the rows satisfy both conditions in the query (Markis and Prescott).

USING the NOT Operator

Suppose that one of your organization's managers requests a listing of employees that work in a specific department, such as department 7. Further, the listing should again be sorted alphabetically by last name. The query's WHERE clause is straight forward:

```
WHERE emp_dpt_number = 7
```

But what if the request is for a listing of employees that do **not** work in department 7? The OR logical operator can be used to identify employees not in department 7 by simply specifying all department numbers except for department 7:

```
WHERE emp_dpt_number = 1 OR emp_dpt_number = 2 OR
      emp_dpt_number = 3 OR . . . (more clauses)!
```

But the WHERE clause given above is unnecessarily complex! Further, in an organization with dozens of departments, the use of the OR logical operator is too unwieldy or even infeasible to use. SQL Example 4.5 uses the NOT operator to simplify the WHERE clause.

```
/* SQL Example 4.5 */
COLUMN "Dept" FORMAT 9999;
SELECT emp_last_name "Last Name", emp_first_name "First Name",
    emp_dpt_number "Dept"
FROM employee
WHERE NOT emp_dpt_number = 7
ORDER BY emp_last_name;

Last Name       First Name      Dept
--------        ---------       ----
Amin            Hyder              3
Bordoloi        Bijoy              1
Joyner          Suzanne            3
Markis          Marcia             3
```

The query can also be written by using a "not equal to" comparison operator as shown in SQL Example 4.6.

```
/* SQL Example 4.6 */
SELECT emp_last_name "Last Name", emp_first_name "First Name",
    emp_dpt_number "Dept"
FROM employee
WHERE emp_dpt_number <> 7
ORDER BY emp_last_name;

Last Name       First Name     Dept
--------        ---------      ----
Amin            Hyder             3
Bordoloi        Bijoy             1
Joyner          Suzanne           3
Markis          Marcia            3
```

Sometimes the "not equal to" comparison operator can become unwieldy in a WHERE clause with several complex conditions. Suppose that a department manager requires a listing of all employees except those assigned to department 7 or those that are female. The NOT operator can simplify this WHERE clause so that it reads in an almost English-like fashion. SQL Example 4.7 demonstrates this use of the NOT operator.

```
/* SQL Example 4.7 */
SELECT emp_last_name "Last Name", emp_first_name "First Name",
    emp_dpt_number "Dept", emp_gender "Gender"
FROM employee
WHERE NOT emp_dpt_number = 7 AND NOT emp_gender = 'F'
ORDER BY emp_last_name;

Last Name       First Name     Dept    Gender
--------        ---------      ----    ------
Amin            Hyder             3     M
Bordoloi        Bijoy             1     M
```

COMBINING OR AND AND OPERATORS

In the last section, you studied examples with the OR logical operator used repeatedly to connect conditional statements. You can also use the AND logical operator repeatedly, and you can combine the AND and OR logical operators to create complex queries. But you must exercise caution! There are pitfalls when combining the AND and OR operators. The next query gives an example of just such a pitfall. Examine the question, the query, and the result table carefully.

Using the *employee* table, provide a list of employees with a last name that begins after the letter "E," and who are either female or work in department 1. SQL Example 4.8 provides the proposed WHERE clause.

```
/* SQL Example 4.8 */
SELECT emp_last_name "Last Name", emp_first_name "First Name",
    emp_dpt_number "Dept", emp_gender "Gender"
FROM employee
WHERE emp_last_name > 'E' AND emp_gender = 'F' OR emp_dpt_number = 1
ORDER BY emp_last_name;

Last Name      First Name      Dept      Gender
---------      ---------       ----      ------
Bordoloi       Bijoy            1        M
Joyner         Suzanne          3        F
Markis         Marcia           3        F
Prescott       Sherri           7        F
```

The SELECT statement executes, but is it correct? The answer is no! The result table should not contain "Bijoy Bordoloi" because his last name does not begin with a letter that is greater than the letter "E." This also underscores the importance of not simply accepting a result table as correct if an Oracle error is not generated by the SELECT statement.

Where does this query go wrong? The answer is that there is a hierarchy of evaluation for the AND, OR, and NOT operators. When the AND operator is combined with the OR operator, Oracle evaluates the conditions connected by the AND operator first. Following this Oracle next evaluates the conditions connected by the OR operator. Let's break the WHERE clause into pieces in order to see how the conditions are evaluated.

There are three conditions to be evaluated. Oracle begins by examining the two conditions connected by the AND operator. With this WHERE clause, a table row will be included in the result table if both conditions connected by the AND operator are true. Essentially, Oracle returns a value of either true or false from the AND operation. In this query, a table row is included in the result if it matches either the first or the second condition.

```
Condition 1 AND Condition 2
emp_last_name > 'E' AND emp_gender = 'F'
```

Next, Oracle combines the result of the AND operation (which is TRUE here) with the remaining condition in an OR operation. Let's suppose that the result of the AND operation was TRUE for a given row. The resulting OR operation looks like the following to Oracle.

```
TRUE OR Condition 3
TRUE OR emp_dpt_number = 1
```

You can force a change in the hierarchy of evaluation for a complex condition by using parentheses to force the order of operation. This works exactly the same way as it does in mathematics. SQL Example 4.9 gives the correct rewritten query.

```
/* SQL Example 4.9 */
SELECT emp_last_name "Last Name", emp_first_name "First Name",
    emp_dpt_number "Dept", emp_gender "Gender"
```

```
FROM employee
WHERE emp_last_name > 'E' AND
  (emp_gender = 'F' OR emp_dpt_number = 1)
ORDER BY emp_last_name;

Last Name      First Name     Dept     Gender
---------      ---------      ----     ------
Joyner         Suzanne          3      F
Markis         Marcia           3      F
Prescott       Sherri           7      F
```

Oracle evaluates the complex condition beginning with the inner most set of parentheses. Here, Oracle will first test a row to see if the employee is female *OR* is in department 1. If a row passes that test, the query then tests to see if the employee's name begins with a letter that is greater than "E."

The order in which the conditions are listed has no effect on the result table that is produced; however, the order of the conditions may affect the efficiency with which the computer processes an SQL statement. Our focus for now is on writing SQL statements that produce correct output. The last query could have been written as shown in SQL Example 4.10 to produce the same result table.

```
/* SQL Example 4.10 */
SELECT emp_last_name "Last Name", emp_first_name "First Name",
    emp_dpt_number "Dept", emp_gender "Gender"
FROM employee
WHERE (emp_gender = 'F' OR emp_dpt_number = 1) AND
    emp_last_name > 'E'
ORDER BY emp_last_name;
```

As you gain experience with SQL, you will find that writing queries becomes second nature. In contrast, it will never be easy to understand exactly what a manager needs in terms of information. When you have doubt about what a manager has requested, ask questions!

LISTS (IN AND NOT IN)

There are two operators that are designed for testing to determine if data stored in a table column is either in or not in a list or set of values. These are the IN and NOT IN operators. These operators greatly simplify the task of writing queries that might otherwise require a large number of either OR logical operators or an unwieldy use of the NOT logical operator.

USING THE IN OPERATOR

Until this point, all queries have required you to compare the value stored in a single column of a table with another single value. In order to compare a column against several values, it is necessary to use the OR operator to combine multiple conditions. One of our organizational managers needs a listing of employees who earn specific annual salary figures of $43,000, $30,000 or $25,000 per year. Further, the listing is to be sorted by employee salary. The query can be written as shown in SQL Example 4.11.

```
/* SQL Example 4.11 */
SELECT emp_last_name "Last Name", emp_first_name "First Name",
    emp_salary "Salary"
FROM employee
WHERE emp_salary = 43000 OR emp_salary = 30000 OR emp_salary = 25000
ORDER BY emp_salary;

Last Name       First Name      Salary
--------        ---------       ---------
Markis          Marcia          $25,000.00
Amin            Hyder           $25,000.00
Prescott        Sherri          $25,000.00
Bock            Douglas         $30,000.00
Joyner          Suzanne         $43,000.00
Zhu             Waiman          $43,000.00
6 rows selected.
```

The use of the OR operator is unnecessarily complex. The IN operator can simplify the query. The revised query in SQL Example 4.12 tests to see the *emp_salary* column value matches any of the values in the list that is enclosed within parentheses.

```
/* SQL Example 4.12 */
SELECT emp_last_name "Last Name", emp_first_name "First Name",
    emp_salary "Salary"
FROM employee
WHERE emp_salary IN (43000, 30000, 25000)
ORDER BY emp_salary;

Last Name       First Name      Salary
--------        ---------       ---------
Markis          Marcia          $25,000.00
Amin            Hyder           $25,000.00
Prescott        Sherri          $25,000.00
Bock            Douglas         $30,000.00
Joyner          Suzanne         $43,000.00
Zhu             Waiman          $43,000.00
6 rows selected.
```

Because the WHERE clause has less code, the query is easier to read. Notice that each value in the list is separated by a comma (,).

But what if the values in the list are character strings as would be the case if we were producing a listing of employees that reside in Marina, Edwardsville, or St. Louis? Character string values must be enclosed in single quotation marks. The resulting query sorted by employee city is shown in SQL Example 4.13.

```
/* SQL Example 4.13 */
SELECT emp_last_name "Last Name", emp_first_name "First Name",
    emp_city "City"
FROM employee
WHERE emp_city IN ('Marina', 'Edwardsville', 'St. Louis')
ORDER BY emp_city;

Last Name      First Name      City
--------       ---------       ----------
Bordoloi       Bijoy           Edwardsville
Prescott       Sherri          Edwardsville
Joyner         Suzanne         Marina
Amin           Hyder           Marina
Zhu            Waiman          St. Louis
Bock           Douglas         St. Louis
```

USING THE **NOT IN** OPERATOR

Okay, you've provided your department manager with the requested list of employees that earn $43,000, $30,000 or $25,000 per year. However, the manager now requests a listing of employees who *did not* earn one of those three salary figures listed in the previous result table. The NOT IN operator was designed exactly to support this type of reporting requirement. The query in SQL Example 4.13 requires very little modification. Simply replace the IN operator with the NOT IN operator as shown in SQL Example 4.14. The result table lists the two employees whose annual salary figures are NOT IN the prescribed list.

```
/* SQL Example 4.14 */
SELECT emp_last_name "Last Name", emp_first_name "First Name",
    emp_salary "Salary"
FROM employee
WHERE emp_salary NOT IN (43000, 30000, 25000)
ORDER BY emp_salary;

Last Name      First Name      Salary
--------       ---------       ---------
Joshi          Dinesh          $38,000.00
Bordoloi       Bijoy           $55,000.00
```

COMMON ERRORS WHEN USING **IN** AND **NOT IN** OPERATORS

There are some common errors that you need to avoid when using the IN and NOT IN operators. The query in SQL Example 4.15 is missing the required commas between list items. Oracle returns the fairly confusing *ORA-00907: missing right parenthesis* error message. This is confusing because an examination of the WHERE clause shows that there is, in fact, no missing parenthesis. The missing commas have confused the Oracle software.

```
/* SQL Example 4.15 */
SELECT emp_last_name "Last Name", emp_first_name "First Name",
    emp_salary "Salary"
FROM employee
WHERE emp_salary NOT IN (43000 30000 25000);

ERROR at line 3:
ORA-00907: missing right parenthesis
```

Another common error is a failure to include parentheses when coding the list of values. The SELECT statement in SQL Example 4.16 returns the *ORA-00933: SQL command not properly ended* error message. Again, this message is somewhat confusing because the WHERE clause *does* have a semicolon at the end of the statement. Again, Oracle has become confused by the syntactical error.

```
/* SQL Example 4.16 */
SELECT emp_last_name "Last Name", emp_first_name "First Name",
    emp_salary "Salary"
FROM employee
WHERE emp_salary IN 43000, 30000, 25000;

ERROR at line 3:
ORA-00933: SQL command not properly ended
```

RANGES (BETWEEN AND NOT BETWEEN)

Writing a query with a condition that satisfies a range of values is similar to writing one that selects rows based on a list of values. Both query types allow you to compare values from a single table column against more than one value. However, with a list of values, your query will specify two or more exact values in the listing. When the number of values is quite large, it is often unwieldy or infeasible to use a simple listing. In this situation, your query needs to specify a range of values that a single table column may satisfy. SQL has two operators, BETWEEN and NOT BETWEEN that can simplify the expression of a range of values. Additionally, this eliminates the need to use a more complex WHERE clause involving the use of the AND logical operator.

USING THE **BETWEEN** OPERATOR

You can use the BETWEEN operator to specify an *inclusive* range of values. When BETWEEN is used, the value from the table column used in the WHERE clause condition must fall within or between the lower and upper values specified by the BETWEEN operator. The range includes the end points specified by the range of values.

Suppose that one of our managers requires a listing of employees with annual salary figures that are between $25,000 and $40,000 per year. The query in SQL Example 4.17 will produce the required result table with the output sorted by employee salary. Notice that the query uses the AND logical operator.

```
/* SQL Example 4.17 */
SELECT emp_last_name "Last Name", emp_first_name "First Name",
    emp_salary "Salary"
FROM employee
WHERE emp_salary >= 25000 AND emp_salary <= 40000
ORDER BY emp_salary;

Last Name       First Name      Salary
--------        ---------       ---------
Markis          Marcia          $25,000.00
Amin            Hyder           $25,000.00
Prescott        Sherri          $25,000.00
Bock            Douglas         $30,000.00
Joshi           Dinesh          $38,000.00
```

This query can be rewritten using the BETWEEN operator as shown in SQL Example 4.18. This may make the WHERE clause easier to understand and less likely to be incorrectly coded by an SQL programmer.

```
/* SQL Example 4.18 */
SELECT emp_last_name "Last Name", emp_first_name "First Name",
    emp_salary "Salary"
FROM employee
WHERE emp_salary BETWEEN 25000 AND 40000
ORDER BY emp_salary;

Last Name       First Name      Salary
--------        ---------       ---------
Markis          Marcia          $25,000.00
Amin            Hyder           $25,000.00
Prescott        Sherri          $25,000.00
Bock            Douglas         $30,000.00
Joshi           Dinesh          $38,000.00
```

SPECIFYING MORE THAN ONE SALARY RANGE

If you need to specify two different salary ranges for employees, that is, 25,000 to 30,000 and 40,000 to 43,000, the query can be to include two BETWEEN clauses as is done in SQL Example 4.19. This query will display rows for employees that have an annual salary that falls within one of the two specified salary ranges. Note that the specified range includes the end points for the two salary ranges.

```
/* SQL Example 4.19 */
SELECT emp_last_name "Last Name", emp_salary "Salary"
FROM employee
WHERE emp_salary BETWEEN 25000 AND 30000
    OR emp_salary BETWEEN 40000 AND 43000
ORDER BY emp_salary;
```

```
Last Name      Salary
--------       ---------
Markis         $25,000.00
Amin           $25,000.00
Prescott       $25,000.00
Bock           $30,000.00
Joyner         $43,000.00
Zhu            $43,000.00
6 rows selected.
```

USING THE **NOT BETWEEN** OPERATOR

The NOT BETWEEN operator is the mirror image of the BETWEEN operator. It is used to exclude a range of column values from a result table. For example, if one of your firm's managers needs a listing of employees with salaries that are either extremely high or extremely low, you can exclude salaries in a middle range of values with the NOT BETWEEN operator. The query in SQL Example 4.20 lists employees with salaries below $28,000 or above $50,000. You might also observe that using the NOT BETWEEN operator in this query is equivalent to using two BETWEEN operators combined with the OR logical operator that was used earlier in SQL Example 4.19.

```
/* SQL Example 4.20 */
SELECT emp_last_name "Last Name", emp_salary "Salary"
FROM employee
WHERE emp_salary NOT BETWEEN 28000 AND 50000
ORDER BY emp_salary;

Last Name      Salary
--------       ---------
Markis         $25,000.00
Amin           $25,000.00
Prescott       $25,000.00
Bordoloi       $55,000.00
```

COMMON ERRORS WHEN USING **BETWEEN** AND **NOT BETWEEN** OPERATORS

Like the IN and NOT IN operators, there are some common errors associated with the BETWEEN and NOT BETWEEN operators that need to be avoided. One typical error that even experienced programmers occasionally make is inserting a comma within a numeric value that is used to express the inclusive range of the BETWEEN search. The query in SQL Example 4.21 has this error. Oracle returns the *ORA-00905: missing keyword* error message. However, there is no keyword missing! Once again, Oracle has been confused by your error!

```
/* SQL Example 4.21 */
SELECT emp_last_name "Last Name", emp_salary "Salary"
FROM employee
WHERE emp_salary BETWEEN 25,000 and 40,000;

ERROR at line 3:
ORA-00905: missing keyword
```

Another error that can occur is the misspecification of a SELECT statement by erroneously including too many AND logical operators in the WHERE clause. The query in SQL Example 4.22 has this particular error. Oracle returns the *ORA-00920: invalid relational operator* error message. This error message does point you toward the problem.

```
/* SQL Example 4.22 */
SELECT emp_last_name "Last Name", emp_salary "Salary"
FROM employee
WHERE emp_salary BETWEEN 25000 AND 40000 AND 43000;

ERROR at line 3:
ORA-00920: invalid relational operator
```

CHARACTER MATCHING (LIKE AND NOT LIKE)

Many of the SELECT statement examples shown thus far in the chapter have tested for specific instances of character data such as employee last names that have a beginning letter that is greater than "E." Example: **WHERE emp_last_name > 'E'**

The LIKE and NOT LIKE operators can be used to search for data rows containing incomplete or partial character strings within a data column. For example, the query in SQL Example 4.23 searches the *employee* table for employee names that begin with the characters 'Bo'. The search is case-sensitive meaning that 'Bo' is not equivalent to 'BO'.

```
/* SQL Example 4.23 */
SELECT emp_last_name "Last Name", emp_first_name "First Name"
FROM employee
WHERE emp_last_name LIKE 'Bo%';

Last Name       First Name
--------        ---------
Bordoloi        Bijoy
Bock            Douglas
```

The percent (%) symbol is a wild card symbol used to represent one or more characters. There are four allowable wild card characters. The wildcard operators and their uses are defined in Table 4.1.

TABLE 4.1	
Wild Card	*Meaning*
% (percent)	any string of zero or more characters
_ (underscore)	any single character
[ ] (brackets)	any single character within a specified range such as '**a**' to '**d**', inclusive [a-d] or a set of characters such as [aeiouy]
[^] (not brackets)	any single character **not** in the specified range or set. (e.g., [^a-f])

Study the examples shown in Table 4.2. They will help you understand how to use the wild card characters with the LIKE operator. Typical results of a search are shown in parentheses ().

The SELECT statement shown in SQL Example 4.24 generates a result table that includes all DISTINCT rows where the employee social security number in the *assignment* table ends with the numbers 555.

```
/* SQL Example 4.24 */
COLUMN "Emp SSN" FORMAT A12;
SELECT DISTINCT work_emp_ssn "Emp SSN"
FROM assignment
WHERE work_emp_ssn LIKE '%555';

Emp SSN
--------
999555555
```

Conversely, the NOT logical operator can be used in conjunction with the LIKE operator to find all DISTINCT employee rows that do not end with 555 as is done in SQL Example 4.25.

```
/* SQL Example 4.25 */
SELECT DISTINCT work_emp_ssn "Emp SSN"
FROM assignment
WHERE work_emp_ssn NOT LIKE '%555';

Emp SSN
--------
999111111
999222222
999333333
999444444
999666666
999887777
999888888
7 rows selected.
```

There is a notable limitation when using wild card characters—you *cannot* use the comparison operators (=, >, <, etc.) with wild card characters. Wild cards used without

TABLE 4.2

LIKE '%inger' will search for every name that ends with 'inger' (**Ringer,** Str**inger**).

LIKE '%en%' will search for every name that has the letters 'en' in the name (Be**n**net, Gr**een**, McBadd**en**).

LIKE '_heryl' will search for every six-letter name ending with 'heryl' (**Cheryl**). Notice how this is different than '%heryl', which would return names that are six characters or more.

LIKE '[CK]ars[eo]n' will search for every six-letter name that begins with a 'C' or 'K' and has the letter 'e' or 'o' between 'ars' and 'n' (e.g., '**Carsen**,' '**Karsen**,' '**Carson**,' and '**Karson**'.

LIKE '[M-Z]inger' will search for all the names ending with 'inger' that begin with any single letter 'M' thru 'Z' (**R**i**nger**).

LIKE 'M[^c]%' will search for all the names that begin with 'M' not having 'c' as the second letter.

the LIKE operator are interpreted as characters for which you wish to search. The query in SQL Example 4.26 attempts to find any employee Social Security Number (SSN) that consists of the four characters '%555' only. It will not find employee SSNs ending with 555. In fact, it returns no rows from the *assignment* table because none of the SSNs have a percent sign as part of the data! In order for this query to execute correctly, you must substitute the LIKE operator for the equal sign (=) comparison operator.

```
/* SQL Example 4.26 */
SELECT DISTINCT work_emp_ssn
FROM assignment
WHERE work_emp_ssn = '%555';
no rows selected
```

When a character search pattern contains single or double quotes within the string of characters, your query must be written by using the opposite type of quote marks to enclose the pattern. For example, the string shown below includes double quote marks around the word **Hello.** In order to search for this word, enclose the entire string with single quote marks as shown.

TABLE 4.3

Expression	*Result*
LIKE '5%'	Returns any row where the column data value is '5' followed by any string of zero or more characters.
LIKE '5[%]'	Returns any row where the data value is 5%.
LIKE '_n'	Returns any row where the column data value is a two-character value ending in the letter 'n' (e.g., an, in, on, etc.).
LIKE '[_]n'	Returns any row where the column data value is _n.
LIKE '[ ]]'	Returns any row where the column data value is].

TABLE 4.4	
Expression	*Result*
LIKE '[a-ef]'	Returns any row where the data value is a, b, c, d, e, or f.
LIKE '[-aef]'	Returns any row where the data value is -, a, e, or f.

When this: "Hello," said Mark.

Do this: ' "Hello," said Mark. '

But what if the string of characters has one of the wild card characters as part of the string? In order to use a wild card such as the percent sign, underscore, or left or right bracket (%), (_) ([ ), or ( ]) as characters in a LIKE match string, enclose each wild card in brackets ([]). Table 4.3 summarizes this usage.

Earlier, you learned that you can use the dash (-) symbol inside square brackets with a LIKE operator to express a range of characters in a search. If you want the dash (-) symbol to be one of the characters for which you are searching, you must place the dash symbol as the first character inside the set of brackets.

To search for a dash in a character string, place the dash as the first character inside a set of brackets. This usage is shown in Table 4.4.

UNKNOWN VALUES (IS NULL AND IS NOT NULL)

The term NULL is a keyword meaning the absence of any stored value. If a column in a data row is NULL, then there is no value stored in that column. One of the rows in the *assignment* table shown in Appendix A has a NULL value for the *work_hours* column. The SELECT statement shown in SQL Example 4.27 uses the IS NULL operator to query the *assignment* table to display all rows with a NULL value for *work_hours*.

```
/* SQL Example 4.27 */
SELECT *
FROM assignment
WHERE work_hours IS NULL;

WORK_EMP_       WORK_PRO_NUMBER      WORK_HOURS
---------       ---------------      ----------
999444444        1
999666666       20
```

This query uses the IS NULL operator to test for a NULL value. You can also use the IS NOT NULL operator to retrieve rows where any value has been stored. You need to understand that a NULL value is *not synonymous* with "zero" (numerical values) or "blank" (character values). Rather, NULL values allow users to distinguish between a deliberate entry of zero/blank and a nonentry of data. You should think of NULL as meaning "unknown." Because of the nature of the NULL, when you compare a NULL with another value the results are *never true;* a NULL value does not match anything, not even another NULL value! Stated another way, one unknown value cannot equal or be compared to another unknown value. However, NULL values are considered the same as each other when using the DISTINCT keyword to limit the number of rows displayed in a result table.

As you saw above, knowing the meaning of NULL allows you to write queries that can test for a NULL value. Rows can be included or excluded from a result table when a column contains a NULL value; but the column must have been defined as being capable of storing a NULL value when it was created. For example, it should be obvious that a column that is specified as a PRIMARY KEY cannot store a NULL value.

The earlier query in SQL Example 4.27 is not the same as the one shown in SQL Example 4.28 that tests to see if the *work_hours* column is equal to zero.

```
/* SQL Example 4.28 */
SELECT *
FROM assignment
WHERE work_hours = 0;
no rows selected
```

The query in SQL Example 4.28 returns no rows for the result table because none of the rows in the *assignment* table have a zero value for *work_hours*. Thus, you can see that zero (0) is a value, not an "unknown value."

On the other hand, the next two queries will produce the same result table. The query in SQL Example 4.29 includes all rows where the *work_hours* column contains a value. The query in SQL Example 4.30 includes all rows where the *work_hours* is greater than or equal to zero.

```
/* SQL Example 4.29 */
SELECT *
FROM assignment
WHERE work_hours IS NOT NULL;
15 rows selected.
```

```
/* SQL Example 4.30 */
SELECT *
FROM assignment
WHERE work_hours >= 0;
15 rows selected.
```

USING EXPRESSIONS IN SELECT CLAUSES

Thus far, we have used the SELECT clause of a SELECT statement to retrieve data and display result tables for data columns from a specified table. However, a SELECT clause can also contain expressions, or computed columns. Expressions, or computed columns can also be used in a WHERE clause to manipulate column data. An expression is formed by combining a column name or constant with an arithmetic operator. The arithmetic operators used in SQL are given in Table 4.5.

Like logical operators, arithmetic operators have a hierarchy or order of evaluation. Multiplication, division, and modulo operations are performed before addition and subtraction. When an expression contains operators of the same order, the expression is evaluated from left to right. Use parentheses to force a specific order of operation. The most deeply nested expression is performed first.

The Company database employee table stores annual salary figures for employees. However, suppose one of the organization's managers needs a result table that lists employee names and their monthly salaries for purposes of preparing a monthly budget of some type. The SELECT statement shown in SQL Example 4.31 produces the required listing.

```
/* SQL Example 4.31 */
COLUMN "Monthly Salary" FORMAT $99,999.99;
SELECT emp_last_name "Last Name", emp_first_name "First Name",
    emp_salary/12 "Monthly Salary"
FROM employee
WHERE emp_salary/12 > 3500
ORDER BY emp_last_name;

Last Name       First Name      Monthly Salary
--------        ---------       -------------
Bordoloi        Bijoy           $4,583.33
Joyner          Suzanne         $3,583.33
Zhu             Waiman          $3,583.33
```

Note that we have formatted the monthly salary and supplied an *alias* column name of "Monthly Salary" for this computed column (expression). Monthly salary is computed as the value from the *emp_salary* column divided by 12 (annual salary divided among 12 months). The alias name is used in the COLUMN-FORMAT command.

When the column title to be used consists of a single word such as "Salary," the double-quote marks around the *alias* column name are not required. However, if double-quote marks are not used, the output column will automatically display the column name in capital letters even if the column title is typed in a combination of upper and lowercase letters as is done for the alias "Salary" in SQL Example 4.32.

TABLE 4.5

Symbol	Operation	Order
*	Multiplication	1
/	Division	1
%	Modulo	1
+	Addition	2
-	Subtraction	2

```
/* SQL Example 4.32 */
SELECT emp_last_name "Last Name", emp_first_name "First Name",
    emp_salary/12 Salary
FROM employee
WHERE emp_salary/12 > 3500
ORDER BY emp_last_name;

Last Name       First Name      Salary
---------       ----------      ---------
Bordoloi        Bijoy           4583.33333
Joyner          Suzanne         3583.33333
Zhu             Waiman          3583.33333
```

You need to take note of two facts about the last two queries and the result tables that are produced. First, the data column *emp_salary* is not actually listed in the SELECT clause. Only an expression that includes *emp_salary* is used. This was done to demonstrate that using expression with a column name has no effect on the table's underlying values. The expression affects only the result table.

Second, when a data column is manipulated, the result table will have a column name for the computed column that is equivalent to the expression. For this reason, we supplied an alias column name to be used for the computed column. The alias column name provides meaning to the data displayed in the result table. However, Oracle will still produce a result table if you do not use an alias column name as is shown in SQL Example 4.33.

```
/* SQL Example 4.33 */
SELECT emp_last_name "Last Name", emp_first_name "First Name",
    emp_salary/12
FROM employee
WHERE emp_salary/12 > 3500
ORDER BY emp_last_name;

Last Name       First Name      EMP_SALARY/12
---------       ----------      -------------
Bordoloi        Bijoy           $4,583.33
Joyner          Suzanne         $3,583.33
Zhu             Waiman          $3,583.33
```

In the three previous SQL queries, *emp_salary* is divided by a numeric constant, 12. You can also form expressions that use column names on both sides of an arithmetic operator.

NULL values that are in columns that are used in computations can produce unexpected and sometimes confusing results. This occurs because the result of an arithmetic operation on a NULL is NULL or "unknown." For example, if you use a NULL value in a column that is used to produce a computed column, the result displayed will be NULL. SQL Example 4.34 displays data from the *assignment* table that is used to store the number of hours employees work on assigned projects. The query computes the average work hours per employee assigned to Project #1 based on a 40-hour work week. Notice that the employee with SSN 999-44-4444 has not reported any work hours for Project 1, thus the *work_hours* column is NULL. The resulting computed "Average Per Week" column is also NULL, and is displayed as a missing or blank value.

```
/* SQL Example 4.34 */
SELECT work_emp_ssn "SSN", work_pro_number "Project",
    work_hours/40 "Avg Hours/Week"
FROM assignment
WHERE work_pro_number = 1
ORDER BY work_emp_ssn;

SSN            Project      Avg Hours/Week
--------       ------       -------------
999111111           1       .785
999444444           1
999888888           1       .525
```

If a NULL value exists, those rows can be eliminated from the result table by including a WHERE clause that filters out rows with NULL values. Let's continue with our *assignment* table example. The query shown in SQL Example 4.35 produces a result table for average work hours that filters out rows where the *work_hours* column value is NOT NULL.

```
/* SQL Example 4.35 */
SELECT work_emp_ssn "SSN", work_pro_number "Project",
  work_hours/40 "Avg Hours/Week"
FROM assignment
WHERE work_pro_number = 1 AND work_hours IS NOT NULL
ORDER BY work_emp_ssn;

SSN            Project      Avg Hours/Week
--------       ------       -------------
999111111           1       .785
999888888           1       .525
```

It may seem redundant, but the output that results from expressions when NULL values are involved is very important and, sometimes, misunderstood. Consider the *contract_employee* table displayed in Table 4.6. The *contract_employee* table has four

TABLE 4.6

TABLE: contract_employee

emp_id, CHAR(2) NOT NULL	emp_job, VARCHAR2(12) NOT NULL	emp_salary, NUMBER NOT NULL	emp_bonus integer null
10	BIG BOSS	100000	NULL
20	LITTLE BOSS	50000	NULL
30	WARRIOR	10000	2000
40	WARRIOR	11000	3000

columns, *emp_id, emp_job, emp_salary,* and *emp_bonus.* The *emp_bonus* column is allowed to be NULL.

Management wants to determine the total compensation for each contract employee. Compensation is the employee salary added to the employee bonus. The query shown in SQL Example 4.36 produces two rows with NULL values for total compensation. This doesn't mean that the big boss and little boss are not paid. It simply means that since *emp_bonus* is NULL (unknown) for those two data rows, the total compensation could not be computed.

```
/* SQL Example 4.36 */
COLUMN emp_id FORMAT A6;
SELECT emp_id, emp_job, emp_salary+emp_bonus "Total Comp"
FROM contract_employee;

EMP_ID      EMP_JOB           Total Comp
------      ----------        ----------
10          BIG BOSS
20          LITTLE BOSS
30          WORKER                 12000
40          WORKER                 14000
```

You may wish to create the *contract_employee* table and execute the query to satisfy yourself that the result table is accurate. This is left as SQL Coding Exercise 15 in the chapter review exercises.

SUMMARY

This chapter focused on adding power to your queries. The logical operators (AND, OR, NOT) can be used to develop complex WHERE clause criteria for row selection. The IN, NOT IN, BETWEEN, and NOT BETWEEN operators help you simplify WHERE clause criteria. The IS NULL and IS NOT NULL operators enable you to write queries that both identify and ignore rows with missing values. You also learned to write queries that use expressions in the SELECT and WHERE clauses. After completing the exercises that follow this chapter, you should feel comfortable using the concepts covered here to add power to your queries.

REVIEW EXERCISES

LEARN THESE TERMS

AND operator. Joins two or more conditions, and returns results only when *all* of the conditions are true.

BETWEEN operator. The value from the table column used in the WHERE clause condition must fall within or between the lower and upper values specified by the BETWEEN operator.

Computed column. A column of output in a result table that is produced by using an expression that con-

tains an arithmetic operator(s) used to manipulate column data.

IN operator. Used to simplify a query by reducing the number of OR operators. This operator searches for column values that match values in a specified list.

LIKE operator. Used to search for data rows containing incomplete or partial character strings within a data column.

OR operator.   Joins two or more conditions, and it returns results when *any* of the conditions are true.

NOT operator.   Negates the expression that follows it.

NOT BETWEEN operator.   Used to exclude a range of column values from a result table.

NOT IN operator.   Negates the IN operator.

NOT LIKE operator.   Negates the LIKE operator.

NULL.   A keyword meaning the absence of any stored value. NOT NULL is the negation of NULL, meaning that there is a stored value. NULL is synonymous with unknown value.

Wild card.   Different symbols used to represent one or more characters when specifying a WHERE clause using the LIKE or NOT LIKE operator, or a similar string search operator.

CONCEPTS QUIZ

1. You are examining the following WHERE clause in a SELECT statement. Explain when the clause evaluates to true and why?

   ```
   WHERE emp_salary > 25000 AND emp_salary <= 45000
   ```

2. You are examining the following WHERE clause in a SELECT statement. Explain when the clause evaluates to true and why? Are there any potential problems with this WHERE clause?

   ```
   WHERE emp_salary > 25000 OR emp_salary <= 45000
   ```

   Situation: Use the following information to answer the next four questions. For a given data row, the column values are as follows: *emp_salary* = 45000, *emp_gender* = 'F', and *emp_superssn* = '123456789'.

3. Is the following WHERE clause True or False? Why?

   ```
   WHERE emp_salary > 30000 AND emp_gender = 'F' OR
       emp_superssn = '44566778899';
   ```

4. Is the following WHERE clause True or False? Why?

   ```
   WHERE emp_salary > 30000 OR emp_gender = 'F' AND
       emp_superssn = '44566778899';
   ```

5. Is the following WHERE clause True or False? Why?

   ```
   WHERE (emp_salary > 30000 OR emp_gender = 'F') AND
       emp_superssn = '44566778899';
   ```

6. Is the following WHERE clause True or False? Why?

   ```
   WHERE NOT (emp_salary > 30000 OR emp_gender = 'F' AND
       emp_superssn = '44566778899');
   ```

7. What is the purpose of the IN and NOT IN operators?
8. What is the purpose of the BETWEEN and NOT BETWEEN operators?
9. What is the purpose of the LIKE and NOT LIKE operators?
10. What data rows will be returned in a result table for a SELECT statement with the following WHERE clause?

    ```
    WHERE emp_zip LIKE '62%';
    ```

11. Explain the concept of a NULL value.
12. What operators are used in expressions to create computed columns?

TABLE 5.1	
Function Syntax	*Function Use*
SUM([ALL | DISTINCT] expression)	The total of the (distinct) values in a numeric column/expression.
AVG([ALL | DISTINCT] expression)	The average of the (distinct) values in a numeric column/expression.
COUNT([ALL | DISTINCT] expression)	The number of (distinct) non-NULL values in a column/expression.
COUNT(*)	The number of selected rows.
MAX(expression)	The highest value in a column/expression.
MIN(expression)	The lowest value in a column/expression.

arithmetic operators. However, aggregate functions are most often used with a column name.

There are two rules that you must understand and follow when using aggregates:

- Aggregate functions can be used in both the SELECT and HAVING clauses (the HAVING clause is covered later in this chapter).
- Aggregate functions cannot be used in a WHERE clause. For example, the query in SQL Example 5.2 is wrong and will produce the Oracle *ORA-00934 group function is not allowed here* error message.

```
/* SQL Example 5.2 */
SELECT *
FROM employee
WHERE AVG(emp_salary) > 40000;
ERROR at line 3: ORA-00934: group function is not allowed here.
```

If you think about what an aggregate function does, and what the purpose of a WHERE clause is, then this error makes perfect sense. Remember, a WHERE clause includes or excludes rows from a result table based on user-defined criteria. The aggregate function then acts on all rows or a subset of rows that satisfy the criteria specified by a WHERE clause. Since the WHERE clause must execute *before* the aggregate function takes effect, you cannot include an aggregate function in a WHERE clause. Later in this chapter you will learn how to use the HAVING clause to filter out rows with grouped data—*after* aggregate functions have been calculated.

USING THE AVG FUNCTION

Suppose that managers need to determine the average salary of employees for the firm for budgeting or some similar purpose. You can use the AVG function to compute the average value for the *emp_salary* column in the *employee* table. For example, the query in SQL Example 5.3 returns the average of the employee salaries. The output column in the result table is formatted and renamed "Average Employee Salary."

```
/* SQL Example 5.3 */
COLUMN "Average Employee Salary" FORMAT $999,999;
SELECT AVG(emp_salary) "Average Employee Salary"
FROM employee;

Average Employee Salary
-------------------
              $35,500
```

Now suppose that a similar, yet different management question is posed. What is the average salary *offered* to employees? This question asks you to incorporate the concept of computing the average of the distinct salaries paid by the organization. The same query with the DISTINCT keyword in the aggregate function returns a different average as shown in SQL Example 5.4.

```
/* SQL Example 5.4 */
SELECT AVG(DISTINCT emp_salary) "Average Employee Salary"
FROM employee;

Average Employee Salary
-------------------
              $38,200
```

The difference between the two queries occurs because the DISTINCT keyword causes SQL to omit duplicate values from the processing. In SQL Example 5.3, there were three employee rows, each with a salary of $25,000 that were selected and used in computing the average displayed in the result table. In SQL Example 5.4, the salary of $25,000 or any other salary figure that is paid to more than one employee is only used once in computing the average DISTINCT salary.

Using the Sum (SUM) Function

Suppose that a senior manager needs to know the total salary being paid currently by the organization. This question can be answered by using the SUM function. This function can compute the total of a numeric table column. The SELECT statement shown in SQL Example 5.5 returns the requested total of the *emp_salary* column from the *employee* table.

```
/* SQL Example 5.5 */
COLUMN "Total Salary" FORMAT $999,999;
SELECT SUM(emp_salary) "Total Salary"
FROM employee;

Total Salary
-----------
    $284,000
```

If management is preparing a budget for various departments, you may be asked to write a query to compute the total salary for different departments. The query shown in SQL Example 5.6 computes the total *emp_salary* for employees assigned to department 7.

```
/* SQL Example 5.6 */
COLUMN "Total Salary Dept 7" FORMAT $999,999;
SELECT SUM(emp_salary) "Total Salary Dept 7"
FROM employee
WHERE emp_dpt_number = 7;

Total Salary Dept 7
----------------
        $136,000
```

Keep in mind that SQL is not case-sensitive with respect to keywords. Query 5.6 could also have been typed in lower case as is shown in SQL Example 5.7.

```
/* SQL Example 5.7 */
select sum(emp_salary) "Total Salary Dept 7"
from employee
where emp_dpt_number = 7;
```

Regardless, the result table will be identical. This is just to remind you that keywords may be entered in either lowercase or uppercase, and this rule also applies to aggregate function names. By convention, we type keywords in uppercase to differentiate between keywords and column/table names.

USING THE MINIMUM (MIN) AND MAXIMUM (MAX) FUNCTIONS

At times, managers need to know which value in a column is the largest or smallest of all values. Questions such as what product was sold the most or least, which employee is paid the largest or smallest salary, and similar questions arise continually in business. SQL provides two aggregate functions to assist you in writing queries to answer these types of questions. The MIN function returns the lowest value stored in a data column. Similarly, the MAX function returns the largest value stored in a data column. However, unlike SUM and AVG, the MIN and MAX functions work with both numeric and character data columns.

SQL Example 5.8 gives a query that uses the MIN function to find the lowest value stored in the *emp_last_name* column of the *employee* table. This is analogous to determine which employee's last name comes first in the alphabet. Conversely, MAX() lists the employee row where last name comes last (highest) in the alphabet.

```
/* SQL Example 5.8 */
SELECT MIN(emp_last_name), MAX(emp_last_name)
FROM employee;

MIN(EMP_LAST_NAME)      MAX(EMP_LAST_NAME)
----------------        ----------------
Amin                    Zhu
```

More often you will use the MIN and MAX functions to manipulate numeric data columns. Let's return to the management question of what are the highest and lowest salaries paid to employees of the firm. The query shown in SQL Example 5.9 uses the MIN and MAX function to answer this question. Notice that the query does not provide the actual names of the employees with these salary values. We will learn later in this chapter how to combine aggregate functions with column names to answer such a question.

```
/* SQL Example 5.9 */
COLUMN "Highest Salary" FORMAT $999,999
COLUMN "Lowest Salary" FORMAT $999,999
SELECT MAX(emp_salary) "Highest Salary",
    MIN(emp_salary) "Lowest Salary"
FROM employee;

Highest Salary    Lowest Salary
-------------     -----------
      $55,000          $25,000
```

USING THE COUNT FUNCTION

At the beginning of this chapter, we used the COUNT(*) function to count the number of rows in a table. The COUNT function does essentially the same thing. The difference is that you can define a specific column to be counted. When the COUNT function processes a specified column, rows containing a NULL value in the named column are omitted from the count. Recall that a NULL value stands for "unknown," and that this should not be confused with a blank or a zero value. The query shown in SQL Example 5.10 counts the number of employees that are assigned a supervisor. Employees not assigned a supervisor will have a NULL value for the supervisor's Social Security Number (SSN) column (*emp_superssn*).

```
/* SQL Example 5.10 */
SELECT COUNT(emp_superssn) "Number Supervised Employees"
FROM employee;

Number Supervised Employees
---------------------------
                          7
```

In contrast, the COUNT(*) function in SQL Example 5.11 counts each employee row regardless of NULL values.

```
/* SQL Example 5.11 */
SELECT COUNT(*) "Number of Employees"
FROM employee;

Number of Employees
-----------------
                 8
```

USING GROUP BY WITH AGGREGATE FUNCTIONS

Now that you've gained familiarity with aggregate functions, you're ready to add power to your queries. The power of aggregate functions is greater when combined with the GROUP BY clause. In fact, the GROUP BY clause is rarely used without an aggregate function. While it is possible to use the GROUP BY clause without aggregates, such a construction has very limited functionality, and could lead to a result table that is confusing or misleading. We will focus on using the GROUP BY clause with aggregate clauses.

When properly used, the GROUP BY clause enables you to use aggregate functions to answer more complex managerial questions such as:

- What is the average salary of employees in each department?
- How many employees work in each department?
- How many employees are working on a particular project?

Examine the queries posed in the previous section. You'll find queries that use aggregate functions to answer questions regarding a single department in the Company database. However, if a manager requests information about the average salary for *each* department, you would need to write a separate query for each department using the approaches demonstrated thus far. Clearly there has to be a better way! SQL comes to the rescue with the GROUP BY clause and enables you to answer questions about each department with a single query.

The query in SQL Example 5.12 answers the managerial question, how many employees work for each department? The count produced by the COUNT(*) aggregate function is grouped by department based on the *emp_dpt_number* column value.

```
/* SQL Example 5.12 */
SELECT emp_dpt_number "Department", COUNT(*) "Employee Count"
FROM employee
GROUP BY emp_dpt_number;

Department     Employee Count
---------      -------------
       1              1
       3              3
       7              4
```

Further, Oracle provides considerable flexibility in specifying the GROUP BY clause. The column name used in a GROUP BY does not have to be listed in the SELECT clause; however, it must be a column name from one of the tables listed in the FROM clause. We can rewrite the query in SQL Example 5.12 without specifying the *emp_dpt_number* column as part of the result table, but as you can see from the result table for SQL Example 5.13, the results are rather cryptic without the *emp_dpt_number* column to identify the meaning of the aggregate count.

```
/* SQL Example 5.13 */
SELECT COUNT(*) "Employee Count"
FROM employee
GROUP BY emp_dpt_number;

Employee Count
------------
            1
            3
            4
```

Note, however, that if your SELECT clause includes *both* column names and aggregate functions (as was the case with the query in SQL Example 5.12) then you must also have a GROUP BY clause in your query. Further, the column name(s) in the GROUP BY clause *must* match the column name(s) listed in the SELECT clause. Otherwise, Oracle will return error messages as shown below in SQL Example 5.14 and SQL Example 5.15.

```
/* SQL Example 5.14 */
SELECT emp_dpt_number "Department", COUNT(*) "Employee Count"
FROM employee;

ERROR at line 1: ORA-00937: not a single-group group function
```

```
/* SQL Example 5.15 */
SELECT emp_dpt_number "Department", COUNT(*) "Employee Count"
FROM employee
GROUP BY emp_city;

ERROR at line 1: ORA-00979: not a GROUP BY expression
```

The GROUP BY clause does have some limitations. For example, you cannot use an aggregate function in a GROUP BY clause. Oracle will return the *ORA-00934: group function not allowed here* error message as demonstrated by SQL Example 5.16.

```
/* SQL Example 5.16 */
SELECT AVG(emp_salary), emp_salary * 1.25
FROM employee
GROUP BY AVG(salary);

ERROR at line 3: ORA-00934: group function is not allowed here
```

USING GROUP BY WITH EXPRESSIONS

In addition to column names, any expression listed in a SELECT clause can also be used with a GROUP BY clause. Suppose one of our managers needs to know the average salary of employees for our organization. Further, the manager needs to know what the new average salary figures will be if all employees receive a 25% raise (a great business year for the firm)! SQL Example 5.17 produces the needed information by using a GROUP BY clause to group on then expression, ***emp_salary * 1.25,*** as opposed to a column name.

```
/* SQL Example 5.17 */
COLUMN "Current Average Salary" FORMAT $999,999;
COLUMN "New Average Salary" FORMAT $999,999;
SELECT AVG(emp_salary) "Current Average Salary",
    AVG(emp_salary * 1.25) "New Average Salary"
FROM employee
GROUP BY emp_salary * 1.25;

Current Average Salary      New Average Salary
--------------------        ----------------
            $25,000                 $31,250
            $30,000                 $37,500
            $38,000                 $47,500
            $43,000                 $53,750
            $55,000                 $68,750
```

Perhaps a more typical management question might be: What is the average salary for each department, and what would be the new average salary after an across-the-board 25% pay raise? The revised query in SQL Example 5.18 changes the condition in the GROUP BY clause to group on department number.

```
/* SQL Example 5.18 */
SELECT emp_dpt_number "Department",
    AVG(emp_salary) "Current Average Salary",
    AVG(emp_salary * 1.25) "New Average Salary"
FROM employee
GROUP BY emp_dpt_number;

Department      Current Average Salary      New Average Salary
---------       --------------------        ----------------
     1                      $55,000                 $68,750
     3                      $31,000                 $38,750
     7                      $34,000                 $42,500
```

NESTING AGGREGATE FUNCTIONS: MAX(AVG( ))

There are two types of values returned by aggregate functions. These are termed *scalar* and *vector* aggregates. As we noted earlier, a *scalar* aggregate function produces a *single value* in a result table from a SELECT statement that does not include a GROUP BY clause. This is true whether the aggregate function operates on all of the rows in a table or only on a subset of rows defined by a WHERE clause condition.

A *vector* aggregate produces a result table that has many values due to the use of a GROUP BY clause, with one row for each grouping. Oracle supports nesting a vector aggregate inside a scalar aggregate—not all DBMS products support this type of query. To understand how this nested query works, let's start with a vector aggregate that returns many values. SQL Example 5.19 shows the use of the AVG function to determine the average salary of employees in each department.

```
/* SQL Example 5.19 */
COLUMN "Average Salary" FORMAT $999,999;
SELECT emp_dpt_number "Department", AVG(emp_salary) "Average Salary"
FROM employee
GROUP BY emp_dpt_number;

Department      Average Salary
---------      ------------
        1           $55,000
        3           $31,000
        7           $34,000
```

Now, because we have only three departments, it is easy to examine the result table to determine that department 1 has the highest average salary. But suppose our organization has several hundred departments. In this situation, scanning a result table visually to determine which department pays employees the highest average salary would be difficult and might cause you to err in identifying the correct department. However, by making two modifications to the query, you can use SQL to find the highest average salary figure for a department. This is accomplished by nesting the AVG(salary) inside the MAX() function and by removing the *emp_dpt_number* column from the SELECT clause as shown in SQL Example 5.20.

```
/* SQL Example 5.20 */
COLUMN "Largest Average Salary" FORMAT $999,999;
SELECT MAX(AVG(emp_salary)) "Largest Average Salary"
FROM employee
GROUP BY emp_dpt_number;

Largest Average Salary
-------------------
            $55,000
```

Conceptually, SQL first creates an interim result table that looks similar to that produced by the query in SQL Example 5.19. Next, the MAX function is applied to the interim result table to produce a final result table with a single figure for the maximum, average departmental employee salary. The drawback of this query is that the department number is not shown in the result table. In order to display the department number with the highest average salary, the query must specify a HAVING clause containing a *subquery*. We will study the HAVING clause later in this chapter. Chapter 7 covers subqueries.

GROUP BY AND NULL VALUES

When a query with a GROUP BY clause processes data columns that contain NULL values, all data rows containing a NULL value are placed into a distinct group. An examination of the *assignment* table in Appendix A reveals that the *work_hours* column contains some NULL values. Because the *assignment* table is used to track the number of hours each employee dedicates to different projects, each employee may have more than one data row in the *assignment* table. The SELECT statement in SQL Example 5.21 produces a result table where *work_hours* are summed and the rows are grouped by the *work_emp_ssn* column. The result table shown lists the total hours (SUM) worked by each employee.

```
/* SQL Example 5.21 */
SELECT work_emp_ssn "SSN",
  SUM(work_hours) "Total Hours Worked"
FROM assignment
GROUP BY work_emp_ssn;

SSN             Total Hours Worked
--------        -----------------
999111111                   39.9
999222222                   39.6
999333333                   42.1
999444444                   44.6
999555555                     34
999666666
999887777                     41
999888888                     43
```

The row for the employee with social security number 999-66-6666 contains a NULL value for the total work hours because the *work_hours* column value is NULL.

USING **GROUP BY** WITH A **WHERE** CLAUSE

You can combine the WHERE and GROUP BY clauses in a SELECT statement. The WHERE clause works to eliminates data table rows from consideration before any grouping takes place. SQL Example 5.22 is a query that produces an average hours worked result table for employees with an SSN that is larger than the specified SSN, 999-66-0000. Here again, you will notice that one employee has a NULL value for the average hours worked.

```
/* SQL Example 5.22 */
SELECT work_emp_ssn SSN, AVG(work_hours) "Average Hours Worked"
FROM assignment
WHERE work_emp_ssn > 999660000
GROUP BY work_emp_ssn;

SSN             Average Hours Worked
--------        ------------------
999666666
999887777                   20.5
999888888                   21.5
```

Using GROUP BY with an ORDER BY Clause

As you learned in studying Chapter 3, the ORDER BY clause allows you to specify how to sort rows in a result table. The default ordering is from smallest to largest value. Similarly, a GROUP BY clause in a SELECT statement determines the sort order of rows in a result table with aggregate results. The sort order can be changed by specifying an ORDER BY clause after the GROUP BY clause. This allows you to specify a sort order based on a data column that is not specified in the GROUP BY clause. SQL Example 5.23 has a query that provides managers with information about the average salary of employees in each department. The result table is sorted from smallest to largest by the average salary figure. Without the ORDER BY clause, the output would be sorted by the *emp_dpt_number* column specified in the GROUP BY clause.

```
/* SQL Example 5.23 */
SELECT emp_dpt_number "Department", AVG(emp_salary) "Average Salary"
FROM employee
GROUP BY emp_dpt_number
ORDER BY AVG(emp_salary);

Department     Average Salary
---------      -------------
        3           $31,000
        7           $34,000
        1           $55,000
```

If management wants the result table to display average salaries from highest to lowest, you can specify the DESC keyword in the ORDER BY clause. SQL Example 5.24 shows the revised query.

```
/* SQL Example 5.24 */
SELECT emp_dpt_number "Department", AVG(emp_salary) "Average Salary"
FROM employee
GROUP BY emp_dpt_number
ORDER BY AVG(emp_salary) DESC;

Department     Average Salary
---------      -------------
        1           $55,000
        7           $34,000
        3           $31,000
```

Using GROUP BY with a HAVING Clause

Earlier you learned that you cannot use an aggregate function in a WHERE clause. Oracle will return an error message and fail to process the query. The HAVING clause is used for aggregate functions in the same way that a WHERE clause is used for column names and expressions. Essentially, the HAVING and WHERE clauses do the same thing, that is filter rows from inclusion in a result table based on a condition.

While it may appear that a HAVING clause filters out groups, it does not. Rather, a HAVING clause filters rows. When all rows for a group are eliminated so is the group.

To summarize, the important differences between the WHERE and HAVING clauses are:

- A WHERE clause is used to filter rows **BEFORE** the GROUPING action (i.e., before the calculation of the aggregate functions).
- A HAVING clause filters rows **AFTER** the GROUPING action (i.e., after the calculation of the aggregate functions).

Suppose that a manager in the Accounting Department requires a listing of departments where the average salary is greater than $33,000. We know that we cannot use the condition "AVG(*emp_salary*) > 33000" in the WHERE clause because Oracle will return an error message due to the AVG aggregate function in the WHERE clause. We can remedy this problem by using a HAVING clause to filter rows after the grouping action. SQL Example 5.25 gives a query with the appropriate SELECT statement.

```
/* SQL Example 5.25 */
SELECT emp_dpt_number "Department", AVG(emp_salary) "Average Salary"
FROM employee
GROUP BY emp_dpt_number
HAVING AVG(emp_salary) > 33000;

Department      Average Salary
---------       -------------
        1             $55,000
        7             $34,000
```

Now, suppose this same manager is not interested in the budget for department 1, but has the same question regarding average salaries for the other departments in our organization. This gives rise to a situation where we can combine the use of the WHERE and HAVING clauses. SQL Example 5.26 gives the SELECT statement needed to produce a result table for this query.

```
/* SQL Example 5.26 */
SELECT emp_dpt_number "Department", AVG(emp_salary) "Average Salary"
FROM employee
WHERE emp_dpt_number <> 1
GROUP BY emp_dpt_number
HAVING AVG(emp_salary) > 33000;

Department      Average Salary
---------       -------------
        7             $34,000
```

Of course, having completed this series of SELECT statements in sequence, we knew in advance that only one department would satisfy all of the conditions of the query, and this helps us to prove the accuracy of the query. Conceptually, SQL performs the following steps in the query given in SQL Example 5.26.

1. The WHERE clause filters rows that do not meet the condition *emp_dpt_number* <> 1.
2. The GROUP BY clause collects the surviving rows into one or more groups for each unique *emp_dpt_number*.
3. The aggregate function calculates the average salary for each *emp_dpt_number* grouping.
4. The HAVING clause filters out the rows from the result table that do not meet the condition: average salary greater than $33,000.

All of this represents quite a bit of work on the part of your SQL query and your Oracle server software. The good news is that you do not have to do the processing by hand, nor do you really have to worry about how it all happens. How the Oracle server handles the query does not matter because it will interpret your query and create its own plan of action.

STANDARD SQL RULES

The most common use of a HAVING clause is to create result tables containing one row per group, with one or more summary values in a row. To do this your query must meet the following conditions:

1. Columns listed in a SELECT clause must also be listed in the GROUP BY expression or they must be arguments of aggregate functions.
2. A GROUP BY expression can only contain column names that are in the SELECT clause listing.
3. Columns in a HAVING expression must be either:
   • Single-valued—arguments of an aggregate function, for instance, or
   • Listed in the SELECT clause listing or GROUP BY clause.

The SELECT statement in SQL Example 5.27 is an example of a query that complies with these rules. First, the *emp_dpt_number* column listed in the SELECT clause listing is also listed in the GROUP BY clause. The second expression in the SELECT clause listing is the aggregate function, COUNT(*). Second, the GROUP BY expression only contains column names listed in the SELECT clause column listing (*emp_dpt_number*). Third, the HAVING expression is an argument of an aggregate function. The query will return a single row per group in the result table, and will group the rows in the *employee* table by the *emp_dpt_number* column. The query eliminates groups that have less than three employees.

```
/* SQL Example 5.27 */
SELECT emp_dpt_number "Department", COUNT(*) "Employee Count"
FROM employee
GROUP BY emp_dpt_number
HAVING COUNT(*) >= 3;

Department     Employee Count
---------      -------------
        3                  3
        7                  4
```

Let's see what happens when two additional aggregate functions are added to the SELECT clause listing. The modified query in SQL Example 5.28 counts the number of employees in a department and simultaneously computes both the largest and smallest employee salary for each department.

```
/* SQL Example 5.28 */
COLUMN "Top Salary" FORMAT $999,999;
COLUMN "Low Salary" FORMAT $999,999;
SELECT emp_dpt_number "Department", COUNT(*) "Employee Count",
    MAX(emp_salary) "Top Salary", MIN(emp_salary) "Low Salary"
FROM employee
GROUP BY emp_dpt_number
HAVING COUNT(*) >= 3;

Department      Employee Count      Top Salary      Low Salary
---------       --------------      ---------       ---------
        3                    3       $43,000         $25,000
        7                    4       $43,000         $25,000
```

By adding the MAX(*emp_salary*) and MIN(*emp_salary*) columns to the query, you gain additional columns in the result table, but the exact same groups are displayed. This query conforms to Standard SQL because the *emp_salary* column name is included as an argument in the MAX and MIN aggregate functions. It is simply chance that the largest and smallest employee salary figures for departments 3 and 7 are identical in the *employee* table.

SQL Extensions to **GROUP BY** and **HAVING** Clauses

Various software vendors, such as Oracle, provide extensions to the standard SQL. These extensions provide flexibility in displaying data in result tables by allowing references to columns and expressions that are not used to create groups or summary calculations. You need to understand that these extensions are *not* part of the ANSI standard for SQL. Before using these, ensure that the database management system software that you are using supports these language extensions.

- A SELECT clause listing that includes aggregate functions can also include columns that are not arguments of aggregate functions, or that are not included in the GROUP BY clause.
- The GROUP BY clause can include column names or expressions that are not included in the SELECT clause listing.
- The GROUP BY ALL clause displays all groups, even those excluded from calculations by a WHERE clause.
- The HAVING clause can include columns or expressions that are not listed in the SELECT clause or in a GROUP BY clause.

Sometimes, an SQL extension can add rows and columns to the result table that are difficult to interpret. This can also occur when a GROUP BY clause is omitted. Table 5.2 summarizes what you need to do if you are writing a query that involves grouping and summarizing column data.

TABLE 5.2	**Grouping and Summarizing**
To Get This Effect:	*Do This:*
Exclude rows before grouping.	Use a WHERE clause.
Divide a result table into groups.	Use a GROUP BY clause.
Calculate summary values for each group.	Include one or more aggregates in the SELECT clause listing.
Exclude groups from the result table.	Use a HAVING clause.
If This Happens:	*Look for This:*
All qualified rows in all qualified groups display.	The SELECT clause listing contains a column name that is not in the GROUP BY clause.

USING HAVING WITHOUT A GROUP BY CLAUSE

The HAVING clause is a conditional option that is directly related to the GROUP BY clause option because a HAVING clause eliminates rows from a result table based on the result of a GROUP BY clause. Many relational database management systems including Oracle will not process a query with a HAVING clause that is not accompanied by a GROUP BY clause. The following query in SQL Example 5.29 attempts to use a HAVING clause without a GROUP BY clause. Oracle generates the *ORA-00937: not a single-group group function* error.

```
/* SQL Example 5.29 */
SELECT emp_dpt_number, AVG(emp_salary)
FROM employee
HAVING AVG(emp_salary) > 33000;

ERROR at line 1: ORA-00937: not a single-group group function
```

SUMMARY

In this chapter, you developed an understanding of the use of aggregate functions. The GROUP BY clause enables you to produce complex data manipulations with ease through the use of clearly understandable queries. You also learned to use the HAVING clause to restrict rows in a result table to those meeting conditions that involve the use of an aggregate function. The WHERE and ORDER BY clauses were also covered in conjunction with the GROUP BY clause and aggregate functions. You learned to use these clauses to order the display of rows in a result table according to management specifications, and to eliminate information that was not desired in a final result table. The chapter also summarized SQL extensions for the GROUP BY and HAVING clauses. You are now ready to reinforce your learning by completing the review exercises.

REVIEW EXERCISES

LEARN THESE TERMS

Aggregate functions. Used to write queries to produce data that can aid in decision making regarding exceptional situations.

AVG. The average of values in a numeric column/expression.

COUNT. The number of non-NULL values in a column/expression.

COUNT(*). The number of selected rows.

DISTINCT. A keyword that causes SQL to omit duplicate values from processing.

GROUP BY clause. Used to specify which rows from a data table will be included when aggregating information by groups.

HAVING clause. Used to filter rows through the use of aggregate functions.

MAX. The highest value in a column/expression.

MIN. The lowest value in a column/expression.

Scalar aggregate. A scalar aggregate function produces a *single value* in a result table from a SELECT statement that does not include a GROUP BY clause.

SUM. The total of values in a numeric column/expression.

Vector aggregate. A vector aggregate yields a result table that has many values due to the use of a GROUP BY clause.

CONCEPTS QUIZ

1. Explain the use of each of the aggregate functions: SUM, AVG, COUNT, COUNT(*), MAX, and MIN.
2. What is the purpose of the DISTINCT keyword when used with an aggregate function?
3. What is the rule regarding the use of aggregate functions in SELECT, HAVING, and WHERE clauses?
4. Which is the aggregate functions work with both numeric and character data columns?
5. If you write a query using the COUNT aggregate function, what happens to rows that contain a NULL value for the column being queried?
6. If you write a query using the COUNT(*) aggregate function, what happens to rows that contain NULL values?
7. What is the purpose of the GROUP BY clause?
8. Name one limitations of the GROUP BY clause with respect to aggregate functions.
9. How many values are in a result table that is produced by using a scalar aggregate function without a GROUP BY clause?
10. How many values are in a result table that is produced by using a vector aggregate function with a GROUP BY clause?
11. What happens to a result table when a GROUP BY clause processes data columns that contain NULL values?
12. How does a WHERE clause affect the production of a result table from a SELECT statement that has a GROUP BY clause?
13. Why would you use an ORDER BY clause to order output when a GROUP BY clause normally determines the sort order of rows in a result table?
14. What is the keyword used to display result table rows from highest to lowest value based on a data column in which the ORDER BY clause is used for sorting?
15. What is the purpose of a HAVING clause, and what advantage does it offer to you in developing queries?

16. If you need to create a result table containing more than one summary value in each row, what conditions must be met in using a HAVING clause along with aggregate functions?

SQL CODING EXERCISES AND QUESTIONS

1. A manager from the human resources department needs you to write a query to count the number of dependents of employees of the company. Count the number of rows in the *dependent* table. Label the output column **Number of Dependents.**

2. The *dep_date_of_birth* column in the *dependent* table stores date of birth information for dependents of employees of the company. Write a query to display the date of birth of the youngest dependent listed in the table. No special output column label is required.

3. The department table stores information about departments within the company. The *dpt_mgr_start_date* column stores the date on which an employee started working as a department manager. Write a query to display the date for the manager that has worked as a department manager the longest. No special output column label is required.

4. Accountants working on the company's annual budgeting process need to know the average salary (*emp_salary*) for employees and the sum of all employee salaries. The information is stored in the *employee* table. The result table should have two columns based on a single query. Label the columns **Average Salary** and **Total Salary.** Format the output as $999,999.

5. A new government reporting regulation requires you to develop a query that will count the number of male dependents of employees of the company. The information is stored in the *dep_gender* column of the *dependent* table. The result table should have a single output column labeled **Number Male Dependents.**

6. A revision to the government reporting regulation cited in question 5 requires the report to count the number of male and female dependents of the company. Display the information as two columns, one for gender and one for the associated count. The result table should have two rows, one for each gender. Use a single query. Additionally, the gender output column should be formatted as A6 and have a heading of **Gender.** The count column should have a heading of **Number Counted.**

7. The government reporting regulation cited in questions 5 and 6 also require a report of the count of each type of dependent (spouse, daughter, and son). Write a query that will produce a result table with two columns labeled **Dependent Type** (use the *dep_relationship* column) and **Dependent Count** from the *dependent* table.

8. Modify the query written for question 7 to restrict output to the result table such that spouses are not listed. Only a count of daughters and sons should be listed in the output. Label the columns as specified in question 7.

9. Modify the query written for question 7 to sort the output by the count of the number of dependents in each category with the largest counts listed first. Label the columns as specified in question 7.

10. Modify the query written for question 7 to restrict the output to include rows for dependents born after December 31, 1970. Use the *dep_date_of_birth* column in your query to refer to each dependent's date of birth. Use the TO_DATE function

for the *dep_date_of_birth* column and the TO_DATE('31-DEC-70') expression in your query. Label the columns as specified in question 7.

11. The company's executive director or project manager needs to know the number of projects each department is working on based on the information stored in the *project* table. The result table should have two columns labeled **Department** and **Project Count.** You will need to refer to the *pro_dept_number* column that stores the department number and the *pro_number* column that stores the project number information.

12. Rewrite the query from question 11 to exclude projects located in Edwardsville. You will need to use the *pro_location* column that stores the project location in writing your query. Label the columns as specified in question 11.

13. Rewrite the query from question 11 to exclude any group that does not have at least two projects. Label the columns as specified in question 11.

14. Write a query to provide the Executive Director with the total hours worked per project. Use the *work_pro_number* and *work_hours* columns from the *assignment* table to obtain the project numbers and hours worked, respectively. Label the two columns **Project Number** and **Total Hours,** respectively. Format the output for the Total Hours column as 999.99.

15. Rewrite the query for question 14 to exclude projects where the average *work_hours* column value is less than 15 hours. Sort the output by **Total Hours** from smallest to largest.

CHAPTER 6

JOINS

This chapter focuses on JOIN operations. Thus far, your study of the SQL has focused on writing queries that retrieve data stored in a single table. However, large databases have many related tables. Often, managers need information that requires the retrieval of data from related rows that are stored in more than one table. These queries are termed JOIN operations, and may include data rows from two, three, or even more related tables.

OBJECTIVES

The related tables of a large database are linked through the use of *foreign keys* or what are often referred to as *common columns*. In this chapter, you will learn to join tables together based on foreign keys. The ability to join tables will enable you to add more meaning to the result table that is produced. Writing table joins is a task SQL programmers routinely accomplish. Your learning objectives for this chapter include:

- Write an equijoin query and inequality join by using the WHERE clause.
- Learn the basic JOIN operation rules.
- Write complex JOIN queries with more than two tables, and more than two columns.
- Write OUTER JOIN queries.
- Write SELF JOIN queries.

A TYPICAL JOIN OPERATION

Figure 6.1 displays the *employee* and *department* tables. The figure illustrates the concept of a JOIN operation by connecting columns within each table with a line. One line connects the *employee* table's *emp_dpt_number* column with the *department* table's *dpt_no* column. Even though these two columns have different names, the data stored in the columns share a common *domain* of values. The domain of values for the *emp_dpt_number* column in the *employee* table is all valid department numbers. This

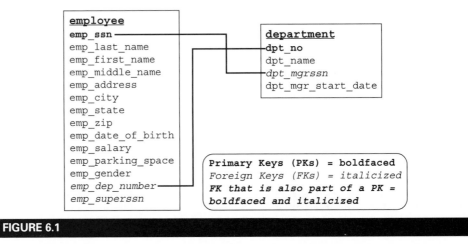

FIGURE 6.1

means that, because of the referential integrity clauses enforced when the tables were created, the values stored in the *emp_dpt_number* column must also appear in the *dpt_no* column for one of the rows in the *department* table.

A second line connects the *employee* table's *emp_ssn* column to the *department* table's *dep_mgrssn* column. This line represents a second, different JOIN operation. This second JOIN operation enables the display of detailed information about a department manager since the only information stored in the *department* table about each department's manager is the manager's social security number (*dep_mgrssn*).

If you review the SQL script in Appendix A that creates the *employee* and *department* tables, you will discover that it is possible for an employee to NOT be assigned to a specific department. However, this situation would only arise if a department is eliminated (deleted) from the database. In this case, the *emp_dpt_number* column value for employees assigned to the deleted department is set to NULL pending the reassignment of each employee to a new department.

We will begin our study of JOIN operations by focusing on the relationship between the *employee* and *department* tables represented by the common department number values. The first query shown in SQL Example 6.1 lists employee names and department numbers. This query only retrieves data from the single *employee* table.

```
/* SQL Example 6.1 */
COLUMN "Last Name" FORMAT A15;
COLUMN "First Name" FORMAT A15;
SELECT emp_last_name "Last Name", emp_first_name "First Name",
    emp_dpt_number "Department"
FROM employee;

Last Name       First Name      Department
--------        ---------       ---------
Bordoloi        Bijoy                   1
Joyner          Suzanne                 3
Zhu             Waiman                  7
more rows will be displayed . . .
```

A large organization can have dozens or even hundreds of departments. Thus, the numbers displayed in the department column shown above may not be very meaningful. In fact, they may be meaningless! In this situation, a manager may want the result table to display the department name instead of the department number. This requires you to retrieve information from two tables since department names are stored in the *department* table. Hence, your query needs to join the *employee* and the *department* tables in order to produce the desired result table.

Oracle SQL uses the WHERE clause to join tables. In fact, the JOIN operation can be easily specified and is straight-forward. Study the query in SQL Example 6.2. In this query, the WHERE clause links the *employee* table's *emp_dpt_number* column to the *department* table's *dpt_no column*. Since the query retrieves row data from two tables, each table is listed in the FROM clause. Further, each table is provided with a table *alias name*. The use of an alias name is optional. The *employee* table's alias name is simply the letter "e" while the *department* table's alias is the letter "d." Table alias names are used to enable an abbreviated method for referencing a table name within the query. This shorthand method for referring to a table simplifies writing a query. The query is also shown without the use of alias names in SQL Example 6.3.

```
/* SQL Example 6.2
   Query with alias names */
SELECT emp_last_name "Last Name", emp_first_name "First Name",
   dpt_name "Department Name"
FROM employee e, department d
WHERE e.emp_dpt_number = d.dpt_no;
```

```
/* SQL Example 6.3
   Same query using full table names */
SELECT emp_last_name "Last Name", emp_first_name "First Name",
   dpt_name "Department Name"
FROM employee, department
WHERE employee.emp_dpt_number = department.dpt_no;

Last Name       First Name      Department Name
--------        ---------       ---------------
Bordoloi        Bijoy           Headquarters
Joyner          Suzanne         Admin and Records
Zhu             Waiman          Production
more rows will be displayed . . .
```

HOW JOINS ARE PROCESSED

Now that you've seen a basic JOIN query, it's time to learn what SQL is doing for you behind the scenes. Conceptually, when two tables are joined, SQL creates a *Cartesian* product of the tables. A Cartesian product consists of all possible combinations of the rows from each of the tables. Therefore, when a table with 10 rows is joined with a table with 20 rows, the Cartesian product is 200 rows ($10 \times 20 = 200$). For example, joining the *employee* table with eight rows and the *department* table with three rows will produce a Cartesian product table of 24 rows ($8 \times 3 = 24$).

It is important to understand how JOIN queries are processed in order to develop your knowledge of this important concept. Therefore, we will examine a series of examples to aid you in understanding the JOIN operation process. Table 6.1 shows two tables simply named *table_1* and *table_2*. Each table has a single column named *col_1*. Each table also has three rows with simple alphabetic values stored in the *col_1* column.

A Cartesian product of these tables yields a result table with nine rows ($3 \times 3 = 9$). The query in SQL Example 6.4 that produces the Cartesian product is elementary.

```
/* SQL Example 6.4 */
COLUMN col_1 FORMAT A5;
SELECT *
FROM table_1, table_2;

COL_1    COL_1
-----    -----
a        a
b        a
c        a
a        b
b        b
c        b
a        c
b        c
c        c
```

An examination of the result table reveals that the first row of *table_1* was joined with every row of *table_2*. Likewise, the second row of the *table_1* was joined with every row of the *table_2*, and so forth.

A Cartesian product result table is normally not very useful. In fact, such a result table can be terribly misleading. If you execute this type of query for the *employee* and *department* tables, the result table implies that every employee has a relationship with every department, and we know that this is simply not the case!

The query in SQL Example 6.4 requires a WHERE clause to specify the nature of the relationship between the two tables. This will prevent the error of joining rows that are not related. SQL Example 6.5 gives the revised query. The WHERE clause specifies that only related rows are to be displayed in the result table, in other words, where values in *table_1* match the values in *table_2*.

TABLE 6.1

Table_1 Col_1	Table_2 Col_1
A	a
B	b
C	c

```
/* SQL Example 6.5 */
SELECT *
FROM table_1 t1, table_2 t2
WHERE t1.col_1 = t2.col_1;

COL_1       COL_1
-----       -----
a           a
b           b
c           c
```

The WHERE clause filters out rows that are not related. Conceptually, it is important to understand that the WHERE clause is the key to joining tables. We will now return to SQL Example 6.3, where we joined *employee* and *department* tables; however, we will now restrict the result table to a listing of employees that work in a specific department. The revised query shown in SQL Example 6.6 specifies the listing of employees in the Production Department (department 7). This is accomplished by using the AND logical operator and adding a condition to the WHERE clause. You need to understand that a WHERE clause can JOIN tables as well as restrict the rows displayed in the result table based on specified criteria.

```
/* SQL Example 6.6 */
SELECT emp_last_name "Last Name", emp_first_name "First Name",
    dpt_name "Department Name"
FROM employee e, department d
WHERE e.emp_dpt_number = d.dpt_no AND e.emp_dpt_number = 7;

Last Name       First Name      Department Name
---------       ----------      ---------------
Zhu             Waiman          Production
Bock            Douglas         Production
Joshi           Dinesh          Production
Prescott        Sherri          Production
```

JOIN OPERATION RULES

JOINS AND THE SELECT CLAUSE

Now that you have seen several JOIN examples, we will review the detailed rules that you need to understand in order to produce successful JOIN operations. As with any query, a JOIN query always begins with a SELECT clause. List the columns to be displayed in the result table after the SELECT keyword. Further, the result table column order reflects the order in which column names are listed in the SELECT clause. If a manager wants the order of the columns modified, you simply rearrange the order of the column listing in the SELECT clause. SQL Example 6.7 moves the Department Name column to the first column position in the result table.

```
/* SQL Example 6.7 */
SELECT dpt_name "Department Name", emp_last_name "Last Name",
    emp_first_name "First Name"
FROM employee e, department d
WHERE e.emp_dpt_number = d.dpt_no AND e.emp_dpt_number = 7;

Department Name      Last Name     First Name
-------------        --------      ---------
Production           Zhu           Waiman
Production           Bock          Douglas
Production           Joshi         Dinesh
Production           Prescott      Sherri
```

JOIN operations also support the specification of all columns by the use of a simple asterisk (*) in a SELECT clause. The result table for a query like the one shown in SQL Example 6.8 contains all columns from both the *employee* and *department* tables. When the asterisk (*) is used, the column order of the result table is based on the order in which tables are listed in the FROM clause; thus, the order in which the columns are listed will be all *employee* columns followed by all *department* columns. For purposes of brevity, we have omitted the result table for this query, but you may wish to execute the query yourself in order to examine the output.

```
/* SQL Example 6.8 */
SELECT *
FROM employee e, department d
WHERE e.emp_dpt_number = d.dpt_no AND e.emp_dpt_number = 7;
```

JOINS AND THE FROM CLAUSE

Any SELECT statement that has two or more table names (or view names—see Chapter 8) listed in a FROM clause is a JOIN query. By definition, a JOIN operation retrieves rows from two or more tables.

You will always use the FROM clause to list the tables from which columns are to be retrieved by a JOIN query. The FROM clause listing has a limit of 16 table names. The order of table name listings is irrelevant to the production of the result table with the one exception noted above—that is, if you use an (*) in the SELECT clause, then the column order in the result table reflects the order in which tables are listed in the FROM clause.

JOINS AND THE WHERE CLAUSE

As we have seen, the WHERE clause specifies the relationship between tables listed in the FROM clause. It also restricts the rows displayed in the result table. The most commonly used JOIN operator is the "equal" sign (=).

QUALIFYING COLUMN NAMES AND ALIASES

Normally, you do not need to create alias names for tables. This is optional. However, when column names are *ambiguous,* you must qualify the column names. A column name is ambiguous when the same column name is used in different tables. The company database described in Appendix A avoids ambiguity by naming each column with a prefix to denote the table to which the column belongs. However, this naming convention is not required. Recall our earlier example with the tables named *Table_1* and *Table_2*. The query used to JOIN these tables is shown in SQL Example 6.9.

```
/* SQL Example 6.9 */
SELECT *
FROM table_1, table_2
WHERE table_1.col_1 = table_2.col_1;
```

Since each table has a column named *col_1*, the column names used in the WHERE clause to accomplish the JOIN operation are *qualified* by referencing the table name, "dot," and the column name. If the column names were not qualified, the query would look like the one shown below, and Oracle will return the *ORA-00918: column ambiguously defined* error message. The query shown in SQL Example 6.10 fails to process because of ambiguity in the column names (*col_1*).

```
/* SQL Example 6.10 */
SELECT *
FROM table_1, table_2
WHERE col_1 = col_1;

ERROR at line 3:
ORA-00918: column ambiguously defined
```

This error message tells you that you have included a column name somewhere in the query that exists in more than one table listed in the FROM clause. Here the error is in the WHERE clause; however, it is also possible to make a similar error in the SELECT clause. The SELECT statement shown below fails to qualify the *col_1* name in the SELECT clause, and Oracle again produces the *ORA-00918* error message.

```
/* SQL Example 6.11 */
SELECT col_1
FROM table_1, table_2
WHERE table_1.col_1 = table_2.col_1;

ERROR at line 1:
ORA-00918: column ambiguously defined
```

As you have seen, an ambiguous column name is qualified by using the DOT (.) connector to connect the table name and column name. Sometimes, it is easier to qualify column names by using table alias names. As was demonstrated earlier, a table can be assigned an alias name for a query by simply listing a unique identifier for the table name in the FROM clause. Often, a single letter is used as an identifier to reduce keystroke requirements as was done earlier in the JOIN query for the *employee* and *department* tables shown here as SQL Example 6.12.

```
/* SQL Example 6.12 */
SELECT dpt_name "Department Name", emp_last_name "Last Name",
    emp_first_name "First Name"
FROM employee e, department d
WHERE e.emp_dpt_number = d.dpt_no AND e.emp_dpt_number = 7;
```

The use of the letters "e" and "d" is completely arbitrary; "t1" and "t2" or any other unique aliases could be used. The important points to learn are:

- The alias name must follow a table name.
- Use a space to separate a table name and its alias name.
- The alias name must be unique within the SELECT statement.

When column names are not identical you are not required to qualify them. Sometimes, they are qualified anyway because it can be helpful in terms of documenting the query.

The query in SQL Example 6.12 can be documented by rewriting it as is shown in SQL Example 6.13. In this fashion, it becomes clear that the *dpt_name* column is retrieved from the *department* table. Likewise, the *emp_last_name* and *emp_first_name* columns are retrieved from the *employee* table.

```
/* SQL Example 6.13 */
SELECT d.dpt_name "Department Name", e.emp_last_name "Last Name",
    —e.emp_first_name "First Name"
FROM employee e, department d
WHERE e.emp_dpt_number = d.dpt_no AND e.emp_dpt_number = 7;
```

While not required by the database management system processing the SQL statement, the additional qualification may help you and future programmers decipher the query should it ever need to be modified.

JOIN–RELATIONAL OPERATORS

The JOIN operators shown in Table 6.2 determine the basis by which columns are matched and are called *relational operators*. You will recognize them as the comparison operators that you learned earlier.

ADDITIONAL WHERE CLAUSE OPTIONS

Thus far, we have focused on using the WHERE clause to specify JOIN operations. You have also studied some examples that use the WHERE clause to specify simple selection criteria, such as the specification of a certain department number for row selection. In fact, all of the selection criteria used in earlier chapters to add power to queries can also be used with JOIN operations. SQL Example 6.14 gives a SELECT statement that retrieves the names of employees based on department numbers by using the IN operator to select employees in either department 3 or 7.

TABLE 6.2

Operator	Meaning
=	equal to
<	less than
>	greater than
>=	greater than or equal to
<=	less than or equal to
!=	not equal to
<>	not equal to
!>	not greater than
!<	not less than

```
/* SQL Example 6.14 */
SELECT emp_last_name "Last Name", emp_first_name "First Name",
    dpt_name "Department Name"
FROM employee e, department d
WHERE e.emp_dpt_number = d.dpt_no AND
    d.dpt_no IN (3, 7)
ORDER BY emp_last_name;

Last Name      First Name     Department Name
---------      ----------     ---------------
Amin           Hyder          Admin and Records
JBock          Douglas        Production
Joshi          Dinesh         Production
more rows will be displayed . . .
```

For all practical purposes, you may specify as many selection criteria as is necessary to produce the desired result table. Additionally, although the queries shown thus far have always specified the JOIN operation first, the order of selection criteria or JOIN operations is not important. Query 6.14 could have been rewritten as is shown in SQL Example 6.15. Notice that the criteria for row selection and table joins in the WHERE clause are reversed, as is the department number listing within the IN listing.

```
/* SQL Example 6.15 */
SELECT emp_last_name "Last Name", emp_first_name "First Name",
    dpt_name "Department Name"
FROM employee e, department d
WHERE d.dpt_no IN (7, 3) AND
    e.emp_dpt_number = d.dpt_no
ORDER BY emp_last_name;
```

JOIN OPERATIONS USING INEQUALITY OPERATORS (<, >, <>)

The JOIN queries covered thus far are termed *equijoins* because the relational operator used in the JOIN operation is the equal sign (=). However, you may use any relational operator in a JOIN query. This query in SQL Example 6.16 uses an inequality operator, the not equal to than (<>) relational operator.

```
/* SQL Example 6.16 */
COLUMN "Emp Last Name" FORMAT A15;
COLUMN "Dependent Name" FORMAT A15;
SELECT emp_last_name "Emp Last Name", dep_name "Dependent Name"
FROM employee e, dependent d
WHERE e.emp_ssn <> d.dep_emp_ssn AND
    e.emp_last_name IN ('Bordoloi', 'Bock')
ORDER BY emp_last_name;

Emp Last Name    Dependent Name
------------     --------------
Bock             Jo Ellen
Bock             Andrew
Bock             Allen
Bock             Susan
Bordoloi         Jo Ellen
Bordoloi         Deanna
Bordoloi         Mary Ellen
Bordoloi         Jeffery
Bordoloi         Allen
Bordoloi         Susan
Bordoloi         Andrew
11 rows selected.
```

Query 6.16 produces a result table in which the dependent names listed are not dependents of the respective employees who are listed. Note that Jo Ellen, Andrew, Allen, and Susan are not dependents of either employee, but only Deanna and Mary Ellen are not dependents of Bordoloi. This must mean that Deanna and Mary Ellen are dependents of Bock. The query may not make a lot of sense to you as an SQL programmer, but its usefulness depends on management's need for the information.

As it happens, JOIN operations using inequality operators are not used very often. Most queries are equijoins because a JOIN operation based on equality often make the most sense. Conceptually, a JOIN operation involving an inequality operator works the same way as an equijoin. A Cartesian product is formed from the *employee* and *dependent* tables. The result table is then populated based on the inequality JOIN condition and selection criteria.

COMPLEX JOIN OPERATIONS

JOINING MORE THAN TWO TABLES

While the examples given thus far have joined rows from two tables, you can specify up to 16 tables in a JOIN operation. Sixteen is a very large number! While it is not uncommon to have three or four tables in a JOIN operation, it would be very unusual to exceed this number; thus, it turns out that 16 is not much of a limitation. You do need to understand that the more tables that are included in a JOIN operation, the longer the query will take to process, especially when the tables are large with millions of rows per table.

The example shown in Figure 6.2 joins three tables to produce a result table based on two different relationships. The bold lines show that the *assignment* table is related to the *employee* table through the employee Social Security Number (SSN) domain of values. Similarly, the *assignment* table is related to the project table through the project number domain of values. The *assignment* table is classified as an *association* table because the rows in it relate to or associate both the *employee* and *project* tables simultaneously.

An association table relates or associates two or more other tables where the other tables would be related in a many-to-many fashion. Here, the *assignment* table depicts the fact that many employees can be assigned to work on a project, and a project can simultaneously have many employees assigned to it. Association tables are also termed *intersection* or *conjunction* tables.

The SELECT statement to join the tables depicted in Figure 6.2 is shown in SQL Example 6.17.

```
/* SQL Example 6.17 */
COLUMN "Raised Salary" FORMAT $999,999;
SELECT emp_last_name "Last Name", emp_first_name "First Name",
    1.10*emp_salary "Raised Salary", p.pro_name "Project"
FROM employee e, assignment a, project p
WHERE e.emp_ssn = a.work_emp_ssn AND
    a.work_pro_number = p.pro_number AND
    p.pro_name = 'Inventory';

Last Name      First Name     Raised Salary     Project
---------      ----------     -------------     --------
Zhu            Waiman               $47,300      Inventory
Markis         Marcia               $27,500      Inventory
Amin           Hyder                $27,500      Inventory
```

FIGURE 6.2

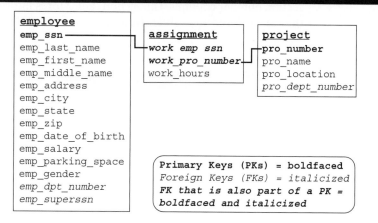

This is a good example of a situation in which joining more than two tables yields information that managers may find extremely helpful. The result table shown provides information about what employee salaries will be if every worker on the inventory project is given a 10 percent raise.

Let's take a closer look at the query in SQL Example 6.17. It may help you to refer to the description of the company database that is provided in Appendix A. This may seem strange, but did you notice that the *assignment* table does not contribute any columns to the result table! Also none of the columns used to specify the JOIN operation are included in the result table. Even when are not represented in a result table, they may be used to formulate a query's WHERE clause.

Examine Figure 6.2 again. The bold lines connecting the tables depict the fact that the JOIN operation involves two different conditions that are stated in query 6.17. The first condition joins the *employee* and *assignment* tables based on each employee's SSN. Thus, only employees who are working on a project are included in the result table. The second condition joins the *assignment* and *project* tables based on the project number columns in each table. This means that only projects that have associated rows in the *assignment* table will be included in the result table.

```
WHERE e.emp_ssn = w.work_emp_ssn AND        /* Condition #1 */
    w.work_pro_number = p.pro_number AND    /* Condition #2 */
    p.pro_name = 'Inventory';               /* Condition #3 */
```

Finally, there is a third condition in the WHERE clause. The third condition does not join any tables; rather, it specifies criteria for row selection in order to restrict the result table to those rows for employees working on the project named "Inventory." Conceptually, a Cartesian product of the three tables is formed, and then only those rows satisfying the conditions stated in the WHERE clause are retained for the result table.

JOINING TABLES BY USING TWO COLUMNS

Study the diagram in Figure 6.3. This diagram depicts the relationship at a university where students enroll in course sections.

The *enrollment* table stores rows describing enrollments in various course sections and is identified by a composite key that includes the student SSN, course number, and section number columns. The *section* table stores information about sections of courses that are offered in a given term, and has rows identified by a composite key that

FIGURE 6.3

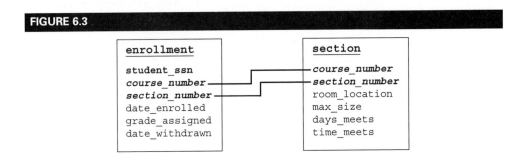

includes the course number and section number. In order to join the *enrollment* and *section* tables, the JOIN operation needs to specify a complex JOIN condition that includes both the *course_number* and *section_number* columns from both tables. This is because neither the *course_number* nor *section_number* columns are sufficient by themselves to identify the associated rows for a given course and section. This example can be extended to three or more columns and to three or more tables.

The SELECT statement that accomplishes the JOIN based on two columns is shown in SQL Example 6.18. Again, this situation arises when the related tables have *composite primary key* columns. You may recall that a composite primary key is required when a single column is not sufficient to guarantee the unique identification of table rows.

```
/* SQL Example 6.18 */
SELECT s.course_title "Course Title", e.student_ssn "Student SSN"
FROM enrollment e, section s
WHERE e.course_number = s.course_number AND
    e.section_number = s.section_number;
```

OUTER JOIN OPERATIONS

Oracle supports an OUTER JOIN operation. This type of join has a limited, but very important and specific purpose. It is used to identify situations where rows in one table do *not* match rows in a second table, even though the two tables are related. Such would be the situation if management wants to know what products are available but have never been sold to a customer. Clearly, management would want to eliminate the stockage of poorly selling products. While a *product* table stores information about all products that are for sale, a *sales* table stores rows only about products that have actually sold. If a product is not listed in the *sales* table, then it has not sold and would have no corresponding rows in the *sales* table. An OUTER JOIN allows rows from one table to appear in a result table even if when is no matching value in the table to which it is joined.

Let's examine an OUTER JOIN situation for the Company database. Suppose management needs a listing of all employees of the firm as well as their dependents. Figure 6.4 shows the relationship between the *employee* and *dependent* tables. The *dep_emp_ssn* column is a foreign key in the *dependent* table and has a shared domain with the *emp_ssn* column of the *employee* table. Each dependent has a single employee to whom they belong, but some employees will not have any dependents. This is analogous to the product sales situation described above since some products have no sales history. We can use an OUTER JOIN to join the *employee* and *dependent* tables even when employees have no dependents.

The query in SQL Example 6.19 produces the desired result table. The plus sign in parentheses (+) tells Oracle to execute an OUTER JOIN operation. In fact, this is a LEFT OUTER JOIN because the query will return ALL of the rows from the employee table that is listed on the left side of the join operation in the WHERE clause. The plus symbol (+) is on the right-side of the equal sign indicating that some value of *dep_emp_ssn* may be NULL. The naming of the LEFT OUTER JOIN may

```
employee                        dependent
emp_ssn                         dep_emp_ssn
emp_last_name                   dep_name
emp_first_name                  dep_gender
emp_middle_name                 dep_date_of_birth
emp_address                     dep_relationship
emp_city
emp_state
emp_zip
emp_date_of_birth
emp_salary                      Primary Keys (PKs) = boldfaced
emp_parking_space               Foreign Keys (FKs) = italicized
emp_gender                      FK that is also part of a PK =
emp_dep_number                  boldfaced and italicized
emp_superssn
```

FIGURE 6.4

seem backwards, but it is the *dependent* table (right side) that is being outer-joined to the *employee* table (left side) because some employees will not have dependents.

```
/* SQL Example 6.19 */
COLUMN "Dependent" FORMAT A14;
COLUMN "Relationship" FORMAT A12;
SELECT emp_last_name "Last Name", emp_first_name "First Name",
    dep_name "Dependent", dep_relationship "Relationship"
FROM employee e, dependent d
WHERE e.emp_ssn = d.dep_emp_ssn(+);

Last Name      First Name     Dependent      Relationship
--------       ----------     ----------     -----------
Bordoloi       Bijoy
Joyner         Suzanne        Allen          SPOUSE
Zhu            Waiman         Andrew         SON
Zhu            Waiman         Jo Ellen       DAUGHTER
Zhu            Waiman         Susan          SPOUSE
Markis         Marcia
Amin           Hyder
Bock           Douglas        Deanna         DAUGHTER
Bock           Douglas        Jeffery        SON
Bock           Douglas        Mary Ellen     SPOUSE
Joshi          Dinesh
Prescott       Sherri
12 rows selected.
```

The result table lists some employees more than once. This happens when an employee has more than one dependent. Also, some employees do not have any dependents listed. The *dep_name* and *dep_relationship* columns of these employees are NULL.

OUTER JOINS AND NULL VALUES

The result table produced by SQL Example 6.19 is useful, but what if your manager wants the listing of employees to be restricted to list only employees who do *not* have any dependents. Again, this is analogous to the sales order situation described earlier in which it might be advantageous to produce a listing of only products that have never sold. This would enable our firm to advertise those products and to get them off of our store's shelves. Similarly, management might desire a listing of employees with no dependents in order to satisfy some governmental reporting requirement.

Now, you may argue that for the small number of rows given in our result table, a manager could manually "line through" any employees that have dependents and obtain the required information. However, if the result table is large, most managers would find this approach to be unacceptable.

We can take advantage of the fact that the *dep_name* column will be NULL for employees with no dependents, and simply add a criteria to the WHERE clause to exclude employees where the *dep_name* column is NULL. The revised query is shown in SQL Example 6.20.

```
/* SQL Example 6.20 */
SELECT emp_last_name "Last Name", emp_first_name "First Name",
    dep_name "Dependent", dep_relationship "Relationship"
FROM employee e, dependent d
WHERE e.emp_ssn = d.dep_emp_ssn(+) AND
    d.dep_name IS NULL;


Last Name      First Name      Dependent      Relationship
--------       ---------       ---------      -----------
Bordoloi       Bijoy
Markis         Marcia
Amin           Hyder
Joshi          Dinesh
Prescott       Sherri
```

Finally, we can tidy up the result table by eliminating the dependent and relationship columns as output since they are blank. We simply remove these column names from the SELECT clause listing. SQL Example 6.21 produces a clean result table that provides only the essential information needed by management.

```
/* SQL Example 6.21 */
SELECT emp_last_name "Last Name", emp_first_name "First Name"
FROM employee e, dependent d
WHERE e.emp_ssn = d.dep_emp_ssn(+) AND
    d.dep_name IS NULL;


Last Name      First Name
--------       ---------
Bordoloi       Bijoy
Markis         Marcia
Amin           Hyder
Joshi          Dinesh
Prescott       Sherri
```

LEFT AND RIGHT OUTER JOIN OPERATIONS

Eventually, as your career as an SQL programmer blossoms, you will hear arguments about the terms RIGHT OUTER JOIN and LEFT OUTER JOIN. These terms refer to ordering of the tables depicted in an entity-relationship diagram. Earlier, we noted that the OUTER JOIN between the *employee* and *dependent* tables is a LEFT OUTER JOIN. However, if the *employee* table were to be depicted on the right side of the relationship in Figure 6.4, and if it is outer-joined with a *dependent* table depicted on the left side of the relationship and in the WHERE clause, this is sometimes referred to as a RIGHT OUTER JOIN.

Now if you think about it, the entity-relationship diagram could just as easily have been drawn with the *dependent* table on the left and the *employee* table on the right. Does the fact that this is now called a RIGHT OUTER JOIN make any difference to SQL? The answer is no. The query in SQL Example 6.19 can be rewritten as is done in SQL Example 6.22. Can you find the slight difference? We have highlighted it for you. The + is now shown on the left side of the equal sign, but the query is still returning ALL of the rows from the *employee* table. The query has the order of the conditions in the JOIN operation reversed from their earlier specification. Regardless, SQL dutifully produces exactly the same result table!

```
/* SQL Example 6.22 */
SELECT emp_last_name "Last Name", emp_first_name "First Name",
    dep_name "Dependent", dep_relationship "Relationship"
FROM employee e, dependent d
WHERE d.dep_emp_ssn(+) = e.emp_ssn;

Last Name       First Name      Dependent       Relationship
--------        ---------       ---------       -----------
Bordoloi        Bijoy
Joyner          Suzanne         Allen           SPOUSE
Zhu             Waiman          Andrew          SON
Zhu             Waiman          Jo Ellen        DAUGHTER
Zhu             Waiman          Susan           SPOUSE
Markis          Marcia
Amin            Hyder
Bock            Douglas         Deanna          DAUGHTER
Bock            Douglas         Jeffery         SON
Bock            Douglas         Mary Ellen      SPOUSE
Joshi           Dinesh
Prescott        Sherri
12 rows selected.
```

So remember, if a colleague wants to "quibble" about whether a JOIN operation is a LEFT versus RIGHT OUTER JOIN, the difference is purely semantic.

SELF JOIN OPERATIONS

A SELF JOIN operation produces a result table when the relationship of interest exists among rows that are stored within a single table. This is the case for the company's *employee* table for the **supervise** relationship depicted in Appendix A and here in Figure 6.5. Each employee is identified by his or her SSN (*emp_ssn*). Likewise, each employee row has a column to store his or her supervisor's SSN (*emp_superssn*). A supervisor is simply an employee who performs supervisory functions, and so we did not create a separate table to store supervisor rows. If you study the data for the *employee* table depicted in Appendix A, you will discover that the employee who is in charge of the company has a NULL value for the *emp_superssn* column.

The query in SQL Example 6.23 produces a listing of employees and their supervisors.

```
/* SQL Example 6.23 */
COLUMN "Employee" FORMAT A28;
COLUMN "Supervisor" FORMAT A28;
SELECT e1.emp_last_name || ', ' || e1.emp_first_name "Supervisor",
    e2.emp_last_name || ', ' || e2.emp_first_name "Employee"
FROM employee e1, employee e2
WHERE e1.emp_ssn = e2.emp_superssn;

Supervisor            Employee
-------------         --------------
Bordoloi, Bijoy       Joyner, Suzanne
Bordoloi, Bijoy       Zhu, Waiman
Joyner, Suzanne       Markis, Marcia
Joyner, Suzanne       Amin, Hyder
Zhu, Waiman           Bock, Douglas
Zhu, Waiman           Joshi, Dinesh
Zhu, Waiman           Prescott, Sherri
```

The SELECT clause uses the concatenation operator, two vertical bars (| |), to concatenate each supervisor's last and first names along with a comma separator between names into a single output column. This is also done for employees who are supervised. The concatenation of columns is covered in detail in Chapter 10.

The FROM clause specifies the *employee* table twice, each time with a different table alias name (*e1* and *e2*). This is necessary in order to create a conceptual Cartesian product between what appear to be two different and separate *employee* tables named

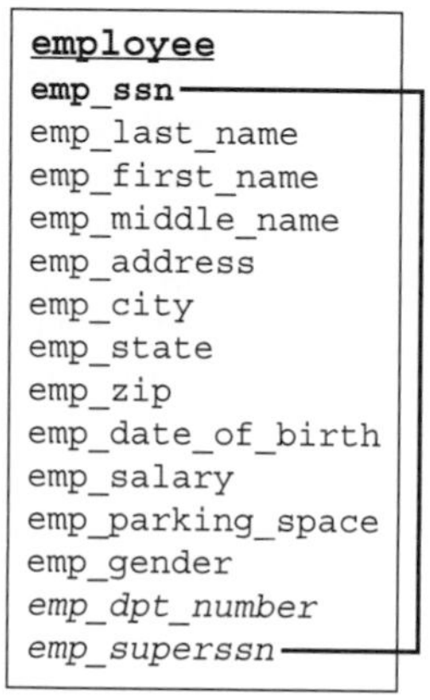

FIGURE 6.5

```
employee
emp_ssn
emp_last_name
emp_first_name
emp_middle_name
emp_address
emp_city
emp_state
emp_zip
emp_date_of_birth
emp_salary
emp_parking_space
emp_gender
emp_dpt_number
emp_superssn
```

e1 and *e2*. The alias table names are used to specify the SELF JOIN operation in the WHERE clause. Rows are joined where the employee's supervisor SSN equals the employee SSN of another row.

Did you notice that one row is missing from the result table? This is the row for employee Bordoloi because he has no supervisor. He is in charge of the company and, as was noted earlier, the *emp_superssn* column value for Bordoloi's row is NULL.

SUMMARY

In this chapter, you learned to write queries to display information that is extracted from related tables. You can use the WHERE clause to produce JOIN operations for up to 16 tables at a time, although two, three, or four tables are more common. A join of more than two tables requires the WHERE clause to include a complex JOIN condition that uses the AND logical operator. You also learned how to join two or more tables that have composite primary keys. You examined how to use the OUTER JOIN operation to produce queries where tables have rows that may or may not be related to rows in other tables. Finally, you learned how to use a SELF JOIN operation to join rows from a table that are related to rows in the same table. After completing the exercises in the review section that follows, you will have mastered the basic concepts associated with joining tables. You should now have a basic understanding of the process that the Oracle Server uses to execute a join query.

REVIEW EXERCISES

LEARN THESE TERMS

Alias name. A shorthand method for referring to a table in order to simplify query writing.

Ambiguous column names. Occurs when two tables have columns named with identical names. The column names must be qualified.

Association table. A table that relates or associates two other tables where the relationship between those two other tables would be many-to-many.

Cartesian product. A result table consists of all possible combinations of the rows from each of the tables.

Common column. Another term for a foreign key in a table.

Composite primary key. When a table is identified uniquely by more than one column because a single column is not sufficient to guarantee uniqueness.

Concatenate operator. Two vertical bars (| |) used to concatenate two or more column values or literals for display as a single column.

Domain. A specified set of values that are valid for store in a column of a database table.

Equijoin. A JOIN operation that uses an equal sign as the relational operator.

Foreign key. A column used to link a table to another related table. It may also be an internal link within the table used to link rows with other related rows.

JOIN. An operation used to connect (link) two or more tables based on a common domain of values stored to common columns or foreign key columns.

OUTER JOIN operation. Allows rows from one table to appear in a result table even if there is no matching value in the table to which it is joined.

SELF JOIN operation. A JOIN that produces a result table when the relationship of interest exists among rows that are stored within a single table.

CONCEPTS QUIZ

1. Explain the concept of a *domain* of values, and relate this concept to JOIN operations.

2. Which clause in a SELECT statement is used to JOIN tables, and how is this typically accomplished?

3. What is an alias table name? Is it optional or mandatory?

4. What is a Cartesian product? Why is it important?

5. What specifies the order by which columns are displayed in a result table produced by a JOIN operation in which only specified columns are selected?

6. What specifies the order by which columns are displayed in a result table produced by a JOIN operation in which all columns are selected through use of an asterisk (*) in the SELECT clause?

7. You have written a query that fails to execute. The Oracle Server returns the following error message. What do you need to do to correct the error condition?

```
ORA-00918: column ambiguously defined
```

8. You need to qualify a column named *emp_ssn* that is stored in both the *employee* and *benefits* tables. How do you refer to this column in a WHERE clause that has no alias names?

9. Assume that the alias names for the *employee* and *benefits* tables referenced in question 8 above are "e" and "b," respectively. Now how would you reference the ambiguous *emp_ssn* columns?

10. Why would you qualify column names that are NOT ambiguous?

11. What is the limit on using different selection criteria in the WHERE clause of a SELECT statement that is joining tables?

12. What is an equijoin as opposed to an inequality join?

13. What is the maximum number of tables that can be listed in a JOIN operation?

14. What is an association table?

15. When would your JOIN query have to join two or more tables by using more than one column from each table in the JOIN condition?

16. What is an OUTER JOIN?

17. Suppose that our firm tracks repair parts inventory in a table named *inventory* and the use of those parts in a second table named *parts_used*. What type of JOIN would be used to produce a listing of parts that have not been used and how would the JOIN operation conceptually produce the listing?

18. Continuing the situation described in question 17, suppose that some parts are manufactured by using other parts from inventory; thus, there is a relationship among the rows within the *inventory* table. What type of JOIN would be used to produce a listing of which parts are used to manufacture other parts?

SQL CODING EXERCISES AND QUESTIONS

In answering the SQL exercises and questions, submit a copy of each command that you execute and any messages that Oracle generates while executing your SQL commands. Also list the output for any result table that is generated by your SQL statements.

1. Write a query to produce a result table that is a Cartesian product of the *department* and *dept_locations* tables. The result table should include the *dpt_no* and *dpt_name* columns from *department* and the *dpt_location* column from *dept_locations*.

2. The Cartesian product produced in question 1 is not terribly useful. A new manager in the production area needs a report that shows where departments are located. Alter the query for question 1 to restrict row output by joining the two tables.

3. The manager in the human resources department needs a listing of department managers and their salaries and assigned parking spaces. The query must display the department number (*dpt_no*), department name (*dpt_name*), employee first and last name (concatenate the *emp_first_name* and *emp_last_name* columns into a single column), employee salary (*emp_salary*) and employee parking space (*emp_parking_space*). Use the *employee* and *department* tables. Name the columns in the result table as follows: Dept Numb., Department, Employee, Salary, and Parking, respectively. Use COLUMN-FORMAT commands to product a listing that fits easily on one page.

4. The company's vice president for project management needs a listing of which projects are being controlled by which departments. The result table needs to display the department name (*dpt_name*), project number (*pro_number*), project name (*pro_name*), and project location (*pro_location*). The query will use the *department* and *project* tables. Give each output column an appropriate column name.

5. Revise the query written for question 4 to restrict output to projects located in Edwardsville or supervised by the production department.

6. The company's vice president for project management needs a listing of all employees and the number of hours they have worked on projects. The result table should list the employee's last and first names (*emp_last_name* and *emp_first_name*), project number (*work_pro_number*), and hours worked (*work_hours*). The query uses the *employee* and *assignment* tables. The result table should list all employees, whether they work on a project or not. Use alias names for the table names. Give each column an appropriate column name. Sort the output by *emp_last_name* and *emp_first_name*. Which employee(s) is (are) assigned to a project, but has (have) not worked any hours on a project?

7. Revise the query for question 6 to list only employees who have *not* worked any hours for an assigned project. This will provide the vice president for project management with a "needs to be motivated" list of employees.

8. Revise the query for question 6. Replace the project number as an output column with the project name (*pro_name*). The project name information must be retrieved from the *project* table. Rename the column Project. All other requirements remain the same.

9. The human resources manager needs a listing of employees by last name, their dependents' first names, and dependents' birth dates. The relevant output columns are *emp_last_name* from the *employee* table and *dep_name* and *dep_date_of_birth* from the *dependent* table. Use alias table names. Name each column appropriately. Sort the result table by *emp_last_name*. Format the *dep_name* column as A15.

10. Produce a listing of employees that are managed by the manager of department 7. The result table should have the following columns: Manager Last Name, Department Name, and Employee Last Name. Name each column "Supervisor," "Department," and "Employee Supervised," respectively. You must determine which tables and columns are required to produce the result table.

11. Produce a query that will list all employee last names, employee gender, dependent names and dependent gender where the employee's have dependents of the opposite gender. Also list the dependent relationship. The columns needed in the result table are *emp_last_name, emp_gender, dep_name, dep_gender,* and *dep_relationship*. Use the *employee* and *dependent* tables. Use the column names and formats shown below. Sort the result table by *emp_last_name*.

```
COLUMN "Employee" FORMAT A10;
COLUMN "Emp Gender" FORMAT A10;
COLUMN "Dependent" FORMAT A10;
COLUMN "Dep Gender" FORMAT A10;
COLUMN "Relationship" FORMAT A12;
```

SUBQUERIES

Thus far, you have learned to write queries where all of the information needed to specify retrieval criteria is known at *design time*. The term *design time* simply means that you are in the processing of writing or designing a query. This contrasts with *run time,* which refers to the actual execution and processing of a query. In this chapter, you will expand your understanding of the SELECT statement to include the topic of subqueries. Quite simply, a *subquery* is a query within a query. Subqueries enable you to write queries that select data rows for criteria that are actually developed while the query is executing at *run time*.

OBJECTIVES

In order to understand the subquery approach to information retrieval, we will first review what you have learned to this point about the SELECT statement. Your learning objectives for this chapter include:

- Learn the formal subquery definition and write a subquery.
- Learn the subquery restrictions.
- Use the IN operator when writing a subquery.
- Nest subqueries at multiple levels.
- Use comparison operators when writing a subquery.
- Use the ALL and ANY keywords when writing a subquery.
- Write a correlated subquery including the use of the EXISTS operator.
- Use the ORDER BY clause when writing a subquery.

A SUBQUERY EXAMPLE

SQL Example 7.1 queries the *employee* table. You know at design time that you want to retrieve employee information where employee salaries are at or above $25,000, and employees work in department 3 or 7. Additionally, the actual criteria values used in row selection are hard-coded — $25,000 for the employee salary and departments 3 and 7 for the department number.

```
/* SQL Example 7.1 */
COLUMN "Last Name" FORMAT A15;
COLUMN "First Name" FORMAT A15;
COLUMN "Dept" FORMAT 9999;
COLUMN "Salary" FORMAT $99,999;
SELECT emp_last_name "Last Name", emp_first_name "First Name",
    emp_dpt_number "Dept", emp_salary "Salary"
FROM employee
WHERE emp_salary >= 25000
      AND emp_dpt_number IN (3, 7);

Last Name       First Name      Dept    Salary
---------       ----------      ----    ------
Joyner          Suzanne            3    $43,000
Zhu             Waiman             7    $43,000
Markis          Marcia             3    $25,000
more rows are displayed . . .
```

But suppose you need to write a query where the criteria values to be used in a WHERE clause are unknown at design time. As an example, consider a requirement to list the names of all employees that earn a salary equal to the minimum salary amount paid within your organization. The problem is that at design time, you do not know what the minimum salary amount is! Further, over time, the minimum salary will surely change. You could break this query into two tasks by first writing a query to determine the minimum salary amount, like the query in SQL Example 7.2.

```
/* SQL Example 7.2 */
COLUMN "Min Salary" FORMAT $999,999;
SELECT MIN(emp_salary) "Min Salary"
FROM employee;

Min Salary
----------
   $25,000
```

Next, you could substitute the value $25,000 for the minimum employee salary into the WHERE clause of a second query. However, the subquery approach allows you to combine these two separate queries into one query as is illustrated in SQL Example 7.3.

```
/* SQL Example 7.3 */
SELECT emp_last_name "Last Name", emp_first_name "First Name",
    emp_salary "Salary"
FROM employee
```

```
WHERE emp_salary =
    (SELECT MIN(emp_salary)
    FROM employee);

Last Name     First Name     Salary
---------     ----------     ------
Markis        Marcia         $25,000
Amin          Hyder          $25,000
Prescott      Sherri         $25,000
```

Notice that the subquery is essentially the first query that you used in the two-part query approach. Also, the subquery is the object of the equal comparison operator (=). Okay, so the subquery doesn't appear to be such a big deal. In fact, you could quickly scan the *employee* table listed in Appendix A and find the same result. But what if the *employee* table has thousands or even millions of rows? Query 7.3 produces a quick listing, while the manual approach could take hours or even days to complete the task!

You should also note that there are no hard-coded parameters in the query except for the table and column names. The criteria for row selection used for the WHERE clause comes from the result table produced by the subquery. We say that data for the subquery are derived at *run time*. As such, the value returned by this subquery can, and most probably will, change depending on the contents of a table, yet the query will always produce accurate and dependable results.

DEFINITION OF A SUBQUERY

FORMAL DEFINITION

Now that you have seen an example subquery, it may help you to learn the concept by formally defining subqueries. As was stated earlier, a subquery is a query inside another query. More formally, it is the use of a SELECT statement inside one of the clauses of another SELECT statement. In fact, a subquery can be contained inside another subquery.

The subquery you studied earlier in SQL Example 7.3 is an example of a subquery inside a WHERE clause. This is termed a *nested subquery* or *inner query*. The term *outer query* is sometimes used to refer to the SELECT statement that contains a subquery. Oracle also allows a subquery to be listed as an object in a FROM clause listing. This is termed an *inline view* because when a subquery is used as part of a FROM clause, it is treated like a virtual table or view (views are covered in Chapter 8). We will focus here on the use of subqueries with WHERE and HAVING clauses. Subqueries with FROM clauses will not be covered as the technique is not used very often.

You are limited to a maximum of 255 subquery levels in a WHERE clause. But this is not really a limit at all because in practice, it is rare to encounter subqueries nested beyond three or four levels. In fact, the practice of nesting one SELECT statement inside another is the reason for the use of the word *structured* in the name Structured Query Language.

SUBQUERY TYPES

There are three basic types of subqueries. We will study each of these in the remainder of this chapter.

1. Subqueries that operate on lists by use of the IN operator or with a comparison operator modified by the ANY or ALL optional keywords. These subqueries can return a group of values, but the values must be from a single column of a table. In other words, the SELECT clause of the subquery must contain only one parameter, that is, **only one column name** *or* **only one expression** *or* **only one aggregate function.**

2. Subqueries that use an unmodified comparison operator (=, <, >, <>)—these subqueries must return only a single, *scalar* value.

3. Subqueries that use the EXISTS operator to test the *existence* of data rows satisfying specified criteria.

SUBQUERY SYNTAX—GENERAL RULES

A subquery SELECT statement is very similar to the SELECT statement used to begin a regular or outer query. The complete syntax of a subquery is:

```
( SELECT [DISTINCT] subquery_select_parameter
  FROM {table_name | view_name}
             {table_name | view_name} ...
  [WHERE search_conditions]
  [GROUP BY column_name [,column_name ] ...]
  [HAVING search_conditions] )
```

You will notice a few minor differences between a subquery and regular query syntax. For example, the ORDER BY clause cannot be used in writing the subquery part of a query. There are additional clauses that are restricted, including the COMPUTE and FOR BROWSE clauses, but these are beyond the scope of this text. Subqueries can be nested inside both the WHERE and HAVING clauses of an outer SELECT or inside another subquery. Additionally, a subquery is always enclosed in parentheses.

SUBQUERY RESTRICTIONS

CLAUSE RESTRICTIONS

Generally speaking, a SELECT clause of a subquery must contain only one expression, only one aggregate function, or only one column name. Additionally, the value(s) returned by a subquery must be *join-compatible* with the WHERE clause of the outer query. This last point is made clearer through the example SELECT statement shown in SQL Example 7.4. This query lists the names of employees that have dependents. The domain of values in the *dependent* table's *dep_emp_ssn* column is all valid employee Social Security Numbers (SSNs). Thus, the values returned from this column in the *dependent* table in the subquery are join-compatible with values stored in the *employee* table's *emp_ssn* column of the outer query because they are the same type of data and the data values come from the same domain of possible values.

```
/* SQL Example 7.4 */
SELECT emp_last_name "Last Name", emp_first_name "First Name"
FROM employee
WHERE emp_ssn IN
    (SELECT dep_emp_ssn
     FROM dependent);

Last Name     First Name
---------     ---------
Bock          Douglas
Zhu           Waiman
Joyner        Suzanne
```

Notice that the *emp_last_name* and *emp_first_name* columns are not stored in the *dependent* table. These columns only occur in the *employee* table. First, we need to produce an intermediate result table that contains the social security numbers of the employees who have dependents. This is accomplished by the subquery. The outer SELECT statement then qualifies the employee names to be displayed (employee rows) through use of the IN operator. Here, any employee with an SSN that is IN the list produced by the subquery has the data row displayed in the final result table.

DATATYPE JOIN-COMPATIBILITY

In addition to concerns about the domain of values returned from a subquery, the datatype of the returned column value(s) must be *join-compatible*. Join-compatible datatypes are datatypes that the Oracle Server automatically converts when matching data in criteria conditions. For example, it would not make any sense to compare the values stored in the *emp_ssn* column of the *employee* table to values stored in *dep_date_of_birth* column of the *dependent* table because the *emp_ssn* column is of datatype CHAR and the *dep_date_of_birth* column is of datatype DATE.

As we learned in Chapter 2, there are a fairly small number of Oracle datatypes, but these datatypes enable you to store all types of data. While Oracle datatypes vary somewhat from those specified by the ANSI standard for SQL, the Oracle server maps the ANSI standard data types to Oracle's datatypes. For example, the Oracle Server will automatically convert among any of the following ANSI numeric datatypes when making comparisons of numeric values because they all map into the Oracle NUMBER datatype:

- int (integer)
- smallint (small integer)
- decimal
- float

Remember that Oracle does not make comparisons based on column names. Columns from two tables that are being compared may have different names as long as they have a shared domain and the same datatype or convertible datatypes.

TABLE 7.1

Column Name	Datatype
stu_id	CHAR
student_id	CHAR

JOIN-COMPATIBLE DATA COLUMNS

Table 7.1 shows columns from two different tables with different column names. Both of these columns store student identification values. They are join-compatible because they store the same datatype.

NOT JOIN-COMPATIBLE

Table 7.2 shows two columns with different types that have the same column name. Even though the column names are identical, and even though both columns store student identification values, one column is CHAR and the other is NUMBER. Because these datatypes are different, the Oracle server will fail to process the join request—they are not join-compatible.

OTHER RESTRICTIONS

There are additional restrictions for subqueries:

- The DISTINCT keyword *cannot* be used in subqueries that include a GROUP BY clause.
- Subqueries cannot manipulate their results internally. This means that a subquery cannot include the ORDER BY clause, the COMPUTE clause, or the INTO keyword. Although we have not covered use of the INTO keyword in earlier chapters, quite simply, the INTO keyword is used to create temporary tables.

SUBQUERIES AND THE IN OPERATOR

THE IN OPERATOR

The IN operator should be familiar to you. In earlier chapters, you used it to write queries that defined row selection criteria based on the use of lists of data enclosed in parentheses. The only difference in the use of the IN operator with subqueries is that the list does not consist of *hard-coded* values. The query shown in SQL Example 7.5 illustrates the use of hard-coded department number values.

TABLE 7.2

Column Name	Datatype
stu_id	CHAR
stu_id	NUMBER

```
/* SQL Example 7.5 */
SELECT emp_last_name "Last Name", emp_first_name "First Name",
    emp_dpt_number "Dept"
FROM employee
WHERE emp_dpt_number IN (1, 7);

Last Name       First Name      Dept
---------       ---------       ----
Bordoloi        Bijoy              1
Zhu             Waiman             7
Bock            Douglas            7
more rows are displayed . . .
```

WHERE clauses of queries that include the IN operator take the general form:

```
WHERE <expression> [NOT] IN (subquery)
```

Suppose that a manager in the human resources department requires a listing of employees that have male dependents, but not a listing of the actual dependents themselves. We can write a subquery that retrieves the employee SSN (*dep_emp_ssn*) from the *dependent* table where the dependent's gender is male. The outer query will then list employees that have an employee SSN (*emp_ssn*) that is found in the listing produced by the subquery as illustrated in SQL Example 7.6.

```
/* SQL Example 7.6 */
SELECT emp_last_name "Last Name", emp_first_name "First Name"
FROM employee
WHERE emp_ssn IN
    (SELECT dep_emp_ssn
    FROM dependent
    WHERE dep_gender = 'M');

Last Name       First Name
---------       ---------
Bock            Douglas
Zhu             Waiman
Joyner          Suzanne
```

Let's review the conceptual steps involved in evaluating the query. First, the subquery returns the SSNs of those employees that have male dependents from the *dependent* table.

```
/* SQL Example 7.7 */
SELECT dep_emp_ssn
FROM dependent
WHERE dep_gender = 'M';

DEP_EMP_S
---------
999444444
999555555
999111111
```

There are three male dependents, and the intermediate result table produced by the subquery lists the SSNs of the employees to which these dependents belong. Next, these SSN values are substituted into the outer query as the listing that is the object of the IN operator. So, from a conceptual perspective, the outer query now looks like the following:

```
/* SQL Example 7.8 */
SELECT emp_last_name "Last Name", emp_first_name "First Name"
FROM employee
WHERE emp_ssn IN (999444444, 999555555, 999111111);

Last Name       First Name
--------        ---------
Joyner          Suzanne
Zhu             Waiman
Bock            Douglas
```

The preceding queries, like many subqueries, can also be formulated as *join queries.* As you will recall from your study of Chapter 6, a join query will join the *employee* and *dependent* tables based on the common domain of values stored in the *employee* table's *emp_ssn* column and the *dependent* table's *dep_emp_ssn* column. The SQL Example 7.9 illustrates this join query approach.

```
/* SQL Example 7.9 */
SELECT emp_last_name "Last Name", emp_first_name "First Name"
FROM employee e, dependent d
WHERE e.emp_ssn = d.dep_emp_ssn AND
      d.dep_gender = 'M';

Last Name       First Name
--------        ---------
Zhu             Waiman
Joyner          Suzanne
Bock            Douglas
```

Both the join and the subquery version will produce identical result tables, although the order of the rows in the result table may differ. Each query is equally correct. This begs the question, "Which approach is most appropriate?" The general, basic rules of thumb are:

- Use a subquery when the result table displays columns from a single table.
- Use a join query when the result displays columns from two or more tables.

THE **NOT IN** OPERATOR

Like the IN operator, the NOT IN operator can take the result of a subquery as the operator object. Earlier we produced a listing of employees with dependents. Suppose that a human resource manager, in order to meet a government reporting requirement, requires a listing of employees who do *not* have any dependents. The NOT IN operator is especially good for producing this type of result table as shown in SQL Example 7.10.

```
/* SQL Example 7.10 */
SELECT emp_last_name "Last Name", emp_first_name "First Name"
FROM employee
WHERE emp_ssn NOT IN
    (SELECT dep_emp_ssn
     FROM dependent);

Last Name       First Name
--------        ---------
Bordoloi        Bijoy
Markis          Marcia
Amin            Hyder
more rows are displayed . . .
```

The subquery produces an intermediate result table containing the SSNs of employees who have dependents in the *dependent* table. Conceptually, the outer query compares each row of the *employee* table against the result table. If the employee SSN is *NOT* found in the result table produced by the inner query, then it is included in the final result table.

MULTIPLE LEVELS OF NESTING

Thus far, we have studied subqueries nested one level in depth. However, subqueries may themselves contain subqueries. When the WHERE clause of a subquery has as its object another subquery, these are termed *nested subqueries*. Remember, Oracle places no practical limit on the number of queries that can be nested in a WHERE clause (did you remember that the limit is 255 subqueries?). Consider the problem of producing a listing of employees who worked more than 10 hours on the project named *Order Entry*. A subquery is appropriate because the result table will list only columns from a single table. The result table produced by SQL Example 7.11 displays only columns from the *employee* table.

```
/* SQL Example 7.11 */
SELECT emp_last_name "Last Name", emp_first_name "First Name"
FROM employee
WHERE emp_ssn IN
    (SELECT work_emp_ssn
     FROM assignment
     WHERE work_hours > 10 AND work_pro_number IN
        (SELECT pro_number
         FROM project
         WHERE pro_name = 'Order Entry') );

Last Name       First Name
--------        ---------
Bock            Douglas
Prescott        Sherri
```

In order to understand how this query executes, we begin our examination with the lowest subquery. We will execute it independently of the outer queries. It is important to note that this subquery is useful where the project name is known, but the associated project number is not known. SQL Example 7.12 gives the query and result table. The result is a single column from a single row known as a *scalar* result.

```
/* SQL Example 7.12 */
SELECT pro_number
FROM project
WHERE pro_name = 'Order Entry';

PRO_NUMBER
---------
        1
```

Now, let's substitute the project number into the IN operator list for the intermediate subquery and execute it as shown in SQL Example 7.13. The intermediate result table lists two employee SSNs for employees that worked more than 10 hours on project 1.

```
/* SQL Example 7.13 */
SELECT work_emp_ssn
FROM assignment
WHERE work_hours > 10 AND work_pro_number IN (1);

WORK_EMP_
---------
999111111
999888888
```

Finally, we will substitute these two social security numbers into the IN operator listing for the outer query in place of the subquery.

```
/* SQL Example 7.14 */
SELECT emp_last_name "Last Name", emp_first_name "First Name"
FROM employee
WHERE emp_ssn IN (999111111, 999888888);

Last Name      First Name
---------      ---------
Bock           Douglas
Prescott       Sherri
```

As you can see, the final result table matches that produced when the entire query with two nested subqueries executed. This *decomposition approach* to studying queries can also help you in writing nested subqueries.

SUBQUERIES AND COMPARISON OPERATORS

COMPARISON OPERATORS AND ERRORS

This section discusses subqueries that use a comparison operator in the WHERE clause. Table 7.3 provides a listing of the SQL comparison operators and their meaning.

The general form of the WHERE clause with a comparison operator is similar to that used thus far in the text. Note that the subquery is again enclosed by parentheses.

```
WHERE <expression> <comparison_operator> (subquery)
```

We saw an earlier example of the equal sign (=) comparison operator as is shown here.

```
WHERE emp_salary =
    (SELECT MIN(emp_salary)
     FROM employee);
```

The most important point to remember when using a subquery with a comparison operator is that the subquery can return only a single or *scalar* value. This is also termed a *scalar subquery* because a single column of a single row is returned by the subquery. If a subquery returns more than one value, the Oracle Server will generate the *ORA-01427: single-row subquery returns more than one row* error message, and the query will fail to execute. Let's examine a subquery that will not execute because it violates the "single value" rule. The query in SQL Example 7.15 returns multiple values for the *emp_salary* column.

```
/* SQL Example 7.15 */
SELECT emp_salary
FROM employee
WHERE emp_salary > 40000;

EMP_SALARY
---------
     55000
     43000
     43000
```

TABLE 7.3	
Comparison Operator	*Meaning*
=	equal to
<	less than
>	greater than
>=	greater than or equal to
<=	less than or equal to
!=	not equal to
<>	not equal to
!>	not greater than
!<	not less than

Now, if we substitute this query as a subquery in another SELECT statement, then that SELECT statement will fail. This is demonstrated in the SELECT statement SQL Example 7.16. Here the SQL code will fail because the subquery uses the greater than (>) comparison operator and the subquery returns multiple values.

```
/* SQL Example 7.16 */
SELECT emp_ssn
FROM employee
WHERE emp_salary >
    (SELECT emp_salary
     FROM employee
     WHERE emp_salary > 40000);

ERROR at line 4:
ORA-01427: single-row subquery returns more than one row
```

In order to use a subquery as the object of a comparison operator, you must be familiar enough with the data stored in the relevant tables and with the nature of the programming problem to know with certainty that the subquery will return a scalar value.

AGGREGATE FUNCTIONS AND COMPARISON OPERATORS

As you will recall, the aggregate functions (AVG, SUM, MAX, MIN, and COUNT) always return a *scalar* result table. Thus, a subquery with an aggregate function as the object of a comparison operator will always execute provided you have formulated the query properly. Suppose that a payroll manager needs a listing of employees that have a salary level that is greater than the average salary for all employees. SQL Example 7.17 uses the AVG aggregate function in the subquery to produce the desired result.

```
/* SQL Example 7.17 */
SELECT emp_last_name "Last Name", emp_first_name "First Name",
    emp_salary "Salary"
FROM employee
WHERE emp_salary >
    (SELECT AVG(emp_salary)
     FROM employee);

Last Name       First Name      Salary
---------       ----------      ------
Bordoloi        Bijoy           $55,000
Joyner          Suzanne         $43,000
Zhu             Waiman          $43,000
Joshi           Dinesh          $38,000
```

The subquery produces a scalar result table with a single value—the average salary of all employees. The outer query then lists employees that have a salary that exceeds the average salary.

COMPARISON OPERATORS MODIFIED WITH THE **ALL** OR **ANY** KEYWORDS

The ALL and ANY keywords can modify a comparison operator to allow an outer query to accept multiple values from a subquery. The general form of the WHERE clause for this type of query is:

```
WHERE <expression> <comparison_operator> [ALL | ANY] (subquery)
```

The ALL and ANY keywords can produce a result table that has zero, one, or more than one value. Subqueries that use these keywords may also include GROUP BY and HAVING clauses.

THE **ALL** KEYWORD

In order to understand the ALL keyword, let's examine its effect on the "greater than" (>) comparison operator in a SELECT statement. Suppose our payroll manager needs an employee list for those employees with a salary that is greater than the salary of all of the employees in department 7. In SQL Example 7.18, the ALL keyword modifies the greater than comparison operator to mean greater than *all* values.

```
/* SQL Example 7.18 */
SELECT emp_last_name "Last Name", emp_first_name "First Name",
    emp_salary "Salary"
FROM employee
WHERE emp_salary > ALL
    (SELECT emp_salary
     FROM employee
     WHERE emp_dpt_number = 7);

Last Name        First Name        Salary
--------         ---------         ------
Bordoloi         Bijoy             $55,000
```

Conceptually, for each row in the *employee* table, the inner query creates a final listing of salaries of employees that work in department 7. We can determine these salaries by executing the inner query by itself.

```
/* SQL Example 7.19 */
SELECT emp_salary
FROM employee
WHERE emp_dpt_number = 7;

EMP_SALARY
---------
     43000
     30000
     38000
     25000
```

The outer query finds the largest salary value in the list for department 7. This is $43,000. Next, the outer query compares the salary of each employee to this largest value one row at a time. The result table includes only employees that have a salary that is larger than that of anyone who works in department 7. In this case, only Bordoloi has such a salary.

THE ANY KEYWORD

The ANY keyword is not as restrictive as the ALL keyword. When used with the greater than comparison operator, "> ANY" means greater than some value. Let's examine the ANY keyword when used within the SELECT statement in SQL Example 7.20. Here, the firm's payroll manager needs the employee name and salary of any employee that has a salary that is greater than that of *any* employee with a salary that exceeds $30,000. This query is not the same as asking for a listing of employees with salaries that exceed $30,000. We shall see how it differs by examining the execution of the SELECT statement in detail.

```
/* SQL Example 7.20 */
SELECT emp_last_name "Last Name", emp_first_name "First Name",
    emp_salary "Salary"
FROM employee
WHERE emp_salary > ANY
    (SELECT emp_salary
     FROM employee
     WHERE emp_salary > 30000);

Last Name      First Name      Salary
--------       ----------      ------
Bordoloi       Bijoy           $55,000
Joyner         Suzanne         $43,000
Zhu            Waiman          $43,000
```

For each employee, the inner query finds a list of salaries that are greater than $30,000. Let's execute the inner query by itself in order to see the listing that is produced.

```
/* SQL Example 7.21 */
SELECT emp_salary
FROM employee
WHERE emp_salary > 30000;

EMP_SALARY
----------
     55000
     43000
     43000
     38000
```

A total of four employee salaries are listed in the intermediate result table produced by the inner query, and the smallest of these is $38,000. The outer query looks at all the values in the list and determines whether the employee currently being considered earns more than *any* of the salaries in the intermediate result table (here, this means more than $38,000). The employees listed in the final result table all earn more than the $38,000 listed in the intermediate result table.

An "= ANY" (Equal Any) Example

The "= ANY" operator is exactly equivalent to the IN operator. For example, to find the names of employees who have male dependents, you can use either IN or "= ANY"—both of the queries in SQL Examples 7.22 and 7.23 produce identical result tables.

```
/* SQL Example 7.22 */
SELECT emp_last_name "Last Name", emp_first_name "First Name"
FROM employee
WHERE emp_ssn IN
    (SELECT dep_emp_ssn
     FROM dependent
     WHERE dep_gender = 'M');
```

```
/* SQL Example 7.23 */
SELECT emp_last_name "Last Name", emp_first_name "First Name"
FROM employee
WHERE emp_ssn = ANY
    (SELECT dep_emp_ssn
     FROM dependent
     WHERE dep_gender = 'M');

Last Name       First Name
---------       ---------
Bock            Douglas
Zhu             Waiman
Joyner          Suzanne
```

A "!= ANY" (Not Equal Any) Example

As we saw above, the "= ANY" is identical to the IN operator. However, the "!= ANY" (not equal any) is *not* equivalent to the NOT IN operator. If a subquery of employee salaries produces an intermediate result table with the salaries $38,000, $43,000, and $55,000, then the WHERE clause shown here means "NOT $38,000" AND "NOT $43,000" AND "NOT $55,000."

```
WHERE NOT IN (38000, 43000, 55000);
```

However, the "!= ANY" comparison operator and keyword combination shown in this next WHERE clause means "NOT $38,000" OR "NOT $43,000" OR "NOT $55,000."

```
WHERE != ANY (38000, 43000, 55000);
```

Let's consider another situation. Suppose a human resource manager needs a listing of employees that do not have dependents. You might write the following erroneous query:

```
/* SQL Example 7.24 */
SELECT emp_last_name "Last Name", emp_first_name "First Name"
FROM employee
WHERE emp_ssn != ANY
    (SELECT DISTINCT dep_emp_ssn
     FROM dependent);

Last Name       First Name
--------        ---------
Bordoloi        Bijoy
Joyner          Suzanne
Zhu             Waiman
Markis          Marcia
Amin            Hyder
Bock            Douglas
Joshi           Dinesh
Prescott        Sherri
8 rows selected.
```

The query fails! The result table lists *every employee* in the employee table! This occurs because the inner query returns all SSNs for employees with dependents from the *dependent* table. Then, for each *dep_emp_ssn* value, the outer query finds all employee SSNs that do not match one of the *dep_emp_ssn* values. However, since there are three values in the intermediate result table, the "!= ANY" operator is like an "OR" operator during the comparison, and of course each employee SSN fails to match at least one of the *dep_emp_ssn* values! In this example, the "**!= ANY**" operator will *always* return a TRUE value. Remember, when OR is used, a value is returned when any of the conditions tested is TRUE.

So, how can we answer the management query? The solution approach was actually covered earlier in this chapter—use the NOT IN operator as is done in SQL Example 7.25.

```
/* SQL Example 7.25 */
SELECT emp_last_name "Last Name", emp_first_name "First Name"
FROM employee
WHERE emp_ssn NOT IN
    (SELECT DISTINCT dep_emp_ssn
     FROM dependent);

Last Name       First Name
--------        ---------
Bordoloi        Bijoy
Markis          Marcia
Amin            Hyder
Joshi           Dinesh
Prescott        Sherri
```

CORRELATED SUBQUERIES

As opposed to a regular subquery, where the outer query depends on values provided by the inner query, a *correlated subquery* is one where the inner query depends on values provided by the outer query. This means that in a *correlated subquery,* the inner query is executed repeatedly, once for each row that might be selected by the outer query. SQL Example 7.26 demonstrates this concept.

Correlated subqueries can produce result tables that answer complex management questions. Suppose our payroll manager needs a listing of the most highly paid employee from each department. Clearly the MAX aggregate function should be used some place in the SELECT statement, and sure enough, it is used in the inner query of the SELECT statement shown in SQL Example 7.26.

```
/* SQL Example 7.26 */
SELECT emp_last_name "Last Name", emp_first_name "First Name",
    emp_dpt_number "Dept", emp_salary "Salary"
FROM employee e1
WHERE emp_salary =
    (SELECT MAX(emp_salary)
     FROM employee
     WHERE emp_dpt_number = e1.emp_dpt_number);

Last Name      First Name    Dept    Salary
--------       ---------     ----    ------
Bordoloi       Bijoy          1      $55,000
Joyner         Suzanne        3      $43,000
Zhu            Waiman         7      $43,000
```

Unlike the subqueries previously considered, the subquery in this SELECT statement cannot be resolved independently of the main query. Notice that the outer query specifies that rows are selected from the *employee* table with an alias name of *e1*. The inner query compares the employee department number column (*emp_dpt_number*) of the *employee* table to the same column for the alias table name *e1*. The value of *e1.emp_dpt_number* is treated like a variable—it changes as the Oracle server examines each row of the employee table. The subquery's results are correlated with each individual row of the main query—thus, the term *correlated subquery*.

In this query, the Oracle server considers each row of the *employee* table for inclusion in the result table by substituting the value of the employee's department number for each row into the inner query. Unlike the previous subqueries, the above query generates a new set of values for each row in the *employee* table.

This may be easier to understand by actually working through the data stored in the *employee* table found in Appendix A. The first row stores data for employee Bijoy Bordoloi of department 1. The Oracle server will retrieve Bordoloi's department number and insert it as the value for *e1.emp_dpt_number* in the inner query. The inner query will use the MAX function to compute the maximum salary for all of the employees in department 1. Since this value is $55,000, and since Bijoy is paid $55,000, his name is included in the final result table.

The second row stores data for employee Suzanne Joyner with a salary of $43,000 in department 3. Again, the Oracle server will retrieve Joyner's department number and insert it as the *new* value for *e1.emp_dpt_number* in the inner query. The maximum salary for department 3 is $43,000. Since Joyner is paid $43,000, her name is also included in the final result table.

Let's skip to the fourth row. This row belongs to Marcia Markis with a salary of $25,000 in department 3. Again, the Oracle server will retrieve Markis' department number and insert it into the inner query. Again, the maximum salary for department 3 will be computed as $43,000. Since Markis' salary is $25,000 and this is less than the maximum for department 3, her row is *not* included in the final result table. You should be able to work through the remaining rows and determine whether or not a row will be included in the final result table.

SUBQUERIES AND THE EXISTS OPERATOR

When a subquery uses the EXISTS operator, the subquery functions as an *existence test*. In other words, the WHERE clause of the outer query tests for the existence of rows returned by the inner query. The subquery does not actually produce any data; rather, it returns a value of TRUE or FALSE.

The general format of a subquery WHERE clause with an EXISTS operator is shown here. Note that the NOT operator can also be used to negate the result of the EXISTS operator.

```
WHERE [NOT] EXISTS (subquery)
```

Again, we will return to the question of listing all employees that have dependents. This query can be written using the EXISTS operator shown in SQL Example 7.27.

```
/* SQL Example 7.27 */
SELECT emp_last_name "Last Name", emp_first_name "First Name"
FROM employee
WHERE EXISTS
    (SELECT *
     FROM dependent
     WHERE emp_ssn = dep_emp_ssn);

Last Name       First Name
---------       ----------
Joyner          Suzanne
Zhu             Waiman
Bock            Douglas
```

Did you notice that this SELECT statement is a *correlated* subquery? The inner query depends on values (the *emp_ssn* column) provided by a table (*employee*) specified in the FROM clause of the outer query. Therefore, the subquery will execute for each row contained in the *employee* table. When the subquery executes, it searches the *dependent* table for row(s) that meets the criteria stated in the subquery's WHERE clause. If at least one row is found, the subquery returns a TRUE value to the outer query. If the subquery cannot find a row that meets the criteria, it returns a FALSE value. When the outer query receives a TRUE value, the employee row being evaluated is included in the result table.

Notice that subqueries using the EXISTS operator are a bit different from other subqueries in the following ways:

- The keyword EXISTS is not preceded by a column name, constant, or other expression.
- The parameter in the SELECT clause of a subquery that uses an EXISTS operator almost always consists of an asterisk (*). This is because there is no real point in listing column names since you are simply testing for the existence of rows that meet the conditions specified in the subquery.
- The subquery evaluates to TRUE or FALSE rather than returning any data.
- A subquery that uses an EXISTS operator will always be a correlated subquery.

The EXISTS operator is very important, because there is often no alternative to its use. All queries that use the IN operator or a modified comparison operator (=, <, >, etc. modified by ANY or ALL) can be expressed with the EXISTS operator. However, some queries formulated with EXISTS cannot be expressed in any other way! Why then shouldn't we simply write all of the earlier queries by using the EXISTS operator? The answer concerns query processing efficiency. Consider the two queries shown in SQL Examples 7.28 and 7.29. Each query produces identical result tables of employees that have dependents.

```
/* SQL Example 7.28 */
SELECT emp_last_name
FROM employee
WHERE emp_ssn = ANY
    (SELECT dep_emp_ssn
     FROM dependent);

EMP_LAST_NAME
------------
Bock
Zhu
Joyner
```

```
/* SQL Example 7.29 */
SELECT emp_last_name
FROM employee
WHERE EXISTS
    (SELECT *
     FROM dependent
     WHERE emp_ssn = dep_emp_ssn);

EMP_LAST_NAME
------------
Bock
Zhu
Joyner
```

Suppose the *employee* table has 5 million rows, as might be the case for a very large government agency. In the first query, the subquery executes only once. The outer query then processes the *employee* table against values returned by the subquery. The *employee* table will have 5 million rows processed. The second query contains a correlated subquery; therefore, the subquery processes once for every row processed by the outer query. If the outer query processes 5 million rows, then the subquery will also process 5 million times! Obviously, the first query is more efficient.

The NOT EXISTS operator is the mirror image of the EXISTS operator. A query that uses NOT EXISTS in the WHERE clause is satisfied if the subquery returns *no* rows.

SUBQUERIES AND THE ORDER BY CLAUSE

Let's return to SQL Example 7.29. If the result table is large, management may request that the output be sorted by employee name. The SELECT statement shown in SQL Example 7.30 adds the ORDER BY clause to specify sorting by first name within last name. Note that the ORDER BY clause is placed after the WHERE clause, and that this includes the subquery as part of the WHERE clause.

```
/* SQL Example 7.30 */
SELECT emp_last_name "Last Name", emp_first_name "First Name"
FROM employee
WHERE EXISTS
    (SELECT *
    FROM dependent
    WHERE emp_ssn = dep_emp_ssn)
ORDER BY emp_last_name, emp_first_name;

Last Name      First Name
--------       ---------
Bock           Douglas
Joyner         Suzanne
Zhu            Waiman
```

SUMMARY

This chapter introduced the topic of subqueries. A subquery is simply a query inside another query. You learned that a subquery can also have a subquery as an object of its WHERE clause. Subqueries can enable the production of result tables without hardcoding the criteria used for row selection. In order to use a subquery, the data type of the value(s) produced by a subquery must be *join-compatible* with the expression in the WHERE clause of the outer query.

You also studied the use of various operators with subqueries. This included the IN and NOT IN operators that are useful for processing subqueries that return a list of values. You also studied the use of multiple levels of nesting and learned to decompose queries when writing them and when studying the way that they process tables. Additionally, you saw how the ALL and ANY keywords can modify the effect of a comparison operator. Aggregate functions are commonly used in subqueries to return a *scalar* result table.

The *correlated subquery* is one where the inner query depends on values provided by the outer query. This type of subquery can produce result tables to answer complex management questions. You also learned to use the EXISTS operator for subqueries that test the existence of rows that satisfy a specified criteria. These subqueries return a TRUE or FALSE value. Finally, you studied the relationship between correlated subqueries that use the EXISTS operator and subqueries that use the IN operator. You also learned where to place the ORDER BY clause for an outer query.

After completing the review exercises given in the next section, you should have good expertise in using subqueries to query a database. In addition, you should understand the method of processing correlated subqueries.

REVIEW EXERCISES

LEARN THESE TERMS

ALL keyword. A keyword that can modify a comparison operator (e.g., the ALL keyword modifies the greater than comparison operator to mean greater than *all* values).

ANY keyword. A keyword that can modify a comparison operator (e.g., the ANY keyword modifies the greater than operator to mean greater than *some* value).

Correlated subquery. A subquery in which the inner query depends on values that are provided by the outer query.

Design time. Refers to your mode of operation when you are writing or designing a query.

EXISTS operator. An operator used in a subquery to function as an "existence test." The subquery returns a value of TRUE or FALSE.

Join-compatible. The values returned by a subquery are compatible in terms of datatype and the domain of values with the WHERE clause specified in an outer query.

Nested subquery. The WHERE clause of a subquery has as its object another subquery.

Run time. Refers to the actual execution and processing of a query.

Scalar result. When a result table is a single column from a single row. Also termed a *scalar subquery*.

Subquery. A query within a query.

CONCEPTS QUIZ

1. What term is used to refer to the SELECT statement that contains a subquery?
2. How many levels of subqueries can be used within a WHERE clause?
3. The IN operator is used for what type of subqueries?
4. Name a clause that *cannot* be used in writing the subquery portion of a query?
5. Complete this sentence: A subquery is always enclosed in _____.
6. Complete this sentence: Generally speaking, the SELECT clause of a subquery must contain _____, _____, or _____.
7. What does the term join-compatible mean with respect to datatypes?
8. Explain conceptually how the following query is processed by the Oracle server:

```
SELECT emp_last_name "Last Name", emp_first_name "First Name"
FROM employee
WHERE emp_ssn IN
    (SELECT dep_emp_ssn
     FROM dependent
     WHERE dep_gender = 'M');
```

9. What are the general, basic rules of thumb regarding when to use a join versus a subquery approach in writing queries?

10. Suppose that you want to produce a listing of employees that are not assigned to work on a specific project listing. What operator is most appropriate for this type of query?

11. Complete this sentence: This _____ _____ to studying queries can also help you in writing nested subqueries.

12. Study the WHERE clause shown here. What will happen when a query executes with this WHERE clause?

```
WHERE emp_salary >
    (SELECT emp_salary
     FROM employee
     WHERE emp_salary > 30000);
```

13. What type of result table do aggregate functions produce?

14. Suppose that a payroll manager desires a list of employees who have a salary that is greater than the salary of all of the employees in department 5. Which keyword would you use to modify the comparison operator?

15. Suppose that a payroll manager wants to know the employee name and salary of any employee who has a salary that is greater than that of any employee with a salary that exceeds $30,000. Which keyword would you use to modify the comparison operator?

16. The "= ANY" comparison operator and keyword is identical to the _____ operator.

17. What is a correlated subquery?

18. When writing a correlated subquery, how is the table name listed in the outer query's FROM clause referenced in the WHERE clause of the subquery?

19. Complete this sentence: When a subquery uses the EXISTS operator, the subquery functions as an _____ _____.

20. Complete this sentence: A subquery that is the object of an EXISTS operator evaluates to either _____ or _____.

SQL CODING EXERCISES AND QUESTIONS

Note: You should create meaningful column names for the result tables produced by the queries that you write in working the following exercises.

1. The *assignment* table stores data about the hours that employees are working on specific projects. Management desires a listing of employees (last and first name) who are currently working on project 10, 20, or 30. Use a subquery approach.

2. Modify the query you wrote for question 1 by sorting the rows of the result table by employee last name.

3. Management needs a listing of employee names (last and first) who have worked on a project, but have not worked on project 10, 20, or 30. You must use the NOT IN operator. Use a subquery approach and sort the rows of the result table by employee last name.

4. Management needs a listing of employee names (last and first) who worked more than eight hours on the 'Payroll' project. Your query should have a subquery within a subquery.

5. Management is concerned with employee's that are nearing retirement. The human resources manager needs a listing of employees (last and first names) and their date of birth, but only if the employee was born before *all* employees in department 3. *Hint:* Use the MIN aggregate function to determine the age of the oldest employee in department 3 based on the *emp_date_of_birth* column.

6. Management is concerned that some employees are not putting in sufficient work hours on assigned projects 1, 2, and 3. List the names (last and first) of employees who worked on one of these three projects who worked fewer hours than the average number of hours worked on each of these three projects combined. *Hint:* Compute the average hours worked on projects 1, 2, and 3 in a subquery.

7. Management is still concerned about work productivity. Write a query that will produce a listing of each employee who worked the least on each project (each project will have only a single employee listed unless two employees tied for putting forth the least effort). Include the employee SSNs (*work_emp_ssn*), hours worked (*work_hours*), and project number (*work_pro_number*) columns in the result table. *Hint:* Use a correlated subquery. Sort the output by *work_pro_number*.

8. Management is again concerned with productivity. It is felt that employees may not be paid sufficiently well to motivate their work. Produce a listing of names (last and first) of each employee that receives the lowest salary in each department (some departments may have more than one poorly paid employee). The result table should list the *emp_ssn, emp_last_name, emp_first_name, emp_dpt_number,* and *emp_salary* columns with meaningful column names, sorted by *emp_dpt_number.* Based on the results of this question and question 7, is there any evidence that employees who are paid poorly also did poorly in terms of their hours worked on assigned projects?

9. Management also has concerns about the salaries of younger employees. Write a query to display the last and first names, department number, salary, and birth date of the youngest employee in each department. *Hint:* Use the MAX function. Based on the results of this question and question 8, is there any evidence that younger employees are paid poorly?

10. Review the requirements for question 4. Rewrite the query to add the number of hours worked (*work_hours*) and project name (*pro_name*) to the result table. This challenging modification requires a combination join query and subquery approach.

11. Using a subquery approach, list the names of employees (last and first name) who are managers of departments. Use the EXISTS operator.

12. The Company's CEO needs to know the department with the *highest* average salary. The result table should have two columns labeled **Department** and **Highest Average Salary.**

VIEWS, SYNONYMS, AND SEQUENCES

This chapter covers three important types of database objects—*views, synonyms,* and *sequences.* A *view* is a *logical* or *virtual table.* Views have several uses. A major advantage of a view is that it can simplify query writing such that system users without an extensive background in SQL can write some of their own queries to access database information. Views can also provide an element of data security by limiting the data that a system user can access.

Synonyms are simply *alias names* for database objects. You can create synonyms as well as use synonyms created by other system users. Synonyms also simplify query writing and provide an element of system security.

Sequences are special database objects that support the automatic generation of integer values, and are often used to generate primary key values for tables. For example, order numbers for customer orders could be automatically generated.

OBJECTIVES

We will explore the creation and maintenance of each of these three specialized database objects. We will also learn how to alter and drop these objects. In the review section of the chapter, you will be presented with a number of exercises designed to reinforce key learning points for views, synonyms, and sequences. Your learning should focus on the following objectives:

- Create a single table view.
- Create a join table view—include functions.
- Insert, update, and delete table rows using a view.
- Create a view with errors.
- Drop a view.
- Create a public and a private synonym.
- Drop a synonym.

- Rename a synonym.
- Create a sequence including all of the CREATE SEQUENCE options.
- Access sequence values when storing rows in related tables.
- Alter a sequence.
- Drop a sequence.

VIEWS

A database view is a *logical* or *virtual table* based on a query. In fact, it is useful to think of a *view* as a stored query. In fact, views are created through use of a CREATE VIEW command that incorporates use of the SELECT statement. Views are queried just like tables. This means that from your perspective as a developer or from a database system user's perspective, a view looks like a table. In fact, a database stores information about the definition of a view as an object. A database also stores the execution plan for creating a view. However, the actual data presented by a SELECT query of a view is not stored as part of a database. Rather, the data is "gathered together" each time that a view is queried from the database tables for which a view is defined.

In order to understand view objects better, let's work with an example. Examine the *employee* table definition provided in Appendix A. The *employee* table has a fairly large number of columns. Clearly these columns will not interest all managers. The manager of employee parking will be concerned with which employees are assigned to which parking spaces, while a human resources department manager will be concerned with other facts such as employee name and gender. The view definition provided in SQL Example 8.1 creates a view named *employee_parking*.

```
/* SQL Example 8.1 */
CREATE VIEW employee_parking (parking_space, last_name,
    first_name, ssn) AS
SELECT emp_parking_space, emp_last_name, emp_first_name, emp_ssn
FROM employee
ORDER BY emp_parking_space;
View Created.
```

One of the nice features of the *employee_parking* view is that it is simple. If you manage employee parking, you can select information about employees without having to deal with columns of data that are irrelevant to your job. This view also limits the information that employee parking personnel can access; thus, the employee salary information, for example, is hidden from members of the parking department. After all, parking managers do not have a "need to know" with regard to everyone's salary in an organization. Let's examine the information provided by the view with a SELECT query as shown in SQL Example 8.2.

```
/* SQL Example 8.2 */
COLUMN last_name FORMAT A15;
COLUMN first_name FORMAT A15;
SELECT *
```

```
FROM employee_parking;

PARKING_SPACE       LAST_NAME       FIRST_NAME      SSN
-------------       ---------       ----------      ---------
            1       Bordoloi        Bijoy           999666666
            3       Joyner          Suzanne         999555555
           32       Zhu             Waiman          999444444
more rows are displayed...
```

Notice that the only columns in the query are those defined as part of the view. Additionally, we have renamed the columns in the view so that they are slightly different than the column names in the underlying employee table. Further, the rows are sorted by *parking_space* column even though there is no ORDER BY in the SELECT command used to access the view. Each of these features adds to the simplicity of data retrieval through view usage.

CREATING A VIEW

Now that you have studied an example view, we will examine the full syntax of the CREATE VIEW command. The general syntax is given below. The CREATE VIEW command has a number of options and we will learn about each of these in this section.

CREATE VIEW Syntax

```
CREATE [OR REPLACE] [FORCE|NOFORCE] VIEW <view name> [(column alias
name....)] AS <query> [WITH [CHECK OPTION] [READ ONLY] [CONSTRAINT]];
```

The OR REPLACE option is used to re-create a view that already exists. This option is useful for modifying an existing view without having to drop or grant the privileges that system users have acquired with respect to the view (Chapter 12 covers user privileges in detail). If you attempt to create a view that already exists without using the OR REPLACE option, Oracle will return the *ORA-00955: name is already used by an existing object* error message and the CREATE VIEW command will fail. The query in SQL Example 8.3 uses the OR REPLACE option.

```
/* SQL Example 8.3 */
CREATE OR REPLACE VIEW junk AS
SELECT *
FROM assignment;
View created.
```

The FORCE option allows a view to be created even if a base table that the view references does not already exist. This option is used to create a view prior to the actual creation of the base tables and accompanying data. Before such a view can be queried, the base tables must be created and data must be loaded into the tables. This option can also be used if a system user does not currently have the privilege to create a view.

The NOFORCE option is the opposite of FORCE and allows a system user to create a view if they have the required permissions to create a view, and if the tables from which the view is created already exist. This is the default option.

The WITH READ ONLY option allows creation of a view that is read-only. You cannot use the DELETE, INSERT, or UPDATE commands to modify data for a read-only view.

The WITH CHECK OPTION clause allows the update of rows that can be selected through the view. It also enables you to specify constraints on values. The CONSTRAINT clause works in conjunction with the WITH CHECK OPTION clause to enable a database administrator to assign a unique name to the CHECK OPTION. If a DBA omits the CONSTRAINT clause, Oracle will automatically assign the constraint a system-generated name that will not be very meaningful.

EXAMPLE **CREATE VIEW** COMMANDS

The CREATE VIEW command shown in SQL Example 8.4 creates a view named *empview7*. This view is defined to display each employee's social security number (SSN), first name, and last name, but only for employees assigned to department 7. The view has a different structure than the employee table in terms of the columns in the view. The view stores a subset of the *employee* table rows because the rows accessible through the view are restricted to employees assigned to department 7.

```
/* SQL Example 8.4 */
CREATE VIEW empview7 AS
SELECT emp_ssn, emp_first_name, emp_last_name
FROM employee
WHERE emp_dpt_number=7;
View created.
```

SQL Example 8.5 shows a simple query of the *empview7* view.

```
/* SQL Example 8.5 */
SELECT *
FROM empview7;

EMP_SSN        EMP_FIRST_NAME       EMP_LAST_NAME
- - - - - - -  - - - - - - - - - -  - - - - - - - - - -
999444444      Waiman               Zhu
999111111      Douglas              Bock
999333333      Dinesh               Joshi
999888888      Sherri               Prescott
```

It is also possible to create a view that has exactly the same structure as an existing database table. The view named *dept_view* in SQL Example 8.6 has exactly the same structure as *department* table. Further, the view provides access to all of the rows of the *department* table.

```
/* SQL Example 8.6 */
CREATE VIEW dept_view AS
SELECT *
FROM department;
View created.
```

Now it appears that the *dept_view* may not be terribly useful since it simply duplicates the *department* table in terms of data row accessibility. However, we can recreate the view by using the OR REPLACE clause to create a view that is *read-only* by specifying a WITH READ ONLY clause. SQL Example 8.7 shows the revised CREATE VIEW command. The new read-only version of *dept_view* restricts data manipulation language operations on the view to selection. Additionally, anyone that previously had access to the *dept_view* will continue to have access to the new view definition. Note that the CONSTRAINT clause is used to name the WITH READ ONLY constraint as *vw_dept_view_read_only*. This enables a DBA to more easily determine the status of constraints for views.

```
/* SQL Example 8.7 */
CREATE OR REPLACE VIEW dept_view AS
SELECT *
FROM department WITH READ ONLY CONSTRAINT vw_dept_view_read_only;
View created.
```

FUNCTIONS AND VIEWS—A JOIN VIEW

In addition to specifying columns from existing tables, you can use single row functions consisting of number, character, date, and group functions as well as expressions to create additional columns in views. This can be extremely useful because the system user will have access to data without having to understand how to use the underlying functions. Consider the query in SQL Example 8.8, which illustrates the usage of the MAX and MIN functions within views.

```
/* SQL Example 8.8 */
CREATE OR REPLACE VIEW dept_salary
    (name, min_salary, max_salary, avg_salary) AS
SELECT d.dpt_name, MIN(e.emp_salary),
    MAX(e.emp_salary), AVG(e.emp_salary)
FROM employee e, department d
WHERE e.emp_dpt_number=d.dpt_no
GROUP BY d.dpt_name;
View created.
```

The *dept_salary* view can be queried to produce a result table with the department name (from the *department* table), as well as three computed columns. These three columns will store the minimum, maximum, and average salaries for members of the department, but the data used to produce a result table with these three columns actually come from the *employee* table. Thus, this view is also known as a *join view* because it joins the *department* and *employee* tables. Further, the data will be grouped by department name.

Now we will execute the SELECT statement shown in SQL Example 8.9 to display data from the *dept_salary* view. Notice how simple the query is to write as compared to the query used to create the view. This query can be executed by a system user with limited SQL training and enable the system user easy access to information that may be used repeatedly over time.

```
/* SQL Example 8.9 */
SELECT *
FROM dept_salary;

NAME                MIN_SALARY    MAX_SALARY    AVG_SALARY
---------------     ----------    ----------    ----------
Admin and Records        25000         43000         31000
Headquarters             55000         55000         55000
Production               25000         43000         34000
```

VIEW STABILITY

Remember that a view does not actually store any data. The data needed to support view queries are retrieved from the underlying database tables and displayed to a result table at the time that a view is queried. The result table is stored only temporarily.

If a table that underlies a view is dropped, then the view is no longer valid. Attempting to query an invalid view will produce an *ORA-04063: view "VIEW_NAME" has errors* error message. We will examine this by creating a *test* table with a single column. SQL Examples 8.10, 8.11, and 8.12 create a table named *test*, store two data rows to the table, and display all the data from the table.

```
/* SQL Example 8.10 */
CREATE TABLE test (
    test_row VARCHAR2(10)
);
```

```
/* SQL Example 8.11 */
INSERT INTO test VALUES ('Test row 1');
INSERT INTO test VALUES ('Test row 2');
```

```
/* SQL Example 8.12 */
SELECT *
FROM test;
```

```
TEST_ROW
---------
Test row 1
Test row 2
```

As you can see, the *test* table was created and we were able to access data from the table. The commands in SQL Example 8.13 create a view named *test_view* with the same structure and data as our *test* table. The query in SQL Example 8.14 displays all the data from the view *test_view*.

```
/* SQL Example 8.13 */
CREATE VIEW test_view AS
SELECT *
FROM test;
```

```
/* SQL Example 8.14 */
SELECT *
FROM test_view;

TEST_ROW
---------
Test row 1
Test row 2
```

Not surprisingly, the result table for the *test_view* is identical to the result table for the *test* table. Now let's drop the *test* table and query the *test_view* again. Oracle returns the *ORA-04063* error message because the *test_view* object is now invalid.

```
/* SQL Example 8.15 */
DROP TABLE test;
```

```
/* SQL Example 8.16 */
SELECT *
FROM test_view;

ERROR at line 2:
ORA-04063: view "TEST_VIEW" has errors
```

INSERTING, UPDATING, AND DELETING TABLE ROWS THROUGH VIEWS

In this section, you will learn basic concepts regarding how to insert, update, and delete table rows through the use of views. The concept of inserting rows into tables through views is a complex one. Likewise, updating existing table rows through views is equally or more complex. Deleting rows is considerably simpler.

INSERTING ROWS

Basically, you can insert a row in a table by inserting a row in a view only if the view is updateable. A view is updateable if the INSERT command does not violate any constraints on the underlying tables and if it is not read-only. The rule concerning constraint violations also applies to UPDATE and DELETE commands. We will focus on a single-table update, although it is possible to update base tables accessed through views that are defined for two or more joined tables.

SQL Example 8.17 creates a *dept_view* object to allow system users to display easily the department number and name columns through use of the view. Note that the *dept_view* view has only two columns whereas the *department* table has four columns. The two *department* table columns not included in *dept_view* are both allowed to store NULL values, and there are no constraints on the columns.

```
/* SQL Example 8.17 */
CREATE OR REPLACE VIEW dept_view AS
SELECT dpt_no, dpt_name
FROM department;
```

The INSERT commands in SQL Example 8.18 insert two new rows into the *department* table by using the *dept_view*. Notice that we have erroneously entered the department name of the new department 19 as "Department 20." We will address this a bit later in this section.

```
/* SQL Example 8.18 */
INSERT INTO dept_view VALUES (18, 'Department 18');
INSERT INTO dept_view VALUES (19, 'Department 20');
```

SQL Example 8.19 confirms the row insertions by selecting from the view. The result table displays the original three rows from the *department* table as well as the newly inserted rows for departments 18 and 19.

```
/* SQL Example 8.19 */
SELECT *
FROM dept_view;

DPT_NO     DPT_NAME
------     --------------
     7     Production
     3     Admin and Records
     1     Headquarters
    18     Department 18
    19     Department 20
```

Now we will use an UPDATE command in SQL Example 8.20 to correct the error in the department name for department 19 by changing the name to "Department 19." SQL Example 8.21 queries the *department* table to determine if the rows in the base table were updated through the view.

```
/* SQL Example 8.20 */
UPDATE dept_view SET dpt_name = 'Department 19' WHERE dpt_no = 19;
1 row updated.
```

```
/* SQL Example 8.21 */
SELECT *
FROM department
WHERE dpt_no >= 5;

DPT_NO      DPT_NAME           DPT_MGRSS        DPT_MGR_S
------      -----------        --------         --------
     7      Production         999444444        22-MAY-98
    18      Department 18
    19      Department 19
more rows are displayed...
```

Success! The *department* table has two new rows. The INSERT commands updated the *department* table through the *dept_view* view. Likewise, the UPDATE command updated the department name for department 19. Note that the department manager's SSN and start date columns are NULL for the two new rows because data for these columns were not entered with the INSERT commands in SQL Example 8.18.

There are some limitations on use of the UPDATE command that you need to understand. If you attempt to update a row in a table through a view by referencing a column that is defined for the table, but not for the view, Oracle will return the *ORA-00904: invalid column name* error message.

Now let's try the DELETE command. SQL Example 8.22 deletes the rows for departments 18 and 19 through the *dept_view* object. SQL Example 8.23 verifies that these two rows no longer exist in the *department* table. That was pretty straightforward.

```
/* SQL Example 8.22 */
DELETE dept_view
WHERE dpt_no = 18 OR dpt_no = 19;
2 rows deleted.
```

```
/* SQL Example 8.23 */
SELECT *
FROM department;
```

```
DPT_NO      DPT_NAME              DPT_MGRSS     DPT_MGR_S
------      ----------------      ---------     ---------
     7      Production            999444444     22-MAY-98
     3      Admin and Records     999555555     01-JAN-01
     1      Headquarters          999666666     19-JUN-81
```

CREATING A VIEW WITH ERRORS

If there are no syntax errors in a CREATE VIEW statement, Oracle will create a view even if the view-defining query refers to a nonexistent table or an invalid column of an existing table. A view will also be created even if the system user does not have privileges to access the tables that a view references. However, the new view will be unusable and is categorized as "created with errors." As was noted earlier, a DBA may create such a view in anticipation of later creating the associated base tables or columns. In order to create such a view, a DBA or system user must use the FORCE option of the CREATE VIEW command.

In the CREATE VIEW command in SQL Example 8.24, the table named *divisions* does not exist and the view is created with errors. Oracle returns an appropriate warning message.

```
/* SQL Example 8.24 */
CREATE FORCE VIEW div_view AS
SELECT *
FROM divisions;
Warning: View created with compilation errors.
```

If we now create a table named *divisions,* as shown in SQL Example 8.25, a query of the invalid *div_view* view will execute, and the view is automatically recompiled and becomes valid. We can also do the compilation manually. Of course, the SELECT statement in SQL Example 8.26 returns *"no rows selected"* because we did not insert any data into the *divisions* table!

```
/* SQL Example 8.25 */
CREATE TABLE divisions (
    Test_Column CHAR(1) );
Table created.
```

```
/* SQL Example 8.26 */
SELECT *
FROM divisions;
no rows selected
```

DROPPING VIEW

A DBA or view owner can drop a view with the DROP VIEW command. SQL Example 8.27 drops the *dept_view* object.

```
/* SQL Example 8.27 */
DROP VIEW dept_view;
View dropped.
```

A SUMMARY OF VIEW FACTS

Now let's summarize the facts that we have learned about views. Some of these facts underscore advantages of views while others underscore limitations of views.

- A view does not store data, but a view does display data through a SELECT query as if the data were stored in the view.
- A view definition as provided by the CREATE VIEW statement is stored in the database. Further, Oracle develops what is termed an *execution plan* that is used to "gather up" the data that need to be displayed by a view. This execution plan is also stored in the database.
- A view can simplify data presentation as well as provide a kind of data security by limiting access to data based on a "need to know."
- A view can display data from more than one table. We say that views hide *data complexity*. For example, a single view can be defined by joining two or more tables. The resulting view is, however, treated as a single table, thereby hiding the fact that the view rows actually originate from several tables. This also simplifies data access.
- Views can be used to update the underlying tables. Views can also be limited to read-only access.
- Views can change the appearance of data. For example, a view can be used to rename columns from tables without affecting the base table.
- A view that has columns from more than one table cannot be modified by an INSERT, DELETE, or UPDATE command if a grouping function GROUP BY clause is part of the view definition.
- A view cannot reference the *nextval* and *currval* pseudocolumns created through the use of sequences. These pseudocolumns are explained later in this chapter under the SEQUENCES section.
- A row cannot be inserted in a view in which the base table has a column with the NOT NULL or other constraint that cannot be satisfied by the new row data.
- If there is any question about whether or not columns in a join view (a view defined with two or more base tables) are updateable, you can query the *user_updateable_columns* data dictionary view (see Chapter 12). This view will display the desired information.

SYNONYMS

A *synonym* is an *alias,* that is, a form of shorthand used to simplify the task of referencing a database object. The concept is analogous to the use of nicknames for friends and acquaintances. It is fairly common to refer to someone named *Robert* by the nickname *Bob.* Study the SELECT statement in SQL Example 8.28.

```
/* SQL Example 8.28 */
SELECT tablespace_name, status
FROM sys.dba_tablespaces;

TABLESPACE_NAME      STATUS
-------------        ------
SYSTEM               ONLINE
RBS                  ONLINE
more rows are displayed...
```

The database object referenced in query 8.28 is a view named *sys.dba_tablespaces.* The actual result table displayed will vary from one database to the next depending on the structure of the database. The *sys.dba_tablespaces* object is part of the Oracle data dictionary and is owned by the user named SYS. The SELECT statement is a bit cumbersome to type because of the syntax of the object name, and is easier to enter if the view is referenced through use of a brief synonym such as *tbs.* In order to do this, the user SYS, as owner of the view, must execute a CREATE SYNONYM command to create the synonym named *tbs.*

CREATING SYNONYMS

The general form of the CREATE SYNONYM command is:

```
CREATE [PUBLIC] SYNONYM synonym_name FOR object_name;
```

SQL Example 8.29 shows the command to create the *tbs* synonym as a public synonym. Since the user SYS is creating the synonym, it is unnecessary to qualify the name of the *dba_tablespaces* object with the object owner name of SYS as part of the CREATE SYNONYM command.

```
/* SQL Example 8.29 */
CREATE PUBLIC SYNONYM tbs FOR sys.dba_tablespaces;
```

Did you notice the use of the optional PUBLIC keyword? There are two categories of synonyms, *public* and *private.* A public synonym can be accessed by any system user. In fact, the individual creating a public synonym does not own the synonym—rather, it will belong to the PUBLIC user group that exists within Oracle. Private synonyms, on the other hand, belong to the system user that creates them and reside in that user's schema. Recall that a schema is storage space allocated to the system user. The schema name is the same as the user's Oracle account user name. In this fashion, two different system users can create their own private synonyms within their individual schemas without having to worry about what they name the synonyms. If a system user selects a private synonym name that another system user has already used, Oracle will not return an error because the actual name of any synonym includes the schema name (e.g., *schema_name.synonym_name*). Note the use of the dot notation when referencing a schema name and a synonym stored in the schema.

A system user can grant the privilege to use private synonyms that they own to other system users. In order to create synonyms, you will need to have the CREATE SYNONYM privilege. Further, you must have the CREATE PUBLIC SYNONYM privilege in order to create public synonyms. These privileges can be granted to you by the DBA for your organization. Detailed information about how to grant privileges is covered in Chapter 12.

If a synonym is declared as public, the synonym name cannot already be in use as a public synonym. Attempting to create a public synonym that already exists will cause the CREATE PUBLIC SYNONYM command to fail, and Oracle will return the *ORA-00955: name is already used by an existing object* error message.

Now let's return to our original SELECT command in SQL Example 8.28. You can now rewrite this command by referencing the *tbs* synonym as shown in SQL Example 8.30. Further, the creation of a public synonym makes the *sys.dba_tablespaces* object available to all system users.

```
/* SQL Example 8.30 */
SELECT tablespace_name, status
FROM tbs;

TABLESPACE_NAME      STATUS
-------------        ------
SYSTEM               ONLINE
RBS                  ONLINE
more rows are displayed...
```

There are three additional advantages to synonym usage:

1. A synonym provides what is termed *location transparency* because the synonym name hides the actual object name and object owner from the user of the synonym.

2. You can create a synonym for a database object and then refer to the synonym in application code. The underlying object can be moved or renamed, and a redefinition of the synonym will allow the application code to continue to execute without errors.

3. A public synonym can be used to allow easy access to an object for all system users.

DROPPING SYNONYMS

If you own a synonym, you have the right to drop (delete) the synonym. The DROP SYNONYM command is quite simple as shown in SQL Example 8.31.

```
/* SQL Example 8.31 */
DROP SYNONYM synonym_name;
```

You can drop any synonym that you own, that is, one that is stored in your schema within the database. In order to drop a public synonym like the *tbs* synonym created earlier, you must include the PUBLIC keyword in the DROP SYNONYM command as shown in SQL Example 8.32. In order to drop a public synonym, you must have the DROP PUBLIC SYNONYM privilege.

```
/* SQL Example 8.32 */
DROP PUBLIC SYNONYM tbs;
```

Dropping synonyms can sometimes lead to problems. If an application program or SQL script references the dropped synonym, the program will fail. If a database object such as a view references the dropped synonym name, then the view object will not be dropped from the database, but it will become *invalid,* that is, not usable. Also, if a table or other database object referenced by a synonym is dropped, the synonym is *not* automatically dropped. If you are uncertain about whether to drop a synonym, you might best consider leaving it since a synonym definition consumes an insignificant amount of database storage space.

RENAMING SYNONYMS

Private synonyms can be renamed with the RENAME SYNONYM command. All existing references to the synonym are automatically updated in the data dictionary. Thus, any system user with privileges to use a synonym will retain those privileges if the synonym name is changed.

The syntax of the RENAME SYNONYM command shown in SQL Example 8.33 is like that for the RENAME command for any other database object such as a view or table.

```
/* SQL Example 8.33 */
RENAME old_synonym_name TO new_synonym_name;
```

Did you note that the RENAME SYNONYM command *only* works for private synonyms? If we attempt to rename a public synonym such as the *tbs* synonym created earlier, Oracle will return an *ORA-04043: object tblspaces does not exist* error message as shown in SQL Example 8.34.

```
/* SQL Example 8.34 */
RENAME tbs TO ts;
ORA-04043: object TBS does not exist
```

However, the RENAME SYNONYM command works as expected for an existing private synonym. The sequence of commands shown in SQL Example 8.35 creates a private synonym *dep_loc* for the table named *dept_locations* in the company database described in Appendix A. The *dep_loc* synonym is then renamed to be simply *dl.*

```
/* SQL Example 8.35 */
CREATE SYNONYM dep_loc FOR dept_locations;

RENAME dep_loc TO dl;
Table renamed.
```

Note that Oracle returns the message *Table renamed* when a private synonym is renamed.

SEQUENCES

Have you ever wondered how certain numeric identifiers are created? For example, suppose a furniture store numbers customer orders. What is the origin of the number used to identify customer orders? If we let sales clerks create order numbers, sooner or later two different sales clerks will use the same order number to identify two different orders. The solution to this type of data processing problem is to let the computer system generate a unique order number. Oracle provides the capability to generate sequences of unique numbers for this type of use, and they are called *sequences*.

Just like tables, views, indexes, and synonyms, a sequence is a type of database object. Generally, sequences are used to generate unique, sequential integer values that are used as primary key values in database tables. The sequence of numbers can be generated in either ascending or descending order.

CREATING SEQUENCES

The syntax of the CREATE SEQUENCE command is fairly complex because it has numerous optional clauses. We will examine each clause one at a time.

```
CREATE SEQUENCE <sequence name>
[INCREMENT BY <number>]
[START WITH <start value number>]
[MAXVALUE <MAXIMUM VALUE NUMBER>]
[NOMAXVALUE]
[MINVALUE <minimum value number>]
[CYCLE]
[NOCYCLE]
[CACHE <number of sequence value to cache>]
[NOCACHE]
[ORDER]
[NOORDER];
```

The CREATE SEQUENCE command must specify a unique sequence name. This is the only required clause in the command. If you do not specify any of the other clauses, all sequence numbers generated will follow the Oracle default settings. The default settings for each clause are explained below.

The INCREMENT BY clause is used to determine how the sequence will increment as each number is generated. The default is an increment of 1; however, if you have a good reason for a sequence to skip numbers, you can provide some other increment. A positive numeric increment generates ascending sequence numbers with an interval equal to the interval you select. A negative numeric increment generates descending sequence numbers.

The START WITH clause specifies the starting numeric value for the sequence. The default for START WITH is one. Additionally, you must specify a start value if you already have some rows with data in the column that will now store sequence values.

The MAXVALUE clause specifies the maximum value to which a sequence can be incremented. In the absence of a MAXVALUE, the maximum allowable value that can be generated for a sequence is quite large, 10 to the 27th power – 1! The default is NOMAXVALUE.

The MINVALUE clause specifies the minimum value of a sequence for a decrementing sequence (one that generates numbers in descending order). The default is NOMINVALUE.

The CYCLE clause specifies that sequence values can be reused if the sequence reaches the specified MAXVALUE. If the sequence cycles, numbers are generated starting again at the MINVALUE.

The CACHE clause can improve system performance by enabling Oracle to generate a specified batch of sequenced numbers to be stored in cache memory. For example, CACHE 40 will cache 40 sequence numbers. These numbers will be used in turn until there are none remaining, then Oracle will generate the next 40 sequence numbers. When you cache sequence numbers, there is the possibility some of the numbers may never be used. Since the numbers are cached in memory, an abnormal shutdown of the system will cause the unused cached numbers to be lost. Generally, if you are generating primary key values, this does not cause a problem with application development and use. If you specify CACHE without specifying a number, the default cache size is 20 sequence numbers. Optionally, you can specify NOCACHE to prevent the cache of sequence numbers.

The ORDER clause is a bit difficult to understand. This clause specifies that sequence numbers are allocated in the exact chronological order in which they are requested. Consider a sequence that starts with one and increments by one. This means that the first system user to request a sequence number will receive sequence 1, the second system user to request a sequence number will receive sequence 2, and so forth. The NOORDER clause ensures that system users or application programs will be allotted unique numbers, just not necessarily in chronological order.

A CREATE SEQUENCE EXAMPLE

Let's return to our furniture store example. Management at the furniture store wishes to identify each sales order by a unique order number. Further, the order number needs to be generated by the application program that is used by sales personnel to record sales information. As the application developer, you coordinate with your organizational DBA for the creation of a new sequence to be named *order_number_sequence*. The CREATE SEQUENCE command in SQL Example 8.36 specifies a sequence for order numbers that will have a maximum numeric value of 100 million and then will cycle back to the value one. Further, the system will cache 10 sequence numbers at a time.

```
/* SQL Example 8.36 */
CREATE SEQUENCE order_number_sequence
```

```
INCREMENT BY 1
START WITH 1
MAXVALUE 100000000
MINVALUE 1
CYCLE
CACHE 10;
Sequence created.
```

ACCESSING SEQUENCE VALUES

Sequence values are generated through the use of two *pseudocolumns* named *currval* and *nextval.* A pseudocolumn behaves like a table column, but psuedocolumns are not actually stored in a table. We can select values from pseudocolumns but cannot perform manipulations on their values.

The first time you select the *nextval* pseudocolumn, the initial value in the sequence is returned. Subsequent selections of the *nextval* pseudocolumn cause the sequence to increment as specified in the INCREMENT BY clause and return the newly generated sequence value. The *currval* pseudocolumn returns the current value of the sequence, which is the value returned by the last reference to *nextval.*

The sequence used to reference a pseudocolumn is best explained by an example. We could return a value through use of the *nextval* pseudocolumn for the *order_number_sequence* sequence by referencing *order_number_sequence.nextval* (read *sequence_name,* dot, *nextval*). Let's practice this on a real table. In order to do this, you need to create a simple table named *sales_order* as shown in SQL Example 8.37. The table will only have two columns, the *order_number* and *order_amount* (dollar value of the order).

```
/* SQL Example 8.37 */
CREATE TABLE sales_order (
    order_number        NUMBER(9)
        CONSTRAINT pk_sales_order PRIMARY KEY,
    order_amount        NUMBER(9,2)
);
```

The INSERT commands in SQL Example 8.38 insert three rows into the *sales_order* table. The INSERT commands reference the *order_number_sequence. nextval* pseudocolumn.

```
/* SQL Example 8.38 */
INSERT INTO sales_order
    VALUES ( order_number_sequence.nextval, 155.59 );
INSERT INTO sales_order
    VALUES ( order_number_sequence.nextval, 450.00 );
INSERT INTO sales_order
    VALUES ( order_number_sequence.nextval, 16.95 );
```

Now, let's examine the *sales_order* table by querying the table (SQL Example 8.39) to display the rows that were inserted. Note that the sequence number values stored in the *order_number* column were properly generated.

```
/* SQL Example 8.39 */
SELECT *
FROM sales_order;

ORDER_NUMBER        ORDER_AMOUNT
-----------         -----------
          1               155.59
          2                  450
          3                16.95
```

Having seen how the *nextval* pseudocolumn is used, you're probably wondering what the purpose of the *currval* pseudocolumn is. Often, a table like *sales_order* will be related to another table that stores sales order details. Let's create a simple *order_details* table, as per SQL Example 8.40, to illustrate the use of the *currval* pseudocolumn.

```
/* SQL Example 8.40 */
CREATE TABLE order_details (
    order_number        NUMBER(9),
    order_row           NUMBER(3),
    product_desc        VARCHAR2(15),
    quantity_ordered    NUMBER(3),
    product_price       NUMBER(9,2),
CONSTRAINT pk_order_details
    PRIMARY KEY (order_number, order_row),
CONSTRAINT fk_order_number FOREIGN KEY (order_number)
    REFERENCES sales_order
);
```

Note that the *order_details* table primary key includes both the *order_number* and *order_row* columns. The *order_row* is simply a way of numbering each item ordered on a specific order. For each order row, the system stores the product description, quantity ordered, and product price. The *order_details* table has a FOREIGN KEY reference to the *sales_order* table through the *order_number* column.

Now, let's return to the use of the INSERT command to store information about sales orders and order details. As each row is inserted into the *sales_order* table, related rows about the products sold on the order are inserted into the *order_details* table. The statements in SQL Example 8.41 stores a *sales_order* totaling $200 along with two *order_detail* rows. Note the use of the *currval* pseudocolumn reference. Additionally, we first delete the rows that were previously inserted into the *sales_order* table.

```
/* SQL Example 8.41 */
/* First delete the existing sales_order rows */
DELETE FROM sales_order;
```

```
/* Now insert a new sales_order row and two order_detail rows */
INSERT INTO sales_order
    VALUES ( order_number_sequence.nextval, 200.00 );
INSERT INTO order_details
    VALUES ( order_number_sequence.currval, 1, 'End Table',
        1, 100.00);
INSERT INTO order_details
    VALUES ( order_number_sequence.currval, 2, 'Table Lamp',
        2, 50.00);
```

The SELECT statements in SQL Examples 8.42 and 8.43 display the rows in these two tables, respectively. The use of *order_number_sequence.nextval* when inserting a row into the *sales_order* table results in the generation of the next sequence number to be used as the *order_number* primary key. The use of *order_number_sequence.currval* when inserting the two rows in the *order_details* table enables the *reuse* of the current sequence number. If the *nextval* pseudocolumn name was used instead, the *order_number* in the *sales_order* table would *not* match the *order_number* column value in the *order_details* table, and we would have a referential integrity problem!

```
/* SQL Example 8.42 */
SELECT *
FROM sales_order;

ORDER_NUMBER    ORDER_AMOUNT
-----------     -----------
          4             200
```

```
/* SQL Example 8.43 */
SELECT *
FROM order_details;

ORDER_NUMBER   ORDER_ROW   PRODUCT_DESC   QUANTITY_ORDERED   PRODUCT_PRICE
-----------    --------    ------------   ----------------   ------------
          4           1   End Table                     1             100
          4           2   Table Lamp                    2              50
```

ALTERING A SEQUENCE

A sequence is usually altered when it is desirable to set or eliminate the values of the MINVALUE or MAXVALUE parameters, or to change the INCREMENT BY value, or to change the number of cached sequence numbers. The ALTER SEQUENCE command in SQL Example 8.44 changes the MAXVALUE of the *order_number_sequence* to 200 million.

```
/* SQL Example 8.44 */
ALTER SEQUENCE order_number_sequence MAXVALUE 200000000;
Sequence altered.
```

There is one important final note on creating and altering sequences. When specifying a MINVALUE clause, the specified value should be less than the MAXVALUE where a sequence generates ascending numbers. In the case of a descending sequence, the MAXVALUE should be less than the MINVALUE.

VIEWING SEQUENCE PROPERTIES

You may need to review the names and properties of your sequences. As illustrated in SQL Example 8.45, you can do this by querying the USER_SEQUENCES system view with a SELECT command. This view is part of the Oracle data dictionary.

```
/* SQL Example 8.45 */
SELECT * FROM USER_SEQUENCES;

SEQUENCE_NAME          MIN_VAL MAX_VALUE INCRE C O CACHE_SIZE LAST_NUMBER
---------------------- ------- --------- ----- - - ---------- -----------
ORDER_NUMBER_SEQUENCE        1 200000000     1 Y N         10           6
```

DROPPING A SEQUENCE

You will use the DROP SEQUENCE command to drop sequences that need to be recreated or are no longer needed. The general format is shown here along with SQL Example 8.46, which drops the *order_number_sequence* object.

```
DROP SEQUENCE <sequence name>;
```

```
/* SQL Example 8.46 */
DROP SEQUENCE order_number_sequence;
Sequence dropped.
```

Do you recall the earlier discussion about the impact that dropping a synonym can have on program execution? Dropping a sequence can have a similar negative impact. If an existing program or procedure references a sequence that is dropped, then that program or procedure will fail.

SUMMARY

In this chapter, you learned about three new types of database objects. Views are an important mechanism to facilitate the display of selected columns from tables. Views can also provide a type of database security by restricting restrict access to database information by limiting the columns displayed by a view. You also learned basic concepts about updating tables through views. Synonyms are shorthand alias names for database objects, and can simplify the access of information as well as provide for location transparency. Finally, the commands necessary to create and use a sequence database object were covered.

REVIEW EXERCISES

LEARN THESE TERMS

ALTER SEQUENCE.   A command used to alter one of the optional parameters of a sequence object.

CREATE SEQUENCE.   A command used to create a new sequence database object.

CREATE SYNONYM.   A command used to create a new synonym for a database object.

CREATE VIEW.   A command that uses a SELECT statement to create a view.

DROP SEQUENCE.   A command used to drop an existing sequence.

DROP SYNONYM.   A command used to drop an existing synonym.

DROP VIEW.   A command used to delete an existing view.

Join view.   A view definition that can be queried to display data that results from a join of two or more database tables.

Private synonym.   A synonym belonging to the system user who created it and resides in that user's schema.

Pseudocolumn.   A database object that behaves like a table column, but psuedocolumns are not actually stored in a table.

Public synonym.   A synonym that can be accessed by any system user.

RENAME SYNONYM.   A command that renames an existing private synonym, and all references to the synonym are automatically updated.

Sequences.   Special database objects that support the automatic generation of integer values.

Synonym.   An alias name for a database object.

View.   A logical table; also termed a virtual table.

CONCEPTS QUIZ

1. Where is the data for a view stored?
2. What data manipulation language operations are allowed for a view that is created with the WITH READ ONLY clause?
3. What is the purpose of the CONSTRAINT clause with a view that is created with the WITH READ ONLY clause?
4. A view named *project_hours* displays the project name from the *project* table and the average hours worked on the project as an aggregated column from the *assignment* table. What will happen to the view if the *assignment* table is dropped? What will happen if you write a SELECT statement to display data from the view?
5. When can you insert a row into a table through use of a view?
6. What happens if your write a CREATE VIEW command to create a view for a nonexistent table?
7. What is the primary purpose of a synonym?
8. What is the difference between public and private synonyms?
9. In addition to making it easier to access database objects, name two of the three additional advantages of synonym usage.
10. What command would you use to change the name of a private synonym named *archived_projects to old_projects?*
11. What is the purpose of the INCREMENT BY clause in the CREATE SEQUENCE command?
12. What is the purpose of the MAXVALUE clause in the CREATE SEQUENCE command?

13. What does the CACHE clause do in the CREATE SEQUENCE command and why would it be used?
14. To what does the pseudocolumn named *nextval* refer?
15. To what does the pseudocolumn named *currval* refer and how is it related to the *nextval* pseudocolumn?

SQL Coding Exercises and Questions

1. The payroll department needs to regularly access information about employee salary information. The DBA of the company has directed you to create a view based on the *employee* table named *salary_view*. This view should include the employee SSN (*emp_ssn*), employee last and first names (*emp_last_name* and *emp_first_name*), and the salary for each employee (*emp_salary*). Name the columns of the view as follows: *ssn, last_name, first_name,* and *salary.* Write the SQL code needed to create this view. Write a SELECT statement to display rows from the view for employees with salaries at or above $30,000.

2. Replace the view named *salary_view* created in question 1 with a new view (same name) that also includes the *emp_dpt_number* column. Name this column *department* in the new view. Write a SELECT statement to display rows from the view where employees are in department 7 and their salary is at or above $30,000.

3. Clerical employees in the human resources department only need read-access to information about employee dependents. Create a read only view named *dependent_view* that has the same structure as the *dependent* table. Name the read-only constraint *vw_dependent_view_read_only.* Use the DESCribe command to describe the *dependent_view* object and list the description.

4. Create a view named *project_hours* that will be used by the senior project manager to access information about work hours that have been reported for different projects. The view should join the *project* and *assignment* tables. The view should show each project's name (*pro_name*) as well as the average hours worked on each project. Name the columns *project_name* and *average_hours* in the view. The rows in the view should be grouped by the project name. Write a SELECT statement to display projects where the average hours is at or greater than 15.

5. The Company's senior project manager needs to access information about departments that manage projects for a specific set of projects, namely those located in either Edwardsville or Marina. Create a view named *department_projects* that includes the *dpt_no* and *dpt_name* columns from the *department* table and the *pro_name* and *pro_location* from the *project* table. The view should only reference rows for projects that are located in either Edwardsville or Marina. The columns in the view should be named *dept_no, department, project,* and *location,* respectively. Write a SELECT statement to display all of the rows that are accessible through the view. Format the output columns of the SELECT statement as A15 for *project* and *location,* and A17 for *department.*

6. The senior project manager has requested that the *department_projects* view also include the project number. Replace the *department_projects* view described in question 5 with a new view that includes the *pro_number* column from the project table. Name this column *pro_no* in the view. All other requirements remain unchanged. Write a SELECT statement to display all of the rows that are accessi-

ble through the view. Format the output columns of the SELECT statement as A15 for *project* and *location,* A17 for *department* and 999999 for *pro_no.*

7. Demonstrate the use of the view named *department_projects* for the senior project manager by writing a SELECT command to query the *department_projects* view created in question 6 to display all row information for projects belonging to department 3.

8. The senior project manager no longer needs the views named *department_projects* and *project_hours.* Write commands to drop these views.

9. You wish to provide location transparency security for the table named *dept_locations* and have decided to do this by creating a public synonym named *locations.* Write the command to create this public synonym. Write a SELECT statement to display the locations of department 7 (use the *dpt_no* column) by using the *locations* synonym.

10. You've decided to create a synonym to be used personally to assist you in referencing the table named *assignment.* The synonym will be named simply *asgn.* Write the command to create this synonym.

11. Write a command to rename the asgn synonym to have a new name of *asign.* Write a SELECT statement to display all column values by using the *asign* synonym where the *work_hours* column value is greater than or equal to 30 hours.

12. The senior vice president for resource management desires to number new departments within the company sequentially beginning with number 40. The department numbering will be in increments of 1. In order to improve system performance, you have recommended that 5 department numbers be cached and this has been approved. No other options are to be set for the new sequence. Name the sequence *department_number_sequence.* Write the code needed to create this sequence.

13. Write an INSERT command to insert two new rows into the *department* table by using the *department_number_sequence* created in question 12. The other information to be inserted is shown below. Write a SELECT statement to display all rows from the *department* table.

   - dpt_name = 'Engineering'
   - dpt_name = 'Inventory Mngt'
   - dpt_mgrssn = NULL for both new rows
   - dpt_mgr_start_date = NULL for both new rows

14. Write a command to insert a new project into the project table. This project will be controlled by the Inventory Management department. Use the *department_number_sequence* created and used in questions 12 and 13 to insert the new row into the project table. The other information to be inserted is shown below. Write a SELECT statement to display the row for project 55. Compare it to the department numbers listed in question 13. Ensure that the correct *pro_dept_number* value is stored to the new project row.

   - pro_number = 55
   - pro_name = 'New Inventory Sys'
   - pro_location = 'Marina'
   - pro_dept_number = (generate this from the sequence)

CHAPTER

SQL*PLUS REPORTS

Chapter 1 introduced you to Oracle's SQL*Plus program. You have since learned to use SQL*Plus to execute SQL statements that both define and manipulate data. In this chapter you will study another aspect of SQL*Plus—the *interactive report writer* capability. It is important to understand this aspect of SQL*Plus because many information systems have been developed over the years that use the SQL*Plus report writer capability. It is very likely that you may one day be assigned to provide programming support for the maintenance of one of these information systems, and that your support requirement may include the modification of SQL*Plus programs. Additionally, you will discover that the report writer capability takes a *nonprocedural* approach to computer programming in which you, as the programmer, describe through SQL*Plus commands what you need in terms of a report, and SQL*Plus then does the work of producing the report.

OBJECTIVES

In this chapter, we will learn the basics of interactive report writing with SQL*Plus. The learning objectives include:

- Create a SQL*Plus program command file.
- Use remarks in SQL*Plus programs.
- Set values for top and bottom titles as well as report headers and footers.
- Set report characteristics including line size, page size, and spacing of output for both printers and computer monitor screens.
- Select columns from tables to display in reports.
- Create a control break report including clearing breaks and using the BREAK and COMPUTE commands.
- Use the SPOOL command to produce report listing files.
- View command file settings.
- Create Master-Detail reports including the use of variables in report titles and footers with the COLUMN command NEW_VALUE clause.

- Use a view in a SQL*Plus program command file.
- Use variables for interactive reporting.
- Display a date and page number in a title.
- Use the ACCEPT, PROMPT, and PAUSE commands for interactive program execution with substitution variables.
- Define user variables.
- Pass parameter values through the START command.
- Format aggregate function titles.
- Change column headings.

AN SQL*PLUS PROGRAM COMMAND FILE

Throughout this chapter, you will learn to create SQL*Plus reports interactively by entering commands at the SQL> prompt and by saving commands to SQL*Plus program command files. Interactive commands can be used to specify report headings, report footers, report titles, page numbers, and other common report features that managers tend to request. You will also learn to modify these features by reissuing the commands with new values. Unfortunately, if you exit SQL*Plus, all of the information about a report's features is lost unless you save your commands in a file. For this reason, we will also focus on creating files that will store SQL*Plus commands. We'll refer to this type of file as a SQL*Plus program command file, or simply a SQL program. The filename extension used for these files is *.sql*.

SQL Example 9.1 shows a sample SQL*Plus program command file. This SQL program will produce the report shown in Figures 9.1a and 9.1b. All of the data for the report is selected from the *assignment* table of the company database described in Appendix A.

The SQL program has numerous commands. We will examine each of these commands in order to learn their function in producing the report shown in Figures 9.1a and 9.1b. You will discover that the commands are quite simple to learn.

```
/* SQL Example 9.1 */
REM Program: ch9-1.sql
REM Programmer: dbock; 3-20-2003
REM Description: A program to list employee work history
REM on projects.

TTITLE 'Project Information'
BTITLE SKIP 1 CENTER 'Not for external dissemination.'
REPHEADER 'Project Report #1 — prepared by D. Bock' SKIP 2
REPFOOTER SKIP 3 '— Last Page of Report —'

SET LINESIZE 55
SET PAGESIZE 24
SET NEWPAGE 1

COLUMN "Emp. Soc. Sec. #" FORMAT A16
COLUMN "Hours Worked" FORMAT 999.99
```

```
Sun Apr 14                                               page 1
                    Project Information

Project Report #1 - prepared by D. Bock

Emp. Soc. Sec. #   Project #      Hours Worked
-----------------  ----------     ------------
999111111                   1            31.40
999111111                   2             8.50
999222222                  10            34.50
999222222                  30             5.10
999333333                   3            42.10
999444444                   1
999444444                   2            12.20
999444444                   3            10.50
999444444                  10            10.10
999444444                  20            11.80
999555555                  20            14.80
999555555                  30            19.20
999666666                  20
999777777                  10            10.20
            Not for external dissemination.
```

FIGURE 9.1a

```
SELECT work_emp_ssn "Emp. Soc. Sec. #",
    work_pro_number "Project #", work_hours "Hours Worked"
FROM assignment
ORDER BY work_emp_ssn, work_pro_number;
```

REMARKS

Optional remarks are typically entered at the beginning of a command file program identify the filename, programmer name, and date of program creation. A brief description of the program is also provided. You may also list modifications made by programmer name, date and description here. Remarks and blank lines are used throughout a program to enhance the understandability and readability of programming code.

TOP AND BOTTOM TITLES

Titles and footers on reports enhance the meaning of reports for managerial system users. Reports are rarely disseminated to managers without appropriate title and footers. SQL*Plus supports the programming of four types of titles and footers: (1) top title, (2) bottom title, (3) report header, and (4) report footer.

```
Sun Apr 14                                                 page 2
                        Project Information

Emp. Soc. Sec. #   Project #       Hours Worked
------------------ -----------     ---------------
999887777                   30             30.80
999888888                    1             21.00
999888888                    2             22.00




-- Last Page of Report --






                   Not for external dissemination.
```

FIGURE 9.1b

The TTITLE command (short for top title) prints a title on *each page* of a report. When a simple TTITLE command like the one shown below is used, the report will automatically display the report date and page number. You can see an example of this type of title in Figure 9.1a and 9.1b.

```
TTITLE 'Project Information'
```

You can also issue the TTITLE command interactively at the SQL> prompt. The first TTITLE command shown below will turn the report title off. The second one will change the report title interactively when followed by a slash (/) command.

```
TTITLE OFF
TTITLE 'Project and Employee Information'
/
```

The BTITLE command prints a bottom title with the specified information at the bottom of *each page* of a report. For example, your organization may want each page of a report marked as not for external dissemination as is shown in the BTITLE command here.

```
BTITLE SKIP 1 CENTER 'Not for external dissemination.'
```

The SKIP clause is optional. SKIP 1 will insert one blank line into the report. You can specify the number of lines to skip. If the SKIP option is specified prior to the bottom title, as is done above, then one line is skipped prior to printing the bottom title. The CENTER option centers the bottom title output. Additionally, as with the TTITLE command, you may elect to interactively turn off the bottom title with the OFF option shown here. Typing this command and then following it with a slash '/' at the SQL> prompt will produce a report without a bottom title line as is shown here.

```
BTITLE OFF
/
```

In addition to CENTER, you can also use the keywords RIGHT and LEFT within both the TTITLE and BTITLE commands to control the display of report information. An example multilined TTITLE command is shown below.

```
TTITLE LEFT date_var -
    RIGHT 'Page: ' FORMAT 99 sql.pno SKIP 1 -
    CENTER 'Project and Employee Information'
```

A dash (-) at the end of a line continues the TTITLE command. The *date_var* entry is a variable name that stores the date. When a complex TTITLE command is used, Oracle does not automatically print the date and page number information as was done earlier in Figure 1.a. You will learn how to store a date variable to a variable name toward the end of this chapter. Likewise, the *sql.pno* entry is a predefined SQL variable that can be used to display the current page number for a report. Here, the *sql.pno* value is formatted to display at the right margin of the top title line. The title 'Project and Employee Information' will be printed centered and one line below the date and page because the SKIP 1 clause after the page number specification will cause the report title to skip down one line.

REPORT HEADERS AND FOOTERS

A report header can be used to add meaningful information to the top of the *first page* of a report. You should use the REPHEADER command whenever you want information to be displayed on only the first page. The REPHEADER command shown below uses the SKIP 2 option to insert two blank lines immediately after the report header is printed. You'll also notice in Figure 9.1a that the report header prints after the top title line.

```
REPHEADER 'Project Report #1 — prepared by D. Bock' SKIP 2
```

Report footers add meaningful information to the bottom of the *last page* of a report. Sometimes it is useful to display a message such as "Last Page of Report" so that managers will know that they have the entire report available for their examination. In the command shown here, the SKIP 3 option provides for three skipped blank lines prior to printing the report footer. You will also note from Figure 9.1b that the report footer prints prior to the bottom title line.

```
REPFOOTER SKIP 3 '— Last Page of Report —'
```

The OFF option also applies to report headers and footers, and will turn the report header and/or footer off.

```
REPHEADER OFF
REPFOOTER OFF
```

SETTING THE LINE AND PAGE SIZE

The SET LINESIZE command specifies the size of an output line in characters. The report in Figures 9.1a and 9.1b have a line size of 55 characters, although a more typical size for a computer monitor or printed paper is 79 characters. You must vary the line size as a function of the font size—larger fonts allow for fewer characters per line. You can also enter this command interactively to vary the line size while experimenting with report formatting.

```
SET LINESIZE 55
```

Similarly, the SET PAGESIZE command specifies the number of lines to be printed per page. A typical setting is 50 to 55 lines of output per page for 10-point or 12-point printer fonts. The command shown below sets the page size to 50 lines.

```
SET PAGESIZE 50
```

The SET NEWPAGE command specifies the number of blank lines to print before the top title line of a report, that is, the line that displays the report date and page number. This is useful for aligning reports produced by various types of printers. The SET NEWPAGE command does not affect the PAGESIZE value. The command shown below specifies 6 blank lines at the top of *each page*. If the page size is set to 55, this will leave 49 lines for displaying output.

```
SET NEWPAGE 6
```

All of these commands can be entered interactively at the SQL> prompt and executed by following them with a slash (/), for example:

```
SET NEWPAGE 6
/
```

OUTPUT TO THE COMPUTER MONITOR SCREEN

When you are testing an SQL program that will produce a printed report, it is sometimes useful to specify values for the LINESIZE, PAGESIZE, and NEWPAGE values so that report output will fit on a computer monitor screen. This will enable you to view the report for accuracy before converting it for output to printed format and will save on paper waste. Typical values for screen output are shown below.

```
SET LINESIZE 79
SET PAGESIZE 24
SET NEWPAGE 0
```

Additionally, you will probably want the computer monitor screen output to pause between pages so that you can review the report. This can be accomplished by the SET PAUSE commands shown below. The first command specifies the prompt that you will see on the computer monitor screen. Here, the prompt will be "More . . ." The second command turns the PAUSE option on. After you have finished debugging your program, you can revise the settings for the LINESIZE, PAGESIZE, and NEWPAGE values and use the SET PAUSE OFF to remove output pauses.

```
SET PAUSE 'More . . .'
SET PAUSE ON
SET PAUSE OFF
```

SELECT STATEMENT

The information displayed in the detailed lines of a report is supplied by a SELECT statement. The SELECT statement for the report in Figure 9.1 extracts rows from the *assignment* table. Here, the SELECT statement also sorts the output rows by employee Social Security Number (SSN) (*work_emp_ssn*), then by project number (*work_ pro_number*).

```
SELECT work_emp_ssn, work_pro_number, work_hours
FROM assignment
ORDER BY work_emp_ssn, work_pro_number;
```

CONTROL BREAK REPORTS

Now that you have learned the basic concepts of the interactive SQL*Plus report writer, you are ready to develop more complex reports. Let's review the report shown in Figures 9.1a and 9.1b. Did you notice any information on the report that is unnecessarily repetitious? That's right, the SSN information for each employee repeats unnecessarily. The report can be improved by removing this redundant information. We'll do this by programming a *control break report.*

A control break report organizes information into meaningful groups. We will organize the new report into groups according to each employee's SSN. The modified program is shown in SQL Example 9.2. The additional lines of code required to produce the control break report are highlighted in bold text. Additionally, the decision was made to remove the report header and report footer.

```
/* SQL Example 9.2 */
REM Program: ch9-2.sql
REM Programmer: dbock; 3-20-2003
REM Description: A sample program control break report.

TTITLE 'Project Information'
BTITLE SKIP 1 CENTER 'Not for external dissemination.'

SET LINESIZE 55
SET PAGESIZE 24
SET NEWPAGE 1

COLUMN "Emp. Soc. Sec. #" FORMAT A16
COLUMN "Hours Worked" FORMAT 999.99
CLEAR BREAKS
BREAK ON "Emp. Soc. Sec. #" SKIP 2 ON REPORT
COMPUTE SUM OF "Hours Worked" ON "Emp. Soc. Sec. #"
COMPUTE SUM OF "Hours Worked" ON REPORT

SPOOL report9-2.1st

SELECT work_emp_ssn "Emp. Soc. Sec. #",
    work_pro_number "Project #", work_hours "Hours Worked"
FROM assignment
ORDER BY work_emp_ssn, work_pro_number;

SPOOL OFF
```

Figure 9.2a shows page 1 of the control break report. The report displays the date of preparation and page number at the top of the report automatically. The top title is unchanged from the program in SQL Example 9.1. The detailed information is similar to our earlier report; however, each employee's SSN is now displayed only once for each grouping on the report. Examine the groupings of information. The first grouping is for employee number "999111111." This employee worked 31.4 and 8.5 hours on projects 1 and 2, respectively. Subsequent groupings are shown for the other employees.

The control break program also produces subtotals showing the total hours worked (sum) for each employee on their assigned projects. Subtotals are often used by managers in support of decision-making activities. Employee "999111111" worked a total of 39.9 hours. We will now examine the commands that produced the control break groupings and accompanying hourly summation figures.

THE BREAK COMMAND

The BREAK command groups data rows for a control break report. The syntax of the BREAK command is:

```
BREAK ON (expression1, ON expression2, ... \row\page\report) ...
[SKIP n | [SKIP] PAGE]
[NODUPLICATES | DUPLICATES];
```

FIGURE 9.2a

```
Sun Apr 14                                                    page 1
                        Project Information

Project Report #1 - prepared by D. Bock

Emp. Soc. Sec. #  Project #    Hours Worked
-----------------  -----------  ---------------
999111111                  1            31.40
                           2             8.50
* * * * * * * * * * * * * *                ---------------
sum                                        39.90


999222222                 10            34.50
                          30             5.10
* * * * * * * * * * * * * *                ---------------
sum                                        39.60


999333333                  3            42.10
* * * * * * * * * * * * * *                ---------------

                Not for external dissemination.
```

The BREAK command can be used to break on an expression, row, page, report, or more than one of these at a time. The BREAK command used in SQL Example 9.2 is shown below.

```
CLEAR BREAKS
BREAK ON "Emp. Soc. Sec. #" SKIP 2 ON REPORT
```

The CLEAR BREAKS command clears any previously established breaks. The BREAK ON command specifies two breaks. The first break is on the alias column name, "Emp. Soc. Sec. #" defined in the SELECT statement given later in the program. Normally, if a break is desired on a column, you would specify the column name in the BREAK command. An example of a BREAK command for the *work_emp_ssn* column is shown below. However, when an alias column name is defined in an associated SELECT command, then the BREAK command must specify the alias column name.

```
BREAK ON work_emp_ssn SKIP 2 ON REPORT
```

The BREAK command works in conjunction with the ORDER BY clause of the SELECT statement. The ORDER BY clause in SQL Example 9.2 sorts output rows by *work_emp_ssn*, then by *work_pro_number.*

```
ORDER BY work_emp_ssn, work_pro_number;
```

This ensures that information on the report is sorted in a manner that will be most easily interpreted by managers. A control break would still occur without the ORDER BY clause; however, the detail output rows would be in *natural order* by their occurrence within the *assignment* table. For a large report, a natural order of presentation is generally not acceptable as managers could experience difficulty finding the desired information on the report without the sorting.

The ON REPORT clause of the BREAK command specifies that a break will also be enforced after all of the data rows from the *assignment* table have been processed. The location of the ON REPORT clause is not important within the BREAK command. When the clause is specified, the report will always issue a final break at the end of the report. This break enables you to produce a final total of hours worked by all employees. Keep this point in mind as we will discuss the production of subtotals and totals in more detail later in this section.

The order of expressions or column names in the BREAK command is critical. For example, suppose employees are assigned to sections, and sections are assigned to departments. This is a purely hierarchical relationship. If you need to produce a control break report listing employee names and counting employees by section within department, the BREAK command would look like the one shown below. The BREAK ON must be ordered from largest to smallest as is shown here.

```
BREAK ON department ON section ON emp_ssn
```

OUTPUT STYLE

The style of output shown in Figure 9.2a is called NODUPLICATES, or NODUP because each group value (employee SSN) is shown only once. This is the default BREAK output method so there is no need to specify it. While this form of output diverges from the relational, two-dimensional, matrix format, it is much easier for managers to read. The NODUP default can be overridden by specifying the keyword DUP with the BREAK command as is shown here. This will yield the purely relational, two-dimensional, matrix format for output.

```
BREAK ON "Emp. Soc. Sec. #" DUP SKIP 2
```

SKIP AND PAGE KEYWORDS

To enhance the readability of a report, one or more blank rows can be inserted after each SSN grouping. As we noted earlier, the SKIP keyword inserts the blank rows. Our program specified to skip two lines prior to beginning the next report group.

Replacing the keyword SKIP with PAGE will cause a *page eject* to occur after each grouping. This will produce a report with each SSN beginning on a new page. This will also cause each group to be preceded by new column headings. This is useful if you are distributing the results of a printed query to various managers and want everyone to receive only the information that is relevant to their needs.

THE COMPUTE COMMAND

Earlier we noted that Figure 9.2a shows subtotals for the hours worked by employee SSN. Appropriate totals and subtotals can improve the managerial value of a report. In addition to summing the hours worked by employee, the total hours worked by all employees are also be summed and displayed at the end of the report as a grand total.

In order for a COMPUTE command to compute subtotals and totals properly it must be used in conjunction with a BREAK command. If you have not specified a BREAK command, then a COMPUTE command will not produce any results! When used with BREAK, a COMPUTE command displays values that are computed for the BREAK expression. The syntax of the COMPUTE command is shown here.

```
COMPUTE {group function} OF {column_name | column_name_alias,
    . . .} ON {break_column_name | ROW | PAGE | REPORT};
```

The semicolon is not required when the command is entered into a program command file. The semicolon is required when the command is entered interactively at the SQL> prompt. Additionally, more than one column may be summed by using multiple COMPUTE commands. Examine the COMPUTE commands in SQL Example 9.2 along with the associated BREAK and SELECT statements shown below.

```
BREAK ON "Emp. Soc. Sec. #" SKIP 2 ON REPORT
COMPUTE SUM OF "Hours Worked" ON "Emp. Soc. Sec. #"
COMPUTE SUM OF "Hours Worked" ON REPORT

SELECT work_emp_ssn "Emp. Soc. Sec. #",
    work_pro_number "Project #", work_hours "Hours Worked"
FROM assignment
ORDER BY work_emp_ssn, work_pro_number;
```

Both of the COMPUTE commands use the SUM aggregate function. The first COMPUTE command sums on the "Hours Worked" alias column name. This is the alias name defined in the SELECT statement for the *work_hours* column. The "Hours Worked" is summed for each employee because the ON clause in the COMPUTE command specifies to use the "Emp. Soc. Sec. #" alias column name. This alias name is defined by the SELECT statement for the *work_emp_ssn* column. Note that this also matches the alias column name specified in the BREAK command.

The second COMPUTE command produces a report total of "Hours Worked" for all employees at the end of the report. This is accomplished by using the ON REPORT clause. Figure 9.2b displays the report total on the last page of output produced by program **ch9-2.sql,** a total of 284.2 hours worked.

You are not limited to using the SUM function in a COMPUTE command. You can also specify the other aggregate functions with this command. These functions are summarized in Table 9.1 for your reference. For example, if management wants a report to display the average hours worked instead of the sum, then the AVG aggregate function would be used with the COMPUTE command as shown below.

```
COMPUTE AVG OF "Hours Worked" ON REPORT
```

The output for the last page of the report based on this COMPUTE modification is displayed in Figure 9.2c.

THE SPOOL COMMAND

SPOOL is the last new command introduced in SQL Example 9.2. The SPOOL command routes the output from a SQL*Plus program to the specified filename. The SPOOL command shown below routes output to a file named **report9-2.lst.** The "lst" filename extension is short for listing; however, you can specify any filename extension that you desire. The SPOOL OFF command terminates writing to the output file.

```
SPOOL report9-2.lst
SPOOL OFF
```

FIGURE 9.2b

```
Sun Apr 14                                              page 4
                        Project Information

Emp. Soc. Sec. #  Project #      Hours Worked
-------------------  -----------    ---------------
sum                                       43.00


                                  ---------------
sum                                      284.20



-- Last Page of Report --




                    Not for external dissemination.
```

TABLE 9.1

Aggregate Function	Action Produced for the Specified Expression in the OF Clause
AVG	Computes and displays the average expression value
COUNT	Computes the total non-NULL expression values
MAXIMUM	Computes the maximum expression value
MINIMUM	Computes the minimum expression value
NUMBER	Computes the number of rows
STD	Computes the standard deviation of the expression value
SUM	Computes the sum or total of the expression value
VARIANCE	Computes the variance of the expression value

The placement of the SPOOL command in the program is important. The command to begin spooling is placed immediately before the SELECT statement. If you place the SPOOL command earlier in the program, the output file will contain the SQL*Plus responses to the earlier program commands as they execute. By placing SPOOL immediately before and SPOOL OFF immediately after the SELECT statement, the output file will contain only the desired report listing.

REVISITING THE BREAK AND COMPUTE COMMANDS

ADDITIONAL BREAK COMMAND DETAILS

The BREAK command in SQL Example 9.2 specifies a break on a column as well as on a report. You can also break on any kind of expression, on rows, and on pages. The BREAK ON ROW command can be used to change report spacing. The BREAK

FIGURE 9.2c

```
Sun Apr 14                                             page 4
                     Project Information

Emp. Soc. Sec. #   Project #      Hours Worked
------------------  ----------    --------------

                                  --------------
avg                                     18.95




                  Not for external dissemination.
```

command shown below will insert a blank line between each row of the *assignment* report.

```
BREAK ON ROW SKIP 1
```

A column break and a row break can be used together. In conjunction, these two breaks create a double-spaced report that is still separated by column values. The command shown here will produce a double-spaced report that also breaks at the end of the report.

```
BREAK ON "Emp. Soc. Sec. #" SKIP 1 ON REPORT ON ROW SKIP 1
```

VIEWING CURRENT **BREAK** AND **COMPUTE** COMMAND SETTINGS

Only one BREAK command can be active at a time. You can interactively replace the current BREAK command by typing a new command at the SQL> prompt. If you forget which BREAK command is active, simply type the command BREAK on a line by itself and SQL*Plus will display the break status. Note that the default for the BREAK command is no duplicates (NODUP).

```
BREAK
break on report nodup
          on Emp. Soc. Sec. # skip 2 nodup
```

Unlike BREAK, the COMPUTE command is cumulative. While you are testing a program, you may accumulate quite a number of COMPUTE settings. You can display the current settings by simply typing the COMPUTE command at the SQL> prompt.

```
COMPUTE
COMPUTE sum LABEL 'sum' OF Hours Worked ON Emp. Soc. Sec. #
COMPUTE sum LABEL 'sum' OF Hours Worked ON REPORT
```

Earlier we learned that the CLEAR BREAK command clears the current break settings. You can also clear COMPUTE settings by typing CLEAR COMPUTE at the SQL> prompt or by placing the command within a program. When the command is used interactively, Oracle will respond as shown below.

```
CLEAR COMPUTE
computes cleared
```

CREATING MASTER-DETAIL REPORTS

A master-detail report is a form of control-break report because the report presents information that is "grouped." However, the report typically displays data rows from more than one table. Consider the one-to-many relationship between the *department* and *project* tables for the company as described in Appendix A.

Each department controls numerous projects, and a project belongs to a single department. In this situation, the rows in the *department* table are "master" rows because the *department* table is on the "one" side of the one-to-many relationship. The associated *project* table rows provide the "detail" information. Managers often prefer to have information from multiple tables presented in either a control-break or master-detail report format.

```
                    Department Number:                 3

DPT_NAME                   PRO_NAME             PRO_LOCATION
------------------         ---------------      ---------------
Admin and Records          Inventory            Marina
Admin and Records          Pay Benefits         Marina




                    Not for external dissemination.
More . . .

                    Department Number:                 7

DPT_NAME                   PRO_NAME             PRO_LOCATION
------------------         ---------------      ---------------
Production                 Order Entry          St. Louis
Production                 Payroll              Collinsville
Production                 Receivables          Edwardsville



                    Not for external dissemination.
```

FIGURE 9.3

Program ch9-3.sql in SQL Example 9.3 produces a master-detail report for the *department–project* relationship. The report is shown in Figure 9.3. You need to study this program in detail in order to understand how the master-detail report is produced. The lines of code that you need to focus on are highlighted in bold text.

```
/* SQL Example 9.3 */
REM Program: ch9-3.sql
REM Programmer: dbock; Date: 3-20-2003
REM Description: A sample Master-Detail report

REM set page size, line size, new page spacing for screen display.
SET LINESIZE 65
SET PAGESIZE 12
SET NEWPAGE 1

REM define department variable
COLUMN pro_dept_number NEW_VALUE dept_number_var NOPRINT

REM set column sizes based on alias column names
COLUMN dpt_name FORMAT A18
COLUMN pro_name FORMAT A15
COLUMN pro_location FORMAT A15
```

```
TTITLE CENTER 'Department Number:' dept_number_var SKIP 2
BTITLE SKIP 1 CENTER 'Not for external dissemination.'

BREAK ON pro_dept_number SKIP PAGE

SELECT pro_dept_number, dpt_name, pro_name, pro_location
FROM department d, project p
WHERE d.dpt_no = p.pro_dept_number AND
    pro_dept_number IN (3, 7)
ORDER BY pro_dept_number;
```

Each master row in Figure 9.3 is printed on a single page along with the associated detail rows. The department number is printed in the top title line on each page of the report. This report lists projects controlled by departments 3 and 7; thus, the report has a total of two pages. We have set the page size at a small size so that both pages of the report can be displayed in a single figure. Also, the report was printed to the computer monitor screen.

This report would be easy to distribute to managers. The appropriate page could be forwarded to each manager for departments 3 and 7. Additionally, an entire copy of the report could be forwarded to the supervisor of the managers for these two departments.

A typical master-detail report format includes information in the top title report line that identifies the "master column" that controls the page breaks. You can reference a column value in a top title by first storing the column value to a *program variable*. You then specify the program variable name in the TTITLE command.

A special form of the COLUMN command is used to define a program variable as shown below. The actual COLUMN command from SQL Example 9.3 is also shown below. The NEW_VALUE clause defines the variable name. You must follow Oracle's naming rules when naming program variables. Here the variable is named *dept_number_var*. This variable will store the current value of the column named *pro_dept_number* from the *project* table. Additionally, the NOPRINT option tells Oracle not to display the *pro_dept_number* value as an output column of the SELECT statement.

```
COLUMN column_name NEW_VALUE variable_name [options]
COLUMN pro_dept_number NEW_VALUE dept_number_var NOPRINT
```

The TTITLE command shown below specifies a title with the literal string 'Department Number:' in the title. This literal is followed by the variable name, *dept_number_var* that was defined in the COLUMN command shown above. The TTITLE command also specifies to skip two lines after the top title for spacing purposes.

```
TTITLE CENTER 'Department Number: ' dept_number_var SKIP 2
```

The BREAK command used in the program must break on the master column for the report. Here, the master column is the department number column (*pro_dept_number*) from the *project* table, although the department number column (*dpt_no*) from the *department* table could also have been used.

```
BREAK ON pro_dept_number SKIP PAGE
```

The SELECT statement selects the columns from the master and detail tables for the report. In this program the department name column (*dpt_name*) from the *department* table is selected to provide additional report information because it will be easier for managers to reference a department by name rather than a department number. The ORDER BY clause also specifies the master column for the report.

```
SELECT pro_dept_number, dpt_name, pro_name, pro_location
FROM department d, project p
WHERE d.dpt_no = p.pro_dept_number AND
    pro_dept_number IN (3, 7)
ORDER BY pro_dept_number;
```

USING VIEWS IN MASTER-DETAIL REPORTS

The report does have some features that can be improved. First, the column headings shown in the report are not be very meaningful because the report uses column names from the tables as default headings. You can improve the report by specifying alias column names for some of the columns or by assigning column headings with a COLUMN command. This option for the COLUMN command is covered later in this chapter. If you use an alias column name for the master column that controls the report, you may experience output errors when the alias name is more than a single word, for example, "Project Number." The output errors occur because you cannot use a variable name in the COLUMN command's NEW_VALUE clause that has blank spaces in the name. The report could also be improved by displaying the department name in the top title line instead of the department number.

One way to overcome these problems is by using a predefined view of the tables in the program. You studied the creation and use of *views* in Chapter 8. SQL Example 9.4 is a revision of SQL Example 9.3 to include a view definition. The report produced by program ch9-4.sql is shown in Figure 9.4. Again, the lines of code that you need to focus on are highlighted in bold text.

```
/* SQL Example 9.4 */
REM Program: ch9-4.sql
REM Programmer: dbock; 3-20-2003
REM Description: The revised Master-Detail program with a View.

REM set page size, line size, new page for screen display.
SET LINESIZE 75;
SET PAGESIZE 12;
SET NEWPAGE 1;

REM Create a view to be used in the SELECT command later.
CREATE OR REPLACE VIEW project_department (project_no, dept_name,
        project_name, location) AS
    SELECT pro_dept_number, dpt_name, pro_name, pro_location
    FROM department d, project p
    WHERE d.dpt_no = p.pro_dept_number AND
        pro_dept_number IN (3, 7)
    ORDER BY pro_dept_number;
```

The PROMPT command can be used on a line by itself or in combination with the ACCEPT command. This also applies to the ACCEPT command, but it is most common to use the two commands together as was done above.

THE MULTILINE **TTITLE** COMMAND

The TTITLE command for program ch9-5.sql shown below has more than one defined line. The *date_var* created earlier is displayed at the left margin of the first top title line. The report name along with the value stored to the project name variable, *pro_name_var,* is displayed centered on the first top title line. Additionally, the page number is formatted and displayed at the right margin of the first top title line. A line is then skipped and the "Project Number:" literal along with the value stored to the project number variable, *pro_number_var,* is displayed centered on the second top title line. Two lines are skipped following the second top title line.

```
TTITLE LEFT date_var CENTER 'Project Name: ' pro_name_var -
       RIGHT 'Page:' FORMAT 999 sql.pno SKIP 1 -
       CENTER 'Project Number:' pro_number_var SKIP 2
```

FORMATTING THE EMPLOYEE SOCIAL SECURITY NUMBER

The employee SSN (*work_emp_ssn*) stored in the *assignment* table, is formatted for display by using a SUBSTR function. The format of the SUBSTR function is shown here and is covered in more detail in Chapter 10.

```
SUBSTR( {character_column | character_string}, start position,
        number of characters)
```

Study the expression shown below. The first SUBSTR function extracts the first three numbers from the employee social security number character string beginning in character position 1. The concatenation operator (||) appends these three numbers to a dash (-) symbol. Another concatenation operator appends these characters to a second SUBSTR function. The second SUBSTR function extracts the next two numbers of the SSN. Another concatenation operator appends another dash, and then the third SUBSTR extracts the last four digits of the social security number. An alias column name of "SSN" is assigned to this expression for use in the COLUMN command that formats the expression as A12. The result is a much nicer formatted display of social security numbers than was used in previous reports.

```
SUBSTR(work_emp_ssn,1,3)||'-'||SUBSTR(work_emp_ssn,4,2)||
'-'||SUBSTR(work_emp_ssn,6,4) "SSN",

COLUMN "SSN" FORMAT A12
```

USING A SUBSTITUTION VARIABLE IN A **WHERE** CLAUSE

The WHERE clause of the SELECT statement in program ch9-5.sql joins four tables: *project, assignment, department,* and *employee.* Additionally, the WHERE clause specifies a criteria for row selection based on values stored in the project number column (*pro_number*) of the *project* table. The value stored to the *project_no_var* that was accepted by the ACCEPT command is used to specify the row selection criteria. Note the use of the ampersand (&) operator. At execution time, the ampersand causes the value stored to the *project_no_var* to be substituted in place of the variable name.

The WHERE clause compares the *pro_number* column of the *project* table to the numeric value stored to the *project_no_var* variable. If you write a WHERE clause that compares a character column to a character value, then the variable name and ampersand operator should be entered within single quote marks.

```
WHERE p.pro_number = a.work_pro_number AND
    a.work_emp_ssn = e.emp_ssn AND
    d.dpt_no = p.pro_dept_number AND
    p.pro_number = &project_no_var
```

ADDITIONAL SQL*PLUS FEATURES

DEFINING USER VARIABLES

SQL*Plus allows interactive report generation and modification. One way to modify a report is by defining additional *program* or *user variables*. In addition to using the NEW_VALUE clause of the COLUMN command, you can also define variables with the SQL*Plus DEFINE command. This command as shown in SQL Example 9.6 defines a variable *name_var*, and assigns it the value "Bordoloi."

```
/* SQL Example 9.6 */
REM Program: ch9-6.sql
DEFINE name_var = Bordoloi
SELECT emp_last_name, emp_first_name, emp_date_of_birth
FROM employee
WHERE emp_last_name = '&name_var'
/

EMP_LAST_NAME       EMP_FIRST_NAME      EMP_DATE_
------------        --------------      --------
Bordoloi            Bijoy               10-NOV-67
```

If you need to know what variables have been defined for your working session, enter the DEFINE command by itself at the SQL> prompt and all current variable definitions will be displayed. You can also delete a variable with the UNDEFINE <variable_name> command.

PASSING PARAMETER VALUES THROUGH THE START COMMAND

You can pass a value to a program at run time as a parameter of the START command. Instead of using a substitution variable as was done in SQL Example 9.5, use an ampersand **(&)** followed by a numeral in the command file; for example, **&1** in place of the substitution variable. Each time you run the command file, the START command replaces the **&1** parameter in the file with the first value (called an argument) listed after a START *filename* command. You can use as many ampersand-parameter variables as is needed in the program. The arguments of the START command are separated by commas. Assume the SELECT statement in SQL Example 9.7 is stored to a command file named **ch9-7.sql.**

```
/* SQL Example 9.7 - Example passing arguments */
REM Program: ch9-7.sql
SELECT emp_last_name, emp_ssn, emp_dpt_number
FROM employee
WHERE emp_last_name = '&1' OR emp_dpt_number = '&2';
REM end of program
```

The program is executed with the START command and two parameter values 'Bock' and '1' are entered where 'Bock' is substituted for the employee last name parameter of &1, and the numeral '1' is substituted for the employee department number parameter of &2. The output is shown here. Can you determine why the two rows were listed in the result table?

```
SQL> start ch9-7.sql Bock 1
old 3: WHERE emp_last_name = '&1' OR emp_dpt_number = '&2'
new 3: WHERE emp_last_name = 'Bock' OR emp_dpt_number = '1'
More . . .

EMP_LAST_NAME     EMP_SSN        EMP_DPT_NUMBER
-----------       --------       -------------
Bordoloi          999666666                  1
Bock              999111111                  7
```

CLEARING THE COMPUTER MONITOR SCREEN

If you need to clear the computer monitor screen before displaying a report (or at any other time), include the CLEAR command with its SCREEN clause at the appropriate point in your command file, using the format shown here.

```
CLEAR SCREEN
```

FORMATTING AGGREGATE FUNCTION TITLES

Recall our use of the COMPUTE command to compute the sum of a column. The COMPUTE command produces a standard title of 'sum' as a label for the column that is aggregated. This also applies to the other aggregate functions; each function has its own standard title. Managers may not find the standard function title to be sufficiently meaningful. SQL*Plus allows you to change the aggregate function title to a more meaningful title. The COMPUTE commands shown below revise those used earlier in SQL Example 9.2 (run program ch9-2a.sql). Each employee's sum of total hours worked is labeled as 'Employee Hours,' and the report sum of total hours is labeled as 'Total Hours.' Figure 9.6 gives pages #1 and #4 of the report produced.

```
COMPUTE SUM LABEL 'Employee Hours' OF "Hours Worked"
    ON "Emp. Soc. Sec. #"
COMPUTE SUM LABEL 'Total Hours' OF "Hours Worked" ON REPORT
```

CHANGING COLUMN HEADINGS

When displaying column headings, you can either use the default heading which is the column name, or you can change the heading with the COLUMN command. Earlier,

FIGURE 9.6

```
Sun Apr 14                                              page 1
                        Project Information

Emp. Soc. Sec. #  Project #      Hours Worked
------------------ -----------    ---------------
999111111                  1            31.40
                           2             8.50
* * * * * * * * * * * * * * *                 ---------------
Employee Hours                           39.90


999222222                 10            34.50
                          30             5.10
* * * * * * * * * * * * * * *                 ---------------
Employee Hours                           39.60


999333333                  3            42.10
* * * * * * * * * * * * * * *                 ---------------
Employee Hours                           42.10


              Not for external dissemination.
--------------pages 2 and 3 would be printed here------------

Sun Apr 14                                              page 4
                        Project Information

Emp. Soc. Sec. #  Project #      Hours Worked
------------------ -----------    ---------------

                                   ---------------
Total Hours                             284.20




              Not for external dissemination.
```

we used alias column names to replace column headings. The COLUMN command's HEADING clause can be used to assign meaningful column headings. Two examples are shown below. If the new heading is a single word, the heading can be typed as is done for the *emp_ssn* column heading of SSN. If the heading is more than one word, the heading must be enclosed in single or double-quotes as is shown for the *emp_last_name* heading of "Last Name." If you want to display a column heading on more than one line, use a vertical bar (|) where you want to begin a new line as is done for the *emp_first_name* column.

```
COLUMN emp_ssn HEADING SSN;
COLUMN emp_last_name HEADING "Last Name";
COLUMN emp_first_name HEADING "First|Name";
```

The new headings will remain in effect until you enter different headings, reset each column's format, or exit SQL*Plus.

SUMMARY

The formatting possibilities that SQL*Plus provides are almost endless. The topics introduced throughout this chapter are meant to provide a brief introduction to report formation and data formatting. After working through this chapter and the chapter review you should feel comfortable creating simple reports with Oracle.

REVIEW EXERCISES

LEARN THESE TERMS

ACCEPT. An interactive command used to store values from the keyboard to program variables.

BREAK. A command that groups data rows for a control break report. Enables breaks on an expression, row, page, report, or more than one of these at a time.

BTITLE. A command is used to print a bottom title or footer on each page of a report.

CENTER. A report option for titles to center output. Associated with the LEFT and RIGHT options that justify output at either the left or right margins, respectively.

CLEAR BREAKS. Clears any previously established breaks.

CLEAR SCREEN. A command to clear the computer monitor screen before displaying a report.

COLUMN...NEW_VALUE. A special form of the COLUMN command used to define a program variable.

COMPUTE. A command used to produce subtotals and totals (or other aggregate function results) when used in conjunction with the BREAK command.

Control break report. Organizes information into meaningful groups.

DEFINE. A command used to define program or user variables for an interactive programming session. Use the UNDEFINE command to delete a variable.

Dual. A pseudo-table in an Oracle database that is used to store system information.

HEADING. A clause of the COLUMN command used to assign a meaningful column heading to an output column of data.

Interactive report writer. The capability of SQL*Plus to generate reports and to issue report formatting commands at the SQL> prompt.

LABEL. An option of the COMPUTE command used to label the output values produced by an aggregate function.

LINESIZE. Used with a SET command to specify the size of an output line in characters for a report.

Master-Detail report. A form of control break report that typically displays data rows from more than one table.

NEWPAGE. Used with a SET command to specify the number of blank lines to print before the top title line of a report.

NODUP. Short for NONDUPLICATES which is the default BREAK output method.

NOPRINT. An option used with the COLUMN command that tells Oracle not to display a value as output for a SELECT statement.

OFF. An interactive option for several commands used to turn the command off during program execution.

PAGESIZE. Used with a SET command to specify the number of lines to be printed on a report page.

Parameter (or argument).   A value passed to a program at run time. Used in a program in place of substitution variables.

PAUSE.   Used with a SET command to pause output that is displayed to a computer monitor screen.

Program variable.   Used to store values manipulated in a SQL*Plus program, for example, by specifying a value in a TTITLE command.

PROMPT.   A command used to display a prompt to the computer monitor screen so that a system user knows that the system requires input from the system user for report preparation.

Remarks.   Comments entered at the beginning of a command file identify the filename, programmer name, and date of program creation, or that are used to document the use of commands throughout a program.

REPHEADER.   A command used to display information at the top of the first page of a report.

REPFOOTER.   A command used to display information at the bottom of the last page of a report.

SKIP.   An optional clause used to insert one or more blank lines into the report.

SPOOL.   A command used to route output from a program to an output file. The OFF option terminates writing to the output file.

Sql.pno.   A predefined SQL variable that can be used to display the current page number for a report.

Substitution variable.   A variable used to substitute values into a SQL*Plus command at the time of program execution.

SUBSTR.   A function used to extract a substring of characters from a string of characters.

TTITLE.   A command used to print a title to each page of a report.

CONCEPTS QUIZ

1. Why would you save SQL*Plus report commands to a program command file?
2. What is the purpose of using remarks in a command file?
3. What is the purpose of report titles and footers?
4. Complete this sentence: The BTITLE command is used to print the specified information at the _____ of _____ _____ of a report.
5. When you specify the SKIP clause in a report command, what effect does this have?
6. What keywords are used to control where output is displayed on a title or footer line?
7. What is *sql.pno?*
8. Complete this sentence: A report header can be used to add meaningful information to the _____ of the _____ _____ of a report.
9. Which command specifies the size of an output line in characters? Of the number of lines on a page?
10. What type of report organizes information into meaningful groups?
11. What two commands are used together to produce control break information and summary information?
12. How many BREAK commands can be in effect at a time? How many COMPUTE commands can be in effect at a time?
13. Which clause is used to cause a break after all of the data rows have been processed?
14. If management wants a report to display the average hours worked for a report about employee work history instead of a sum, which aggregate function would be used with the COMPUTE command as shown below.
15. Complete this sentence: The _____ command routes the output from an SQL*Plus program to the filename specified in the command.
16. If you want an output listing file to contain only the desired report listing, where do you place the SPOOL <filename> and SPOOL OFF commands?

17. How can you display current BREAK and COMPUTE command settings?
18. What differentiates a control break report from a master-detail report?
19. You wish to produce a report listing a department number as a variable in the top title line of a report. How do you accomplish this? What command and clause is used to define the program variable?
20. When producing a master-detail report, which column does a BREAK command break on?
21. What is the name of the pseudo-table that stores system information such as the system date?
22. What two commands are used together to store values entered from the keyboard by a system user during program execution?
23. How is a substitution variable typically used in an SQL*Plus program?
24. What is the operator that is used with a substitution variable and what effect does it have on program execution?
25. If you wish to create a variable not associated with a column where the variable will store a value that can be used as part of a condition in a WHERE clause, which command is used?
26. Complete this sentence: You can pass a value to a program at run time as a _____ of the _____ command.
27. Which option of a COMPUTE command is used to produce a meaningful aggregate function title for report display?
28. What is the alternative to defining alias column names to display meaningful headings at the top of columns of output?

SQL CODING EXERCISES AND QUESTIONS

1. Write a SQL*Plus program to produce a report that lists dependents of employees. Your report should look like the one shown in Figure 9.7. Your report needs to have the following characteristics:

   - Display the values shown in both top title and bottom title lines including date and page number.
   - Assign meaningful column names as shown.
   - Display detail line data from the *dependent* table of the company database.
   - Order the detail lines by the *dep_emp_ssn* column.

2. Modify the program for question 1 to produce a control break report like the one shown in Figure 9.8. Your report needs to have the following additional characteristics:

   - Display each employee SSN only once for each group of dependents belonging to each employee.
   - Use the COUNT aggregate function to count the number of dependents and display this count at the end of the report.

3. Write an SQL*Plus program that will use a view named *employee_dependent*. This view should include the following columns from the *employee* and *dependent* tables specified in Table 9.1 below. The program will produce a master-detail report like the one shown in Figure 9.9. Your report needs to have the following characteristics:

```
Sun Apr 14                                                  page 1
                      Dependent Information

Emp SSN        Dependent      Gender    Date Birth    Relationship
-----------    -----------    --------  -----------   ---------------
999111111      Deanna         F         31-DEC-78     DAUGHTER
999111111      Jeffery        M         01-JAN-78     SON
999111111      Mary Ellen     F         05-MAY-57     SPOUSE
999444444      Andrew         M         25-OCT-98     SON
999444444      Jo Ellen       F         05-APR-96     DAUGHTER
999444444      Susan          F         03-MAY-75     SPOUSE
999555555      Allen          M         29-FEB-68     SPOUSE


                Not for external dissemination.
```

FIGURE 9.7

- List each employee's name at the top of a new report page with a page number.
- Break on the employee's SSN value.
- Display the number of dependents per employee as a subtotal with the subtotal label shown in the figure.

FIGURE 9.8

```
Sun Apr 14                                                  page 1
                      Dependent Information

SSN            Dependent      Gender    Date Birth    Relationship
-----------    -----------    --------  -----------   ---------------
999111111      Deanna         F         31-DEC-78     DAUGHTER
               Jeffery        M         01-JAN-78     SON
               Mary Ellen     F         05-MAY-57     SPOUSE

999444444      Andrew         M         25-OCT-98     SON
               Jo Ellen       F         05-APR-96     DAUGHTER
               Susan          F         03-MAY-75     SPOUSE

999555555      Allen          M         29-FEB-68     SPOUSE
-----------
          7


                Not for external dissemination.
```

TABLE 9.1

—Employee.emp_ssn

—Employee Name—defined as a concatenated column that includes the Employee.emp_last_name and Employee.emp_first_name columns.

—Dependent.dep_name

—Dependent.dep_gender

—Dependent.dep_relationship

FIGURE 9.9

```
              Employee Name: Bock, Douglas          Page: 1

  SSN              DEPENDENT_NAME     GENDER     RELATIONSHIP
  ----------       ----------------   --------   --------------
  999111111        Jeffery            M          SON
                   Deanna             F          DAUGHTER
                   Mary Ellen         F          SPOUSE
  * * * * * * * *                                --------------
  No Dep                                                     3


              Not for external dissemination.



              Employee Name: Zhu, Waiman           Page: 2

  SSN              DEPENDENT_NAME     GENDER     RELATIONSHIP
  ----------       ----------------   --------   --------------
  999444444        Jo Ellen           F          DAUGHTER
                   Andrew             M          SON
                   Susan              F          SPOUSE
  * * * * * * * *                                --------------
  No Dep                                                     3


              Not for external dissemination.



              Employee Name: Joyner, Suzanne       Page: 3

  SSN              DEPENDENT_NAME     GENDER     RELATIONSHIP
  ----------       ----------------   --------   --------------
  999555555        Allen              M          SPOUSE
  * * * * * * * *                                --------------
  No Dep                                                     1


              Not for external dissemination.
```

```
04/14/02            Employee Name: Bock, Douglas       Page: 1

SSN                DEPENDENT_NAME    GENDER    RELATIONSHIP
--------------     -----------------  --------  ---------------
999-11-1111        Jeffery            M         SON
                   Deanna             F         DAUGHTER
                   Mary Ellen         F         SPOUSE
* * * * * * * *                                 ---------------
No Dep                                                    3




                   Not for external dissemination.
```

FIGURE 9.10

4. Alter the program you wrote for question 3 to display the employee SSN formatted with dashes (-) in the appropriate location. *Hint:* This can be accomplished by altering the view definition. A sample page from the report is shown in Figure 9.10.

5. Alter the program for question 3 to include a top title for each page that is two separate lines. The first top title line will display the date at the left margin and page number at the right margin. The second top title line will display the employee name prompt and actual employee name.

6. Alter the program for question 3 to use the ACCEPT and PROMPT commands to ask the system user to enter a value for the employee SSN. The new report should print a single page like that shown in Figure 9.10 where the detail lines listing dependent and employee information is listed only for the employee matching the SSN entered at the prompt. Additionally, you are to remove the view definition from the program and produce the detail lines by specifying the output through use of a SELECT statement (do not use the previously defined view). You may optionally include the use of two separate top title lines with the information specified in question 5.

7. Alter the program you wrote for question 6 to use parameter values such that the program will execute by specifying the employee SSN as a parameter of the START command.

10

ADDITIONAL FUNCTIONS

Earlier you learned to use numeric, aggregate functions such as AVG and MAX. Oracle has many additional functions that can add power to your queries. Most of these can be classified as string, number, and date functions. This chapter introduces you to a selected subset of the Oracle functions used most often by programmers.

OBJECTIVES

Character functions allow you to manipulate a string of characters where the string can include letters, numbers, and special characters. Number functions, as the name implies, manipulate values stored in tables defined as NUMBER columns. Date functions manipulate data stored in DATE columns of tables. Remember, a DATE column stores both date and time information so date functions also enable you to manipulate the time values stored in these columns. You will also study functions that convert values from one datatype to another, such as character data to date. Additionally, the DECODE function is a form of If-Then-Else function that enables value-by-value substitutions of data stored in table columns. Your learning objectives are:

- Use character functions to manipulate CHAR type data.
- Use number functions to manipulate NUMBER type data.
- Use date functions to manipulate DATE type data.
- Use the DECODE function to complete value substitutions.

GENERAL NOTATION

Functions will be formally defined by using the general notation shown below.

```
FUNCTION (value, [option])
```

The function name will be given in capital letters. The word *value* is a placeholder that may be filled by either a string of characters enclosed in single-quote marks, or a column name. As was the case with aggregate functions, each function has a single set of parentheses, and all values and options are enclosed by these parentheses. The optional clauses will vary among the different functions.

CHARACTER (STRING) FUNCTIONS

Quite simply, a character string refers to a group of characters where the characters can be alphabetic letters, numbers, spaces, and special characters. Examples of character string values are shown in Table 10.1.

Did you notice that numeric values are treated as character strings if they are not manipulated mathematically? For example, you would never add two telephone numbers together, nor would you subtract two product numbers; therefore, telephone numbers and product numbers are actually character strings—not numbers. Table 10.2 summarizes the character functions that you will examine in this section.

UPPER, LOWER, AND INITCAP FUNCTIONS

The UPPER, LOWER, and INITCAP functions can alter the appearance of information displayed in a result table. The UPPER function will convert data stored in a character column to upper case letters. The LOWER function, on the other hand, converts data stored in a character column to lower case letters. The INITCAP function will capitalize the first letter of a string of characters. The general form of these functions is:

```
LOWER(char_value)

UPPER(char_value)

INITCAP(char_value)
```

The query in SQL Example 10.1 selects data from the *employee* table. The *emp_gender* column stores a single-character coded value of "M" for male or "F" for female, and these values are stored in capitalized format. The first expression in the SELECT clause uses the LOWER function to display these coded values in lower case. The second expression in the SELECT clause uses the UPPER function to display employee last names as all capital letters. Each employee's state of residence is stored as a two-character abbreviation, such as "CA" for California and "NY" for New York. If it is desirable to display these values with only the first letter capitalized, the LOWER function can first return the lowercase equivalents of these two-character abbreviations. By nesting the LOWER function inside the INITCAP function, these lowercase equivalents will be displayed with just the first letter capitalized.

TABLE 10.1	
Type of Data to Be Stored	*Example Values*
Customer street address	100 South Main Street
Customer telephone number	(618) 555-1212
Customer name	Bijoy Bordoloi or Douglas Bock
Social Security number	999-99-9999
Product number	13496

TABLE 10.2	
FUNCTION	**Use/Definition**
INITCAP	Capitalizes the first letter of a string of characters
INSTR	Searches a character string for a character string subset and returns the start position and/or occurrence of the substring
LENGTH	Returns a numeric value equivalent to the number of characters in a string of characters
LOWER	Returns a character value that is all lower case
LTRIM	Trims specified characters from the left end of a string
RTRIM	Trims specified characters from the right end of a string
SUBSTR	Returns a string of specified *length* from a larger character string beginning at a specified character *position*
UPPER	Returns a character value that is all uppercase

```
/* SQL Example 10.1 */
COLUMN "Gender" FORMAT A6;
COLUMN "Last Name" FORMAT A15;
COLUMN "State 1" FORMAT A7;
COLUMN "State 2" FORMAT A7;
SELECT LOWER(emp_gender) "Gender",
    UPPER(emp_last_name) "Last Name",
    emp_state "State 1", INITCAP(LOWER(emp_state)) "State 2"
FROM employee;

Gender     Last Name     State 1     State 2
------     ---------     -------     -------
m          BORDOLOI      IL          Il
f          JOYNER        CA          Ca
m          ZHU           MO          Mo
more rows will be displayed...
```

LENGTH Function

The general form of the LENGTH function is:

```
LENGTH(char_value)
```

This function returns a numeric value equivalent to the number of characters comprised by the specified *char_value*. This function is usually used in conjunction with other functions for tasks such as determining how much space needs to be allocated for a column of output on a report. We have seen that Oracle stores character string data using the CHAR or VARCHAR2 datatypes. CHAR columns are fixed-length and Oracle blank-pads, that is, add blanks to character strings that do not completely fill a CHAR column. VARCHAR2 columns are variable length. Thus, the column datatype can affect the value returned by the LENGTH function.

The SELECT statement in SQL Example 10.2 produces a result table listing the cities where employees of the company reside. It also specifies the numeric length of each city name. Note that blank characters count as part of the length.

Additionally, since the *emp_city* column is defined as VARCHAR2, the field is not blank-padded.

```
/* SQL Example 10.2 */
COLUMN "City" FORMAT A15;
COLUMN "Length" FORMAT 999999;
SELECT DISTINCT emp_city "City", LENGTH(emp_city) "Length"
FROM employee;

City            Length
----------      -----
Collinsville        12
Edwardsville        12
Marina               6
Monterey             8
St. Louis            9
```

SUBSTR FUNCTION AND CONCATENATION

The SUBSTR function is a very powerful function that can extract a substring from a string of characters. The general format of the function is:

```
SUBSTR(char_value, start_position [, number_of_characters])
```

The SELECT statement in SQL Example 10.3 extracts the last four digits of each employee's Social Security number (SSN) for display in a result table for department 3.

```
/* SQL Example 10.3 */
COLUMN "Last Name" FORMAT A15;
COLUMN "First Name" FORMAT A15;
COLUMN "Last 4 SSN" FORMAT A10;
SELECT emp_last_name "Last Name", emp_first_name "First Name",
    SUBSTR(emp_ssn,6,4) "Last 4 SSN"
FROM employee
WHERE emp_dpt_number = 3;

Last Name       First Name      Last 4 SSN
--------        ---------       ---------
Joyner          Suzanne         5555
Markis          Marcia          7777
Amin            Hyder           2222
```

The SUBSTR function can be combined with the *concatenation operator* (| |). The concatenation operator in SQL is two vertical lines. This enables you to concatenate substrings in order to achieve special formatted output. Recall that employee SSNs (*emp_ssn*) are stored without the normal dashes used when displaying these values. SQL Example 10.4 demonstrates formatting of employee SSNs in the result table. The concatenation operator is also used to format each employee name (last and first name) for display as a single column.

```
/* SQL Example 10.4 */
COLUMN "Employee Name" FORMAT A30;
COLUMN "SSN" FORMAT A12;
SELECT emp_last_name||', '||emp_first_name "Employee Name",
    SUBSTR(emp_ssn,1,3)||'-'||SUBSTR(emp_ssn,4,2)||'-'||
    SUBSTR(emp_ssn,6,4) "SSN"
FROM employee
WHERE emp_dpt_number = 3;

Employee Name            SSN
-------------            ----------
Joyner, Suzanne          999-55-5555
Markis, Marcia           999-88-7777
Amin, Hyder              999-22-2222
```

The SELECT clause concatenates each employee last name with a comma and blank space ', '. This is, in turn, concatenated to the employee first name. The SSN is formatted by using the first SUBSTR function to extract the first three numbers from the employee SSN character string beginning in character position 1. The concatenation operator appends these three numbers to a dash (-) symbol. Another concatenation operator appends a second SUBSTR function that extracts the next two numbers of the SSN. Another set of concatenation operators append another dash, and then the third SUBSTR extracts the last four digits of the SSN. An alias column name of "SSN" is assigned to this expression for use in the COLUMN command that formats the expression as A12. You'll also note that this particular expression is quite long. SQL allows you to break the expression to start a new line—a convenient break point is right before or after the use of a concatenation operator.

LTRIM AND RTRIM FUNCTIONS

The LTRIM and RTRIM functions trim characters from the left and right ends of strings, respectively. If no *character_set* to be trimmed is specified, then the functions trim blank spaces from the *char_value*. The format for each of these functions is:

```
RTRIM(char_value [,'character_set'])
LTRIM(char_value [,'character_set'])
```

Suppose that a data table has a fixed-length column defined as CHAR(20), and that this column stores values that actually vary in length, such as the names of the month in a year. Further, suppose that there is a need to compute the length of each value stored in this column. Since CHAR data fields are automatically blank-padded when values are not sufficiently large to fill up all of the column space, the LENGTH function would return a length of 20 for each column value! However, you can combine the RTRIM function with the LENGTH function to return a true length of the values stored in the column.

Let's test this by creating a table named *month_table,* and by inserting three rows of data into the table as exemplified by the sequence of commands in SQL Example 10.5.

```
/* SQL Example 10.5 */
CREATE TABLE month_table (
month_name      CHAR(20));

INSERT INTO month_table VALUES ('January');
INSERT INTO month_table VALUES ('February');
INSERT INTO month_table VALUES ('March');
```

Now, the SELECT statement in SQL Example 10.6 displays the month names, length of the untrimmed month names, and length of the trimmed month names. The RTRIM function is enclosed in the LENGTH function to produce the third output column.

```
/* SQL Example 10.6 */
SELECT month_name "Month", LENGTH(month_name) "Untrimmed",
   LENGTH(RTRIM(month_name)) "Trimmed"
FROM month_table;

Month          Untrimmed      Trimmed
-------        ---------      ------
January             20             7
February            20             8
March               20             5
```

You can also use the LTRIM and RTRIM functions to trim unwanted characters from column values. For example, if some data values stored in the *emp_address* column of the *employee* table have been stored with a period at the end of the address, it may be desirable to trim this period prior to displaying a result set. The expression to trim the period from the right end of the column values is shown below. Notice that the character string to be trimmed is given inside single quote marks.

```
RTRIM(emp_address,'.')
```

INSTR Function

The INSTR function is used to search a character string for a character substring. The general format is:

```
INSTR(char_string, sub_string [, start_position [, occurrence]])
```

The INSTR function returns a numeric value specifying the position within the *char_string* where the substring begins. By default, the search for the substring begins at character position 1; however, you can specify a different start position to begin the search. Optionally, you can specify a search that finds substrings that occur more than once in a string. By specifying a numeric value for *occurrence,* such as 2, you can return the numeric value specifying where the second occurrence of a substring begins.

Suppose that you need to know if any employee lives at a street address that includes the word 'Oak'. The SELECT statement in SQL Example 10.7 produces a result table listing employee addresses and the position where the word 'Oak' begins within the address. When the *Position* column (the second column) displays zero this means that the address does not contain the word 'Oak'.

```
/* SQL Example 10.7 */
COLUMN "Address" FORMAT A20;
COLUMN "Position" FORMAT 99999999;
SELECT emp_address "Address", INSTR(emp_address,'Oak') "Position"
FROM employee;

Address              Position
---------------      -------
South Main #12              0
202 Burns Farm             0
303 Lindbergh              0
High St. #14               0
S. Seaside Apt. B          0
#2 Mont Verd Dr.           0
#10 Oak St.                5
Overton Way #4             0
```

Now the above query works, but managers are more likely to want a listing that is restricted to just employees with the word 'Oak' in the street address. We can use the INSTR function in the WHERE clause of a SELECT statement as shown in SQL Example 10.8 to produce the desired result table where the value returned by the INSTR clause is not equal to zero.

```
/* SQL Example 10.8 */
COLUMN "Address" FORMAT A20;
SELECT emp_last_name "Last Name", emp_address "Address"
FROM employee
WHERE INSTR(emp_address,'Oak') != 0;

Last Name     Address
--------      ---------
Joshi         #10 Oak St.
```

NUMBER FUNCTIONS

Oracle has a large number of functions for manipulating columns that store NUMBER data. We studied the aggregate functions used to manipulate NUMBER data earlier in the text in Chapter 5. Here, we will focus our learning on two additional types of numeric functions—those that act on single values and those that act on lists of values.

SINGLE-VALUE FUNCTIONS

You'll find that the single-value functions are really quite simple. These functions can be combined with the arithmetic operator symbols (+ - * /) to develop complex expressions for display in result tables. Numeric functions accept numeric arguments, such as expressions or column names defined as datatype NUMBER, and return numeric values. The values returned are generally accurate to 38 decimal digits. Table 10.3 lists most of the single-value numeric functions and their use/definition. We will examine several of these functions in detail.

TRANSCENDENTAL FUNCTIONS

The transcendental functions include ACOS, ASIN, ATAN, ATAN2, COS, COSH, EXP, LN, LOG, SIN, SINH, TAN, and TANH. Business programming rarely requires

TABLE 10.3

Function	Use/Definition
ABS	The absolute value of a number. ABS(–5) returns 5
ACOS	The arc cosine of a number. Arguments must be between –1 and 1 and the returned value ranges from 0 to *pi* in radians. ACOS(0.5) = 1.047
ASIN	The arc sine of a number. Arguments must be between –1 and 1 and the returned value ranges from *pi*/2 to *pi*/2 in radians. ASIN(0.5) = 0.534
ATAN	The arc tangent of a number. Arguments are unbounded and the returned value ranges from –*pi*/2 to *pi*/2 in radians. ATAN(0.5) = 0.464
ATAN2	The arc tangent of two related numbers. Arguments are unbounded and the returned value ranges from –*pi* to *pi*. ATAN2(0.5, 5.0) = 0.0997
CEIL	The smallest integer value that is greater than a number. CEIL(6.6) = 7
COS	The cosine of a number expressed in radians. COS(0.5) = 0.8776
COSH	The hyperbolic cosine of a number. COSH(0.5) = 1.128
EXP	The value of the mathematical constant 'e' raised to the nth power. EXP(1) = 2.718
FLOOR	The largest integer value that is less than or equal to a number. FLOOR(6.7) = 6
LN	The natural logarithm of a number where the number is greater than zero. LN(0.5) = –0.693
LOG	The logarithm of base number1 of number2. Number1 is any base other than 0 or 1 and number2 is any positive number. LOG(10, 0.5) = –0.301
MOD	The modulus division function, returns the remainder of number1 divided by number2. MOD(7, 3) = 1
NVL	A replacement function, if value1 is NULL, NVL returns value2; otherwise, NVL returns value1. NVL(work_hours,'Zero') substitutes a value of Zero for any NULL value in the *work_hours* column.
POWER	The number1 raised to the number2 power. If number1 is negative, number2 must be an integer. POWER(5, 0.5) = 2.236
ROUND	Rounds a number1 to number2 decimal places. ROUND(15.34563, 2) = 15.35
SIGN	Evaluates number1; returns –1 if number1 is negative; 0 if number1 is 0; 1 if number1 is positive. SIGN(0.5) = 1
SIN	The Sine of a number expressed in radians. SIN(0.5) = 0.479
SINH	The Hyperbolic Sine of a number expressed in radians. SINH(0.5) = 0.521
SQRT	The square root of a number; the number must be positive. SQRT(5) = 2.236
TAN	The Tangent of a number expressed in radians. TAN(0.5) = 0.546
TANH	The Hyperbolic Tangent of a number expressed in radians. TANH(0.5) = 0.462
TRUNC	Truncates a number1 to number2 decimal places. TRUNC(15.34563,2) = 15.34

these functions, and we will not define each of them here. For the most part, they are used in scientific applications. There is limited applicability in the area of quantitative business areas such as finance and marketing research. The query in SQL Example 10.9 demonstrates how to generate values for selected transcendental functions from the *dual* table. Recall that the *dual* table automatically exists in every Oracle database.

```
/* SQL Example 10.9 */
SELECT COS(0.5), EXP(1), LN(0.5), LOG(10,0.5)
FROM dual;

   COS(0.5)        EXP(1)       LN(0.5)    LOG(10,0.5)
--------        ---------    ---------    ----------

.877582562    2.71828183    -.69314718      -.30103
```

NVL FUNCTION FOR NULL VALUE SUBSTITUTION

You have learned that NULL values actually represent an unknown value. Sometimes when values in tables are unknown, it is possible to substitute a reasonable guess or average value where a NULL value exists. At other times you may wish to highlight the absence of a value by substituting another value, such as zero for the NULL value. The query in SQL Example 10.10 reveals that some employees have NULL values for the *work_hours* column in the *assignment* table for projects 1 and 20.

```
/* SQL Example 10.10 */
COLUMN "Hours" FORMAT 9990.9
SELECT work_emp_ssn "SSN", work_pro_number "Project",
work_hours "Hours"
FROM assignment
WHERE work_pro_number IN (1,20);

SSN            Project    Hours
--------       ------     -----
999111111          1       31.4
999888888          1       21.0
999444444          1
999444444         20       11.8
999555555         20       14.8
999666666         20
```

Suppose that the senior project manager has requested that we produce a result table and substitute the value 0.0 where NULL values exist in the *assignment* table. We can accomplish this task with the NVL function. NVL is a substitution function and it allows you to substitute a specified value where the stored value in a row is NULL. The general format of the NVL function is:

```
NVL(value1, value2)
```

The NVL function works with character, date and other datatypes as well as numbers. If *value1* is NULL, NVL returns *value2;* otherwise, NVL returns *value1.* The following query in SQL Example 10.11 will produce the result requested by the senior project manager by listing a value of 0 where work_hours is NULL.

```
/* SQL Example 10.11 */
COLUMN "Hours" FORMAT 9990.9
SELECT work_emp_ssn "SSN", work_pro_number "Project",
    NVL(work_hours, 0) "Hours"
FROM assignment
WHERE work_pro_number IN (1,20);

SSN           Project    Hours
--------      ------     -----
999111111          1      31.4
999888888          1      21.0
999444444          1       0.0
999444444         20      11.8
999555555         20      14.8
999666666         20       0.0
```

ABS Function

The absolute value is a mathematical measure of magnitude. The general format of the ABS function is:

```
ABS(value)
```

Oracle provides the ABS function for use in computing the absolute value of a number or numeric expression. Business managers may be interested in the magnitude by which a particular value deviates from some standard or average value. For example, suppose that the senior project manager has established 20 hours as the desired standard for working on assigned projects. The manager may wish to know which employees have deviated significantly from this standard, either by not working enough (less than 10 hours) or by exceeding expectations (more than 30 hours). The query in SQL Example 10.12 addresses the senior project manager's concerns.

```
/* SQL Example 10.12 */
COLUMN "Hours" FORMAT 9990.9
COLUMN "Avg Hrs" FORMAT 9990.99
COLUMN "Difference" FORMAT 90.99
SELECT work_emp_ssn "SSN", work_hours "Hours",
    ABS(work_hours - 20) "Difference"
FROM assignment
WHERE ABS(work_hours - 20) >= 10
ORDER BY ABS(work_hours - 20);

SSN           Hours    Difference
--------      -----    ---------
999887777      30.8        10.80
999111111      31.4        11.40
999111111       8.5        11.50
999222222      34.5        14.50
999222222       5.1        14.90
999333333      42.1        22.10
```

The result table lists each employee SSN, hours worked, and the number of hours by which the hours worked deviates from the standard of 20 hours. Note how the ABS function is used in the SELECT clause to compute the Difference column, in the WHERE clause to specify the criteria for row selection, and in the ORDER BY clause to order the result table by the degree of work deviation.

POWER AND SQRT FUNCTIONS

The POWER and SQRT (square root) functions are typically used in scientific computing, but they may also be used in writing expressions for queries in the financial or marketing research areas. The general format for these functions is:

```
POWER(value1, value2)
SQRT(value)
```

The POWER function raises numeric *value1* to a specified positive exponent, *value2*. The SQRT function computes the square root of a numeric value, expression or NUMBER column value. You may also note that SQRT(value) is equivalent to POWER(value, 0.5). The sample query in SQL Example 10.13 demonstrates the use of these functions by selecting from the *dual* pseudo-table.

```
/* SQL Example 10.13 */
SELECT POWER(10, 3), POWER(25, 0.5), SQRT(25)
FROM dual;

POWER(10,3)      POWER(25,0.5)      SQRT(25)
---------       -----------        -------
     1000                  5              5
```

ROUND AND TRUNC FUNCTIONS

The ROUND and TRUNC (truncate) functions are used to display numeric values to specific levels of mathematical precision. The general format of these functions is:

```
ROUND(value1, integer_value2)
TRUNC(value1, integer_value2)
```

The ROUND function rounds *value1* to the specified number of digits of precision, an integer value shown in the formal definition as *integer_value2*. The TRUNC function drops digits from a number. Usually, we round or truncate numbers to some number of digits after the decimal. Suppose that a manager needs a listing of hours worked by employees assigned to projects, but wishes the listing to be rounded to the nearest whole hour. Perhaps a different manager wishes to simply truncate the hours worked to the nearest whole hour. The query in SQL Example 10.14 produces a result table that supports both managerial needs. Note that the highlighted rows show differences in output produced by rounding versus truncating.

```
/* SQL Example 10.14 */
SELECT work_emp_ssn "SSN", work_hours "Hours",
    ROUND(work_hours,0) "Rounded", TRUNC(work_hours,0) "Truncated"
FROM assignment
ORDER BY work_emp_ssn;
```

```
SSN             Hours      Rounded     Truncated
---------       -----      ------      ---------
999111111        31.4          31            31
999111111         8.5           9             8
999222222        34.5          35            34
999222222         5.1           5             5
999333333        42.1          42            42
999444444        12.2          12            12
999444444        10.5          11            10
more rows will be displayed...
```

List Functions—GREATEST and LEAST

The list functions, GREATEST and LEAST enable you to extract values from a group of columns. The general format for these two functions is:

```
GREATEST(column1, column2, ... )
LEAST(column1, column2, ... )
```

Contrast this with aggregate functions that work on groups of rows. Suppose that we have a data table that tracks the total hours worked by employees on a monthly basis over the course of three months. Table 10.4 depicts this type of data.

Using the sequence of commands in SQL Example 10.15, let's create a table like Table 10.4 and name it *monthly_hours*. We'll also insert the values from Table 10.4 into the *monthly_hours* data table.

```
/* SQL Example 10.15 */
CREATE TABLE monthly_hours (
    emp_ssn             CHAR(9),
    jan_hours           NUMBER(5,1),
    feb_hours           NUMBER(5,1),
    mar_hours           NUMBER(5,1) );

INSERT INTO monthly_hours VALUES ('999666666',162.5,158.9,157.7);
INSERT INTO monthly_hours VALUES ('999555555',165.5,170.4,177.4);
INSERT INTO monthly_hours VALUES ('999444444',158.9,161.2,160.8);
INSERT INTO monthly_hours VALUES ('999887777',146.4,188.2,178.2);
```

TABLE 10.4

Employee SSN	January Hours	February Hours	March Hours
999666666	162.5	158.9	157.7
999555555	165.5	170.4	177.4
999444444	158.9	161.2	160.8
999887777	146.4	188.2	178.2
More rows . . .			

Now suppose that a project manager needs to know both the greatest and least number of hours each employee worked during the three-month period. The query in SQL Example 10.16 uses the GREATEST and LEAST functions to produce the desired result table.

```
/* SQL Example 10.16 */
SELECT emp_ssn "SSN",
    GREATEST(jan_hours, feb_hours, mar_hours) "Greatest Hrs",
    LEAST(jan_hours, feb_hours, mar_hours) "Least Hrs"
FROM monthly_hours;

SSN            Greatest Hrs     Least Hrs
--------       -----------      --------
999666666          162.5          157.7
999555555          177.4          165.5
999444444          161.2          158.9
999887777          188.2          146.4
```

DATE FUNCTIONS

From your study of Chapter 2, you'll recall that the DATE datatype stores both date and time information including the hour, minute, and second. Oracle provides a seemingly endless multitude of date functions that can transform a date into almost any display format that you could desire. Oracle also provides functions that can convert date values to character and character values to date. We will focus on the date functions that are used most often. These are described in Table 10.5.

SYSDATE Function

The SYSDATE function returns the current date and time from the computer's operating system. You can select SYSDATE from any table, so in this respect, SYSDATE is a sort of pseudo-column. In the example shown in SQL Example 10.17, the SYSDATE is selected from the *employee* table.

```
/* SQL Example 10.17 */
SELECT emp_ssn, SYSDATE
FROM employee;
```

TABLE 10.5

Function	Use/Definition
ADD_MONTHS	Adds the specified number of months to the specified date and returns that date
SYSDATE	Returns the current system date and time
TO_CHAR	Converts a date value to a character string
TO_DATE	Converts a character string or number to a date value

```
EMP_SSN        SYSDATE
---------      ---------
999666666      21-APR-02
999555555      21-APR-02
999444444      21-APR-02
```

The query shown above simply demonstrates the ability to select SYSDATE from a table—the SYSDATE value shown has no particular significance. This also shows the standard format for most Oracle systems when returning date values: DD-MON-YY. Later, you will learn how to format date output to meet unique system user requirements.

DATE ARITHMETIC

Oracle provides the capability to perform date arithmetic. For example, if you add seven (7) to a value stored in a date column, Oracle will produce a date that is one week later than the stored date. Adding 7 is equivalent to adding 7 days to the date. Likewise, subtracting 7 from a stored date will produce a date that is a week earlier than the stored date.

You can also subtract or compute the difference between two date values. Subtracting two date columns will produce the number of days between the two dates. Suppose that a human resources manager needs to know how long the department manager of department 3 has worked in his assigned position. The query in SQL Example 10.18 produces the desired result table.

```
/* SQL Example 10.18 */
COLUMN SSN FORMAT A10;
COLUMN "Last Name" FORMAT A15;
COLUMN "Number Days" FORMAT 99999999999;
SELECT dpt_mgrssn "SSN", emp_last_name "Last Name",
    SYSDATE - dpt_mgr_start_date "Number Days"
FROM department, employee
WHERE dpt_mgrssn = emp_ssn AND
    dpt_no = 3;

SSN             Last Name       Number Days
---------       ---------       ----------
999555555       Joyner                 476
Your answer will vary depending on when you execute the query.
```

ADD_MONTHS FUNCTION

The approach taken above computes how long a manager has been assigned to a specific job position in terms of days; however, managers often are more interested in having this value expressed in months or years. Suppose that a human resources manager needs to know the ten-year anniversary dates for current department managers in order to determine if any of the managers are eligible for a service award. You could execute a query that adds 3,650 days (10 years at 365 days/year) to the *dep_mgr_* *start_date* column of the *department* table; however, this type of date arithmetic would fail to take into consideration leap years that have 366 days. The ADD_MONTHS function solves this problem by adding the specified number of months to a specified date. The format of the function is:

```
ADD_MONTHS(start_date, number_of_months)
```

The query in SQL Example 10.19 will display the required 10-year anniversary information.

```
/* SQL Example 10.19 */
SELECT dpt_mgrssn "SSN", emp_last_name "Last Name",
    dpt_mgr_start_date "Start Date",
    ADD_MONTHS(dpt_mgr_start_date, 120) "10 Yr Anniversary"
FROM department, employee
WHERE dpt_mgrssn = emp_ssn;

SSN             Last Name       Start Dat    10 Yr Ann
--------        ---------       ---------    ---------
999444444       Zhu             22-MAY-98    22-MAY-08
999555555       Joyner          01-JAN-01    01-JAN-11
999666666       Bordoloi        19-JUN-81    19-JUN-91
```

TO_CHAR AND TO_DATE FUNCTIONS

The functions are used to format output and to convert data from one datatype to another. The general form of these functions is:

```
TO_CHAR(date_value, {'format_string','NLS_parameter'})
TO_DATE(char_value, {'format_string','NLS_parameter'})
```

The TO_CHAR function converts a date value to a VARCHAR2 character string. When the *format_string* is omitted, the date conversion is to the default date format—generally DD-MON-YY. The *NLS_parameter* is an optional value used to specify the national language to use if one other than the current default is required.

The TO_DATE function is the mirror-image of TO_CHAR and converts a date value to a character string. Both of these functions can be used to format output by using a wide range of formatting options.

The default date format for use with TO_CHAR and TO_DATE can be set by assigning a value to the NLS_DATE_FORMAT (national language support date format) parameter. The ALTER SESSION command shown in SQL Example 10.20 sets the format from the default of DD-MON-YY to DD-MON-YYYY to display a full, four-digit year.

```
/* SQL Example 10.20 */
ALTER SESSION SET NLS_DATE_FORMAT = 'DD-MON-YYYY';
SELECT SYSDATE
FROM dual;

SYSDATE
----------
21-APR-2002
```

Table 10.6 specifies some of the more common date formats that can be used with the TO_CHAR and TO_DATE functions. A complete listing can be obtained from Oracle's Web site: *http://otn.oracle.com/docs/products/oracle9i/content.html.*

The SELECT statement in SQL Example 10.21 demonstrates formatting output for the *employee* table's *emp_date_of_birth* column.

```
/* SQL Example 10.21 */
SELECT emp_date_of_birth "Birth Date",
    TO_CHAR(emp_date_of_birth, 'MONTH DD, YYYY') "Spelled Out"
FROM employee;

Birth Dat    Spelled Out
---------    ---------------
10-NOV-67    NOVEMBER 10, 1967
20-JUN-71    JUNE 20, 1971
08-DEC-75    DECEMBER 08, 1975
More rows will be displayed ...
```

This query in SQL Example 10.22 displays the time information stored to the *emp_date_of_birth* column, if that is of interest to one of the Company managers.

```
/* SQL Example 10.22 */
SELECT TO_CHAR(emp_date_of_birth, 'HH:MI:SS') "Time Stored"
FROM employee;
```

TABLE 10.6

Format	Use/Description
D	Day of week
DD	Days in month
DDD	Days in year
DY	Three-letter day abbreviation
DAY	Day spelled out—padded with blank characters to 9 characters in length
HH, HH12, and HH24	Hour of day; Hour of day (hours 1–12); Hour of day (hours 1–24)
MI	Minute (0–59)
MM	Month—numbered 01 to 12
MON	Month spelled out in abbreviated 3-character format
MONTH	Month spelled out—padded with blank characters to 9 characters in length
SS	Second (0–59)
Y, YY, YYY, and YYYY	Year in 1-, 2-, 3-, or 4-year formats

```
Time Sto
--------
12:00:00
12:00:00
12:00:00
More rows will be displayed ...
```

Each row in the table has the same time information stored to the *emp_date_of_birth* column because time information was not specified when the sample database was created. The default time used when dates are entered is 12:00:00 (midnight).

The TO_DATE function is often used with the INSERT command to convert a literal string into an Oracle date format for purposes of data storage. The example in SQL Example 10.23 will insert a new row into the *dependent* table. Here the date format specifies the month and day as two digits each followed by a four-digit year value.

```
/* SQL Example 10.23 */
INSERT INTO dependent VALUES ( '999111111', 'Rachael', 'F',
    TO_DATE('10-04-1975', 'MM-DD-YYYY'), 'DAUGHTER');
```

TO_DATE is also used in WHERE clauses as is done in the query in SQL Example 10.24 that displays dependents born before January 1, 1990.

```
/* SQL Example 10.24 */
SELECT dep_name, dep_date_of_birth
FROM dependent
WHERE dep_date_of_birth < TO_DATE('01-JAN-1990');

DEP_NAME        DEP_DATE_
---------       ---------
Susan           03-MAY-75
Allen           29-FEB-68
Jeffery         01-JAN-78
Deanna          31-DEC-78
Mary Ellen      05-MAY-57
```

The TO_DATE function used above will fail if the character string used to specify the date in the TO_DATE function does not match the default Oracle format of DD-MON-YY. In this situation, as SQL Example 10.25 demonstrates, Oracle will return the *ORA-1843: not a valid month* error message.

```
/* SQL Example 10.25 */
SELECT dep_name, dep_date_of_birth
FROM dependent
WHERE dep_date_of_birth < TO_DATE('01-01-1990');
```

```
ERROR at line 3:
ORA-01843: not a valid month
```

ROUND AND TRUNC FUNCTIONS WITH DATES

The ROUND function rounds dates in the same fashion as it rounds numbers. If the time value stored in a date column is before noon, ROUND will return a value of 12:00:00 (midnight). Any time stored that is exactly noon or later returns a value of 12:00:00 (midnight) the next day. The TRUNC function truncates times to 12:00:00 (midnight) of the date stored in the date column. These functions can be used to prevent Oracle from returning a fraction of a date in a "difference" type of calculation as demonstrated in SQL Example 10.26.

```
/* SQL Example 10.26 */
COLUMN dep_name FORMAT A15;
SELECT dep_name, TO_DATE('25-FEB-68') - SYSDATE "Not Rounded",
    TO_DATE('25-FEB-68') - ROUND(SYSDATE) "Rounded"
FROM dependent
WHERE dep_emp_ssn = '999555555';

DEP_NAME       Not Rounded    Rounded
-------        ----------     ------
Allen            -12474.906     -12475
```

DECODE FUNCTION

The DECODE function is an Oracle extension to ANSI SQL. The DECODE function enables you to use If-Then-Else logic when displaying values. The general format is:

```
DECODE(expression, search1, result1, search2, result2, ..., else
default)
```

The *expression* can be a column value of any datatype, or a result from some type of computation or function. The *expression* is compared to *search1* and if *expression* = *search1,* then *result1* is returned. If not, then the search continues to compare *expression* = *search2* in order to return *result2,* etc. If the *expression* does not equal any of the *search* values, then the *default* value is returned. The *else default* can be a column value or the result of some type of computation or function.

Suppose that the senior project manager requests a listing that highlights employee work activities for project 10. Employees who work more than 30 hours on a project are to be designated as having "worked very hard" while others "worked ok." The SELECT statement in SQL Example 10.27 uses the DECODE function to produce the desired result table. The TRUNC function truncates the result of the work_hours column divided by 30. For employees working 30 or more hours, this yields a truncated value that is greater than or equal to 1. The DECODE function tests for a value of zero (0). The TRUNC function yields zero for employees working less than 30 hours and displays the appropriate message in the Work Status column of the result table.

```
/* SQL Example 10.27 */
SELECT work_emp_ssn "SSN", work_hours "Hours Worked",
    DECODE(TRUNC(work_hours/30),0,'Worked OK','Worked Very Hard') "Work
Status"
FROM assignment
WHERE work_pro_number = 10;

SSN             Hours Worked   Work Status
---------       -----------    --------------
999444444           10.1       Worked OK
999887777           10.2       Worked OK
999222222           34.5       Worked Very Hard
```

SUMMARY

In this chapter, you learned numerous additional functions that add power to SQL queries. Character functions are used to manipulate CHAR data. The UPPER, LOWER, and INITCAP functions alter the appearance of information displayed in a result table by displaying data as all upper- or lowercase letters, or by capitalizing the first letter of a string. The LEN function computes the number of characters in a string while the SUBSTR function extracts a substring form a character string. The LTRIM and RTRIM functions trim character strings of any leading and trailing blank characters while the INSTR function searches for a substring within a larger string.

Number functions manipulate NUMBER data. There are numerous transcendental functions such as ACOS and ASIN used for scientific applications. The NVL function is used to substitute values where data are otherwise NULL in value. The ABS function can be used to compute absolute differences between two values. The POWER and SQRT functions are used to raise numeric values to specified exponential values and to compute square roots, respectively. The ROUND and TRUNC (truncate) functions display numeric values to specific levels of mathematical precision. The GREATEST and LEAST functions extract the largest and smallest values from a group of columns.

The Date functions TO_CHAR and TO_DATE are used to convert a date value to a character string, and a character string or number to a date value, respectively. These functions can also be used to format date and time output in a result table and to format data for row insertions when combined with the INSERT command. The SYSDATE function returns the current system date and time. The ADD_MONTHS function adds the specified number of months to a specified date in order to return a specific date in the future as part of a query.

The DECODE function is an Oracle extension to standard ANSI SQL and enables the use of If-Then-Else logic to display values.

REVIEW EXERCISES

LEARN THESE TERMS

ABS. Computes the absolute value of a number or numeric expression.

ADD_MONTHS. Adds the specified number of months to the specified date and returns that date.

GREATEST. Extracts the largest (greatest) value from a group of columns.

INITCAP. Capitalizes the first letter of a string of characters.

INSTR. Searches a character string for a character string subset and returns the start position and/or occurrence of the substring.

LEAST. Extracts the smallest (least) value from a group of columns.

LENGTH. Returns a numeric value equivalent to the number of characters in a string of characters.

LOWER. Returns a character value that is all lower-case.

LTRIM. Trims specified characters from the left end of a string.

NVL. A substation function that allows a programmer to substitute a specified value wherein stored values are NULL.

CONCEPTS QUIZ

POWER. Raises a numeric value to a specified positive exponent.

ROUND. Rounds a value to a specified number of digits of precision.

RTRIM. Trims specified characters from the right end of a string.

SQRT. Computes the square root of a numeric value, expression or NUMBER column value.

SUBSTR. Returns a string of specified length from a larger character string beginning at a specified character position.

SYSDATE. Returns the current system date and time.

TO_CHAR. Converts a date value to a character string.

TO_DATE. Converts a character string or number to a date value.

TRUNC. Truncates digits from a numeric value.

UPPER. Returns a character value that is all upper-case.

CONCEPTS QUIZ

1. Are numbers such as telephone numbers and product numbers treated as character or numeric data? Why?
2. What is the purpose of the UPPER, LOWER, and INITCAP functions?
3. What does the LENGTH function do?
4. What is the purpose of the SUBSTR function? What will the following SELECT statement do?

```
SELECT SUBSTR(emp_ssn,6,4)
FROM employee;
```

5. What is the purpose of the LTRIM and RTRIM functions?
6. When using the INSTR function to search a character string, what does the function return if the character string is found? Not found?
7. Is the NVL function limited to use with the NUMBER datatype?
8. Which function would you use to measure the magnitude by which a particular value deviates from some standard or average value?
9. How do the GREATEST and LEAST functions differ from the aggregate functions MAX and MIN?
10. What values are turned by the SYDATE function?
11. What is the standard format for date values in Oracle?

12. What value is returned by the following expression: SYSDATE + 1
13. You wish to know the date six months from now. Which function is best for displaying this value?
14. What is the purpose of the TO_CHAR and TO_DATE functions?
15. How does the ROUND function work with date values?
16. Which function provides If-Then-Else logic?

SQL CODING EXERCISES AND QUESTIONS

In answering the SQL exercises and questions, submit a copy of each command that you execute and any messages that Oracle generates while executing your SQL commands. Also list the output for any result table that is generated by your SQL statements.

1. Management requires a listing of employees by last name, first name, and middle initial. The last name should be displayed in all capital letters. The entire name should be concatenated together so as to display in a single field with a column heading of "Employee Name." The rows should be sorted by employee last name, then employee first name.
2. Write a query that displays the *department* name and the length in number of characters of each department's name. Use the *department* table. Label the column headings appropriately.
3. Rewrite the query for question 1 to only list employees that have the character string "oy" in the name.
4. Management wants a listing of department numbers and locations (use the *dept_locations* table)—display the output as a single column with the heading "Department Locations."
5. Write a query that displays the first four characters of each employee's last name and the last four digits of each employee's SSN. Label the column headings "Name" and "SSN." Order the result table rows by employee last name.
6. Create the table named month_table that is discussed in the chapter. Add the first six months of the year to the table. Write a SELECT statement to display the month name, untrimmed month name length, and trimmed month name length as was done in the chapter.
7. Write a query to display a listing of employee last names and the SSN of the employee's supervisor. If the employee has no supervisor, display the message "Top Supervisor." Provide appropriate headings. Sort the result table by employee last name.
8. Develop a listing for the company's senior project manager that lists employees that reported working between 15 and 25 hours on assigned projects. List the employee last name, project number, and hours worked. Use the ABS function. Use meaningful column headings. Sort the rows of the result table by employee last name. *Hint:* 20 is the midpoint between 15 and 25 hours, the absolute value of the difference would be 5 hours.
9. The senior project manager needs a listing by employee last name, project number, and hours worked with the work_hours column rounded to the nearest integer value for projects 2 and 10. Sort the result table by employee last name within project number. Use meaningful column names.

10. Write a query to display dependent information for the human resources manager. Display each dependent's name, gender, and date of birth. The date of birth should be displayed as: Month Name (spelled out), two-digit day, and four-digit year (e.g., December 05, 1970). Use the COLUMN commands shown here to format the first two columns of output.

```
COLUMN "Gender" Format A6;
COLUMN "Dep Name" FORMAT A15;
```

11. In question 10, the month values are displayed blank-padded to nine characters in length. Rewrite the query by using the RTRIM function and concatenation operators to display the birth date column by removing the blank-padding for the month part of the string of characters forming the date.

12. Write a query to display each dependent's name, date of birth, and date on which the dependent turned or will turn 65 years of age. Use meaningful column names. Display each date using the DD-MON-YYYY format. Use the ADD_MONTHS and TO_CHAR functions. *Hint:* 65 years equals 780 months.

13. Write a short query to display the current day of the week from the operating system date.

14. The human resources manager needs a listing of dependents including their name and gender. Instead of displaying the coded values for gender, your result table must display the terms "male" and "female," as appropriate. Use meaningful column headings. Sort the result table by dependent name.

EMBEDDED SQL

Did you know that the Structured Query Language is used in conjunction with many different procedural and object-oriented programming host languages? This approach to programming is termed *embedded SQL* and simply means that the host language includes the ability to use SQL statements to both retrieve and store records in a nonprocedural fashion. You will be a more effective SQL programmer if you have a basic understanding of the principles of embedding SQL commands.

OBJECTIVES

We will explore methods for embedding SQL in three different procedural languages, Visual Basic 6.0, Visual Basic.NET, and COBOL. The Visual Basic language is one of the most popular in the world and is used extensively to develop desktop systems that execute in a Microsoft Windows interface. We will examine how SQL is embedded in Visual Basic 6.0 programming code for both the retrieval and storage of table rows.

Visual Basic.NET is the latest evolution of the Visual Basic language. Understanding how SQL is embedded in Visual Basic.NET is important because the object-oriented nature and powerful Web coding capabilities of this language makes it a likely language for use for many years into the future.

Finally, we will examine the COBOL language because it has been used extensively in business for several decades. While COBOL is an older language, it is still used to build large business systems that interface with both flat files and database management systems. A large number of systems have been written in COBOL, and these systems are still in use today and will be used for many years to come. Your learning objectives for this chapter are:

- Learn the benefits of embedding SQL in a host language.
- Use ActiveX Data Object (ADO) control properties to specify a SQL statement in Visual Basic that retrieves data rows.
- Use ADO control properties to store (update) data rows.
- Use ADO.NET to connect a Visual Basic.NET program to a database.

- Use ADO.NET to execute a SELECT statement.
- Use the EXEC SQL in COBOL to define a relational table structure in the Working-Storage section.
- Use SELECT statements in a COBOL Procedure Division to read and write records.

BENEFITS OF EMBEDDING SQL IN A PROCEDURAL LANGUAGE

As you have learned from your studies thus far, SQL is a very powerful language for nonprocedural data processing. Recall that the term *nonprocedural* means that a single SQL command tells the information system *what* to do as opposed to *how* to accomplish the intended data processing task. Unfortunately, nonprocedural languages have some serious limitations in terms of building computer system interfaces to support unique processing requirements. Thus, there is a need to use procedural languages, such as Visual Basic, Visual Basic.NET, or COBOL to meet specialized or unique processing requirements.

As an example, consider how difficult it would be for a worker with no SQL training to extract information needed to support decision making. Such a worker might be a manager that is reviewing the status of employee personnel records, or a worker at a large retail store who needs to enter sales data for goods being purchased by customers. These types of workers cannot be expected to formulate SQL commands in order to accomplish their work; still, we would often find these workers using computers to automate the record review or sales order processing tasks.

Programmers use procedural languages to build the computer interfaces that these workers use as part of their daily work. Procedural languages have the following advantages:

- A rich command set that provides the capability to program a graphical user interface to match unique system processing requirements.
- Language constructs such as iterative (WHILE and UNTIL loops) and decision structures (IF and SELECT CASE statements) that enable specialized record-at-a-time processing.
- The ability to program computer interfaces so that system users do not need specialized training in writing queries in order to use information systems coded with procedural languages.

EMBEDDING SQL IN VISUAL BASIC 6.0

THE ACTIVEX DATA OBJECTS CONTROL

Microsoft Visual Basic provides a visual programming language that is encased within an integrated development environment (IDE). The IDE enables computer programmers to develop information systems rapidly by dragging and dropping various control objects, such as textboxes and labels onto windows-like forms. As a programmer literally paints the interface, Visual Basic writes the programming code behind the forms to implement the interface that is being visually designed.

Visual Basic provides all of the normal procedural programming constructs used by computer programmers including decision structures using IF statements and looping structures using both WHILE and UNTIL loops. Database processing is primarily accomplished through use of the ActiveX Data Objects (ADO) control. This specialized control enables a computer programmer to connect an application program written in Visual Basic to an existing database. Further, it is easy to create the database connection. Figure 11.1 shows an example employee processing form with an ADO control.

The ADO control is used to process employee records. The employee processing form displays a subset of the data columns from the *employee* table. This is a very common approach to visual programming with Visual Basic. The ADO control provides First, Previous, Next, and Last buttons (arrows) to make it easy to navigate from one row of data to the next. When one of the ADO control navigation buttons is clicked, the form display updates to a new record. The ADO control also has properties that can be visually programmed to make a database connection.

The *ConnectionString* property stores a character string that specifies how to connect to a database. Part of the *ConnectionString* information specifies where the database is located. The *ConnectionString* also specifies the type of database as well as information about provider software that is used to make a database connection. In the coding segment shown in VB6 Example 11.1, a connection is made to an Oracle database named *Company*.

FIGURE 11.1

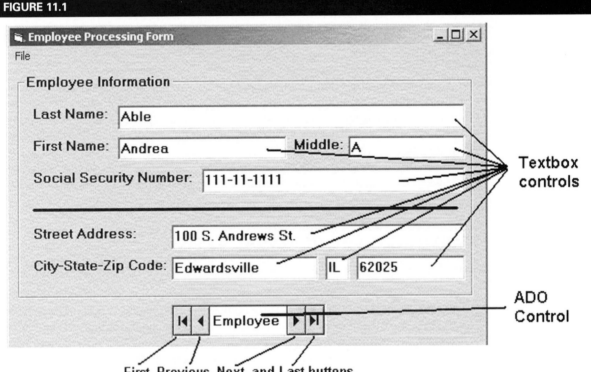

```
REM VB6 Example 11.1
ConnectionString = "Provider=MSDAORA.1; User ID=dbock;
Password=mypassword; Data Source=Company; Persist Security Info=True"

(Note: All of the above code will be entered on a single coding line).
```

The *CommandType* property specifies how data will be retrieved from a database. Data rows are retrieved from disk and stored in a memory object called a *recordset*. While Visual Basic supports processing an entire table, the most common approach is to process a subset of table rows; thus, a recordset usually consists of one or just a few table rows. This is because it is unwieldy to try to navigate through a large set of records where a table may store thousands and thousands of rows. Additionally, retrieving an entire table from a server over a network can cause network traffic to be unacceptably high. A programmer specifies a value for the *CommandType* property of "1-adCmdText," which means that an SQL statement will be used to retrieve the records for the recordset.

The *RecordSource* property stores the actual SQL statement used to create a recordset. For example, the records displayed for the recordset in Figure 11.1 were retrieved with the SELECT statement shown in VB6 Example 11.2. As you can see, the SELECT statement is exactly like those you have learned while studying this textbook.

```
REM VB6 Example 11.2
SELECT emp_last_name, emp_first_name, emp_middle_name, emp_ssn,
    emp_address, emp_city, emp_state, emp_zip
FROM employee
WHERE emp_zip = '62025';
```

VB6 Example 11.2 creates a *recordset* that can have zero, one, or more data rows from the *employee* table. Where there is more than one row, the ADO control navigation buttons are used to move from one row to the next. If the ADO control enables both reading and writing rows (this is also an ADO property that can be set), any changes made to a value displayed on the form while the system user navigates to another row will cause the changed data to be saved automatically to the database.

There are two additional properties for each textbox control that must be set in order for a Visual Basic form to display database data. These are the *DataField* and *DataSource* properties shown in Figure 11.2 that displays a Visual Basic property window that is associated with the textbox control that displays the employee first name.

The *DataSource* property of each textbox is set to the name of the ADO control. Here the ADO control is named *adoEmployee*. Setting the *DataSource* property of a textbox links the textbox control to the ADO control. Next, the *DataField* property is set to the appropriate column name from the *employee* table in order to specify the exact value to display in a textbox. Each textbox on the employee processing form will have the same value for the *DataSource* property, but the *DataField* property for each textbox will reflect the column of data to be displayed in that particular textbox. This same approach is used for other Visual Basic controls that display database rows—labels, list boxes, data combo boxes, data grids, and the like.

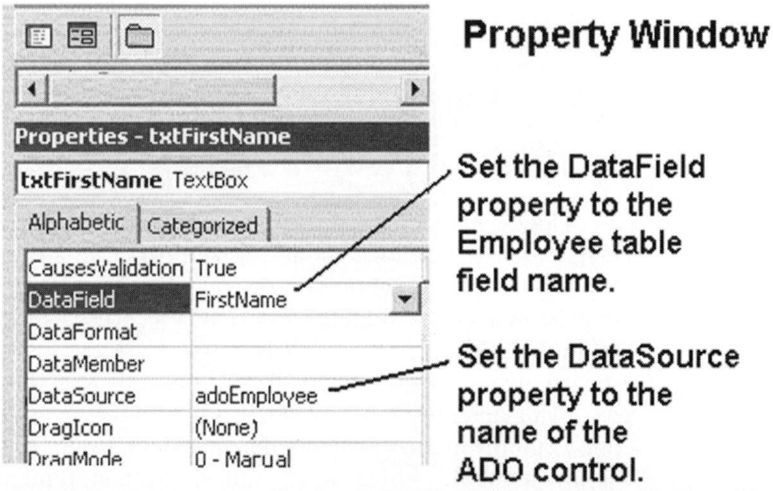

Set the DataField property to the Employee table field name.

Set the DataSource property to the name of the ADO control.

FIGURE 11.2

SELECTING DATA SPECIFIED BY A USER INPUTTED VALUE

The SELECT statement in VB6 Example 11.2 has an obvious limitation. Did you notice it? The SELECT statement has the zip code value "hard-coded"—the statement will always retrieve data rows in which the zip code equals '62025'. Hard coding data values such as a zip code may work well if managers often execute the same query over and over. However, a system user often needs to retrieve records based on values that are specified through some type of user input.

Figure 11.3 shows the use of an InputBox dialog box to allow a system user to enter employee Social Security number (SSN) values. The SSN entered is used to retrieve an individual *employee* table data row. The system user types an SSN into the InputBox text area, and clicks the OK button. The SELECT statement in VB6 Example 11.3 is the command that we wish to execute for an employee with a SSN of '111-11-1111'.

FIGURE 11.3

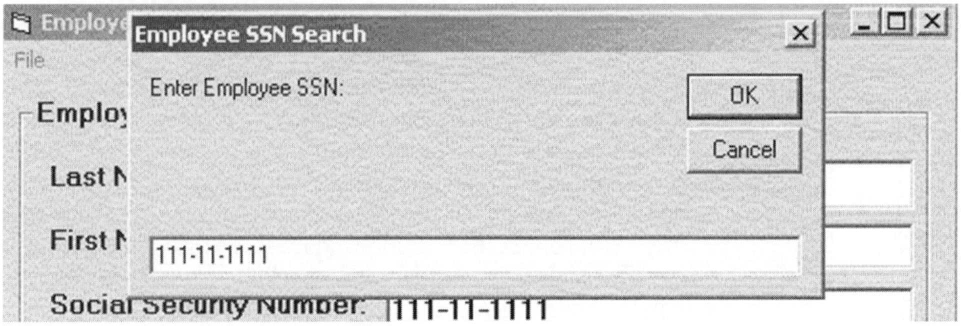

```
REM VB6 SQL Example 11.3
SELECT emp_last_name, emp_first_name, emp_middle_name, emp_ssn,
    emp_address, emp_city, emp_state, emp_zip
FROM employee
WHERE emp_ssn = '111-11-1111';
```

However, the programmer must avoid hard-coding the SSN. Instead, the query must use the SSN that is entered in the InputBox. It should be obvious that simply setting the *emp_ssn* column value in the WHERE clause to '111-11-1111' will not work! This problem is solved by storing the value entered into the InputBox to a Visual Basic memory variable that stores string or character data. The Visual Basic code to produce the InputBox and store the value is shown in VB6 Example 11.4. The value entered for the SSN is stored to the *strSSN* variable.

```
REM VB6 SQL Example 11.4
Dim strSSN As String
strSSN = InputBox("Enter Employee SSN:", _
    "Employee SSN Search", vbOKCancel)
```

The program stores the SELECT statement to a second string variable named *strSQL* in the code segment shown in VB6 Example 11.5. Note that the entire SELECT statement is stored inside double quote marks. Each piece of the SELECT statement is a string of characters that are concatenated together with the Visual Basic concatenation operator (the ampersand—&). The WHERE clause has the *emp_ssn* column name set equal to the value stored to the *strSSN* variable that was captured through use of the InputBox. Thus, at execution time, the SELECT statement stored to the *strSQL* variable includes the SSN stored to the *strSSN* variable.

```
REM VB6 Example 11.5
'Store SQL statement to a string variable
strSQL = "SELECT emp_last_name, emp_first_name, " & _
        "emp_middle_name, emp_ssn, emp_address, " & _
        "emp_city, emp_state, emp_zip" & _
        "FROM employee" & _
        "WHERE emp_ssn = " & strSSN
```

Finally, the *RecordSource* property of the ADO control is updated by storing the *strSQL* string variable to the *RecordSource* property as shown in VB6 Example 11.6. The ADO control is refreshed with the *Refresh* method. The *Refresh* method automatically creates a new recordset, and the correct employee row will be retrieved and displayed on the employee processing form.

```
REM VB6 Example 11.6
'Update the recordset retrieved by the ADO control
adoEmployee.RecordSource = strSQL
adoEmployee.Refresh
```

The code from these examples would typically be located within a Click event procedure that is linked either to a menu option under the File menu shown on the employee processing form, or to a command button. The advantage of embedding SQL for a programmer is that the Visual Basic code is fairly simple to write, and the system can be developed rapidly by combining the power of the nonprocedural SQL SELECT statement with the versatility of the Visual Basic procedural programming language. Of course, additional code would be needed to handle the situation where an invalid employee SSN is entered or where the database connection is lost due to some network failure, but the basic code needed to retrieve and save data to and from a database table is fairly simple.

EMBEDDING SQL IN VISUAL BASIC.NET

WHY USE VISUAL BASIC.NET

Microsoft's Visual Basic.NET language is one of the core programming languages in Microsoft's new .NET framework. In fact, the programming language you elect to use within the .NET framework is not as critical as it has been in the past. This is because all of the programming languages within the .NET framework compile to the same intermediate Common Language Runtime. Visual Basic.NET continues to support the development of application program interfaces that are Windows-based, but now it also provides powerful features for programming Web-based interfaces. This means that the systems you program can be run by using any Web browser software and data can be retrieved and stored over the Internet. Visual Basic.NET can also be used to program a wide range of newer computing devices such as personal digital assistants and TV-based Internet terminals.

THE SYSTEM.DATA NAMESPACE

Within the .NET framework, all objects are members of *classes.* For example, the forms used to build an application interface are members of the *Forms class.* A *namespace* is an abstract object used to group classes together in order to make the classes easier to access. The *System.Data* namespace contains all of the classes that you will need in order to access almost any type of database. The *System.Data* namespace is divided into two sets of classes. One is termed ***System.Data.OleDB,*** and is used to connect to any database with an OLEDB provider (short for Object Linking and Embedding Database—a software driver used to connect to databases), such as the Oracle database. The other is termed ***System.Data.SQLClient,*** and is designed to connect to the Microsoft SQL Server database engine. SQL Server is Microsoft's relational database management system software.

ADO.NET

Visual Basic 6.0 uses the ActiveX Data Objects (ADO) approach to connect to databases through OLEDB providers (software drivers). ADO has evolved into ADO.NET in Visual Basic.NET. ADO.NET still uses OLEDB providers to connect to databases such as Oracle, Microsoft SQL Server, and Microsoft Access.

The major tasks facing a database programmer are:

- Connecting to a database.
- Executing SQL statements to add, delete, modify, or retrieve table rows.
- Working with datasets. Datasets replace the recordsets used in VB 6.0.

We will examine the first two of these tasks. The third task, working with datasets is beyond the scope of this text.

MAKING A DATABASE CONNECTION

As with Visual Basic 6.0, the information needed to connect to a database is stored to a *connection string* and the connection string is used in conjunction with the appropriate *connection object,* either the OLEDB or SQL Server connection object. A sample VB.NET connection string for an Oracle database named Company is shown in VB.NET Example 11.1.

```
REM VB.NET Example 11.1
strConnection = "Provider=MSDAORA.1; User ID=dbock;
Password=mypassword; Data Source=Company; Persist Security Info=True"
```

The connection string value is stored to a string constant named *strConnection.* VB.NET Example 11.2 shows the declaration of a connection object named *objConnection.* The value of the *strConnection* constant is passed to the *objConnection* object as an argument inside parentheses. Following this the database connection is opened by using the Open method.

```
REM VB.NET Example 11.2
Module MyConnection
    Private Const strConnection As String = & _
        "Provider = MSDAORA.1; User ID=dbock; Password=mypassword; & _
        "Data Source=Company; Persist Security Info=True"
    Sub Main()
        Dim objConnection As New _
            System.Data.OleDb.OleDbConnection(strConnection)
        objConnection.Open()
    End Sub
End Module
```

EXECUTING SQL STATEMENTS

Visual Basic.NET uses a command object (*OleDBCommand*) to execute SQL statements. The approach is again similar to that used in Visual Basic 6.0 in that a programmer creates a string memory variable to store the SQL statement to be executed. Suppose that we again wish to issue a SELECT statement to retrieve data rows from the *employee* table of the Company database. The SELECT statement is shown in VB.NET Example 11.3.

```
REM VB.NET Example 11.3
SELECT emp_last_name, emp_first_name, emp_middle_name, emp_ssn,
    emp_address, emp_city, emp_state, emp_zip
FROM employee
WHERE emp_zip = '62025';
```

The .NET code module named *MyConnection* shown earlier in VB.NET Example 11.2 needs to be modified to accommodate reading data. The modified code is shown in VB.NET Example 11.4. Note that the *strSQL* memory variable stores the SELECT command as a series of concatenated character strings. A command object named *objCommand* is created and the value of *strSQL* and the *objConnection* connection object are passed to the *objCommand* object as parameters inside parentheses. A reader object (*objReader*) is created to store the actual rows returned when the *ExecuteReader* method of the *objCommand* object executes. This code simply creates the connection and stores rows to the dataset. Additional code would need to be added to process the data rows retrieved by the SELECT statement.

```
REM VB.NET Example 11.4
Module MyConnection
    Private Const strConnection As String = & _
        "Provider = MSDAORA.1; User ID=dbock; Password=mypassword; & _
        "Data Source=Company; Persist Security Info=True"
    Sub Main()
        Dim strSQL As String
        strSQL = "SELECT emp_last_name, emp_first_name, " & _
                "emp_middle_name, emp_ssn, emp_address, " & _
                "emp_city, emp_state, emp_zip " & _
                "FROM employee " & _
                "WHERE emp_zip = '62025';"
        Dim objConnection As New _
            System.Data.OleDb.OleDbConnection(strConnection)
        Dim objCommand As New _
            System.Data.OleDb.OleDbCommand(strSQL, objConnection)
        Dim objReader As _
            System.Data.OleDB.OleDBReader
        objConnection.Open()
        objReader = objCommand.ExecuteReader()
        'Additional code goes here to process the rows returned
        'by the SQL query.
    End Sub
End Module
```

As with Visual Basic 6.0, the SELECT statement can be modified to allow the system user to specify which rows to return based on values captured through either an InputBox or based on values typed into a textbox on a form. The Visual Basic.NET code used to retrieve or update data is beyond the scope of this textbook; however, the above example clarifies how SQL can be embedded within this procedural language.

Additionally, you need to understand that embedding SQL in this fashion simplifies the data retrieval task tremendously.

EMBEDDING SQL IN COBOL

COBOL is an old programming language that is has been used extensively for business programming for decades. It is still in heavy use today. Throughout the years, the COBOL language standard has been revised to add new capabilities. Embedding SQL within the COBOL language is one of these capabilities. A COBOL program with embedded SQL requires additional commands or statements not used in a standard or regular COBOL program. These statements are used within the DATA and PROCEDURE divisions.

DATA DIVISION MODIFICATIONS

The Data Division of a COBOL program is used to declare both the structure of files or databases that a program will access. It is also used to declare memory variables known as Working-Storage variables. The Working-Storage Section of a COBOL program is also used to declare tables in memory that will store data rows that are retrieved from database tables. You will also note in COBOL Example 11.1 that all SQL statements are preceded by an EXEC SQL command and followed by an END-EXEC command. These two commands are used to mark the beginning and end of SQL statements so that a COBOL compiler can properly compile the program. The code in COBOL Example 11.1 shows the declaration of a table named *employee* that will store data rows retrieved from the *employee* table of our company database. Again, this code is located in the Working-Storage Section. You will also note that only the table columns that will be retrieved for processing need to be defined in the table. The other columns in the *employee* table are ignored.

```
* COBOL Example 11.1
EXEC SQL
    DECLARE EMPLOYEE TABLE
        (EMP_SSN              CHAR(9),
        EMP_LAST_NAME         CHAR(25),
        EMP_FIRST_NAME        CHAR(25),
        EMP_MIDDLE_NAME       CHAR(25),
        EMP_ADDRESS           CHAR(50),
        EMP_CITY              CHAR(25),
        EMP_STATE             CHAR(2),
        EMP_ZIP               CHAR(9)  )
END-EXEC.
```

In order to process the *employee* table, rows that are retrieved are stored to standard COBOL variables. These are also declared in the Working-Storage Section. Row data is moved from the *employee* table to the COBOL variables. The Working-Storage declaration of these variables is shown in COBOL Example 11.2. Since the variable naming rules for COBOL prohibit the use of the underscore (_) character, the character is replaced by the dash (-) symbol.

```
* COBOL Example 11.2
01 EMPLOYEE-WORK.
    05  EMP-SSN            PIC X(9).
    05  EMP-LAST-NAME      PIC X(25).
    05  EMP-FIRST-NAME     PIC X(25).
    05  EMP-MIDDLE-NAME    PIC X(25).
    05  EMP-ADDRESS        PIC X(50).
    05  EMP-CITY           PIC X(25).
    05  EMP-STATE          PIC X(2).
    05  EMP-ZIP            PIC X(9).
```

In order to process SQL statements and the *employee_data* table declared in COBOL Example 11.2, a *SQL communications area* (SQLCA) must be defined in the server's memory. The SQL communications area includes a SQLCODE parameter. The SQLCODE parameter stores coded values that represent what occurs within an information system whenever any SQL statement executes. The normal execution of an SQL statement causes the SQLCODE parameter to store a value of zero. Program code must be written for the COBOL program Procedure Division in order to test the value of SQLCODE through the use of IF statements. The IF statements will determine if a given SQL statement executes successfully. The SQL communications area is created by the INCLUDE command shown in COBOL Example 11.3.

```
* COBOL Example 11.3
EXEC SQL
    INCLUDE SQLCA
END-EXEC.
```

PROCEDURE DIVISION MODIFICATIONS

The retrieval of data rows through use of an embedded SQL SELECT statement in COBOL requires the storage of data values to *host* variables. For the *employee* table, this simply means that data row values will be stored to the `01 EMPLOYEE-WORK` memory variable created in COBOL Example 11.2. A SELECT statement embedded in a Procedure Division looks like the one shown in COBOL Example 11.4. Note that the host variables are preceded by a colon (:) symbol that is used to differentiate these variables to the program compiler. Additionally, the SELECT statement is NOT ended by a semicolon when it is embedded in COBOL. The code is located within a paragraph named PROCESS-EMPLOYEE-DATA.

```
* COBOL Example 11.4
PROCESS-EMPLOYEE-DATA.
    EXEC SQL
        SELECT EMP_SSN, EMP_LAST_NAME, EMP_FIRST_NAME,
            EMP_MIDDLE_NAME, EMP_ADDRESS,
```

```
                    EMP_CITY, EMP_STATE, EMP_ZIP
           INTO :EMP-SSN, :EMP-LAST-NAME, :EMP-FIRST-NAME,
                :EMP-MIDDLE-NAME, :EMP-ADDRESS, :EMP-CITY,
                :EMP-STATE, :EMP-ZIP
           FROM EMPLOYEE
           WHERE EMP_ZIP = "62025"
      END-EXEC.
      IF SQLCODE = 0
*          (Place additional code here to process the employee row)
      ELSE
*          (Insert additional code here to handle the retrieval
*           error - no employees with the specified Zip Code)
      END IF.
```

Additional code would be added to process the data rows retrieved from the *employee* table by calling the PROCESS-EMPLOYEE-DATA paragraph through use of a standard PERFORM UNTIL command within COBOL. The embedded SQL command replaces the use of a COBOL READ command for the simple retrieval of data.

Data can be inserted into the *employee* table by using the SQL INSERT statement in place of the COBOL WRITE command as shown in COBOL Example 11.5. Let's assume that the data values to be inserted have already been moved to the work variables defined within the **01 EMPLOYEE-WORK** memory variable created earlier. This could be accomplished by using a series of ACCEPT commands to enable data entry from the keyboard. Alternatively, the data values could be READ from a sequential or indexed data file.

```
* COBOL Example 11.5
EXEC SQL
    INSERT INTO EMPLOYEE (EMP_SSN, EMP_LAST_NAME,
           EMP_FIRST_NAME, EMP_MIDDLE_NAME, EMP_ADDRESS,
           EMP_CITY, EMP_STATE, EMP_ZIP)
        VALUES (:EMP-SSN, :EMP-LAST-NAME, :EMP-FIRST-NAME,
           :EMP-MIDDLE-NAME, :EMP-ADDRESS, :EMP-CITY,
           :EMP-STATE, :EMP-ZIP)
END-EXEC.
```

Note that the values inserted from the Working-Storage variables match up on a one-for-one basis with the column names defined for the *employee* table in the Working-Storage Section of the program.

SUMMARY

In this chapter you learned that SQL can be embedded within different procedural programming languages. The advantages of using embedded SQL for a computer programmer is an increase in work productivity because SQL commands add the power of a nonprocedural language to a procedural language. This simplifies data retrieval, manipulation, and storage. In Visual Basic 6.0 and Visual Basic.NET, database connections are created through the use of various types of Command and Connection objects, and through the use of OLEDB provider software. In COBOL, the Data and Procedure Divisions are modified to include the use of special SQL processing commands. Embedded SQL statements and code that define internal COBOL tables are used to process database tables, and are marked for the compiler by using the EXEC SQL and END-EXEC commands.

REVIEW EXERCISES

LEARN THESE TERMS

ActiveX Data Objects (ADO). An approach using a specialized control to enable the computer programmer to create database connections very rapidly.

Class. In Visual Basic.NET, a class includes all object members that are grouped with similar characteristics. For example, the forms used to build an application interface are members of the *Forms class*.

CommandType. An ADO control property that specifies how data will be retrieved from a database.

ConnectionString. An ADO control property used to specify how to connect to a database.

Data Division. The division within a COBOL program that is used to declare both the structure of files or databases, as well as Working-Storage variables.

DataField. A property of a control that is used to set to the actual column name from a table to be displayed in a form control such as a textbox.

DataSource. A property of a control such as a textbox that specifies the name of the ADO control (recordset) that links the textbox control to the database through the ADO control.

Embedded SQL. The use of SQL commands in conjunction with procedural and object-oriented programming host languages where the SQL command is embedded within the host language.

END-EXEC. The end of every SQL statement within a COBOL program is marked for the compiler by an END-EXEC command.

EXEC SQL. The beginning of every SQL statement within a COBOL program is marked for the compiler by an EXEC SQL command.

Nonprocedural. A single SQL command tells the information system *what* to do as opposed to *how* to accomplish the intended data processing task.

OLEDB. Object linking and embedding database provider.

Procedure Division. The division within a COBOL program used to specify the logic for processing data.

Recordset. A memory object that includes all data rows retrieved to memory from a database for processing.

RecordSource. An ADO control property that stores the actual SQL statement used to create a recordset.

SQLCA. An area within a COBOL program's Data Division (*SQL communications area*) that *must* be defined in order to process embedded SQL statements. The SQL communications area includes a SQLCODE parameter.

System.Data.OleDB. One of the classes within the System.Data namespace that is used to connect to any database with an OLEDB provider.

CONCEPTS QUIZ

1. Why is it useful to embed SQL statements within a host language?
2. What is the purpose of an ADO control in Visual Basic?
3. How are controls on a Visual Basic form able to display data from relational database columns?
4. What advantages does Visual Basic.NET have over Visual Basic 6.0?
5. What type of object is used in Visual Basic.NET to execute SQL statements? How is the SQL statement passed to the host program?

6. Which two divisions within a COBOL program require modification in order to use embedded SQL statements?
7. What two special commands are used to mark the beginning and end of SQL statements that are embedded within a COBOL program?
8. Conceptually, how is a Data Division in a COBOL program modified in order to allow the retrieval of data from a relational DBMS table?
9. What is the purpose of the SQLCODE parameter in a COBOL program with embedded SQL commands?

SQL CODING EXERCISES AND QUESTIONS

In answering the SQL exercises and questions, submit a copy of each command that you execute and any messages that Oracle generates while executing your SQL commands. Also list the output for any result table that is generated by your SQL statements.

1. Study the company database in Appendix A. You plan to build a form in Visual Basic 6.0 to display all of the columns in the *department* table. Write the SELECT statement to retrieve all rows from the table.
2. Suppose that in question 1 only a single *department* table row should be retrieved to display on the Visual Basic form. The form will have a textbox named *txtDepartment* and the value of the department to display will be referenced by the *txtDepartment.Text* property. Write an embedded SQL statement to retrieve the desired department. Store the SQL statement to a Visual Basic string variable named *strSQL*.
3. The ADO control used to process the department table referenced in question 2 is named *adoDepartment*. Write the code necessary to store the *strSQL* variable to the appropriate property of the ADO control and to retrieve the desired department row.
4. You are using Visual Basic.NET to connect to an Oracle database named *MyDatabase*. Write code needed to declare a Private Constant (Private Const) named *strConnection* and to store the appropriate connection string value to this constant to make a connection to *MyDatabase*. The User ID is **user350** and the password is **abracadabra.**
5. Write a DECLARE statement to declare a table named DEPT_LOC to be used to define the *dept_locations* table (see the company database schema in Appendix A) within a COBOL program.
6. One of your colleagues has written a portion of the Working-Storage Section of a COBOL program to define variables to be used to process the *dept_locations* table from the company database. Your colleague's code is shown below. Write a COBOL paragraph named PROCESS-DEPT-LOC-DATA that will select rows from the *dept_locations* table and store the values into the Working-Storage Section variables where the department number is 1. Remember that the table is named DEPT_LOC in the DECLARE statement.

```
01 DEPT-LOC-WORK.
   05  DPT-NO          PIC 99.
   05  DPT-LOCATION    PIC X(20).
```

CHAPTER 12

ORACLE DATABASE ADMINISTRATION

As an SQL programmer, you can expect to work regularly with an Oracle database administrator. In fact, you will be a more effective SQL programmer if you have a basic understanding of database administration principles. Experienced SQL programmers are often given limited access to various tables and views that comprise an Oracle database data dictionary. Access to data dictionary components can enable you to do your job better.

OBJECTIVES

In Chapter 2 you learned some database administration basics—how to create tables and indexes. In this chapter, we will extend your understanding of Oracle database administration by surveying topics with the following learning objectives:

- Develop a general understanding of database administration.
- Understand the duties of a database administrator.
- Learn about the organization of an Oracle database.
- Learn concepts concerning the Oracle data dictionary.
- Learn about the special SYS and SYSTEM Oracle database user accounts
- Learn commands used to manage user accounts including creating, altering, and dropping user accounts.
- Learn to allocate and deallocate system and object privileges
- Study the use of roles to simplify common database administration tasks and the commands used to create/alter roles.
- Familiarize with various data dictionary tables and views.

DATABASE ADMINISTRATION OVERVIEW

Database administration is a specialized area within a large information systems department that is separate from the application development area. Generally, application development includes systems analysis, systems design, programming, and systems testing. Database administration is concerned with administrative tasks that must be accomplished in order for application developers and information system users to access an organization's databases. A database administrator (DBA) is neither superior to nor inferior to an application developer. DBAs and application developers must be both technically competent and capable of working close with other professionals in a support type of relationship. One of the primary roles of a DBA is to provide the support needed by an application developer so that the application developer can accomplish the task of building and maintaining information systems.

DATABASE ADMINISTRATOR DUTIES

A *DBA* is the individual assigned primary responsibility for administering a database. In addition to working closely with application developers, DBAs also work hand in hand with operating system administrators. Many of the tasks associated with administering an operating system and the associated computer servers are similar to the tasks of a DBA. Both system administrators and DBAs are concerned with issues such as system backup and recovery, system security, and user account allocation. The DBA's task list, however, focuses exclusively on an organization's databases. A DBA must be able to do the following detailed tasks:

- Install relational database management system software and upgrades.
- Design and create a database including the allocation of system disk storage for current and future database storage requirements.
- Start up and shut down a database.
- Create user accounts and monitor user activities.
- Grant database privileges to control data security and data access.
- Backup and recover a database in the event of system failure.
- Tune a database to optimize database performance.
- Manage database network connectivity.
- Migrate a database to a new version of the DBMS software.

Large organizations often have many DBAs. A DBA may be assigned responsibility for managing one or more individual databases or groups of databases. Large systems may require more than one DBA to manage an individual database.

ORGANIZATION OF AN ORACLE DATABASE

An Oracle relational database is typical of databases running on larger relational database management systems, and includes both memory and disk storage components. Figure 12.1 provides a fairly detailed conceptual model of what is termed an *Oracle Instance*.

Oracle Instance

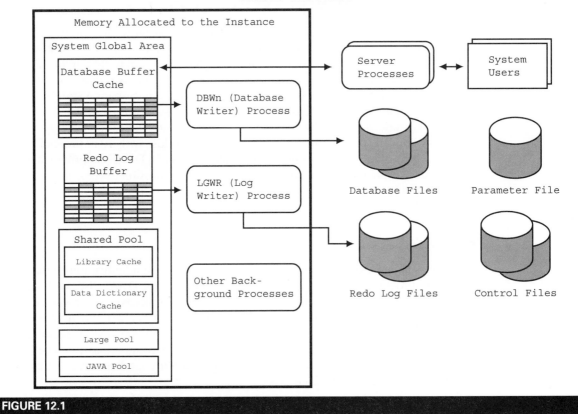

FIGURE 12.1

AN ORACLE INSTANCE

The large rectangle in Figure 12.1 labeled *Memory Allocated to the Instance* represents part of a server computer's random access memory (RAM). This part of RAM is strictly allocated to a running *instance* of an Oracle database. The instance includes the *system global area (SGA),* and the SGA is divided into the *database buffer cache, redo log buffer, shared pool, large pool,* and *JAVA pool.*

The *instance* also includes memory is also allocated for computer programs called *background processes.* The background processes are part of the Oracle *instance,* and are actually computer programs. These programs provide the services needed to enable system developers and system users to save database objects such as data tables and data rows in tables. The background processes also enable database recovery, database backup, data archiving, and other data management tasks as necessary.

Figure 12.1 also shows several types of *disk* objects (files). An Oracle database does not normally run on a personal computer, although there is a version of Oracle called Personal Oracle that will do just that. Usually, an Oracle database is very large and resides on a powerful server computer. A server computer is typically connected to many disk drives. In fact, it is common for a server to access dozens of hard disk drives. You are probably used to thinking in terms of drive "C" on your personal computer. If you've never seen a server computer, you might imagine a much more powerful personal computer with a powerful operating system and separate hard disks for drives "D, E, F," and so on, all the way through "Z" and beyond.

The *database files* shown in Figure 12.1 typically include many different physical files stored on many disk drives. Database files provide the primary storage for all objects stored in a database. This is where user tables and data are stored.

The *redo log files* in Figure 12.1 store information that is used to recover a database if some type of database failure occurs. The *control files* store information about the actual physical organization of an Oracle database. The *parameter file* stores information that Oracle needs in order to operate the database as specified by the DBA. The DBA can change information in the parameter file in order to change operating characteristics of the database.

When a system user logs onto an Oracle database or when an application program executes (an application program is simply another type of system user), Oracle allocates a memory object called as a *server process* as shown in Figure 12.1. The dedicated server version of Oracle allocates one server process to each system *user process*. The multithreaded server version of Oracle allows server processes to be shared by more than one system user process. A server process communicates with a user process in order to service the data requests from the connected user process. In this sense, a server process is like a program; it is *not* a separate server computer—do not confuse these different uses of the term *server*. The server process actually interprets the SQL commands passed from the user process through the server process to Oracle, and moves the requested data from the database files into the database buffer cache.

Suppose that a system user executes a SQL command that will modify an existing data row stored in an Oracle database. The data row is moved from a database file to the server process allocated to the system user, and then to the *database buffer cache* in the *system global area*. The database buffer cache is a memory object that is shared by all system users. This sharing improves system performance because more than one user process may need to access the same data row. Data inside the database buffer cache is constantly being modified as data rows are added, deleted, and updated. Over time, modified data blocks (a single data block typically contains many rows of data) are written from the database buffer cache by a background process called the *database writer (DBWn)* back to the appropriate disk data file, thereby saving the data to the magnetic hard disk.

As existing data rows in the database buffer cache are modified or new data rows are created, memory images of these modifications and new rows are stored to the *redo log buffer* in the system global area. As the redo log buffer in memory fills up, the modified row images are written to the redo log files on disk by a different background process called the *log writer (LGWR)*. This is necessary because the redo log buffer is a memory object, and if electrical power is lost, the redo log buffer contents are lost and the Oracle database would not be able to recover modified and new data rows that have not yet been written to the database files. The redo log files are a magnetic hard disk objects; thus, their data are not lost if electrical power fails. Over time, the redo log files can be archived to provide a more permanent record of database changes. The data in redo log buffers and in redo log files are used to recover a database in the event of some type of system failure.

In addition to the database writer and log writer background processes, there are other background processes that perform additional database administration tasks such as managing memory space allocated to Oracle by the operating system, archiving data, and performing backup and recovery. Some of these processes manage the *shared pool, large pool,* and *JAVA pool* shown in Figure 12.1.

The shared pool is shared by all server processes in order to improve performance efficiency of an Oracle database. The large pool is memory that can be used to store variables and other memory values that would be part of an individual system user's allocated server process. The Java pool is used for memory allocation in support of the execution of Java commands for Internet-based applications accessing an Oracle database. A detailed explanation of the shared pool, large pool, and JAVA pool is beyond the scope of this text.

TABLESPACES AND FILES

In order to provide for optimal system performance, an Oracle database is normally divided into logical components termed *tablespaces.* Most tablespaces are created by a DBA when a database is initially created. Over time, additional tablespaces can be added to a database. As the term implies, a tablespace is used to store tables. But, tablespaces are actually used to store *all* types of database objects. These objects include indexes, sequences, procedures, views, and other database objects. A typical Oracle database will have most of the tablespaces listed here.

- *SYSTEM*—used to store the data dictionary for the database. The data dictionary is described in detail in the next section. This tablespace is required.
- *USER*—used to store objects created and owned by individual system users of the database. This is normally where tables and indexes are stored that are created by system users like yourself.
- *DATA*—used to store all permanent tables that store data accessed by an organization's information systems.
- *INDEXES*—used to store all permanent indexes that allow efficient storage and retrieval of data stored in tables in the DATA tablespace.
- *TEMP*—used to store temporary objects created by user processes such as those associated with sorting data (by using the ORDER BY clause in a SELECT statement), or the storage of temporary tables created by a JOIN of two tables.
- *UNDO*—used to store undo segments. These special objects enable the system to recover from minor database errors and enable you to rollback or undo a transaction that you do not wish to commit. Recall from your study of Chapter 2 that committing a transaction means to save a database change permanently.
- *IDS*—used to store objects created when a system developer uses Oracle's Internet Developer Suite (IDS) computer-aided, software-engineering (CASE) tools such as Oracle Designer, Reports and Forms when building an information system.
- *SPECIAL_APPS*—used to store objects such as tables and indexes for special, large applications that require considerable space and/or time resources.

So, why is there a need for different tablespaces? It is because different types of database objects have different performance characteristics, and separating the database objects into different storage areas can enable a DBA to improve or "tune" system performance. Exactly how this improves system performance is very complex and is beyond the scope of this text. Suffice to say that you will almost always find Oracle databases organized into different tablespaces.

Tablespaces are *logical,* not *physical* objects. Tablespaces are actually stored in *data files.* Data files are the corresponding physical objects. A very large tablespace may require more than one data file in order to store all of its objects. This is intuitive if you stop and think about the nature of a disk drive. A disk drive, even a large one, has a finite, fixed amount of storage capacity. Even if a DBA allocates most of a very large disk drive to a single data file, the system may eventually fill the data file with data. For example, the database table that stores Social Security system information about U.S. citizens is enormous. It encompasses thousands of data files. Still, the individual tables that store worker wage and retirement benefit data history data are managed as a single, logical tablespace.

On the other hand, a data file can only store data for a single tablespace. A DBA cannot allocate more than one tablespace to a data file, but a DBA can allocate additional data files to a tablespace as the need for more storage space becomes evident.

Tablespaces are created with the CREATE TABLESPACE command. This is a complex command and the database privileges needed to execute the command are only allocated to DBAs.

ABOUT THE DATA DICTIONARY

The Oracle *data dictionary* consists of *read-only, base tables* that store information about the database. The data dictionary is stored in the *system* tablespace. Some of the information stored in the data dictionary includes:

- All schema object definitions—the definitions of the tables, indexes, sequences, views, and other database objects.
- The amount of space allocated for each object, and the amount of space currently used by each object.
- The names of the Oracle user accounts, and the privileges and roles granted to each account.
- Information needed to enforce integrity constraints.
- Other database information.

Information stored in the data dictionary is termed *metadata,* that is, data about data. When you execute an SQL command such as CREATE TABLE, CREATE INDEX, or CREATE SEQUENCE to create an object, all of the information about column names, column size, default values, constraints, index names, sequence starting values, and other information are stored in the form of metadata to the data dictionary tables.

The read-only, base tables that comprise the data dictionary are rarely ever accessed by system developers or system users. Usually only the various Oracle processes will access these tables. In order to make it easier to access information and manage a database, the tables of the data dictionary are organized into various *user-accessible views*. These views are also part of the data dictionary.

THE SYSTEM AND SYS ACCOUNTS

When an Oracle database is created, two special user accounts named SYS and SYSTEM are created. The user account SYS is the owner of all base tables and user-accessible views in the data dictionary. As you can imagine, the security of the SYS account is quite tight and only DBAs can access this account.

During database operation, Oracle accesses the base tables through the SYS account. For this reason, only Oracle can write new data or modify existing data in the base tables. Individual system users should never be given privileges to UPDATE, INSERT, or DELETE rows for these data dictionary tables. Individual system users will, on occasion, have privileges to SELECT rows from the data dictionary but, for the most part, they will actually be extracting information from the user-accessible *views*. Access to user-accessible views is made easier by creating public synonyms for the views.

When Oracle software or third-party software adds new tables and views to the data dictionary, the owner of these new objects is the user SYSTEM. Again, access to the SYSTEM account is also tight and is typically restricted to DBAs.

DIFFERENT TYPES OF VIEWS–USER, ALL, AND DBA

There are many different types of data dictionary views. In order to assist system users in using the data dictionary, the views are divided into three different categories: USER, ALL, and DBA.

- *USER*—The *user* prefix is added to all views that display information about objects that belong to an individual user. We term this the user's schema of the database.
- *ALL*—The *all* prefix is added to all views that display information about all objects in the global database schema. This expands on an individual user's perspective of the database.
- *DBA*—The *dba* prefix is added to all views that fall within the database administrator's schema of the database.

VIEWS WITH THE USER PREFIX

Users are interested in objects that belong to them. As a system user, you will want to know about grants that you have given for your objects to other system users. You will want to display information about tables and other objects that you have created. One of the most useful user views is the *user_objects* view. Let's examine the structure of *user_objects* by executing the DESCRIBE command shown in SQL Example 12.1.

```
/* SQL Example 12.1 */
DESC user_objects;

Name                    Null?     Type
-------------           -----     -----------
OBJECT_NAME                       VARCHAR2(128)
SUBOBJECT_NAME                    VARCHAR2(30)
OBJECT_ID                         NUMBER
DATA_OBJECT_ID                    NUMBER
OBJECT_TYPE                       VARCHAR2(18)
CREATED                           DATE
more rows are displayed...
```

As you can see, the *user_objects* view has columns named *object_name, subobject_name,* and so on. Let's display some of the information stored in the *user_objects* view. Execute a SELECT statement to display the *object_name, object_type,* and *created* columns from *user_objects* like the one shown in SQL Example 12.2. Your listing of objects will differ from that shown below depending upon the objects that you created during your study of this textbook. We have used the COLUMN command to format the output since the *object_name* column is normally up to 128 characters in size.

```
/* SQL Example 12.2 */
COLUMN object_name FORMAT A25;
COLUMN object_type FORMAT A10;
SELECT object_name, object_type, created
FROM user_objects
ORDER BY object_name;

OBJECT_NAME             OBJECT_TYP     CREATED
----------------        ---------      ---------
BED                     TABLE          18-JAN-03
BED_TYPE                TABLE          18-JAN-03
CDB_LOG_SESSION         SYNONYM        16-AUG-03
CDDL_TMP_TBL            SYNONYM        16-AUG-03
EMPLOYEE                TABLE          17-JAN-02
EMPTY                   TABLE          17-AUG-01
EXU7CPO                 VIEW           15-AUG-02
MEDICAL_SPECIALTY       TABLE          18-JAN-03
MEDICINE                TABLE          18-JAN-03
PATIENT                 TABLE          18-JAN-03
PK_SERVICE_CAT          INDEX          18-JAN-03
PK_STAFF                INDEX          18-JAN-03
PK_STAFF_MEDSPEC        INDEX          18-JAN-03
PK_TREATMENT            INDEX          18-JAN-03
more rows are displayed...
```

As you can see, this particular system user has created a number of table, view, synonym, and index objects. This view of the data dictionary can assist a system user with identifying a particular object of interest.

VIEWS WITH THE ALL PREFIX

A view with the *all* prefix will expand your perspective of the database by adding access to information about objects that do not belong to you. These are objects that you can access because some *other* system user has granted you the privilege to do so. These views also include access to objects through roles that have been granted to you, and to objects that have a defined *public* synonym.

An interesting view similar to the *user_objects* view is the *all_objects* view. If you execute a DESCRIBE command for *all_objects,* you'll find a view description that is quite similar to *user_objects*. An additional key column in *all_objects* not found in *user_objects* is the column labeled *owner.* If you execute the SELECT statement shown in SQL Example 12.3 for *all_objects,* the listing of objects may be quite extensive; depending upon how many objects you are authorized to access. You may wish to terminate the listing (try pressing ctrl and 'C' simultaneously) without listing all objects.

```
/* SQL Example 12.3 */
COLUMN owner FORMAT A15;
SELECT owner, object_name, object_type, created
FROM all_objects;

OWNER          OBJECT_NAME          OBJECT_TYP     CREATED
-----          ------------------   ----------     ---------
SYS            ACCESS$              TABLE          14-AUG-01
SYS            ALL_ALL_TABLES       VIEW           14-AUG-01
SYS            ALL_ARGUMENTS        VIEW           14-AUG-01
SYS            ALL_ASSOCIATIONS     VIEW           14-AUG-01
more rows are displayed...
```

VIEWS WITH THE DBA PREFIX

This category of views is only meant to be queried by a DBA. The DBA views provide a global perspective of the database. You may be given limited access to this category of views during your instruction on SQL in order for you to learn about this part of the data dictionary. You can access most DBA views if you have been granted the SELECT ANY TABLE system privilege. System privileges are discussed later in this chapter.

By default, public synonyms for the DBA views are not created; however, a DBA can create a set of public synonyms for these views, if that is desirable. In the absence of a public synonym, you must access these views by referencing both the view owner (SYS) and the view name. For example, the view *sys.dba_objects* can be used to obtain basic information about all of the objects in the database. The structure of the *sys.dba_objects* view is almost identical to the *all_objects* view, differing only in the size of some of the columns and the constraint listing. A sample SELECT statement for this view is shown in SQL Example 12.4. The listing of objects from a DBA view is often quite extensive.

```
/* SQL Example 12.4 */
SELECT owner, object_name, object_type, created
FROM sys.dba_objects
ORDER BY object_type;
```

If you do not have the privileges to access the sys.dba_objects view, Oracle will return an error message, *ORA-00942: table or view does not exist* telling you that the view does not exist. Of course it does exist, but since you do not have access privileges, Oracle will not even admit that it exists. This is part of the normal system security.

USER ACCOUNTS AND PRIVILEGES

Individual accounts, including those that belong to DBAs must be created. When a database is initially created, a DBA will logon to the database as the user SYS or SYSTEM, and create a personal DBA account. The DBA account will be granted all of the privileges needed to administer the database. During subsequent database administration sessions, the DBA will almost always logon by using the newly created DBA account.

CREATING, ALTERING, AND DROPPING USER ACCOUNTS

The DBA creates individual accounts for each system user. A simple form of the CREATE USER command is shown in SQL Example 12.5. Note that the user name specified in this sample command is *bock*. The user name must be unique within the database.

```
/* SQL Example 12.5 */
CREATE USER bock IDENTIFIED BY secret_password;
```

A DBA or other system administrator must have the CREATE USER system privilege in order to create a user account. Even though *bock* now has an account, *bock* still cannot connect to the database until the DBA grants *bock* the CREATE SESSION system privilege. Hereafter, *bock* will own a *schema* named *bock* and all of *bock's* objects will be stored to the bock schema. Thus, two system users can create two different objects with the same object name because each object is stored to their respective schemas, and the actual name of each object will have the general form: *schema_name.object_name.* For example, if *bock* creates a table named *employee,* then this table's complete name is *bock.employee.* If another user named *bordoloi* creates a table named *employee,* then this table's complete name is *bordoloi.employee.* There are two separate tables, each stored to a separate schema!

SQL Example 12.6 gives a more complete form of the CREATE USER command. This CREATE USER command creates a user account and also allocates space for the storage of objects in various tablespaces. This command will only execute if your database has the tablespaces named here. Your instructor will provide you with the name of the tablespaces for your database.

```
/* SQL Example 12.6 */
CREATE USER bock IDENTIFIED BY secret_password
    DEFAULT TABLESPACE users
    TEMPORARY TABLESPACE temp
```

```
    QUOTA 10M ON users
    QUOTA UNLIMITED ON temp
    QUOTA 5M ON data
    PASSWORD EXPIRE;
```

In addition to creating *bock's* user account, *bock* is assigned a default tablespace named *users.* This means that all objects created by *bock* will be stored in the *bock* schema to the *users* tablespace; further, the space quota for storing objects in the *users* tablespace is limited to 10 megabytes for *bock. Bock* has also been assigned a temporary tablespace of *temp* with an unlimited quota, as well as a quota of five megabytes on the *data* tablespace. Recall from Chapter 2 that the *temp* tablespace is used to store temporary objects such as table rows generated through execution of a SELECT statement with the ORDER BY sorting clause or by joining tables. The *data* tablespace stores any objects belonging to permanent information systems currently used by the organization, such as inventory systems and payroll systems. The PASSWORD EXPIRE clause will force *bock* to change the *secret_password* the first time that this system user connects to the database.

Suppose that we suspect *bock* is doing something with the database that is unauthorized! We can stop *bock* from creating additional objects by altering the *bock* account. The commands shown in SQL Example 12.7 will alter *bock's* quota on the *users* and *data* tablespaces. Existing objects *bock* has created will not be modified, but he will be unable to create new objects.

```
/* SQL Example 12.7 */
ALTER USER bock QUOTA 0 ON users;
ALTER USER bock QUOTA 0 ON data;
```

Of course, you can also use the ALTER USER command to allocate additional space and to restore quota allocations. When bock logs onto his account, he will use the ALTER USER command to change his password as shown in SQL Example 12.8.

```
/* SQL Example 12.8 */
ALTER USER bock IDENTIFIED BY new_secret_password;
```

The DROP USER command will delete a user account. It is necessary to use the CASCADE option if the user has created any objects.

```
/* SQL Example 12.9 */
DROP USER bock;
DROP USER bock CASCADE;
```

If you fail to specify CASCADE, then the DROP USER command will fail if the user has created objects. But wait, we need to EXERCISE CAUTION! What if *bock* is a system developer who has created some critical objects such as tables that our organization uses to store inventory and payroll information? If we drop *bock* with a CAS-CADE, the applications will fail because the tables and indexes that *bock* created will be destroyed. A better alternative is to lock *bock* out of his account because his employment has terminated. We can do this by revoking his privilege to connect to the system. Privilege allocation and revocation are covered in the next section.

GRANTING AND REVOKING PRIVILEGES

We noted earlier that user accounts require the CREATE SESSION privilege in order to logon to SQL*PLUS or any of Oracle's tools. The GRANT command in SQL Example 12.10 will grant user *bock* this privilege.

```
/* SQL Example 12.10 */
GRANT PRIVILEGE create session TO bock;
```

There are many different privileges. In fact, there are so many privileges that they are divided into two categories: *system privileges* and *object privileges.* System privileges allow a system user to perform specific types of operations such as creating, dropping, and altering objects. Object privileges allow a system user to perform a specific operation on a specific object such as a view, table, or index.

SYSTEM PRIVILEGES

System privileges are also termed *system-wide* privileges, and include privileges that focus on managing objects that you own, and privileges that focus on managing objects that any system user may own. Here are example system privileges:

- CREATE SESSION; ALTER SESSION
- CREATE TABLE
- CREATE ANY TABLE; ALTER ANY TABLE
- CREATE ANY INDEX
- UNLIMITED TABLESPACE

Basically, if you can create an object, you can also drop the object. The CREATE TABLE privilege also includes the privilege to create indexes for a table and to subsequently drop those indexes as necessary. A privilege may be granted to more than one user at a time, and several privileges may be granted to one or more users at a time. Some example GRANT commands are shown in SQL Example 12.11. Note that the privileges being granted are separated by a comma as are the user account names:

```
/* SQL Example 12.11 */
GRANT create session TO bock, bordoloi, user001;
GRANT create table, unlimited tablespace TO bock;
GRANT create table, create any table TO bock, bordoloi;
```

Once a DBA has created a user account, a system privilege may be granted to the user account with the WITH ADMIN OPTION. In fact, this option may be used in any GRANT command that grants a system privilege. The WITH ADMIN OPTION enables the grantee (the account receiving the privilege) to, in turn, grant the privilege to other user accounts. SQL Example 12.12 grants CREATE SESSION and CREATE TABLE to *bock,* and also gives *bock* the authority to grant these two privileges to other system user accounts.

```
/* SQL Example 12.12 */
GRANT create session, create table TO bock WITH ADMIN OPTION;
```

You can display system privileges that have been granted, including whether or not the grantee has WITH ADMIN OPTION by querying the *dba_sys_privs* view.

```
/* SQL Example 12.13 */
SELECT *
FROM dba_sys_privs;

GRANTEE       PRIVILEGE              ADMIN
-------       ------------------     ----
BORDOLOI      UNLIMITED TABLESPACE   YES
BOCK          CREATE VIEW            YES
BOCK          EXECUTE ANY PROCEDURE  NO
BOCK          SELECT ANY TABLE       NO
BOCK          UNLIMITED TABLESPACE   NO
CONNECT       ALTER SESSION          NO
CONNECT       CREATE SESSION         NO
more rows are displayed...
```

OBJECT PRIVILEGES

As was noted earlier, object privileges work on a specific object, so the form of the GRANT command is a bit different. The general form is:

```
GRANT privilege1, privilege2, . . .
    ON object_name TO user1, user2, . . . | public;
```

For example, if *bock* has created a table named *employee* and wants to give the user named *bordoloi* the privilege to select rows from the table, the GRANT command in SQL Example 12.14 enables *bordoloi* to select from the table.

```
/* SQL Example 12.14 */
GRANT select ON bock.employee TO bordoloi;
```

Suppose that *bock* also wants *bordoloi* to be able to insert rows into the *employee* table so as to *relieve* bock of some of the workload associated with loading new data. The revised GRANT command in SQL Example 12.15 includes the INSERT privilege.

```
/* SQL Example 12.15 */
GRANT select, insert ON bock.employee TO bordoloi;
```

If *bock* is going to give everyone privileges to select from the *employee* table, the GRANT command will give the SELECT privilege to PUBLIC.

```
/* SQL Example 12.16 */
GRANT select ON bock.employee TO PUBLIC;
```

If *bock* wants *bordoloi* to be able to grant the privilege to insert rows for the *employee* table to other system users, then *bock* would execute a GRANT command with the WITH GRANT OPTION.

```
/* SQL Example 12.17 */
GRANT insert ON bock.employee TO bordoloi WITH GRANT OPTION;
```

REVOKING PRIVILEGES

System privileges may be revoked with the REVOKE command. You can only revoke a privilege that was specifically granted previously with a GRANT command. There are no cascading effects of revoking privileges. This means that if DBA1 grants system privileges WITH ADMIN OPTION to DBA2, and then DBA1 subsequently changes jobs and is no longer authorized DBA privileges, all privileges granted to DBA1 can be revoked without worrying about privileges that DBA1 might have granted to DBA2 or to any system user account, for that matter. SQL Example 12.18 shows the revocation of the SELECT ANY TABLE privilege from the user account *bordoloi*.

```
/* SQL Example 12.18 */
REVOKE select any table FROM bordoloi;
```

Object privileges are revoked in a similar fashion, except that the object for which privileges are revoked must be named in the REVOKE command. The keyword ALL can be used to revoke all privileges for an object from a user account.

```
/* SQL Example 12.19 */
REVOKE select ON bock.employee FROM bordoloi;
REVOKE ALL ON bock.employee FROM bordoloi;
```

ROLES

The concept of a *role* is a simple one, and its purpose is to make it easier for a DBA to manage privileges. You should think of a role as a container of a group of privileges for a specific type of system user, such as an inventory manager. Each time we hire an inventory manager, we would assign the manager a new system user account and authorize that account all of the privileges contained in the role called *inventory_mgr*. Further, we can simplify the management of privileges because we can allocate a role to another role! Figure 12.2 depicts privileges being allocated to roles, and the roles being allocated to system users.

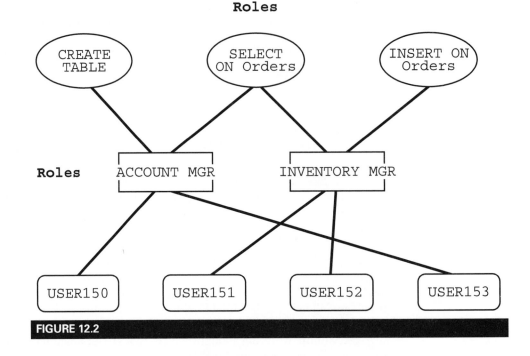

FIGURE 12.2

From studying Figure 12.2, it should be obvious that if you add a new system user who works as an account manager, then you can allocate almost all of the privileges this user will need by simply allocating the role named *account_mgr* to the system user. Further, if it is determined that all account managers need an additional privilege, such as DELETE ON ORDERS, that privilege can be granted to the *account_mgr* role, and all of the system users who are granted the role named *account_mgr* will inherit the new privilege! This considerably simplifies user account management.

A role name must be unique within the database. Additionally, a role can be allocated both system and object privileges. Roles are not owned by anyone so they do not appear in any user account schema. Further, you allocate privileges to roles the same way that you allocate them to a system user account; however, you must first create the role by using the CREATE ROLE command. The example commands shown in SQL Example 12.20 create the role named *inventory_mgr* and grant several privileges to the role. Next the role is allocated to the system user account for *bordoloi*. Finally, the system user *bock* is granted the *inventory_mgr* role with the privilege to grant the role to other system users through the WITH ADMIN OPTION.

```
/* SQL Example 12.20 */
CREATE ROLE inventory_mgr;
GRANT select ON bock.employee TO inventory_mgr;
GRANT select, unlimited tablespace TO inventory_mgr;
GRANT inventory_mgr TO bordoloi;
GRANT inventory_mgr TO bock WITH ADMIN OPTION;
```

There are several predefined roles that are created as part of the task of creating a new database. The CONNECT role is provided for backward compatibility with earlier versions of Oracle. Anyone granted the DBA role will be granted all system privileges needed to function as a DBA and these privileges will include the WITH ADMIN OPTION.

When a role is dropped, Oracle revokes the role and all privileges granted through the role from all system users and from other roles. If you wish to alter a role, the best approach is to create a new role with the desired privileges, grant that role to the system users/roles that possess the role to be dropped; then, you can drop the first role.

A role that is dropped is removed from the data dictionary. If you were granted a role with the ADMIN OPTION, then you can drop the role. You may also drop a roll if you have the DROP ANY ROLE system privilege. The DROP ROLE command is very simple. SQL Example 12.21 shows the command used to drop the *account_mgr* role.

```
/* SQL Example 12.21 */
DROP ROLE account_mgr;
```

EXAMINING DATA DICTIONARY TABLES AND VIEWS

There are a number of data dictionary views that will interest you and further your understanding of database administration. There is also a special set of views named *dynamic performance views* that are used to accumulate information and statistics about the performance of the database. Each dynamic performance view begins with a prefix of **v$.** You are encouraged to examine each of these tables and views for your database installation in order to learn more about the data dictionary.

Dynamic Performance Views

- *v$fixed_table*—lists all x$ tables that underline and store the dynamic performance information that can be displayed in v$ views.
- *v$session*—lists information about the current sessions. You can use this information to "kill" a session if necessary where a session may be hung up or where the system user may no longer be authorized database access.
- *v$sysstat*—gives information about system performance that are used by a DBA to perform database tuning.
- *v$sga*—lists summary information about the system global area.

Object Privilege Views

- *dba_tab_privs*—lists all object privileges granted to a user.
- *dba_col_privs*—lists all privileges granted on specific columns of a table.
- *session_privs*—lists the privileges held by a user for the current logon session.
- *table_privileges*—lists information on object grants for which you are the grantor, grantee, or owner, or where PUBLIC is the grantee.

ROLE AND PRIVILEGE VIEWS

- *dba_roles*—lists all roles in the database.
- *dba_role_privs*—lists roles granted to system users and to other roles.
- *dba_sys_privs*—lists system privileges granted to users and roles.
- *role_role_privs*—lists roles granted to roles.
- *role_sys_privs*—lists all system privileges granted to roles.
- *role_tab_privs*—lists table privileges granted to roles.

OTHER DATA DICTIONARY VIEWS

- *all_all_tables*—lists information about all object tables and relational tables that you can access as a system user.
- *all_users*—simply lists all users that are visible to you as a system user, but this view does not describe the users.
- *sys.dba_tablespaces*—lists information about tablespaces that exist in the system.
- *sys.dba_data_files*—lists information about data files including which tablespaces are allocated to which data files.
- *user_constraints*—lists constraint definitions for tables in your schema.
- *user_indexes*—lists information about your indexes for tables.
- *user_sequences*—lists information about sequences you have created.
- *user_tables*—lists information about your tables.

SUMMARY

In this chapter you learned some basic principles of database administration from a system users perspective. As you have seen, an oracle database is complex. An instance of an Oracle database includes both memory and disk objects, as well as the background processes (programs) that manage these objects. An Oracle database is divided into logical structures termed tablespaces, and tablespaces are allocated to physical objects in the form of data files.

The system tablespace stores the data dictionary for the database. The data dictionary stores all metadata for all objects that exist within the database. You can access this metadata in order to learn more about various objects such as tables, indexes, and sequences, or even the tablespaces themselves.

You have learned how to create both system users accounts and roles, and how to allocate both system and object privileges to system user accounts and roles. Additionally, you have learned how to alter system user accounts and to revoke privileges that have been granted.

REVIEW EXERCISES

LEARN THESE TERMS

ALL. A prefix that is added to all views that display information about all objects in the global database schema.

ALTER USER. A DBA command used to alter user database privileges and resources.

Background processes. Part of an Oracle Instance that provide services that enable system developers and system users to save database objects such as data tables and data rows in tables. They also perform database recovery, database backup, data archiving, and other data management tasks as necessary.

CASCADE.   An option with the DROP command to cause related or owned objects to be deleted when an object or account is dropped—this option deletes referential integrity constraints between objects.

Control files.   Used to store information about the actual physical organization of an Oracle database.

CREATE ROLE.   A DBA command used to create a role name.

CREATE SESSION.   A privilege that allows a system user to logon to SQL*PLUS and use Oracle tools.

CREATE TABLE privilege.   A type of privilege that includes the ability to create tables and indexes for those tables, as well as to drop the table and indexes.

CREATE TABLESPACE.   A DBA command used to create a tablespace.

CREATE USER.   A DBA command used to create a user account.

Data dictionary.   Read-only, base tables that store information about the database.

Data files.   Physical database objects that correspond to the logical tablespace objects. Each tablespace has one or more data files, but a data file belongs to only a single tablespace.

Database administration.   A specialized area within a large information systems department concerned with administrative tasks that must be accomplished in order for application developers and information system users to access an organization's databases.

Database writer.   A background process that writes data from the database buffer cache to the appropriate disk file for data blocks that have been modified.

DBA.   The individual assigned primary responsibility for administering a database; also a prefix that added to all views that fall within the database administrator's schema of the database.

DROP ROLE.   A DBA command used to delete a role from an Oracle database.

DROP USER.   A DBA command used to delete a user account from an Oracle database.

Dynamic performance views.   Data dictionary views used to accumulate information and statistics about the performance of the database.

Instance.   An Oracle database instance includes the memory objects allocated to the system global area and background processes.

GRANT <privilege>.   A DBA command used to grant different privileges to users and to roles.

Log writer.   A background process that writes data from the redo log buffer to redo log files to enable per-

manent archival storage of changes made to an Oracle database.

Metadata.   Data stored in the data dictionary; data about data.

Object privileges.   Allow a system user to perform a specific operation on a specific object such as a view, table, or index.

Parameter file.   Used to store information that Oracle needs in order to operate the database as specified by the DBA. The DBA can change information in the parameter file in order to change operating characteristics of the database.

PASSWORD EXPIRE.   A clause in the CREAT USER command that forces a system user to change their password the first time they connect to a database.

Redo log buffer.   Part of the system global area that stores information that enables recovery.

Redo log files.   Used to store information that would be needed to recover the database to an earlier point in time should some type of database failure occur.

Role.   A container type of object to which privileges can be allocated, then the role can be allocated to a system user so that the system user inherits the privileges associated with the role; simplifies management of privileges.

REVOKE and REVOKE ALL.   A DBA command used to revoke system and object privileges. The keyword ALL can be used to revoke all privileges for an object from a user account.

Schema.   Area within an Oracle database allocated to an individual user; used to store the individual's database objects.

Shared pool.   A part of the SGA that is shared by all server processes in order to improve performance efficiency of an Oracle database.

Server process.   This memory object communicates with the user process in order to service the data requests from the connected user process.

SYS and SYSTEM.   Two special user accounts. SYS is the owner of all base tables and user-accessible views in the data dictionary. SYSTEM owns tables and views created by other Oracle software or third-party software.

System global area (SGA).   Memory allocated to an Oracle instance that is divided into the *database buffer cache, redo log buffer,* and *shared pool.*

System privileges.   Allows a user to perform specific types of operations such as creating, dropping, and altering objects.

Tablespace.   A logical component of an Oracle database that is a place to store tables and other database objects.

USER.   A prefix that is added to all views that display information about objects that belong to an individual user.

User-accessible views.   Views that are part of the data dictionary. In order to make it easier to access information and manage a database, the tables of the data dictionary are organized into various *user-accessible views*.

WITH ADMIN OPTION.   An option with the GRANT command that enables the grantee to, in turn, grant a system privilege to another user account.

WITH GRANT OPTION.   Used with the GRANT command to enable a grantee of an object privilege to grant the object privilege to another user account.

CONCEPTS QUIZ

1. Name three of the detailed tasks normally completed by database administrators.
2. One of the memory components of an Oracle database instance is the system global area. The system global area includes three components: 1)_____, 2)_____, and 3)_____.
3. Which disk object component of an Oracle database instance is used to store information that would be needed to recover the database to an earlier point in time should some type of database failure occur?
4. What is the term for the logical component of an Oracle database that is used to store tables?
5. Which tablespace stores the data dictionary for an Oracle database?
6. Why is an Oracle database divided into different tablespaces?
7. List the information that is stored in a data dictionary.
8. A system user or system developer rarely ever accesses the read-only, base tables that comprise the data dictionary. Instead it is common to access information organized into various _____.
9. What is the name of the user account that owns all base tables and user-accessible views in the data dictionary?
10. What are the three different types (or categories) of views in the data dictionary?
11. Which data dictionary view can be used to obtain a description of objects owned by you as a system user?
12. What is the prefix that is used to denote a view as a dynamic performance view?
13. Which view lists information on all object grants for which you are the grantor, grantee, or owner, or where PUBLIC is the grantee?

SQL CODING EXERCISES AND QUESTIONS

In answering the SQL exercises and questions, submit a copy of each command that you execute and any messages that Oracle generates while executing your SQL commands. Also list the output for any result table that is generated by your SQL statements.

In order to work these exercises while using SQL*Plus, your instructor must grant you the following privileges:

- CREATE SESSION WITH ADMIN OPTION
- CREATE USER WITH ADMIN OPTION
- ALTER USER
- DROP USER
- UNLIMITED TABLESPACE WITH ADMIN OPTION
- CREATE TABLE WITH ADMIN OPTION
- CREATE ROLE WITH ADMIN OPTION

1. Connect to SQL*Plus with your user account. Write the command to create a user account named *bob* that is identified by the password *wonderful.* Write the command to create a user account named *matilda* that is identified by the password *bootcamp.* Write the command to create a user named *makita* that is identified by the password *swordfish.*

2. Write a command to grant *bob* the system privilege needed in order to connect to the database. Bob should have the privilege to grant the system privilege to connect to the database to other system users.

3. Write a command to create a user account named *sally* that is identified by the password *exciting. Sally* is to be granted a 15-megabyte storage limitation on the *users* tablespace, an unlimited storage limitation on the *temp* tablespace, and must be forced to change the password the first time that *sally* connects to the database. The default tablespace will be users and the temporary tablespace will be *temp.* Write a command to grant *sally* the system privilege needed in order to connect to the database.

4. Write a command that will change *sally's* quota on the temp tablespace to 5 megabytes.

5. Connect to SQL*Plus as the user *sally.* Change *sally's* password to *metal* when you connect. Assume that *sally* has changed her mind and wants her password to be *metalmusic.* Write the command that *sally* will execute to change her logon password to *metalmusic.*

6. Connect to SQL*Plus using your own user account. Write the command to drop the user named *matilda,* assuming that *matilda* has not created any objects in the database.

7. Write the command needed to grant *bob* an unlimited tablespace quota privilege.

8. Write the command to grant *bob* the privilege to create a table. *Bob* should also have the authority to grant this privilege to other system users.

9. *Bob* needs to create a table named *books* that will be used to store information about books that the organization has in its library. The CREATE TABLE command is shown below. Connect to the database as *bob* and execute this command as part of this exercise. Which privilege does system user *bob* need in order to create an index on the *books* table?

```
CREATE TABLE books (
    Book_Id    CHAR(6),
    Book_Title VARCHAR(50),
    ISBN       CHAR(15),
    Book_Price NUMBER(6,2) );
```

10. System user *bob* wishes to grant system user *sally* the privilege to query the *books* table. Write this command.

11. The *books* table is so popular that the head of our organization has directed *bob* to grant everyone in the organization the privilege to query the *books* table. Write this command.

12. System user *sally* is to be trusted by *bob* to insert rows into the *books* table. Further, she is to be granted the right to grant the insert privilege to other system users as she deems necessary. Write the command needed to grant this privilege to *sally.*

13. Write a command that will revoke all privileges that system user *sally* has on the *books* table. Does this command keep *sally* from querying the *books* table with a SELECT statement? Why or why not?

14. Connect to the database using your own user account. Write a command that will create a role named *books_mgr* (someone that will manage books).

15. Write the command needed to grant the role *books_mgr* to the system users named *sally* and *makita*.

16. Write the command needed to grant the role *books_mgr* to the system user named *bob* such that *bob* can also grant this role to other system users or to other roles.

17. Write the command that will drop the role named *books_mgr*.

APPENDIX A

THE COMPANY DATABASE SCHEMA

Throughout the textbook you will study SQL statements that query and modify information stored in tables for the **Company** database. This is one of two databases that are used with this textbook, the second being the **Riverbend Hospital** database described in Appendix B.

DATABASE SCHEMA

Figure A.1 shows a diagram of the six tables that comprise the company database. The table names are underlined in the figure, for example, *employee;* and the column names are shown inside the rectangles, for example, *emp_ssn*.

Relationships between the tables are shown with connecting lines. Consider the line connecting the *employee* and *dependent* tables. Figure A.2 shows you how to interpret the relationship connecting lines.

Reading from the *employee* toward the *dependent* table, the line has a circle and three-legged "crow's foot," meaning this is an optional relationship (circle) such that each employee can optionally (circle) have no dependents. The three-legged crow's foot means an employee can have one or more dependents. Reading from the *dependent* toward the *employee* table, the line is crossed by two short lines indicating that this relationship is mandatory in this direction such that each dependent can belong to one and only one employee—a dependent cannot exist without an employee.

Figure A.2 shows two other symbol combinations. The mandatory relationship with one or more dependent table rows per employee row—this would be the situation if the company hired only employees who already had a dependent, but this is not the case so this symbol was not used in Figure A.1. The other is the optional zero or one employee per dependent and this is also not the case so this symbol was not used in Figure A.1. However, you may find other relationships that use these symbol combinations.

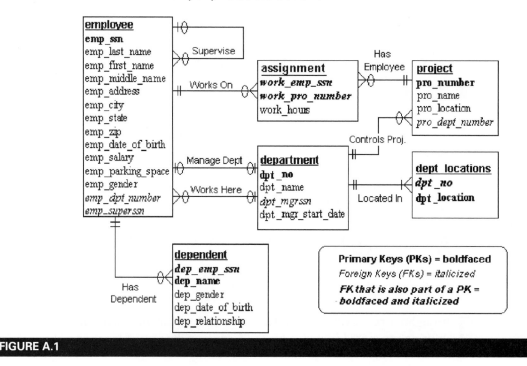

FIGURE A.1

TABLE DEFINITIONS

DEPARTMENT TABLE

The company is organized into separate departments. Tables A.1 and A.2 describe the columns in the *department* table and show the test data stored for each department. Each department is identified by a unique department number (*dpt_no*) and has a department name. Each department has a manager and date on which the manager started managing the department. The manager's Social Security number (*dpt_mgrssn*) stored in the *department* table provides a FOREIGN KEY link to the specific employee that manages a department.

SQL Example A.1 gives the CREATE TABLE command for the *department* table. Two constraints are named, one for the department primary key and the other to ensure that each department row must have a department name (NOT NULL).

```
/* SQL Example A.1 */
CREATE TABLE department (
    dpt_no                  NUMBER(2)
        CONSTRAINT pk_department PRIMARY KEY,
    dpt_name                VARCHAR2(20)
        CONSTRAINT nn_dpt_name NOT NULL,
    dpt_mgrssn              CHAR(9),
    dpt_mgr_start_date      DATE
);
```

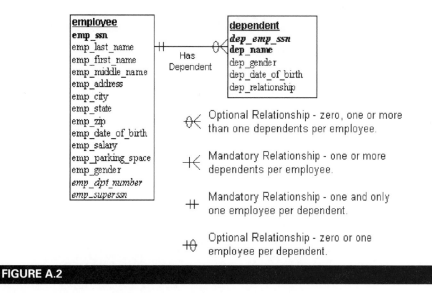

FIGURE A.2

DEPT_LOCATIONS TABLE

Each department may have multiple city locations within the company. In order to provide for normalized data maintenance, a separate *dept_locations* table stores location information. Tables A.3 and A.4 describe the columns and actual data stored in the *dept_locations* table. The primary key of the *dept_locations* table is a composite of *dpt_no* and *dpt_location*. There are no nonkey columns in the table. The *dpt_no* column also serves as a FOREIGN KEY link back to the *department* table.

SQL Example A.2 shows the code to create dept_locations. As you will learn from your study of Chapter 2, the constraint to create the primary key is a special form of the PRIMARY KEY clause that is used to create composite keys from two or more columns. There is also a FOREIGN KEY clause to specify that *dpt_no* references the *department* column.

TABLE A.1

TABLE NAME: department

Column Name	Datatype	Size	Comments
dpt_no	NUMBER	2	**Primary Key.** Number assigned by the company.
dpt_name	VARCHAR2	20	Department name.
dpt_mgrssn	CHAR	9	**Foreign Key** link to *employee* that manages this department.
dpt_mgr_start_date	DATE		Date a manager was assigned to supervise the department.

TABLE A.2

TABLE DATA: department

dpt_no	dpt_name	dpt_mgrssn	dpt_mgr_start_date
7	Production	999444444	05-22-1998
3	Admin and Records	999555555	01-01-2001
1	Headquarters	999666666	06-19-1981

```
/* SQL Example A.2 */
CREATE TABLE dept_locations (
    dpt_no                      NUMBER(2),
    dpt_location                VARCHAR2(20),
CONSTRAINT pk_dept_locations
    PRIMARY KEY ( dpt_no, dpt_location ),
CONSTRAINT fk_dept_loc_no
    FOREIGN KEY (dpt_no) REFERENCES department
) ;
```

EMPLOYEE TABLE

Employee information is stored in the *employee* table. Tables A.5 and A.6 describe the columns in the *employee* table and the data stored in the table. Each employee is identified by their SSN (*emp_ssn*) as a primary key.

Employees work in departments. Employees also manage departments. Thus, Figure A.1 shows these two relationships: *Manage-Dept* and *Works-Here*. The *Manage-Dept* relationship links each row in the *department* table to the *employee* table row for the employee who manages the department. The *Works-Here* relationship links the *employee* table to the *department* table for the department to which each employee is assigned to work.

You should interpret the *Works-Here* relationship as meaning that a department can have zero, one, or more than one assigned employees (crow's foot), and that each employee is assigned to one and only one (mandatory) department. SQL Example A.3 shows the CREATE TABLE command for the *employee* table. The *Works-Here* relationship is implemented by the FOREIGN KEY constraint named *fk_emp_dpt*.

TABLE A.3

TABLE NAME: dept_locations

Column Name	Datatype	Size	Comments
dpt_no	NUMBER	2	**Primary Key.** Number assigned by the company. Also **Foreign Key** link to *department* table.
dpt_location	VARCHAR2	20	**Primary Key.** Department name.

TABLE A.4

TABLE DATA: dept_locations

dpt_no	dpt_location
1	Edwardsville
3	Marina
7	St. Louis
7	Collinsville
7	Edwardsville

The *Manage-Dept* relationship is interpreted as each department has one and only one manager, and any given employee may optionally manage a department. Of course, most employees will not manage a department. You will not find the FOREIGN KEY constraint to enforce the *Manage-Dept* relationship in the CREATE TABLE command for either the *employee* or *department* tables. This is because a constraint cannot be created for a nonexistent table and one of the two tables has to be created first! Instead, this constraint is added to the database after all of the tables are created.

Employees are supervised by other employees. This is a unary or recursive relationship between rows within a single table and is shown as the *Supervise* relationship

TABLE A.5

TABLE NAME: employee

Column Name	Datatype	Size	Comments
emp_ssn	CHAR	9	**Primary Key.** Employee SSN
emp_last_name	VARCHAR2	25	Employee last name
emp_first_name	VARCHAR2	25	Employee first name
emp_middle_name	VARCHAR2	25	Employee middle name
emp_address	VARCHAR2	50	Employee street address
emp_city	VARCHAR2	25	City where employee resides
emp_state	CHAR	2	Two-character abbreviation of the state of residence
emp_zip	CHAR	9	Zip code for mailing
emp_date_of_birth	DATE		Employee date of birth
emp_salary	NUMBER	(7,2)	Employee annual salary
emp_parking_space	NUMBER	4	Number of parking space allocated to the employee
emp_gender	CHAR	1	Code – M = male; F = female
emp_dpt_number	NUMBER	2	**Foreign Key** link to department table. Department to which an employee is assigned
emp_superssn	CHAR	9	**Foreign Key** link to employee record supervising this employee

TABLE A.6

emp_ssn	emp_last _name	emp_first _name	emp_ middle_ name	emp_address	emp_city	emp_ state
999666666	Bordoloi	Bijoy		South Main #12	Edwardsville	IL
999555555	Joyner	Suzanne	A	202 Burns Farm	Marina	CA
999444444	Zhu	Waiman	Z	303 Lindbergh	St. Louis	MO
999887777	Markis	Marcia	M	High St. #14	Monterey	CA
999222222	Amin	Hyder		S. Seaside Apt B	Marina	CA
999111111	Bock	Douglas	B	#2 Mont Verd Dr.	St. Louis	MO
999333333	Joshi	Dinesh		#10 Oak St	Collinsville	IL
999888888	Prescott	Sherri	C	Overton Way #4	Edwardsville	IL

emp_zip	emp_date_ of_birth	emp_salary	emp_parking_ space	emp_ gender	emp_dpt_ number	emp_ superssn
62025	11-10-1967	55000	1	M	1	
93941	06-20-1971	43000	3	F	3	999666666
63121	12-08-1975	43000	32	M	7	999666666
93940	07-19-1978	25000	402	F	3	999555555
93941	03-29-1969	25000	422	M	3	999555555
63121	09-01-1955	30000	542	M	7	999444444
66234	09-15-1972	38000	332	M	7	999444444
62025	07-31-1972	25000	296	F	7	999444444

in Figure A.1. The *Supervise* relationship is enforced by the FOREIGN KEY constraint named *fk_emp_superssn* that links a given employee to his or her supervisor; thus, the employee supervisor's SSN (*emp_superssn*) is stored as a column in the table. This relationship is covered in detail in Chapter 6.

```
/* SQL Example A.3 */
CREATE TABLE employee (
    emp_ssn                CHAR(9)
        CONSTRAINT pk_employee PRIMARY KEY,
    emp_last_name          VARCHAR2(25)
        CONSTRAINT nn_emp_last_name NOT NULL,
    emp_first_name         VARCHAR2(25)
        CONSTRAINT nn_emp_first_name NOT NULL,
    emp_middle_name        VARCHAR2(25),
    emp_address            VARCHAR2(50),
    emp_city               VARCHAR2(25),
    emp_state              CHAR(2),
    emp_zip                CHAR(9),
    emp_date_of_birth      DATE,
    emp_salary             NUMBER(7,2)
        CONSTRAINT ck_emp_salary
            CHECK (emp_salary <= 85000),
    emp_parking_space      NUMBER(4)
```

```
            CONSTRAINT un_emp_parking_space UNIQUE,
    emp_gender                  CHAR(1),
    emp_dpt_number              NUMBER(2),
    emp_superssn                CHAR(9),
CONSTRAINT fk_emp_dpt FOREIGN KEY (emp_dpt_number)
    REFERENCES department
        ON DELETE SET NULL,
CONSTRAINT fk_emp_superssn FOREIGN KEY (emp_superssn)
    REFERENCES employee
        ON DELETE SET NULL
) ;
```

PROJECTS TABLE

Projects for the company are controlled or supervised by departments. Each project is identified by a project number (*pro_number*) and the firm tracks each project by name, and location. Tables A.7 and A.8 show the columns and data for the *project* table. Figure A.1 shows the *Controls-Proj* relationship. A department may have zero, one or more than one active projects and a project belongs to one and only one department.

SQL Example A.4 gives the CREATE TABLE command for the *project* table. The *fk_pro_dept_number* FOREIGN KEY constraint implements the *Controls-Proj* relationship.

```
/* SQL Example A.4 */
CREATE TABLE project (
    pro_number              NUMBER(2)
        CONSTRAINT pk_project PRIMARY KEY,
    pro_name                VARCHAR2(25)
        CONSTRAINT nn_pro_name NOT NULL,
    pro_location            VARCHAR2(25),
    pro_dept_number         NUMBER(2),
CONSTRAINT fk_pro_dept_number FOREIGN KEY (pro_dept_number)
    REFERENCES department
);
```

TABLE A.7

TABLE NAME: project

Column Name	Datatype	Size	Comments
pro_number	NUMBER	2	**Primary Key.** Number assigned by the company
pro_name	VARCHAR2	25	Project name
pro_location	VARCHAR2	25	Project location
pro_dept_number	NUMBER	2	**Foreign Key** link to *department* controlling the project

TABLE A.8

TABLE DATA: project

pro_number	pro_name	pro_location	pro_dept_number
1	Order Entry	St. Louis	7
2	Payroll	Collinsville	7
3	Receivables	Edwardsville	7
10	Inventory	Marina	3
20	Personnel	Edwardsville	1
30	Pay Benefits	Marina	3

ASSIGNMENT TABLE

Each employee is assigned to work on zero, one or more projects. This is reflected in Figure A.1 by the *assignment* table and two relationships: *Works-On* and *Has-Employee*. The *assignment* table is an **association** table because it associates the *employee* and *project* tables. Tables A.9 and A.10 show the columns and data for the *assignment* table. The primary key for *assignment* is a composite of the primary key from the *employee* table combined with the primary key of the *project* table: the *work_emp_ssn* and *work_pro_number* columns.

SQL Example A.5 gives the CREATE TABLE command to create the *assignment* table. The PRIMARY KEY clause implements the primary key in the same fashion as was done earlier for the *dept_locations* table. Two FOREIGN KEY constraints, *fk_work_emp* and *fk_work_pro_number* implement the *Works-On* and *Has-Employee* relationships by referencing back to the respective *employee* and *project* tables. You will learn about the ON DELETE clauses when you study Chapter 2.

```
/* SQL Example A.5 */
CREATE TABLE assignment (
    work_emp_ssn              CHAR(9),
    work_pro_number           NUMBER(2),
    work_hours                NUMBER(5,1),
CONSTRAINT pk_assignment
    PRIMARY KEY ( work_emp_ssn, work_pro_number ),
CONSTRAINT fk_work_emp
```

TABLE A.9

TABLE NAME: assignment

Column Name	Datatype	Size	Comments
work_emp_ssn	CHAR	9	**Primary Key.** Employee SSN. Also **Foreign Key** link to *employee* table
work_pro_number	NUMBER	2	**Primary Key.** Project number. Also **Foreign Key** link to the *project* table
work_hours	NUMBER	(5,1)	Number of hours an employee has worked on a project

TABLE A.10

TABLE DATA: assignment

work_emp_ssn	work_pro_number	Work_hours
999111111	1	31.4
999111111	2	8.5
999333333	3	42.1
999888888	1	21.0
999888888	2	22.0
999444444	2	12.2
999444444	3	10.5
999444444	1	
999444444	10	10.1
999444444	20	11.8
999887777	30	30.8
999887777	10	10.2
999222222	10	34.5
999222222	30	5.1
999555555	30	19.2
999555555	20	14.8
999666666	20	

```
    FOREIGN KEY (work_emp_ssn) REFERENCES employee
        ON DELETE CASCADE,
CONSTRAINT fk_work_pro_number
    FOREIGN KEY (work_pro_number) REFERENCES project
        ON DELETE CASCADE
) ;
```

DEPENDENT TABLE

Figure A.1 shows the *Has-Dependent* relationship between the *employee* and *dependent* tables. Tables A.11 and A.12 describe the columns and data for the *dependent* table. An employee may have zero, one or more dependents, and a dependent belongs to one and only one employee. The firm only tracks minimal information about dependents in order to satisfy governmental reporting requirements for taxation and education purposes. Each *dependent* table row must reference an existing employee row in the *employee* table. The primary key of dependent is a composite of *dep_emp_ssn* and *dep_name*. The *dep_emp_ssn* column also serves to link *dependent* rows to the *employee* table.

SQL Example A.6 gives the CREATE TABLE command for the *dependent* table. The PRIMARY KEY constraint named *pk_dependent* enforces the composite primary key. The FOREIGN KEY constraint named *fk_dep_emp_ssn* implements the Has-Dependent relationship.

TABLE A.11

TABLE NAME: dependent

Column Name	Datatype	Size	Comments
dep_emp_ssn	CHAR	9	**Primary Key.** Employee social security number for this dependent. Also **Foreign Key** link to *employee* table
dep_name	VARCHAR2	50	**Primary Key.** Dependent name.
dep_gender	CHAR	1	Dependent gender coded: M = male; F = female
dep_date_of_birth	DATE		Dependent date of birth.
dep_relationship	VARCHAR2	10	Relationship of dependent to employee (e.g., daughter, spouse, son)

```
/* SQL Example A.6 */
CREATE TABLE dependent (
    dep_emp_ssn             CHAR(9),
    dep_name                VARCHAR2(50),
    dep_gender              CHAR(1),
    dep_date_of_birth       DATE,
    dep_relationship        VARCHAR2(10),
CONSTRAINT pk_dependent PRIMARY KEY (dep_emp_ssn, dep_name),
CONSTRAINT fk_dep_emp_ssn
    FOREIGN KEY (dep_emp_ssn) REFERENCES employee
        ON DELETE CASCADE
) ;
```

ADDITIONAL TABLE CONSTRAINTS

Recall that earlier we discussed the *Manage-Dept* relationship between the *department* and *employee* tables. The FOREIGN KEY constraint for this relationship can be added to the *department* table definition now that the *employee* table has been created. You will study how to alter tables to add constraints in Chapter 2.

TABLE A.12

TABLE DATA: dependent

dep_emp_ssn	dep_name	dep_gender	dep_date_of_birth	dep_relationship
999444444	Jo Ellen	F	04-05-1996	DAUGHTER
999444444	Andrew	M	10-25-1998	SON
999444444	Susan	F	05-03-1975	SPOUSE
999555555	Allen	M	02-29-1968	SPOUSE
999111111	Jeffery	M	01-01-1978	SON
999111111	Deanna	F	12-31-1978	DAUGHTER
999111111	Michelle	F	05-05-1957	SPOUSE

```
/* SQL Example A.7 */
ALTER TABLE department ADD CONSTRAINT fk_dept_emp
    FOREIGN KEY (dpt_mgrssn)
        REFERENCES employee (emp_ssn);
```

CREATE COMPANY TABLES AND INDEXES

The **CreateCompanyDatabase.sql** script code creates the Oracle tables and indexes for the Company database. The script also populates the tables with data. The script assigns explicit names to all table constraints and indexes. When you study Chapter 12, this will make it easier for you to examine the data dictionary tables and views that store constraint and index information for the database.

The script first drops each table to facilitate re-creating the tables and indexes if necessary. This script can be accessed from the textbook website and is stored in a script file named **CreateCompanyDatabase.sql.** Chapter 1 provides you with a detailed explanation of the procedure you need to follow in order to create your own copy of the company database.

```
REM CreateCompanyDatabase.sql
REM Script to create the Company database to
REM accompany Bordoloi/Bock — An Introduction to SQL

REM First drop necessary constraints and tables that
REM might already exist in order to create a clean database.

ALTER TABLE department
    DROP CONSTRAINT fk_dept_emp;
DROP TABLE dependent;
DROP TABLE assignment;
DROP TABLE employee;
DROP TABLE project;
DROP table dept_locations;
DROP table department;

REM Create tables

REM Create department table
CREATE TABLE department (
    dpt_no                    NUMBER(2)
        CONSTRAINT pk_department PRIMARY KEY,
    dpt_name                  VARCHAR2(20)
        CONSTRAINT nn_dpt_name NOT NULL,
    dpt_mgrssn                CHAR(9),
    dpt_mgr_start_date        DATE
);

REM Create dept_locations table
CREATE TABLE dept_locations (
    dpt_no                    NUMBER(2),
    dpt_location              VARCHAR2(20),
CONSTRAINT pk_dept_locations
    PRIMARY KEY ( dpt_no, dpt_location ),
CONSTRAINT fk_dept_loc_no
    FOREIGN KEY (dpt_no) REFERENCES department
) ;
```

```
REM Create project table
CREATE TABLE project (
    pro_number                  NUMBER(2)
        CONSTRAINT pk_project PRIMARY KEY,
    pro_name                    VARCHAR2(25)
        CONSTRAINT nn_pro_name NOT NULL,
    pro_location                VARCHAR2(25),
    pro_dept_number             NUMBER(2),
CONSTRAINT fk_pro_dept_number FOREIGN KEY (pro_dept_number)
    REFERENCES department
);

REM Create employee table
CREATE TABLE employee (
    emp_ssn                     CHAR(9)
        CONSTRAINT pk_employee PRIMARY KEY,
    emp_last_name               VARCHAR2(25)
        CONSTRAINT nn_emp_last_name NOT NULL,
    emp_first_name              VARCHAR2(25)
        CONSTRAINT nn_emp_first_name NOT NULL,
    emp_middle_name             VARCHAR2(25),
    emp_address                 VARCHAR2(50),
    emp_city                    VARCHAR2(25),
    emp_state                   CHAR(2),
    emp_zip                     CHAR(9),
    emp_date_of_birth           DATE,
    emp_salary                  NUMBER(7,2)
        CONSTRAINT ck_emp_salary
            CHECK (emp_salary <= 85000),
    emp_parking_space           NUMBER(4)
        CONSTRAINT un_emp_parking_space UNIQUE,
    emp_gender                  CHAR(1),
    emp_dpt_number              NUMBER(2),
    emp_superssn                CHAR(9),
CONSTRAINT fk_emp_dpt FOREIGN KEY (emp_dpt_number)
    REFERENCES department
        ON DELETE SET NULL,
CONSTRAINT fk_emp_superssn FOREIGN KEY (emp_superssn)
    REFERENCES employee
        ON DELETE SET NULL
) ;

REM Create assignment table
CREATE TABLE assignment (
    work_emp_ssn                CHAR(9),
    work_pro_number             NUMBER(2),
    work_hours                  NUMBER(5,1),
CONSTRAINT pk_assignment
    PRIMARY KEY ( work_emp_ssn, work_pro_number ),
CONSTRAINT fk_work_emp
    FOREIGN KEY (work_emp_ssn) REFERENCES employee
        ON DELETE CASCADE,
CONSTRAINT fk_work_pro_number
    FOREIGN KEY (work_pro_number) REFERENCES project
        ON DELETE CASCADE
) ;
```

```
REM Create dependent table
CREATE TABLE dependent (
    dep_emp_ssn                 CHAR(9),
    dep_name                    VARCHAR2(50),
    dep_gender                  CHAR(1),
    dep_date_of_birth           DATE,
    dep_relationship            VARCHAR2(10),
CONSTRAINT pk_dependent PRIMARY KEY (dep_emp_ssn, dep_name),
CONSTRAINT fk_dep_emp_ssn
    FOREIGN KEY (dep_emp_ssn) REFERENCES employee
        ON DELETE CASCADE
) ;

REM Add FOREIGN KEY constraint between the department
REM and employee tables.
ALTER TABLE department ADD CONSTRAINT fk_dept_emp
    FOREIGN KEY (dpt_mgrssn)
        REFERENCES employee (emp_ssn);

REM POPULATE TABLES

REM Department rows. Department manager SSN
REM and date_mgr_startdate are null.
INSERT INTO department VALUES ( 7, 'Production', NULL, NULL );
INSERT INTO department VALUES ( 3, 'Admin and Records', NULL,
    NULL );
INSERT INTO department VALUES ( 1, 'Headquarters', NULL, NULL );

REM Dept_locations rows.
INSERT INTO dept_locations VALUES ( 1, 'Edwardsville');
INSERT INTO dept_locations VALUES ( 3, 'Marina');
INSERT INTO dept_locations VALUES ( 7, 'St. Louis');
INSERT INTO dept_locations VALUES ( 7, 'Collinsville');
INSERT INTO dept_locations VALUES ( 7, 'Edwardsville');
COMMIT;

REM Project rows.
INSERT INTO project VALUES ( 1, 'Order Entry', 'St. Louis', 7 );
INSERT INTO project VALUES ( 2, 'Payroll', 'Collinsville', 7 );
INSERT INTO project VALUES ( 3, 'Receivables', 'Edwardsville', 7 );
INSERT INTO project VALUES ( 10, 'Inventory', 'Marina', 3 );
INSERT INTO project VALUES ( 20, 'Personnel', 'Edwardsville', 1 );
INSERT INTO project VALUES ( 30, 'Pay Benefits', 'Marina', 3 );
COMMIT;

REM Employee rows.
INSERT INTO employee VALUES( '999666666', 'Bordoloi', 'Bijoy',
    NULL, 'South Main #12', 'Edwardsville', 'IL', 62025,
    TO_DATE('11-10-1967', 'MM-DD-YYYY'), 55000, 1, 'M', 1, NULL );
INSERT INTO employee VALUES( '999555555', 'Joyner', 'Suzanne',
    'A', '202 Burns Farm', 'Marina', 'CA', 93941,
    TO_DATE('06-20-1971', 'MM-DD-YYYY'), 43000, 3, 'F',
    3, '999666666' );
INSERT INTO employee VALUES( '999444444', 'Zhu', 'Waiman',
    'Z', '303 Lindbergh', 'St. Louis', 'MO', 63121,
    TO_DATE('12-08-1975', 'MM-DD-YYYY'), 43000, 32, 'M',
    7, '999666666' );
```

```
INSERT INTO employee VALUES( '999887777', 'Markis', 'Marcia',
    'M', 'High St. #14', 'Monterey', 'CA', 93940,
    TO_DATE('07-19-1978', 'MM-DD-YYYY'), 25000, 402, 'F',
    3, '999555555' );
INSERT INTO employee VALUES( '999222222', 'Amin', 'Hyder',
    NULL, 'S. Seaside Apt. B', 'Marina', 'CA', 93941,
    TO_DATE('03-29-1969', 'MM-DD-YYYY'), 25000, 422, 'M',
    3, '999555555' );
INSERT INTO employee VALUES( '999111111', 'Bock', 'Douglas',
    'B', '#2 Mont Verd Dr.', 'St. Louis', 'MO', 63121,
    TO_DATE('09-01-1955', 'MM-DD-YYYY'), 30000, 542, 'M',
    7, '999444444' );
INSERT INTO employee VALUES( '999333333', 'Joshi', 'Dinesh',
    NULL, '#10 Oak St.', 'Collinsville', 'IL', 66234,
    TO_DATE('09-15-1972', 'MM-DD-YYYY'), 38000, 332, 'M',
    7, '999444444' );
INSERT INTO employee VALUES( '999888888', 'Prescott', 'Sherri',
    'C', 'Overton Way #4', 'Edwardsville', 'IL', 62025,
    TO_DATE('07-31-1972', 'MM-DD-YYYY'), 25000, 296, 'F',
    7, '999444444' );
COMMIT;

REM Assignment rows.
INSERT INTO assignment VALUES ( '999111111', 1, 31.4);
INSERT INTO assignment VALUES ( '999111111', 2, 8.5);
INSERT INTO assignment VALUES ( '999333333', 3, 42.1);
INSERT INTO assignment VALUES ( '999888888', 1, 21.0);
INSERT INTO assignment VALUES ( '999888888', 2, 22.0);
INSERT INTO assignment VALUES ( '999444444', 2, 12.2);
INSERT INTO assignment VALUES ( '999444444', 3, 10.5);
INSERT INTO assignment VALUES ( '999444444', 1, NULL);
INSERT INTO assignment VALUES ( '999444444', 10, 10.1);
INSERT INTO assignment VALUES ( '999444444', 20, 11.8);
INSERT INTO assignment VALUES ( '999887777', 30, 30.8);
INSERT INTO assignment VALUES ( '999887777', 10, 10.2);
INSERT INTO assignment VALUES ( '999222222', 10, 34.5);
INSERT INTO assignment VALUES ( '999222222', 30, 5.1);
INSERT INTO assignment VALUES ( '999555555', 30, 19.2);
INSERT INTO assignment VALUES ( '999555555', 20, 14.8);
INSERT INTO assignment VALUES ( '999666666', 20, NULL);
COMMIT;

REM Dependent rows.
INSERT INTO dependent VALUES ( '999444444', 'Jo Ellen', 'F',
    TO_DATE('04-05-1996', 'MM-DD-YYYY'), 'DAUGHTER');
INSERT INTO dependent VALUES ( '999444444', 'Andrew', 'M',
    TO_DATE('10-25-1998', 'MM-DD-YYYY'), 'SON');
INSERT INTO dependent VALUES ( '999444444', 'Susan', 'F',
    TO_DATE('05-03-1975', 'MM-DD-YYYY'), 'SPOUSE');
INSERT INTO dependent VALUES ( '999555555', 'Allen', 'M',
    TO_DATE('02-29-1968', 'MM-DD-YYYY'), 'SPOUSE');
INSERT INTO dependent VALUES ( '999111111', 'Jeffery', 'M',
    TO_DATE('01-01-1978', 'MM-DD-YYYY'), 'SON');
INSERT INTO dependent VALUES ( '999111111', 'Deanna', 'F',
    TO_DATE('12-31-1978', 'MM-DD-YYYY'), 'DAUGHTER');
```

```
INSERT INTO dependent VALUES ( '999111111', 'Mary Ellen', 'F',
    TO_DATE('05-05-1957', 'MM-DD-YYYY'), 'SPOUSE');
COMMIT;

REM Update department rows to add manager ssn and start date.
UPDATE department SET dpt_mgrssn = '999444444',
    dpt_mgr_start_date = TO_DATE('05-22-1998', 'MM-DD-YYYY')
    WHERE dpt_no = '7';
UPDATE department SET dpt_mgrssn = '999555555',
    dpt_mgr_start_date = TO_DATE('01-01-2001', 'MM-DD-YYYY')
    WHERE dpt_no = '3';
UPDATE department SET dpt_mgrssn = '999666666',
    dpt_mgr_start_date = TO_DATE('06-19-1981', 'MM-DD-YYYY')
    WHERE dpt_no = '1';
COMMIT;

REM Count table rows to ensure the script executed properly.
SELECT COUNT(*) "Department Count Is 3" FROM department;
SELECT COUNT(*) "Dept Locations Count Is 5" FROM dept_locations;
SELECT COUNT(*) "Project Count Is 6" FROM project;
SELECT COUNT(*) "Employee Count IS 8" FROM employee;
SELECT COUNT(*) "Assignment Count Is 17" FROM assignment;
SELECT COUNT(*) "Dependent Count Is 7" FROM dependent;

REM End of Script
```

THE RIVERBEND HOSPITAL CASE

The Riverbend Hospital of Alton, Illinois, is a regional, acute care facility. The hospital maintains a moderate-sized information systems (IS) department that includes 20 to 25 employees. The IS department manager, Mr. John Blasé, directly supervises the senior employees in the department. The department has a senior database administrator, a senior network administrator, two senior operating systems administrators (one for UNIX and one for Windows), and two project managers. The IS staff also includes several senior programmer/analysts, and approximately 10 junior programmer/analysts.

You were recently hired as a junior programmer/analyst based on your collegiate training in use of SQL. Recently, you met with Ms. Juanita Benitez, the senior programmer/analyst in charge of the project team to which you are assigned. Ms. Benitez has assigned you responsibility for developing SQL queries to support a portion of the firm's database. She has directed you to study the entity relationship diagram and database schema for the portion of the database that you will access.

ENTITY RELATIONSHIP DIAGRAMS AND TABLE DEFINITIONS

Figure B.1 depicts the entity relationship diagram. The Riverbend Hospital database is large. Many of the hospital's applications require access to data about patients. The central entity is the Patient. Patient data is stored in the *patient* table described in Table B.1. Each patient is identified by a *patient_number* value that is assigned to the patient by the hospital. Additionally, each patient is assigned an account number that is referenced by the hospital's billing system.

Each time a patient receives treatment or attention from a member of the nursing or physician medical staff at the hospital, an entry is made into the patient's automated hospital record. This information is stored to the *patient note* table in the *note_comment* column. This table allows storage of an individual note comment that is up to 4000 characters in size. The table allows for storage of an unlimited number of comments for a patient. The relationship between *patient* and *patient_note* is one-to-many as shown in Figure B.1. Table B.2 describes the *patient_note* table.

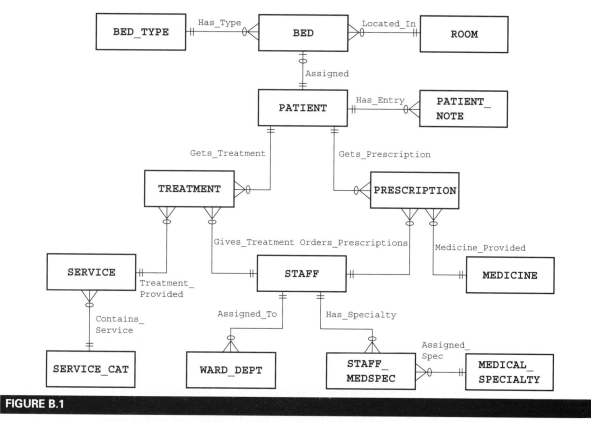

FIGURE B.1

TABLE B.1

TABLE NAME: *patient*

Column Name	Datatype	Size	Comments
Pat_id	CHAR	6	**Primary Key** patient identifier, value assigned by hospital. This value is also used to access patient account information
pat_ssn	CHAR	9	SSN, unique value
pat_last_name	VARCHAR2	50	Last name
pat_first_name	VARCHAR2	50	First name
pat_middle_name	VARCHAR2	50	Middle name
pat_street_address	VARCHAR2	50	Street address
pat_city	VARCHAR2	50	City
pat_state	CHAR	2	State abbreviation
pat_zip	CHAR	9	Zip code
pat_date_of_birth	DATE		Date of birth
pat_telephone_number	CHAR	10	Telephone number
bed_number	NUMBER	4	**Foreign Key** link to the *bed* table
date_last_updated	DATE		Date record last updated

TABLE B.6

TABLE NAME: *ward_dept*

Column Name	Datatype	Size	Comments
ward_id	CHAR	5	**Primary Key;** coded value to identify ward or department
ward_dept_name	VARCHAR2	50	Ward or department name
office_location	VARCHAR2	25	Office location for the ward or department
telephone_number	CHAR	10	Office primary telephone number
date_last_updated	DATE		Date record last updated

ment. Information about medicines that are stocked is stored in the *medicine* table. The prescription of medicine is an association table that relates the *staff, patient,* and *medicine* tables, and is implemented as the table named *prescription* with three one-to-many relationships named *Orders-Prescription, Gets-Prescription,* and *Medicine-Provided.* Only one medicine may be prescribed for each prescription. The *medicine* and *prescription* tables are described in Tables B.13 and B.14.

TABLE B.7

TABLE NAME: *staff*

Column Name	Datatype	Size	Comments
staff_id	CHAR	5	**Primary Key;** value assigned by the hospital
staff_ssn	CHAR	9	Social security number; unique value
staff_last_name	VARCHAR2	50	Last name
staff_first_name	VARCHAR2	50	First name
staff_middle_name	VARCHAR2	50	Middle name
ward_dept_assigned	CHAR	5	**Foreign Key** link to *ward_dept* table
office_location	VARCHAR2	10	Office location
date_hired	DATE		Date employee staff member was hired
hospital_title	VARCHAR2	50	Hospital title; examples: Radiologist; Registered Nurse; Medical Technician
work_phone	CHAR	10	Work telephone number
phone_extension	CHAR	4	Work telephone number extension
license_number	CHAR	20	Medical licensure number assigned by the state medical board; NULL value for nonmedical staff members
salary	NUMBER	(9,2)	Salary for salaried workers; NULL for hourly workers
wage_rate	NUMBER	(5,2)	Hourly wage rate for hourly employees; NULL for salaried workers
date_last_updated	DATE		Date record last updated

TABLE B.8

TABLE NAME: medical_specialty

Column Name	Datatype	Size	Comments
specialty_code	CHAR	3	**Primary Key;** medical specialty code
spec_title	VARCHAR2	50	Title of the specialty
how_awarded	VARCHAR2	100	How the specialty is awarded (e.g., by completion of medical board examination)
date_last_updated	DATE		Date record last updated

TABLE B.9

TABLE NAME: staff_medspec

Column Name	Datatype	Size	Comments
staff_id	CHAR	3	**Primary Key;** also serves as *Foreign Key* link to *staff* table. Staff number
specialty_code	CHAR	8	**Primary Key;** also serves as **Foreign Key** link to *medical_specialty* table. Medical specialty code
date_awarded	DATE		Date the specialty was awarded to the staff member
date_last_updated	DATE		Date record last updated

TABLE B.10

TABLE NAME: service

Column Name	Datatype	Size	Comments
service_id	CHAR	5	**Primary key;** standard medical service identifier
service_description	VARCHAR2	50	Description of service provided
service_charge	NUMBER	(9,2)	Standard fee for a service; may be modified by the individual administering the service as required by the medical situation
service_comments	VARCHAR2	2000	Comments regarding the service including how it should be administered, contraindications, etc.
service_cat_id	CHAR	3	**Foreign Key** link to *service_cat* table; Service category identifier
date_last_updated	DATE		Date record last updated

TABLE B.11

TABLE NAME: service_cat

Column Name	Datatype	Size	Comments
service_cat_id	CHAR	3	**Primary key;** Service category identifier
service_cat_desc	VARCHAR2	50	Service category description
date_last_updated	DATE		Date record last updated

TABLE B.12

TABLE NAME: treatment

Column Name	Datatype	Size	Comments
treatment_number	NUMBER	9	**Primary Key;** unique for a treatment within a given date
treatment_date	DATE		**Primary Key;** required to ensure uniqueness of the Treatment_number column
pat_id	CHAR	6	**Foreign Key** link to *patient* table
staff_id	CHAR	5	**Foreign Key** link to *staff* table
service_id	CHAR	5	**Foreign Key** link to *service* table
actual_charge	NUMBER	(9,2)	Actual charge for the service provided
treatment_comments	VARCHAR2	2000	Additional comments regarding the treatment such as diagnosis information
date_last_updated	DATE		Date record last updated

TABLE B.13

TABLE NAME: medicine

Column Name	Datatype	Size	Comments
medicine_code	CHAR	7	**Primary Key;** medicine standard code
med_name_sci	VARCHAR2	50	Scientific name of the medicine
med_name_common	VARCHAR2	50	Common name of the medicine
normal_dosage	VARCHAR2	300	Normal dosage of the medicine for a prescription
medicine_comments	VARCHAR2	500	Comments about the medicine
quantity_stock	NUMBER	5	Quantity stocked
unit_measure	VARCHAR2	20	Unit of measure (e.g., liters, grams, tablet, capsules)
date_last_updated	DATE		Date record last updated

TABLE B.14

TABLE NAME: prescription

Column Name	Datatype	Size	Comments
pre_number	NUMBER	9	**Primary Key;** Prescription number system generated
pre_date	DATE		Prescription Date
medicine_code	CHAR	7	**Foreign Key** link to *medicine* table
pat_id	CHAR	6	**Foreign Key** link to *patient* table
staff_id	CHAR	5	**Foreign Key** link to *staff* table
dosage_prescribed	VARCHAR2	50	Dosage prescribed (e.g., 50-mg tablet)
dosage_directions	VARCHAR2	500	Directions for administering the medicine (e.g., two times daily)
date_last_updated	DATE		Date record last updated

CREATE RIVERBEND TABLES AND INDEXES

The *CreateRiverbendDatabase.sql* program script contains the SQL statements that create the Riverbend database tables and indexes. We provide the CREATE TABLE commands in this appendix to make it easy for you to understand the table and column names used in the end-of-book exercises provided in Appendix C. The complete script can be downloaded from the textbook Web site.

```
REM CreateRiverbendDatabase.sql script.
REM Table room
CREATE TABLE room (
    room_id             CHAR(6) CONSTRAINT pk_room PRIMARY KEY,
    room_description    VARCHAR2(25),
    date_last_updated   DATE );

REM Table bed_type
CREATE TABLE bed_type (
    bed_type_id         CHAR(2) CONSTRAINT pk_bed_type PRIMARY KEY,
    bed_description     VARCHAR2(50),
    date_last_updated   DATE );

REM Table bed
CREATE TABLE bed (
    bed_number          NUMBER(4)  CONSTRAINT pk_bed PRIMARY KEY,
    room_id             CHAR(6)    CONSTRAINT fk_bed_room
        REFERENCES room(room_id),
    bed_type_id         CHAR(2)    CONSTRAINT nn_bed_type_id NOT NULL
        CONSTRAINT fk_bed_bedtype REFERENCES bed_type(bed_type_id),
    bed_availability    CHAR(1),
    date_last_updated   DATE );

REM Table patient
CREATE TABLE Patient (
    pat_id              CHAR(6)   CONSTRAINT pk_patient PRIMARY KEY,
    pat_ssn             CHAR(9)   CONSTRAINT nn_pat_ssn NOT NULL,
```

```
    pat_last_name              VARCHAR2(50)   CONSTRAINT nn_pat_last_name NOT NULL,
    pat_first_name             VARCHAR2(50)   CONSTRAINT nn_pat_first_name NOT NULL,
    pat_middle_name            VARCHAR2(50),
    pat_street_address         VARCHAR2(50),
    pat_city                   VARCHAR2(50),
    pat_state                  CHAR(2),
    pat_zip                    CHAR(9),
    pat_date_of_birth          DATE,
    pat_telephone_number       CHAR(10),
    bed_number                 NUMBER(4)   CONSTRAINT fk_pat_bed
        REFERENCES bed(bed_number),
    date_last_updated          DATE );

REM Table patient_note
CREATE TABLE patient_note (
    pat_id                     CHAR(6),
    note_date                  DATE,
    note_comment               VARCHAR2(4000),
    date_last_updated          DATE,
    CONSTRAINT fk_pat_note_patient FOREIGN KEY (pat_id)
        REFERENCES patient ON DELETE CASCADE,
    CONSTRAINT pk_section PRIMARY KEY (pat_id, note_date) );

REM Table ward_dept
CREATE TABLE ward_dept (
    ward_id                    CHAR(5)   CONSTRAINT pk_ward_dept PRIMARY KEY,
    ward_dept_name             VARCHAR2(50)   CONSTRAINT nn_ward_dept_name NOT NULL,
    office_location            VARCHAR2(25)   CONSTRAINT nn_ward_dept_location NOT NULL,
    telephone_number           CHAR(10),
    date_last_updated          DATE );

REM Table staff
CREATE TABLE staff (
    staff_id                   CHAR(5)   CONSTRAINT pk_staff PRIMARY KEY,
    staff_ssn                  CHAR(9)   CONSTRAINT nn_staff_ssn NOT NULL,
    staff_last_name            VARCHAR2(50)   CONSTRAINT nn_staff_last_name NOT NULL,
    staff_first_name           VARCHAR2(50)   CONSTRAINT nn_staff_first_name NOT NULL,
    staff_middle_name          VARCHAR2(50),
    ward_dept_assigned         CHAR(5)   CONSTRAINT fk_staff_ward_dept
        REFERENCES ward_dept(ward_id),
    office_location            VARCHAR2(50),
    date_hired                 DATE DEFAULT NULL,
    hospital_title             VARCHAR2(50)   CONSTRAINT nn_staff_title NOT NULL,
    work_phone                 CHAR(10),
    phone_extension            VARCHAR2(4),
    license_number             VARCHAR2(20),
    salary                     NUMBER,
    wage_rate                  NUMBER(5,2),
    date_last_updated          DATE );

REM Table medical_specialty
CREATE TABLE medical_specialty (
    specialty_code             CHAR(3)   CONSTRAINT pk_medical_specialty PRIMARY KEY,
    spec_title                 VARCHAR2(50)   CONSTRAINT nn_medical_spec_title NOT NULL,
    how_awarded                VARCHAR2(100),
    date_last_updated          DATE );
```

```
REM Table staff_medspec
CREATE TABLE staff_medspec (
    staff_id                CHAR(5),
    specialty_code          CHAR(3),
    date_awarded            DATE DEFAULT SYSDATE,
    date_last_updated       DATE,
    CONSTRAINT fk_staff_medspec FOREIGN KEY (staff_id) REFERENCES staff,
    CONSTRAINT fk_medspec_med_spec FOREIGN KEY (specialty_code)
        REFERENCES medical_specialty,
    CONSTRAINT pk_staff_medspec PRIMARY KEY (staff_id, specialty_code) );


REM Table service_cat
CREATE TABLE service_cat (
    service_cat_id          CHAR(3)   CONSTRAINT pk_service_cat PRIMARY KEY,
    service_cat_desc        VARCHAR2(50)   CONSTRAINT nn_service_cat_desc NOT NULL,
    date_last_updated       DATE );


REM Table service
CREATE TABLE service (
    service_id              CHAR(5)   CONSTRAINT pk_service PRIMARY KEY,
    service_description     VARCHAR2(50)   CONSTRAINT nn_service_description NOT NULL,
    service_charge          NUMBER(9,2)   CONSTRAINT ck_service_charge
        CHECK (service_charge >= 0),
    service_comments        VARCHAR2(2000),
    service_cat_id          CHAR(3)   CONSTRAINT fk_service_service_cat
        REFERENCES service_cat(service_cat_id),
    date_last_updated       DATE );


REM Table treatment
CREATE TABLE treatment (
    treatment_number        NUMBER(9),
    treatment_date          DATE,
    pat_id                  CHAR(6)   CONSTRAINT nn_treatment_pat_id NOT NULL,
    staff_id                CHAR(5)   CONSTRAINT nn_treatment_staff_id NOT NULL,
    service_id              CHAR(5)   CONSTRAINT nn_treatment_service_id NOT NULL,
    actual_charge           NUMBER(9,2)   CONSTRAINT ck_treatment_actual_charge
        CHECK (actual_charge >= 0),
    treatment_comments      VARCHAR2(2000),
    date_last_updated       DATE,
    CONSTRAINT fk_treatment_patient FOREIGN KEY (pat_id) REFERENCES patient,
    CONSTRAINT fk_treatment_staff FOREIGN KEY (staff_id) REFERENCES staff,
    CONSTRAINT fk_treatment_service FOREIGN KEY (service_id) REFERENCES service,
    CONSTRAINT pk_treatment PRIMARY KEY (treatment_number, treatment_date) );


REM Table Medicine
CREATE TABLE medicine (
    medicine_code           CHAR(7) CONSTRAINT pk_medicine PRIMARY KEY,
    med_name_sci            VARCHAR2(50) CONSTRAINT nn_medicine_name_sci NOT NULL,
    med_name_common         VARCHAR2(50) CONSTRAINT nn_medicine_name_common NOT NULL,
    normal_dosage           VARCHAR2(300) CONSTRAINT nn_medicine_dosage NOT NULL,
    medicine_comments       VARCHAR2(500),
    quantity_stock          NUMBER(12) CONSTRAINT ck_medicine_qty_stock
        CHECK (quantity_stock >= 0),
    unit_measure            VARCHAR2(20),
    date_last_updated       DATE );
```

```
REM Table prescription
CREATE TABLE prescription (
    pre_number              NUMBER(9)   CONSTRAINT pk_prescription PRIMARY KEY,
    pre_date                DATE,
    medicine_code           CHAR(7)   CONSTRAINT nn_prescription_medicine_code NOT NULL,
    pat_id                  CHAR(6)   CONSTRAINT nn_prescription_pat_id NOT NULL,
    staff_id                CHAR(5)   CONSTRAINT nn_prescription_staff_id NOT NULL,
    dosage_prescribed       VARCHAR2(50)
        CONSTRAINT nn_prescription_dosage_presc NOT NULL,
    dosage_directions       VARCHAR2(500),
    date_last_updated       DATE,
    CONSTRAINT fk_prescription_medicine FOREIGN KEY (medicine_code)
        REFERENCES medicine,
    CONSTRAINT fk_prescription_patient FOREIGN KEY (pat_id) REFERENCES patient,
    CONSTRAINT fk_prescription_staff FOREIGN KEY (staff_id) REFERENCES staff );
```

APPENDIX C

END-OF-BOOK SQL CODING EXERCISES

This appendix provides additional SQL coding exercises to supplement those provided at the end of each chapter. The exercises are divided into sections by chapter. All of the exercises are based on the Riverbend Hospital Case described in Appendix B.

CHAPTER 1

1. Study the *patient* and *patient_note* tables in Appendix B. Is the relationship between these two tables one-to-one, one-to-many, or many-to-many? Explain why.
2. Write a SELECT statement to display the patient identifier (*pat_id*) and patient last name (pat_last_name) for all patients with a last name of 'Young'.
3. Write a SELECT statement to display all columns for a patient with the ID of 100306.
4. Study the patient, bed, room, and bed_type tables in Appendix B. What are the relationships between these tables? Explain why.
5. Write a SELECT statement to display all rows and all columns from the *bed_type* table.
6. The Riverbend Hospital has many different wards and departments. Information about these areas of the hospital is stored to a table named *ward_dept*. Study the *ward_dept* table and the relationship to a table named *staff* in Appendix B. What is the relationship?
7. Write a SELECT statement to display the *ward_id* and *ward_dept_name* columns from the *ward_dept* table (all rows).
8. Based on your study of Appendix B, how is the relationship between the *staff* and *medical_specialty* tables implemented?

9. Write a SELECT statement to display the staff_id and specialty_code columns for all staff members with a specialty code of 'RN1' which is a code for registered nurse.

10. The Riverbend Hospital provides various medical services to patients. These services are categorized for purposes of insurance reporting. Information about these service categories is stored in the service_cat table. Write a SELECT statement to list all columns and rows from this table.

11. Staff members provide services to patients. Based on your study of Appendix B, what is the name of this relationship? What are the names of the tables that implement this relationship?

12. Rows stored to the treatment table are identified by a combination of the *treatment_number* and *treatment_date* columns. Write a SELECT statement to the *treatment_number, treatment_date,* and *treatment_comments* columns from the *treatment* table where the *treatment_number* = 10.

13. Prescriptions are provided by staff members for medicine to be given to patients. What is the name of the table used to store information about prescriptions, and what are the names of the tables that participate in relationships with the table used to store prescription information?

14. Write a SELECT statement to list the medicine_code, med_name_sci (scientific name), and med_name_common (common names) columns from the medicine table. List all rows with your query, but only submit output listing the first eight rows. Execute the following COLUMN commands prior to executing your query.

```
COLUMN med_name_sci FORMAT A23;
COLUMN med_name_common FORMAT A23;
```

15. Use the INPUT command to save the SELECT statement shown here to a file named Staff-Info.sql. Use the START command to execute the file to display a result table. Your code will look similar to that shown here; the system will produce the column numbers—do not type them into your file.

```
SQL> INPUT
  1 REM Displays staff information
  2 COLUMN "Last Name" FORMAT A20;
  3 COLUMN "First Name" FORMAT A20;
  4 COLUMN Title FORMAT A5;
  5 SELECT staff_id, staff_last_name "Last Name",
  6     staff_first_name "First Name", date_hired,
  7 hospital_title "Title"
  8 FROM staff
  9 WHERE hospital_title = 'M.D.'
 10
SQL> SAVE Staff-Info.sql
Created file Staff-Info.sql

START Staff-Info.sql
```

CHAPTER 2

1. Create a table named *patient_archive*. This table will be used to store patient rows for inactive patients. Inactive patients are patients who have not visited the hospi-

tal facility for five years or more. The *patient_archive* table should have the same structure as the *patient* table except that it should *not* have a column to store the *bed_number*—leave this column out of the table definition. Store information about yourself as sample test data to the *patient_archive* table. For the *date_last_updated* column use the value SYSDATE. Name each constraint as is done for the patient table except add the suffix *_archive* to each of the constraint names.

2. Use the DESCRIBE command to describe the *patient_archive*.

3. Use the following SELECT command to display the rows in the *patient_archive*.

```
SELECT * FROM patient_archive;
```

4. Use the DROP command to drop the *patient_archive*.

5. Create the *ward_dept* table described in Appendix B. Include all constraint specifications required to ensure data integrity.

6. Add the data shown here to the *ward_dept* table. Commit your row insertions to the *ward_dept* table.

Ward_id	Ward_dept_name	Office_location	Telephone_number	Date_last_updated
MEDS1	Medical Surgical Ward 1	SW1020	1005559201	SYSDATE
MEDS2	Medical Surgical Ward 2	NW1018	1005559202	SYSDATE
RADI1	Radiology Dept	RA0070	1005559203	SYSDATE

7. Use the DESCRIBE command to describe the *ward_dept* table.

8. Use the following SELECT command to display the rows in the *ward_dept* table.

```
SELECT * FROM ward_dept;
```

9. Create a table like the *staff* table described in Appendix A. Name your table *staff2*. Include all constraint specifications required to ensure data integrity. Create the referential integrity constraints needed to ensure that the *ward_dept* to which staff members are assigned for work exists within the *ward_dept* table. Your integrity constraints should also allow staff members to *not* be assigned to a ward or department. When naming the integrity constraints, replace the word *staff* with the word *staff2*.

10. Add data to the *staff2* table as shown below in the INSERT commands. Add an additional row to the employee data consisting of data that describes yourself (your own employee row). Make up your own data. Commit your row insertions in the *employee* table.

```
INSERT INTO staff2 VALUES ('23232', '310223232', 'Eakin', 'Maxwell',
'E', 'MEDS1', 'SW4208', TO_DATE('6-JAN-98'), 'M.D.',
'1005559268', '0001', 'IL54386', 150000, NULL, SYSDATE);
INSERT INTO staff2 VALUES ('23244', '316223244', 'Webber', 'Eugene',
NULL, 'RADI1', 'SW4392', TO_DATE('16-FEB-95'), 'M.D.',
'1005559270', '4410', 'IL383815', 175000, NULL, SYSDATE);
INSERT INTO staff2 VALUES ('10044', '216223308', 'Sumner', 'Elizabeth',
NULL, 'EMER1', 'SW4393', TO_DATE('16-FEB-01'), 'M.D.', '1005559271',
'3201', 'IL419057', 165000, NULL, SYSDATE);
```

11. Select specific columns from the *staff2* table by using the SELECT statement shown here.

```
SELECT staff_id, staff_ssn, staff_last_name
FROM staff2;
```

12. Delete your data row from the *staff2* table. Execute the SELECT statement given for question 11 to demonstrate that the row has been deleted. Verify your record has been deleted. Assume that the deletion of your row was an error. Execute the command that will undelete your row (*Note:* Do not simply reinsert the row to the table). Use the SELECT statement again to verify that your row has been restored to the table.

13. Execute an UPDATE command that will change the office_location column value for Eugene Webber to SW4000. Execute the SELECT statement shown here to demonstrate that Webber's office has been updated.

```
SELECT staff_last_name, office_location
FROM staff2
WHERE staff_last_name = 'Webber';
```

14. Download the script needed to create the remaining tables of the Riverbend Hospital Database schema shown in Appendix B. Run the script to create the entire database.

15. Alter the *medicine* table to add a column that will be used to store the unit cost of each medicine. Name this column *med_unit_cost* and use an appropriate NUMBER datatype specification. You do not need to store any data to this column.

16. Create a nonunique index on the *service_cat_id* column of the *service* table. Name the index *service_cat_id*.

CHAPTER 3

1. The Riverbend hospital administrator is new to the organization. She requests a listing of the rooms available at the hospital. Write a query to display all information about the rooms from the *room* table. Execute the following COLUMN command to format the *room_id* column.

```
COLUMN room_id FORMAT A7;
```

2. Write a query to display all information about rooms as was done in question 1 without using the asterisk (*) in your query. You may need to use the DESC command to describe the *room* table.

3. The new head surgeon needs a listing of services provided by the hospital. Write a query to display the identifier, description, and charge for each service in the *service* table. Execute the following COLUMN commands to format the service_description column.

```
COLUMN service_id FORMAT A10;
COLUMN service_description FORMAT A30;
```

4. Rewrite the query from question 3, but list the identifier, charge, and description in that order.

5. The hospital's human resources manager requires a listing of staff members from the organization's *staff* table in order to meet the reporting requirements for a government agency. The listing must include each employee's last name (*staff_last_name*), first name (*staff_first_name*), date hired (*date_hired*) and license number (*license_number*). Write the query to display the output sorted by *staff_last_name*. Use the COLUMN commands shown here to format the result table display.

```
COLUMN staff_last_name FORMAT A15;
COLUMN staff_first_name FORMAT A15;
```

6. Rewrite the last query to add the staff middle name in the result table. Display the output with the staff first name followed by the staff middle name and staff last name. Use the appropriate command to limit the output column width for the staff last and first names to 12 characters. Limit the output column width for the staff middle name to 1 character. Do not allow data beyond the specified column widths to wrap. Execute the query to display the new result table.

7. Rewrite the query from question 6 to sort the output by staff first name (minor sort) within staff last name (major sort). Keep all column width settings from question 6.

8. The new hospital facilities coordinator needs a listing of beds of type 'RE' including the *bed_number, room_id,* and *bed_type_id* columns from the *bed* table. Sort the result table by *room_id* in ascending order.

9. The hospital pharmacist and head surgeon are concerned about prescription medicines and the dosage prescribed for patients. Write a query to list each medicine code and dosage prescribed from the *prescription* table. Sort the rows of the result table by the medicine code.

10. Rewrite the query from question 9 to eliminate duplicate rows in the result table.

11. The chief of nurses for the hospital needs a listing of *staff_id, specialty_code,* and date the specialty was awarded (*date_awarded*) for nurses with *specialty_code* of 'RN1' from the *staff_medspec* table. Sort the output by *staff_id.* Write COLUMN commands to display the full title for each column.

12. Rewrite the query for question 11 to display information for licensed practicing nurses with *specialty_code* of 'LPN' from the *staff_medspec* table.

CHAPTER 4

1. A hospital administrator needs a listing of all patients with a zip code of '62025'. The result table should list each patient's, last name, first name, city, state, and zip code. In order to display each row on a single output line, format the patient first and last name and patient city columns as A15. Use meaningful column names such as "First Name."

2. A hospital administrator needs a listing of staff members who are doctors (hospital_title = 'M.D.') in the Oncology Department (ward_dept_assigned = 'ONCOL'). The result table should include the staff member's last name, first name, hospital

title, and ward/department to which they are assigned. Use meaningful column names such as "First Name."

3. Rewrite the query for question 2. The hospital administrator has determined that the listing must also include physicians assigned to medical surgical department 1 (MEDS1).

4. Rewrite the query for question 2. The hospital administrator needs the listing to include physicians assigned to any of four different wards/departments (ONCOL, MEDS1, CARD1, or RADI1). Use the IN operator. Sort the rows of the result table by the ward/department of assignment.

5. Rewrite the query for question 4, but list physicians not assigned to one of the four specified wards/departments.

6. A hospital administrator needs a listing of all patients assigned to specific beds. The result table should list each patient's last name, first name, and bed number of assignment. In order to display each row on a single output line, format the patient first and last name as A15. Use meaningful column names such as "First Name." Use the BETWEEN operator. Sort the result table by bed number.

7. The hospital inventory manager needs a listing of medicines that are both over-stocked and potentially under stocked. List each medicine's code, common name, and quantity in stock (*medicine_code, med_name_common,* and *quantity_stock*) from the *medicine* table. List only medicines that have a *quantity_stock* value that is not between 500 and 25,000. Use the NOT BETWEEN operator. Use meaningful column names such as "Med Code."

8. An administrative worker needs a listing of all staff members who have a last name that begins with the letter 'B' and that have a hospital title of 'M.D.' List each staff member's last and first names as well as hospital title. Sort the output by last name then by first name. Use meaningful column names.

9. Rewrite the query for question 8, but list staff members who have a last name that contains the lowercase letter 'o' with all other requirements remaining the same.

10. The administrator in charge of payroll budgeting needs a listing that displays each salaried staff member's last name, first name, annual salary, monthly salary, and weekly salary. Label the column names for annual salary, monthly salary and weekly salary as Annual, Monthly, and Weekly, respectively. Sort the output by employee last name, then first name. Format the columns named Annual, Monthly and Weekly as $999,999, $99,999 and $9,999, respectively. Do not display output for hourly workers (the value of *wage_rate* is NULL for salaried workers).

11. The hospital administrator in charge of patient census needs a listing of current patients that have not been assigned a bed number in order to complete bed assignments for the day. The result table should list the patient last name and bed number (which will be NULL). Use the IS NULL operator. Use meaningful column names.

12. Dr. Quattromani, a cardiologist at the Riverbend Hospital has requested a listing of patient identifications to whom she prescribed (*prescription* table) either Lanoxin or Alupent (medicine_code is 9999012 or 9999013). Dr. Quattromani's staff identification is 66425. List the prescription number, patient ID, medicine code, and staff ID.

CHAPTER 5

1. A manager from the human resources department needs you to write a query to count the number of staff members of the Riverbend Hospital. Count the number of rows in the *staff* table. Label the output column **Number of Staff Members.**

2. The *date_hired* column in the *staff* table stores date hired information for staff members of the Riverbend Hospital. A hospital administrator wishes to present an award at an upcoming organizational award ceremony to the staff member who has worked the longest at the hospital. Write a query to display the date hired for the oldest staff member listed in the table. No special output column label is required.

3. Rewrite the query for question 2 to display the date hired for the newest staff member at the hospital. No special output column is required.

4. Accountants working on the hospital's annual budgeting process need to know the average salary (*emp_salary*) for staff members and the sum of all staff member salaries. The information is stored in the staff table. The result table should have two columns based on a single query. Label the columns **Average Salary** and **Total Salary.** Format the output as $99,999,999. Keep in mind that not all staff members are salaried.

5. Write a query that is comparable to that for question 4, but this query should list the average wage and total wage for staff members who are paid a wage. Format the output as $999,999. Label the columns **Average Wage** and **Total Wage.**

6. A new government reporting regulation the hospital to report the number of regular beds in use by the hospital. The bed_type codes for these beds is 'R1' and 'R2'. The information is stored in the *bed_type_id* column of the bed table. The result table should have a single output column labeled **Number Regular Beds.**

7. A change in the government reporting regulation regarding available hospital beds requires a count by type of all types of beds that are available. Display the information as two columns, one for *bed_type_id* and one for the associated count. The result table should have several rows, one for each bed type. Use a single query. Additionally, the *bed_type_id* output column should be formatted as A15 and have a heading of **Bed Type.** The count column should have a heading of **Number Counted.** Use a GROUP BY clause.

8. Another government regulation requires a report of the number of services provided by the hospital counted by the standard service categories. Display the result table as two columns, one for *service_cat_id* and one for the associated count. The result table should have several rows, one for each service category. Use a single query. The column headings should be "Service Category" and "Number of Services" and the data comes from the *service* table. You will need to use a GROUP BY clause.

9. Rewrite the query for question 8 to exclude the counting of services in categories injections and laboratories (codes = INJ, LAB).

10. Modify the query written for question 9 to sort the output by the count of the number of services in each category with the largest counts listed first. Label the columns as specified in question 8.

11. The Hospital's Chief of Surgery needs to know the number of treatments provided by each staff member (use *treatment* table). The result table should have two columns labeled **Staff Member ID** and **Treatment Count.** You will need to refer to the *staff_id* column that stores the staff member identification and the *service_id* column that stores the service identification provided as a treatment to a patient.

12. Rewrite the query for question 11 to exclude from the listing staff members providing fewer than 10 treatments. *Hint:* Use a HAVING clause.

13. Rewrite the query for question 12 to exclude from the listing staff members providing fewer than 10 treatments and staff members with *staff_id* values of 66432 and 66444.

14. Write a query to provide the hospital budgeting officer with information about the average charge of each treatment for patients by *service_id*. Base the average value on the *service_id* and *actual_charge* columns of the *treatment* table. Order the output by *service_id*. Format the average charge as $9,999.99.

15. Rewrite the query for question 14 to exclude average charges that are less than $1,000. Order the output by average charge.

CHAPTER 6

1. You are assigned to create a query that will display the patient history for hospital patients. Your result table will display the *pat_id* and *pat_last_name* columns from the *patient* table and the *note_comment* column from the *patient_note* table. Join the tables and use the default column headings. Submit just the output from the first three patient records displayed. Use the COLUMN commands shown here to format the output. How many rows of output are produced by your query?

```
COLUMN p.pat_id FORMAT A6;
COLUMN pat_last_name FORMAT A15;
COLUMN note_comment FORMAT A45;
```

2. Modify the query for question 1 to only list the patient history for the patient with identification #100303. All other requirements remain the same.

3. The hospital's human resources manager needs a listing of staff members and the name of the ward/department to which they are assigned. The result table should display each staff member's last and first name (*staff_last_name* and *staff_first_name*) concatenated as a single column with the heading "Staff Member" as well as a column listing the ward or department name (*ward_dept_name*). These columns come from the *staff* and *ward_dept* tables. The tables must be joined on the common *ward_id* from *ward_dept* table and *ward_dept_assigned* from the *staff* table. Sort the output by the ward/department name first, then by staff member name. Use the COLUMN commands shown here to format the output.

```
COLUMN "Staff Member" FORMAT A25;
COLUMN "Ward or Dept" FORMAT A36;
```

4. The Chief of Surgery requires a listing of services provided by service category. Your query will use the *service* and *service_cat* tables. Display three columns as fol-

lows: *service_cat_id, service_cat_desc, service_id,* and *service_description.* Use headings of "Category," "Category Description," "Service," and "Service Description," respectively. Format the *service_cat_desc* and *service_description* columns as A25. Sort the output by *service_cat_id,* then by *service_id.*

5. Revise the query for question 4 to restrict the output to service categories with identifiers of 'CAR' and 'LAB.' All other requirements remain the same.

6. The Chief of Hospital Resource Utilization needs a listing of patients assigned to beds. The result table needs to include the patient name (last and first names concatenated as a single column), bed number, and bed type identifier. These columns are *pat_last_name, pat_first_name, bed_number,* and *bed_type_id* from the *patient* and *bed* tables. Use meaningful column names and sort the result table rows by the bed number.

7. Revise the query for question 6 to replace the *bed_type_id* column with the *bed_description* column from the *bed_type* table. Your new query will join three tables.

8. Revise the query for question 7 to add a fourth column from the room table to display the *room_description.* Format this column as A15. Set TRUNC ON as necessary to display the result table with one display row per row of output. Your new query will join four tables.

9. Revise the query for question 6 to list patients NOT yet assigned to a bed. The result table needs to include the patient name (last and first names concatenated as a single column) and bed number. This second column should be null. Sort the result table by patient last and then first names.

10. The Chief of Physicians requires a listing of patients receiving treatment. The result table must display the patient name (last and first concatenated from the *patient* table), *service_description* column (*service* table), and staff member name providing the treatment (last and first name concatenated from the *staff* table). Sort the result tables by the patient last then first name. *Hint:* Your query will join four tables. Truncate the output for each column as necessary and format each of the three columns as A20.

11. The Chief of Pharmacy requires a listing of patients receiving prescriptions. The result table must display the patient name (last and first concatenated from the *patient* table), medicine common name (*med_name_common* from the *medicine* table), and staff member who prescribed the medicine (last and first name concatenated from the *staff* table). Sort the result tables by the patient last then first name. *Hint:* Your query will join four tables. Truncate the output for each column as necessary and format each of the three columns as A20.

12. Modify the query for question 11 to display rows only for patients prescribed Demerol.

13. Modify the query for question #11 to only display rows for patients prescribed medicine by Dr. Toni Quattromani (*staff_id* = 66425).

14. Modify the query for question 11 to display rows for patients who were either prescribed Lanoxin or where the doctor writing the prescription was Dr. Quattromani.

CHAPTER 7

1. The *treatment* table stores data about the treatment services that patients have received. The Chief of Physicians needs a listing of patients (last and first name) that have received either a blood glucose or antibiotic injection (*service_id* = '82947' or '90788'). Use a subquery approach.

2. Modify the query you wrote for question 1 to sort the output by patient last name, then patient first name.

3. Modify the query for question #1 to produce a listing of patient names that have NOT received either a blood glucose or antibiotic injection (*service_id* = '82947' or '90788'). Use a subquery approach. Use the NOT IN operator. Sort the output by patient last name, then patient first name.

4. The *prescription* table stores data about the medicine that have been prescribed for patients. The Chief of Pharmacology needs a listing of patients (last and first name) that have received either Valium or Flexeril (*medicine_code* = '9999003' or '9999008'). Use a subquery approach.

5. Modify the query for question 4 to display the output sorted by patient last name, then patient first name.

6. Management needs a listing of patient names (last and first) who have received a service treatment **'General Panel'**; however, you do not know the *service_id* for this service. Your query should have a subquery within a subquery using the *patient, treatment,* and *service* tables. Sort the output by patient last name, then patient first name.

7. The Director of Human Resources for the hospital is concerned about employee retention. One of the hospital directors has suggested that the hospital has difficulty retaining registered nurses (*hospital_title* = 'R.N.'). Produce a listing of staff members (last and first names) and the date they were hired to work at the hospital, but only list staff members who were hired before any nurse with a hospital title of 'R.N.' *Hint:* Use the MIN aggregate function to determine the date hired for the oldest registered nurse based on the *date_hired* column. The result table must also list the employee's hospital title and date hired. Use COLUMN commands to format the result table.

8. Management is concerned about the prescribed charge for services versus the actual charge for services in the surgery category of services (*service_cat_id* = 'SUR'). Produce a listing of surgery services listed in the *treatment* table by *service_id* where the prescribed *service_charge* differs from the *actual_charge* recorded in the *treatment* table. The result table should also include the *service_charge* and *actual_charge*. Use a subquery approach to produce a listing of *service_id* values from the *service* table that belong to the 'SUR' category of services.

9. Alter the above query to only list services where the difference between the *service_charge* and *actual_charge* is greater than the *average* difference between these two charges for services in the 'SUR' category of services. The result table should only list the *service_id* and *service_description* columns from the *service* table. *Hint:* Compute the average difference between these two charges for 'SUR' services in a subquery.

10. Management wants to know which patients were charged the most for a treatment. The result able should list three columns from the *treatment* table appropriately labeled: *pat_id, actual_charge,* and *service_id.* Only list rows where the patient was charged the most for a treatment. This may result in some rows where patients were charged identical amounts to other patients. Sort the rows by *service_id.* Use a correlated subquery. Use the following COLUMN commands to format the output.

```
COLUMN "Patient" FORMAT A7;
COLUMN "Amt Charged" FORMAT $999,999.99;
COLUMN "Treatment" FORMAT A9;
```

11. The Chief of Administration for the hospital is concerned with productivity. It is felt that physicians may not be paid sufficiently well to motivate their work. Produce a listing of names (last and first) of each physician (*hospital_title* = 'M.D.') that receives the lowest salary in each ward/department (some wards/departments may have more than one poorly paid physician). The result table should list the *staff_last_name, staff_first_name, ward_dept_assigned,* and *salary* columns with meaningful column names, sorted by *ward_dept_assigned.* Use the COLUMN commands shown here to format the output.

```
COLUMN "Last Name" FORMAT A15;
COLUMN "First Name" FORMAT A15;
COLUMN "Ward-Dept" FORMAT A9;
COLUMN salary FORMAT $9,999,999;
```

12. Modify the query for question 11 to list physicians from each ward/department who are paid the highest salaries.

13. Management has decided to extend the study of salary payments to employees in all salaried categories (do not include hourly wage employees). Write a query to display the last and first names, ward/department assigned id code, salary, and date hired of the employee in each ward/department who has worked the least amount of time at the hospital. *Hint:* Use the MAX function and a correlated subquery.

14. Review the requirement for question 13. Rewrite the query to add the ward/department name to the result table. Delete the employee first name and the ward/dept assigned id code. This requires a combination join and subquery approach.

CHAPTER 8

1. The pharmacy at the Riverbend Hospital regularly accesses information about medicines that are stocked. The hospital DBA has directed you to create a view based on the *medicine* table named *medicine_view.* This view should include the medicine code (*medicine_code*) common medicine name (*med_name_common*), scientific medicine name (*med_name_sci*), quantity in stock (*quantity_stock*) and unit of measure (*unit_measure*) for each medicine. Name the columns of the view as follows: *med_code, common_name, scientific_name, quantity,* and *units.* Write the SQL code needed to create this view. Write a SELECT statement to display rows from the view for medicines with a quantity in stock level that is at or below 1,000. Format the output to display one row per line in the result table.

2. Replace the view named *medicine_view* created in question 1 with a new view (same name) that also includes the *normal_dosage* column. Name this column *dosage* in the new view. Write a SELECT statement to display rows from the view where medicine code is greater than or equal to 9999010 and the quantity in stock is at or above 10,000. List the medicine code, common name, quantity, and dosage for the medicines.

3. Employees in the patient services department only need read-access to information about patients. Create a read only view named *patient_view* that has the same structure as the *patient* table. Name the read only constraint *vw_patient_view_read_only*. Use the DESCribe command to describe the *patient_view* object and list the description.

4. Create a view named *patient_record* that will be used by hospital physicians and nurses to access information about patients and the notes recorded for patients. The view should join the *patient* and *patient_note* tables. The view should show each patient's name (*pat_last_name* and *pat_first_name* concatenated as a single column), SSN (*pat_ssn*), bed assigned (*bed_number*), note comments (*note_comment*) and date the note was taken (*note_date*) for each patient. Name the columns in the view appropriate names. The rows in the view should be grouped by the patient SSN. Write a SELECT statement to display the patient record where the patient's SSN is 666-66-6666.

5. The hospital pharmacy directory needs a view created named *prescription_view* that has the following information: prescription number, prescription date, dosage prescribed, dosage directions, medicine common name, patient name (last and first as a single column), and staff member identification (*staff_id*) and name (*staff_last_name*) who wrote the prescription. Name the columns in the view appropriate names. Write a SELECT statement to display prescription information for prescription 755444020.

6. The directory of patient treatment planning needs a view created named *treatment_view* that has the following information: treatment number, service identifier, service description, treatment date, patient name (last and first as a single column), staff member identification (*staff_id*) and name (*staff_last_name*) who provided the treatment, actual charge for the treatment, and comments on the treatment. Name the columns in the view appropriate names. Write a SELECT statement to display treatment information for treatment 18.

7. The chief of physicians requests a view named *staff_location_view* that will list staff members and the ward or department to which they are currently assigned. The view should list the staff member's name (last and first as a single column), staff identifier, ward or department ID and ward or department name to which assigned and work telephone number (not the office telephone number), and phone extension. Name the columns in the view appropriate names. Write a SELECT statement to display staff location information for staff members assigned to the ward with identifier MEDS1.

8. Revise the view named *staff_location_view* to only include rows for staff members assigned to wards or departments with the following identifiers: MEDS1, CARD1, ONCOL, and SURG1. Write a SELECT statement to display staff location infor-

mation for staff members in ward CARD1. Your result table should just display the staff member name, ward/department identifier, and ward/department name.

9. The hospital's management no longer needs the views named *staff_location_view* or *treatment_view*. Write commands to drop these views.

10. The Riverbend Hospital DBA needs to provide location transparency security for the table named *medical_specialty* and have decided to do this by creating a public synonym named *med_spec*. Write the command to create this public synonym. Write a SELECT statement to display the specialty code and specialty title (*specialty_code*, *spec_title*) by using the *med_spec* synonym.

11. You've decided to create a synonym to be used personally to assist you in referencing the table named *ward_dept*. The synonym will be named simply *wd*. Write the command to create this synonym.

12. Write a command to rename the *wd* synonym to have a new name of *ward*. Write a SELECT statement to display all column values by using the *ward* synonym where the *ward_id* column value is ONCOL.

13. The hospital chief of administration wants to assign patient identifiers for new patients arriving at the hospital numbers sequentially beginning with number 700000. The patient numbering will be in increments of 1. In order to improve system performance, you have recommended that 10 patient numbers be cached and this has been approved. No other options are to be set for the new sequence. Name the sequence *patient_number_sequence*. Write the code needed to create this sequence.

14. Write an INSERT command to insert two new rows into the patient table by using the *patient_number_sequence* created in question 13. The patient SSNs as well as last and first names are shown below. Leave the other column values NULL. Write a SELECT statement to display the *pat_id*, *pat_ssn*, *pat_last_name*, and *pat_first_name* columns for all rows from the *patient* table with patient identifiers greater than or equal to 700000.

Patient SSN (pat_ssn)	Last Name (pat_last_name)	First Name (pat_first_name)
900-00-0000	Zucker	Zina
900-00-0001	Zucker	Zachary

15. Write two INSERT commands. The first will insert information for a new patient in the *patient* table as was done in question 14. The second will insert a row in the *patient_note* table. The information to be inserted in each table is indicated below.

Patient SSN (pat_ssn)	Last Name (pat_last_name)	First Name (pat_first_name)
900-00-0002	Zucker	Zumwalt

Patient ID (pat_id)	Note Date (note_date)	Comment (note_comment)	Date_last_updated
Generate from sequence.	SYSDATE	Patient admitted from surgery at 0815 hours	SYSDATE

Write a SELECT statement to join the patient and patient_note tables and to display the information for the patient with a social security number of 900-00-0002. Display the following columns: *patient.pat_ssn, patient.pat_last_name, patient.pat_first_name, patient.pat_id, patient_note.pat_id, note_date, and note_comment.*

CHAPTER 9

1. Write a SQL*Plus program to produce a report that lists patient information. Your report should look like the one shown in Figure C.1. Your report needs to:
   - Display the values shown in both top title and bottom title lines including date and page number.
   - Assign meaningful column names as shown.
   - Display detail line data from the *patient* table of the company database.
   - Order the detail lines by the *pat_id* column.

   Your report will produce additional pages to the one shown in Figure C.1.

2. Write an SQL*Plus program to produce a report that lists room and bed information. This report will be used by the hospital patient services coordinator. Your report should look like the one shown in Figure C.2. Your report needs to:
   - Display the values shown in both top title and bottom title lines including date and page number.
   - Assign meaningful column names as shown.
   - Display detail line data from the *bed* table of the company database.
   - Order the detail lines by the *bed_number* within *room_id* columns.

   Your report will produce additional pages to the one shown in Figure C.2.

FIGURE C.1

```
Sat Jul 13                                              page 1
                    Patient Information

Pat ID      Last Name      First Name      Date Birth      Bed
--------    -----------    ------------    ------------    -----
100001      Able           Andrew          02-JAN-91       5001
100002      Benton         Barbara         02-FEB-61          1
100003      Chen           Rue             14-FEB-73          4
100024      Davis          David           14-MAR-83          6
100025      Earnhardt      Earnest         15-DEC-75          7
100026      Franken        Frank           16-DEC-76         11
100027      Grant          Gregory         05-DEC-51         14
100028      Harnett        Harold          03-NOV-48         15
100029      Iona           Ivy             13-OCT-73         16
100030      Juneau         Juliet          15-OCT-75         18
100031      Kraut          Keith           11-OCT-79         20
100050      Lima           Linda           21-MAY-79         23
100051      Monday         Mandy           21-MAY-52         24
100301      Nunn           Nancy           21-JUN-63         26
100302      Ophelia        Opal            04-JUN-72         28
100303      Pauley         Paul            04-JUN-83         30

              Not for external dissemination.
```

```
Sat Jul 13                                                    page 1
                        Room-Bed Information

Room ID        Bed       Type        Available
---------      -----     ------      ------------
ER0001          50       ER          Y
ER0001          51       ER          N
ER0001          52       E2          Y
ER0001          53       E2          Y
ER0001          59       E3          Y
ER0002          54       ER          N
ER0002          55       ER          Y
ER0002          56       E2          Y
ER0002          57       E2          N
ER0002          58       E3          Y
NW3001         2100      R2          Y
NW3011         2101      R2          Y
NW3021         2102      R2          N
NW3031         2103      R2          Y
NW3031         2104      R2          Y
NW3051         2105      R2          Y


              Not for external dissemination.
```

FIGURE C.2

3. Modify the program for question 2 to produce a control break report like the one shown in Figures C.3a and C.3b. Your report needs to:
   - Display each *room_id* column only once for each group of beds located in a room.
   - Use the COUNT aggregate function to count the number of beds and display this count at the end of the report.

4. Write an SQL*Plus program that will use a view named *patient_view*. This view should include the following columns from the *patient* and *patient_note* tables specified in Table C.1 below. The program will produce a master-detail report like the one shown in Figure C.4. Your report needs to:
   - List each patient's name at the top of a new report page with a page number.
   - Break on the patient's *pat_id* column value.
   - Display the number of patient notes per patient as a subtotal with the subtotal label shown in the figure.
   - Display the report lines sorted in *pat_id* order.

5. Alter the program for question 4. The new program should display the current date at the left margin of the top line of each report page (to the left of the patient name). The first output page for the report is shown in Figure C.5.

```
Sat Jul 13                                              page 1
                        Room-Bed Information

Room ID       Bed       Type       Available
---------     -----     ------     ------------
ER0001         50       ER         Y
               51       ER         N
               52       E2         Y
               53       E2         Y
               59       E3         Y

ER0002         54       ER         N
               55       ER         Y
               56       E2         Y
               57       E2         N
               58       E3         Y

NW3001        2100      R2         Y

NW3011        2101      R2         Y

              Not for external dissemination.
```

FIGURE C.3a

FIGURE C.3b

```
Sat Jul 13                                              page 10
                        Room-Bed Information

Room ID       Bed       Type       Available
---------     -----     ------     ------------

SW3008        2011      RE         Y
              2012      RE         Y
---------
       98




              Not for external dissemination.
```

TABLE C.1

—Patient.pat_id
—Patient Name—defined as a concatenated column that includes the patient.pat_last_name and patient.pat_first_name columns.
—Note.note_date
—Note.note_comment

6. Alter the program for question 4. The new program will have a top title for each page that is two separate lines. The top title line #1 must display the date at the left margin and page number at the right margin. The second top title line must display the patient name prompt and actual patient name. The correct report will look like the page shown in Figure C.5 except that the top title line will be two separate lines.

7. Alter the program for question 4 to use the ACCEPT and PROMPT commands to ask the system user to enter a value for the patient identifier (*pat_id*). The new report should print a single page like that shown in Figure C.5 where the detail lines listing *patient* and *patient_note* table information is only listed for the patient matching the *pat_id* value entered at the prompt. Additionally, you are to remove the view definition from the program and produce the detail lines by specifying the output through use of a SELECT statement (do not use the previously defined view). You may optionally include the use of two separate top title lines with the information specified in question 6.

FIGURE C.4

```
                 Patient Name: Able, Andrew          Page:   1

    PAT_ID        NOTE_DATE    COMMENTS
    ----------    ----------   ----------------------------------------
    100001        13-JUL-02    Patient admitted from surgery at 1715
                               hours

                  13-JUL-02    Abdominal dressing dry and intact fol
                               lowing liver surgery. Biliary draina
                               ge tube with moderate amount (50cc) o
                               f dark greenish drainage noted this s
                               hift.

    * * * * * * * *            ----------------------------------------
    No. Notes                                                        2



                   Not for external dissemination.
```

```
07/14/02              Patient Name: Able, Andrew        Page:   1

PAT_ID       NOTE_DATE   COMMENTS
----------   ----------  ------------------------------------------
100001       13-JUL-02   Patient admitted from surgery at 1715
                         hours

             13-JUL-02   Abdominal dressing dry and intact fol
                         lowing liver surgery. Biliary draina
                         ge tube with moderate amount (50cc) o
                         f dark greenish drainage noted this s
                         hift.

* * * * * * * *          ------------------------------------------
No. Notes                                                        2


                  Not for external dissemination.
```

FIGURE C.5

8. Alter the program you wrote for question 7 to use parameter values such that the program will execute by specifying the patient identifier (*pat_id*) as a parameter of the START command. Your report will look like that shown in Figure C.5.

CHAPTER 10

1. The Chief of Physicians requires a listing of staff members by last name, first name, and middle name. The last name should be displayed in all capital letters. The entire name should be concatenated together so as to display in a single field with a column heading of "Staff Name." The rows should be sorted by staff member last name, then first name, then middle name.

2. Write a query that displays the scientific medicine name and the length in number of characters of each medicine name. Use the *medicine* table. Label the column headings appropriately.

3. Rewrite the query for question 1 to only list staff members that have the character string "dr" in the name. Use lowercase letters only.

4. Rewrite the query for question 3 to list staff members that have the character strings "dr" or "rd" in the name. Use lowercase letters only.

5. Rewrite the query for question 4 to list staff members where the character strings of "OR" or "RO" are either capitalized or lowercase, or a combination of the two. Use the UPPER function.

6. The hospital's Chief of Administration wants a listing of rooms and bed numbers. Display the *room_id* and *bed_number* columns from the *bed* table as a single column with the heading **Rooms/Beds.** Order the output by *room_id.*

7. Write a query that displays the first four characters of each staff member's last name and the last four digits of each staff member's SSN. Label the column headings "Name" and "SSN." Order the result table rows by staff member last name.

8. Write a query to display a listing of staff member last names and the salary. If the staff member is paid a wage, the salary will be NULL. In this situation, display the value $0.00. Provide appropriate headings. Sort the result table by staff member last name.

9. Write a query to compare treatment charges to normal service charges. Display the *service_id* and *service_charge* columns from the *service* table, and the *actual_charge* from the *treatment* table. Only display the value if the difference between the service and actual charge is more than $50.00 in difference (either high or low). Also display a computed column that is the difference between the service and actual charge (as a positive number). Use appropriate column sizes and headings.

10. Modify the query for question 9 to display any rows where there is a difference between the service and actual charge where the actual charge was less than the service charge. Order the output by differences from largest to smallest.

11. List the *service_id* and *service_charge* for services and round the *service_charge* to the nearest $10 dollars. Order the output by *service_id*. A sample result table looks like this:

```
Service     Rounded Charge
------      ------------
10060           $260.00
10061           $320.00
10120           $230.00
```

12. Write a query to display staff member information for the human resources manager. Display each staff member's last and first name (concatenated), hospital title, and date hired. The date hired should be displayed as: Month Name (spelled out), two-digit day, and four-digit year (e.g., December 05, 2002). Use the COLUMN commands shown here to format the first two columns of output. Sort the output by date hired.

```
COLUMN "Hospital Title" Format A20;
COLUMN "Staff Name" FORMAT A30;
```

13. The month values produced by your solution to question 12 are displayed blank-padded to nine characters in length. Use the RTRIM function with concatenation operators to rewrite the query to display the birth date column without blank-padding for the month part of the string of characters forming the date.

14. Write a query to display each staff member's name (last and first), date hired, and date on which the staff member will celebrate 10 years of employment with the Riverbend hospital. Use meaningful column names. Display each date using the DD-MON-YYYY format. Use the ADD_MONTHS and TO_CHAR functions. *Hint:* 10 years equals 120 months. Order the rows in the result table by the date hired.

15. Write a query to display each patient's name (last and first), date of birth, and date on which the patient will be 60 years old. Use meaningful column names. Display each date using the DD-MON-YYYY format. Use the ADD_MONTHS and

TO_CHAR functions. *Hint:* 60 years equals 720 months. Order the rows in the result table by the patient's date of birth.

16. The hospital's patient census manager needs a listing of beds by room and whether or not a bed is available or occupied. Instead of displaying the coded values for the *bed_availability* column, your result table must display the terms "Occupied" and "Available," as appropriate. Use meaningful column headings. Sort the result table by *bed_number* within *room_id*. The result table will display the *room_id*, *bed_number*, and *bed_availability* columns.

17. Modify the query you wrote for question 16 to include the *bed_description* column from the *bed_type* table.

18. Modify the query you wrote for question 17 to only list beds that have as part of the bed_description the word "fixed" (upper- or lower-case or any combination).

CHAPTER 11

1. Study the Riverbend database in Appendix B. You are building a form using Visual Basic 6.0 that will display all of the columns for the *medical_specialty* table. Write the SELECT statement to retrieve all rows from the table.

2. You now plan to revise the form design that displays *medical_specialty* information such that only a single row from the table will be retrieved for display on the form. The form will have a textbox named *txtSpecialtyCode*. The value displayed in the textbox is referenced by the *txtSpecialtyCode.Text* property. Write an embedded SQL statement to retrieve the desired row. Store the SQL statement to a Visual Basic string variable named *strSQL*.

3. The ADO control used to process the *medical_specialty* table referenced in question 2 is named *adoMedSpec*. Write the code necessary to store the *strSQL* variable to the appropriate property of the ADO control and to retrieve the desired *medical_specialty* row by refreshing the *adoMedSpec* control.

4. You need to write a Visual Basic.NET program to connect to an Oracle database named *Riverbend*. Write code needed to declare a Private Constant (Private Const) named *strConnection*. Store the correct connection string value to *strConnection* to make a connection to *Riverbend*. The User ID is **doctor** and the password is **getwell.**

5. Write a DECLARE statement to declare a table named ROOM_DATA to be used to define the *room* table of the Riverbend Hospital database for a COBOL program.

6. A systems analyst in your department has written a portion of the Working-Storage Section of a COBOL program to define variables for processing the *room* table from the Riverbend Hospital database. This code is shown below. Write a COBOL paragraph named PROCESS-ROOM-DATA that will select rows from the *room* table and store the values into the Working-Storage Section variables where the room identifier is 'SW1001'. The table is named ROOM_DATA in the DECLARE statement.

```
01 ROOM-WORK.
   05   ROOM-ID                 PIC X(6).
   05   ROOM-DESCRIPTION        PIC X(25).
   05   DATE-LAST-UPDATED       PIC X(10).
```

```
PROCESS-ROOM-DATA.
   EXEC SQL
       SELECT ROOM_ID, ROOM_DESCRIPTION, DATE_LAST_UPDATED
       INTO :ROOM-ID, :ROOM-DESCRIPTION, :DATE-LAST-UPDATED
       FROM ROOM_DATA
       WHERE ROOM-ID = "SW1001"
   END-EXEC.
```

CHAPTER 12

In order to work the exercises for Chapter 12 while using SQL*Plus, your instructor must grant you the following system privileges:

- CREATE SESSION WITH ADMIN OPTION
- CREATE USER WITH ADMIN OPTION
- ALTER USER
- DROP USER
- UNLIMITED TABLESPACE WITH ADMIN OPTION
- CREATE TABLE WITH ADMIN OPTION
- CREATE ROLE WITH ADMIN OPTION

1. Write the command to create a user account named *jim* that is identified by the password *superuser*. Write the command to create a user account named *henrietta* that is identified by the password *hogwarts*. Write the command to create a user account named *chen* that is identified by the password *li*.

2. Write a command to grant *jim* the system privilege needed in order to connect to the database. *Jim* should have the privilege to grant the system privilege to connect to the database to other system users.

3. Write a command to create a user account named *mita* that is identified by the password *bordoloi*. *Mita* is to be granted a 4-megabyte storage limitation on the *users* tablespace, an unlimited storage limitation on the *temp* tablespace, and must be forced to change the password the first time that *mita* connects to the database. The default tablespace will be *users* and the temporary tablespace will be *temp*. Write a command to grant *mita* the system privilege needed in order to connect to the database.

4. Write a command that will change *mita's* quota on the temp tablespace to 3 megabytes.

5. Connect to SQL*Plus as the user *mita*. Change mita's password to *rook* when you connect. Assume that *mita* has changed her mind and wants her password to be *castle*. Write the command that *mita* will execute to change her logon password to *castle*.

6. Connect to SQL*Plus using your own user account. Write the command to drop the user named *henrietta*, assuming that *henrietta* has not created any objects in the database.

7. Write the command needed to grant *jim* an unlimited tablespace quota privilege.

8. Write the command to grant *jim* the privilege to create a table. *Jim* should also have the authority to grant this privilege to other system users.

9. *Jim* plans to create a table named *autos* that will store information about automobiles that the organization sells on its automobile lot. The CREATE TABLE com-

mand is shown below. Connect to the database as *jim* and execute this command as part of this exercise. Which privilege does system user *jim* need in order to create an index on the *autos* table?

```
CREATE TABLE autos (
    Auto_Id             CHAR(22),
    Auto_Description    VARCHAR(50),
    Auto_Price          NUMBER(7,2) );
```

10. System user *jim* wishes to grant system user *mita* the privilege to query the *autos* table. Write this command.

11. The *autos* table is used by many different managers in our organization. *Bob* needs to grant everyone in the organization the privilege to query the *autos* table. Write this command.

12. Jim intends to trust *mita* to insert rows into the *autos* table. Further, she is to be granted the right to grant the insert privilege to other system users as she deems necessary. Write the command needed to grant this privilege to *mita*.

13. Write a command that will revoke ALL privileges that system user *mita* has on the *autos* table. Does this command keep *mita* from querying the *autos* table with a SELECT statement? Why or why not?

14. Connect to the database using your own user account. Write a command that will create a role named *auto_sales_mgr* (someone that will manage automobile sales operations).

15. Write the command needed to grant the role *auto_sales_mgr* to the system users named *mita* and *chen*.

16. Write the command needed to grant the role *auto_sales_mgr* to the system user named *mita* such that *mita* can also grant this role to other system users or to other roles.

17. Write the command that will drop the role named *auto_sales_mgr*.

APPENDIX D

SOLUTIONS TO ODD-NUMBERED EXERCISES

This appendix provides you with solutions to the odd-numbered end-of-chapter and end-of-book (from Appendix C) SQL coding exercises and questions.

END-OF-CHAPTER EXERCISE SOLUTIONS

CHAPTER 1

1. It is the primary statement in SQL that is used to query, or extract information from a database.
3. You simply list the columns from the table or tables to be displayed. The columns are listed in the order in which they are displayed.
5. A comma is used between column names as well as table names.
7. Using uppercase or lowercase commands has no effect; however, by convention, we type commands and clauses such as SELECT, FROM, and WHERE in uppercase and column names, table names, and conditions in lowercase.
9. The ORDER BY clause.

CHAPTER 2

1.
```
CREATE TABLE test_table (
    test_id                 NUMBER(3),
    test_description        VARCHAR2(25) );
INSERT INTO test_table VALUES ( 1, 'Test row #1');
INSERT INTO test_table VALUES ( 2, 'Test row #2');
```

3.
```
SELECT * FROM test_table;

TEST_ID    TEST_DESCRIPTION
-------    ---------------
      1         Test row #1
      2         Test row #2
```

5.
```
REM Create department table
CREATE TABLE department (
     dpt_no          NUMBER(2) CONSTRAINT pk_department PRIMARY KEY,
     dpt_name        VARCHAR2(20) CONSTRAINT nn_dep_name NOT NULL,
     dpt_mgrssn      CHAR(9),
     dpt_mgr_start_date DATE );
```

7.
```
DESC department;
Name                    Null?         Type
----------------        -------       -----------
DPT_NO                  NOT NULL      NUMBER(2)
DPT_NAME                NOT NULL      VARCHAR2(20)
DPT_MGRSSN                            CHAR(9)
DPT_MGR_START_DATE                   DATE
```

9.
```
CREATE TABLE employee (
     emp_ssn         CHAR(9) CONSTRAINT pk_employee PRIMARY KEY,
     emp_last_name   VARCHAR2(25) CONSTRAINT nn_emp_last_name NOT NULL,
     emp_first_name  VARCHAR2(25) CONSTRAINT nn_emp_first_name NOT NULL,
     emp_middle_name VARCHAR2(25),
     emp_address     VARCHAR2(50),
     emp_city        VARCHAR2(25),
     emp_state       CHAR(2),
     emp_zip         CHAR(9),
     emp_date_of_birth DATE,
     emp_salary      NUMBER(7,2) CONSTRAINT ck_emp_salary
        CHECK (emp_salary <= 85000),
     emp_parking_space NUMBER(4) CONSTRAINT un_emp_parking_space UNIQUE,
     emp_gender      CHAR(1),
     emp_dpt_number  NUMBER(2),
     emp_superssn    CHAR(9),
CONSTRAINT fk_emp_dpt FOREIGN KEY (emp_dpt_number) REFERENCES department
     ON DELETE SET NULL,
CONSTRAINT fk_emp_superssn FOREIGN KEY (emp_superssn) REFERENCES employee
     ON DELETE SET NULL ) ;
```

11. The output should display 9 rows of data including the row for the student.

13.
```
UPDATE employee
SET emp_address = '#6 Main St'
WHERE emp_last_name = 'Zhu';
```

15.
```
ALTER TABLE employee ADD (salary_year_to_date NUMBER(7,2));
```

17.
```
CREATE INDEX employee_zip_last_name
ON employee (emp_zip, emp_last_name);
```

CHAPTER 3

1.
```
DESCRIBE assignment;

Name                    Null?         Type
--------------          -------       ----------
WORK_EMP_SSN            NOT NULL      CHAR(9)
WORK_PRO_NUMBER         NOT NULL      NUMBER(2)
WORK_HOURS                           NUMBER(5,1)

SELECT *
FROM assignment;
```

```
WORK_EMP_        WORK_PRO_NUMBER        WORK_HOURS
--------         -------------          ---------
999111111                    1               31.4
999111111                    2                8.5
999333333                    3               42.1
. . . .
17 rows selected.
```

3.
```
SELECT work_emp_ssn, work_hours
FROM assignment;
```

```
WORK_EMP_        WORK_HOURS
--------         ---------
999111111             31.4
999111111              8.5
999333333             42.1
. . . .
17 rows selected.
```

5.
```
SELECT emp_last_name, emp_first_name, emp_middle_name, emp_date_of_birth,
    emp_gender
FROM employee
ORDER BY emp_last_name;
```

```
EMP_LAST_NAME      EMP_FIRST_NAME      EMP_MIDDLE_NAME      EMP_DATE_    E
------------       -------------       -------------        --------     -
Amin               Hyder                                    29-MAR-69    M
```

7.
```
SELECT emp_gender, emp_last_name,
    emp_first_name, emp_middle_name, emp_date_of_birth
FROM employee
ORDER BY emp_gender, emp_last_name;
```

```
E      EMP_LAST_NAME      EMP_FIRST_NAME      E      EMP_DATE_
-      -----------        -----------         -      --------
F      Joyner             Suzanne             A      20-JUN-71
F      Markis             Marcia              M      19-JUL-78
F      Prescott           Sherri              C      31-JUL-72
8 rows selected.
```

9.
```
SELECT dep_emp_ssn, dep_name, dep_relationship
FROM dependent
WHERE dep_relationship <> 'SPOUSE'
ORDER BY dep_emp_ssn DESC;
```

```
DEP_EMP_S        DEP_NAME       DEP_RELATI
--------         -------        ---------
999444444        Jo Ellen       DAUGHTER
999444444        Andrew         SON
999111111        Jeffery        SON
999111111        Deanna         DAUGHTER
```

11.
```
SELECT dpt_no, dpt_location
FROM dept_locations
ORDER BY dpt_no DESC;
```

```
DPT_NO      DPT_LOCATION
------      -----------
     7      St. Louis
     7      Edwardsville
     7      Collinsville
5 rows selected.
```

CHAPTER 4

1.  ```
    COLUMN "First Name" FORMAT A15;
    COLUMN "Last Name" FORMAT A15;
    COLUMN "Gender" FORMAT A6;
    COLUMN "Dept" FORMAT 9999;
    SELECT emp_first_name "First Name", emp_last_name "Last Name",
        emp_gender "Gender", emp_dpt_number "Dept"
    FROM employee
    WHERE emp_gender = 'M' AND emp_dpt_number = 7;
    ```

First Name	Last Name	Gender	Dept
Waiman	Zhu	M	7
Douglas	Bock	M	7
Dinesh	Joshi	M	7

3.  ```
    SELECT emp_first_name "First Name", emp_last_name "Last Name",
        emp_salary "Salary"
    FROM employee
    WHERE emp_salary IN (43000, 50000, 55000);
    ```

First Name	Last Name	Salary
Bijoy	Bordoloi	$55,000.00
Suzanne	Joyner	$43,000.00
Waiman	Zhu	$43,000.00

5.  ```
    SELECT emp_first_name "First Name", emp_last_name "Last Name",
        emp_salary "Salary"
    FROM employee
    WHERE emp_salary BETWEEN 35000 AND 45000
    ORDER BY emp_salary;
    ```

First Name	Last Name	Salary
Dinesh	Joshi	$38,000.00
Suzanne	Joyner	$43,000.00
Waiman	Zhu	$43,000.00

7.  ```
    SELECT emp_first_name "First Name", emp_last_name "Last Name"
    FROM employee
    WHERE emp_first_name LIKE 'D%';
    ```

First Name	Last Name
Douglas	Bock
Dinesh	Joshi

9.  ```
    COLUMN Annual FORMAT $99,999.99;
    COLUMN Monthly FORMAT $99,999.99
    COLUMN Weekly FORMAT $99,999.99;
    SELECT emp_last_name "Last Name", emp_salary "Annual",
        emp_salary/12 "Monthly", emp_salary/52 "Weekly"
    FROM employee
    ORDER BY emp_last_name;
    ```
    ```

Last Name	Annual	Monthly	Weekly
Amin	$25,000.00	$2,083.33	$480.77
Bock	$30,000.00	$2,500.00	$576.92
Bordoloi	$55,000.00	$4,583.33	$1,057.69

8 rows selected.

11. COLUMN State FORMAT A5;
    SELECT emp_last_name "Last Name", emp_superssn "SSN",
        emp_gender "Gender", emp_state "State"
    FROM employee
    WHERE emp_gender = 'F' AND emp_state = 'CA';

Last Name	SSN	Gender	State
Joyner	999666666	F	CA
Markis	999555555	F	CA

13. SELECT work_emp_ssn, work_pro_number, work_hours
    FROM assignment
    WHERE work_pro_number IN (1, 15, 20, 22, 25, 28, 30);

WORK_EMP_	WORK_PRO_NUMBER	WORK_HOURS
999111111	1	31.4
999888888	1	21
999444444	1	

9 rows selected.

15. CREATE TABLE contract_employee (
        emp_id   CHAR(2),
        emp_job   VARCHAR(12),
        emp_salary NUMBER(6),
        emp_bonus   NUMBER(4));

    INSERT INTO contract_employee VALUES ('10', 'BIG BOSS', 100000, NULL);
    INSERT INTO contract_employee VALUES ('20', 'LITTLE BOSS', 50000, NULL);
    INSERT INTO contract_employee VALUES ('30', 'WORKER', 10000, 2000);
    INSERT INTO contract_employee VALUES ('40', 'WORKER', 11000, 3000);

    COLUMN emp_id FORMAT A6;
    SELECT emp_id, emp_job, emp_salary+emp_bonus "Total Comp"
    FROM contract_employee;

EMP_ID	EMP_JOB	Total Comp
10	BIG BOSS	
20	LITTLE BOSS	
30	WORKER	12000
40	WORKER	14000

CHAPTER 5

1. SELECT COUNT(*) "Number of Dependents"
   FROM dependent;

   Number of Dependents

3. ```
   SELECT MAX(dpt_mgr_start_date)
   FROM department;

   MAX(DPT_M
   --------
   22-MAY-98
   ```

5. ```
   SELECT COUNT(dep_gender) "Number Male Dependents"
   FROM dependent
   WHERE dep_gender = 'M';

   Number Male Dependents
   ----------------------
                        3
   ```

7. ```
   SELECT dep_relationship "Dependent Type",
        COUNT(dep_relationship) "Dependent Count"
   FROM dependent
   GROUP BY dep_relationship;

   Dependent    Dependent Count
   ---------    ---------------
   DAUGHTER                   2
   SON                        2
   SPOUSE                     3
   ```

9. ```
   SELECT dep_relationship "Dependent Type",
        COUNT(dep_relationship) "Dependent Count"
   FROM dependent
   GROUP BY dep_relationship
   ORDER BY COUNT(dep_relationship) DESC;

   Dependent    Dependent Count
   ---------    ---------------
   SPOUSE                     3
   DAUGHTER                   2
   SON                        2
   ```

11. ```
    SELECT pro_dept_number "Department", COUNT(pro_number) "Project Count"
    FROM project
    GROUP BY pro_dept_number;

    Department    Project Count
    ----------    -------------
             1                1
             3                2
             7                3
    ```

13. ```
    SELECT pro_dept_number "Department", COUNT(pro_number) "Project Count"
    FROM project
    GROUP BY pro_dept_number
    HAVING COUNT(pro_number) >= 2;

    Department    Project Count
    ----------    -------------
             3                2
             7                3
    ```

15. ```
    COLUMN "Total Hours" FORMAT 999.99;
    SELECT work_pro_number "Project Number", SUM(work_hours) "Total Hours"
    ```
    ```

```
FROM assignment
GROUP BY work_pro_number
HAVING AVG(work_hours) >= 15
ORDER BY SUM(work_hours);

Project Number     Total Hours
------------       ----------
           1           52.40
           3           52.60
          10           54.80
          30           55.10
```

CHAPTER 6

1.
```
SELECT d.dpt_no, dpt_name, dpt_location
FROM department d, dept_locations;

DPT_NO    DPT_NAME            DPT_LOCATION
------    ---------------     -----------
     7    Production          Edwardsville
     3    Admin and Records   Edwardsville
     1    Headquarters        Edwardsville
15 rows selected.
```

3.
```
COLUMN "Department" FORMAT A17;
COLUMN "Employee" FORMAT A20;
COLUMN "Parking" FORMAT 9999999;
COLUMN "Salary" FORMAT $999,999;
SELECT dpt_no "Dept Numb", dpt_name "Department",
    emp_first_name || ' ' || emp_last_name "Employee",
    emp_salary "Salary", emp_parking_space "Parking"
FROM department, employee
WHERE dpt_mgrssn = emp_ssn;

Dept Numb   Department          Employee          Salary     Parking
---------   ---------------     ---------------   --------   -------
        7   Production          Waiman Zhu        $43,000         32
        3   Admin and Records   Suzanne Joyner    $43,000          3
        1   Headquarters        Bijoy Bordoloi    $55,000          1
```

5.
```
SELECT dpt_name "Department", pro_number "Proj. Numb",
    pro_name "Project", pro_location "Location"
FROM department, project
WHERE dpt_no = pro_dept_number AND
    (dpt_name = 'Production' OR pro_location = 'Edwardsville');

Department     Proj. Numb   Project        Location
-----------    ----------   ----------     -----------
Production              1   Order Entry    St. Louis
Production              2   Payroll        Collinsville
Production              3   Receivables    Edwardsville
Headquarters          20   Personnel      Edwardsville
```

7.
```
SELECT e.emp_last_name || ', ' || e.emp_first_name "Employee",
    a.work_pro_number "Proj. Numb", a.work_hours "Hours"
FROM employee e, assignment a
WHERE e.emp_ssn = a.work_emp_ssn(+) AND
    a.work_hours IS NULL
```

```
ORDER BY emp_last_name, emp_first_name;
```

```
Employee              Proj. Numb    Hours
-------------         ---------     -----
Bordoloi, Bijoy            20
Zhu, Waiman                 1
```

9.
```
COLUMN "Dependent" FORMAT A15;
SELECT e.emp_last_name "Employee", d.dep_name "Dependent",
    d.dep_date_of_birth "Birth Date"
FROM employee e, dependent d
WHERE e.emp_ssn = d.dep_emp_ssn
ORDER BY e.emp_last_name;
```

```
Employee      Dependent     Birth Dat
-------       ---------     --------
Bock          Jeffery       01-JAN-78
Bock          Deanna        31-DEC-78
Bock          Mary Ellen    05-MAY-57
7 rows selected.
```

11.
```
COLUMN "Employee" FORMAT A10;
COLUMN "Emp Gender" FORMAT A10;
COLUMN "Dependent" FORMAT A10;
COLUMN "Dep Gender" FORMAT A10;
COLUMN "Relationship" FORMAT A12;
SELECT emp_last_name "Employee", emp_gender "Emp Gender",
    dep_name "Dependent", dep_gender "Dep Gender",
    dep_relationship "Relationship"
FROM employee, dependent
WHERE emp_ssn = dep_emp_ssn AND
    emp_gender <> dep_gender
ORDER BY emp_last_name;
```

```
Employee    Emp Gender    Dependent     Dep Gender    Relationship
-------     ---------     ---------     ---------     ----------
Bock        M             Deanna        F             DAUGHTER
Bock        M             Mary Ellen    F             SPOUSE
Joyner      F             Allen         M             SPOUSE
Zhu         M             Jo Ellen      F             DAUGHTER
Zhu         M             Susan         F             SPOUSE
```

CHAPTER 7

1.
```
COLUMN "Last Name" FORMAT A15;
COLUMN "First Name" FORMAT A15;
SELECT emp_last_name "Last Name", emp_first_name "First Name"
FROM employee
WHERE emp_ssn IN
    (SELECT work_emp_ssn
     FROM assignment
     WHERE work_pro_number IN (10, 20, 30) );
```

```
Last Name     First Name
--------      ---------
Amin          Hyder
Zhu           Waiman
Joyner        Suzanne
5 rows selected.
```

3.
```
COLUMN "Last Name" FORMAT A15;
COLUMN "First Name" FORMAT A15;
SELECT emp_last_name "Last Name", emp_first_name "First Name"
FROM employee
WHERE emp_ssn IN
    (SELECT work_emp_ssn
     FROM assignment
     WHERE work_pro_number NOT IN (10, 20, 30) )
ORDER BY emp_last_name;
```

```
Last Name       First Name
--------        ---------
Bock            Douglas
Joshi           Dinesh
Prescott        Sherri
Zhu             Waiman
```

5.
```
COLUMN "Last Name" FORMAT A15;
COLUMN "First Name" FORMAT A15;
SELECT emp_last_name "Last Name", emp_first_name "First Name",
    emp_date_of_birth "Birth Date"
FROM employee
WHERE emp_date_of_birth <
    (SELECT MIN(emp_date_of_birth)
     FROM employee
     WHERE emp_dpt_number = 3);
```

```
Last Name       First Name      Birth Dat
--------        ---------       --------
Bordoloi        Bijoy           10-NOV-67
Bock            Douglas         01-SEP-55
```

7.
```
SELECT work_emp_ssn "Emp SSN", work_hours "Hours Worked",
    work_pro_number "Project"
FROM assignment a1
WHERE work_hours =
    (SELECT MIN(work_hours)
     FROM assignment
     WHERE a1.work_pro_number = work_pro_number)
ORDER BY work_pro_number;
```

```
Emp SSN         Hours Worked    Project
--------        -----------     ------
999888888              21          1
999111111             8.5          2
999444444            10.5          3
```
6 rows selected.

9.
```
SELECT emp_last_name "Last Name", emp_first_name "First Name",
    emp_dpt_number "Dept", emp_salary "Salary",
    emp_date_of_birth "Birth Date"
FROM employee e1
WHERE emp_date_of_birth =
    (SELECT MAX(emp_date_of_birth)
     FROM employee
     WHERE e1.emp_dpt_number = emp_dpt_number)
ORDER BY emp_dpt_number;
```

Last Name	First Name	Dept	Salary	Birth Dat
Bordoloi	Bijoy	1	$55,000	10-NOV-67
Markis	Marcia	3	$25,000	19-JUL-78
Zhu	Waiman	7	$43,000	08-DEC-75

11.
```
SELECT emp_last_name "Last Name", emp_first_name "First Name"
FROM employee e1
WHERE EXISTS
     (SELECT dpt_mgrssn
      FROM department
      WHERE e1.emp_ssn = dpt_mgrssn);
```

Last Name	First Name
Bordoloi	Bijoy
Joyner	Suzanne
Zhu	Waiman

CHAPTER 8

1.
```
CREATE OR REPLACE VIEW salary_view (ssn, last_name, first_name,
     salary) AS
SELECT emp_ssn, emp_last_name, emp_first_name, emp_salary
FROM employee;

COLUMN last_name FORMAT A15;
COLUMN first_name FORMAT A15;
COLUMN salary FORMAT $999,999;
SELECT *
FROM salary_view
WHERE salary >= 30000;
```

SSN	LAST_NAME	FIRST_NAME	SALARY
999666666	Bordoloi	Bijoy	$55,000
999555555	Joyner	Suzanne	$43,000
999444444	Zhu	Waiman	$43,000

5 rows selected.

3.
```
CREATE OR REPLACE VIEW dependent_view AS
SELECT *
FROM dependent
     WITH READ ONLY CONSTRAINT vw_dependent_view_read_only;

DESC dependent_view
```

Name	Null?	Type
DEP_EMP_SSN	NOT NULL	CHAR(9)
DEP_NAME	NOT NULL	VARCHAR2(50)
DEP_GENDER		CHAR(1)
DEP_DATE_OF_BIRTH		DATE
DEP_RELATIONSHIP		VARCHAR2(10)

5.
```
COLUMN department FORMAT A17;
COLUMN project FORMAT A15;
COLUMN location FORMAT A15;
```

```
CREATE OR REPLACE VIEW department_projects (dept_no, department,
    project, location) AS
SELECT dpt_no, dpt_name, pro_name, pro_location
FROM department, project
WHERE dpt_no = pro_dept_number AND
    (pro_location = 'Edwardsville' OR pro_location = 'Marina');

SELECT *
FROM department_projects;

DEPT_NO       DEPARTMENT           PROJECT          LOCATION
------        ---------------      -----------      -----------
     7        Production           Receivables      Edwardsville
     3        Admin and Records    Inventory        Marina
     1        Headquarters         Personnel        Edwardsville
     3        Admin and Records    Pay Benefits     Marina
```

7.
```
SELECT *
FROM department_projects
WHERE dept_no = 3;

DEPT_NO       DEPARTMENT           PROJECT          LOCATION     PRO_NO
------        ---------------      -----------      -------      ------
     3        Admin and Records    Inventory        Marina           10
     3        Admin and Records    Pay Benefits     Marina           30
```

9.
```
CREATE PUBLIC SYNONYM locations FOR dept_locations;

SELECT *
FROM locations
WHERE dpt_no = 7;

DEP_NO       DEP_LOCATION
------       -----------
     7       Collinsville
     7       Edwardsville
     7       St. Louis
```

11.
```
RENAME asgn TO asign;

SELECT *
FROM asign
WHERE work_hours >= 30;

WORK_EMP_     WORK_PRO_NUMBER      WORK_HOURS
--------      -------------        ---------
999111111                   1           31.4
999333333                   3           42.1
999887777                  30           30.8
999222222                  10           34.5
```

13.
```
INSERT INTO department
    VALUES (department_number_sequence.nextval, 'Engineering',
    NULL, NULL);
INSERT INTO department
    VALUES (department_number_sequence.nextval, 'Inventory Mngt',
    NULL, NULL);

SELECT *
FROM department;
```

```
     DPT_NO     DPT_NAME            DPT_MGRSS     DPT_MGR_S
     ------     ---------------     --------      --------
          7     Production          999444444     22-MAY-98
          3     Admin and Records   999555555     01-JAN-01
          1     Headquarters        999666666     19-JUN-81
         41     Inventory Mngt
         40     Engineering
```

CHAPTER 9

1.  ```
    REM Program: ch9-7.sql
    REM Programmer: dbock; 3-20-2003
    REM Description: A dependent report - solution to SQL Exercise 1.

    TTITLE 'Dependent Information'
    BTITLE SKIP 1 CENTER 'Not for external dissemination.'
    REM REPHEADER 'Project Report #1 — prepared by D. Bock' SKIP 2
    REM REPFOOTER SKIP 3 '— Last Page of Report —'

    SET LINESIZE 60
    SET PAGESIZE 24
    SET NEWPAGE 1

    COLUMN "Emp SSN" FORMAT A12
    COLUMN "Dependent" FORMAT A15
    COLUMN "Gender" FORMAT A6
    COLUMN "Date Birth" FORMAT A10
    COLUMN "Relationship" FORMAT A12
    SELECT dep_emp_ssn "Emp SSN", dep_name "Dependent", dep_gender "Gender",
        dep_date_of_birth "Date Birth", dep_relationship "Relationship"
    FROM dependent
    ORDER BY dep_emp_ssn;
    ```

3.  ```
    REM Program: ch9-9.sql
    REM Programmer: dbock; 3-20-2003
    REM Description: A master-detail employee and dependent report -
    REM solution to SQL Exercise 3.

    SET LINESIZE 60
    SET PAGESIZE 14
    SET NEWPAGE 1

    CREATE OR REPLACE VIEW employee_dependent (ssn, employee_name,
        dependent_name, gender, relationship) AS
        SELECT e.emp_ssn, e.emp_last_name||', '||e.emp_first_name,
            d.dep_name, d.dep_gender, d.dep_relationship
        FROM employee e, dependent d
        WHERE e.emp_ssn = d.dep_emp_ssn
        ORDER BY e.emp_ssn;

    COLUMN employee_name NEW_VALUE employee_name_var NOPRINT
    COLUMN ssn FORMAT A12
    COLUMN dependent_name FORMAT A15
    COLUMN gender FORMAT A6
    COLUMN relationship FORMAT A12

    TTITLE RIGHT 'Page: ' FORMAT 999 sql.pno -
            CENTER 'Employee Name: ' employee_name_var SKIP 2
    BTITLE SKIP 1 CENTER 'Not for external dissemination.'
    ```

```
CLEAR BREAKS
CLEAR COMPUTES
BREAK ON ssn SKIP PAGE
COMPUTE COUNT LABEL 'No Dep' OF "relationship" ON ssn
REM COMPUTE COUNT LABEL 'Total Dep' OF "relationship" ON REPORT

SELECT ssn, employee_name, dependent_name, gender, relationship
FROM employee_dependent;
```

5.  ```
    REM the revised and new code is:
    COLUMN today NEW_VALUE date_var
    SELECT TO_CHAR(SYSDATE, 'MM/DD/YY') today
    FROM dual;
    TTITLE LEFT date_var RIGHT 'Page: ' FORMAT 999 sql.pno SKIP 1 -
          CENTER 'Employee Name: ' employee_name_var SKIP 2
    ```

7.  ```
    REM Program: ch9-12.sql
    REM Programmer: dbock; 3-20-2003
    REM Description: A master-detail employee and dependent report -
    REM solution to SQL Exercise 6. Program ch9-11.sql altered.

    SET LINESIZE 60
    SET PAGESIZE 14
    SET NEWPAGE 1

    COLUMN today NEW_VALUE date_var
    SELECT TO_CHAR(SYSDATE, 'MM/DD/YY') today
    FROM dual;

    COLUMN employee_name NEW_VALUE employee_name_var NOPRINT
    COLUMN ssn NEW_VALUE ssn_var
    COLUMN ssn FORMAT A12
    COLUMN dependent_name FORMAT A15
    COLUMN gender FORMAT A6
    COLUMN relationship FORMAT A12

    TTITLE LEFT date_var RIGHT 'Page: ' FORMAT 999 sql.pno SKIP 1 -
          CENTER 'Employee Name: ' employee_name_var SKIP 2
    BTITLE SKIP 1 CENTER 'Not for external dissemination.'

    CLEAR BREAKS
    CLEAR COMPUTES
    BREAK ON ssn SKIP PAGE
    COMPUTE COUNT LABEL 'No Dep' OF "relationship" ON ssn

    SELECT SUBSTR(e.emp_ssn,1,3)||'-'||SUBSTR(e.emp_ssn,4,2)||'-'||
        SUBSTR(e.emp_ssn,6,4) "ssn", e.emp_last_name||', '||e.emp_first_name
        "employee_name", d.dep_name "dependent_name", d.dep_gender "gender",
        d.dep_relationship "relationship"
    FROM employee e, dependent d
    WHERE e.emp_ssn = d.dep_emp_ssn AND
        e.emp_ssn = '&1'
    ORDER BY e.emp_ssn;
    ```

CHAPTER 10

1.  ```
    COLUMN "Employee Name" FORMAT A30;
    SELECT UPPER(emp_last_name) || ', ' || emp_first_name || ' '
        || emp_middle_name "Employee Name"
    FROM employee
    ORDER BY emp_last_name, emp_first_name;
    ```
    ```

```
Employee Name
-------------
AMIN, Hyder
BOCK, Douglas B
BORDOLOI, Bijoy
8 rows selected.
```

3.
```
COLUMN "Employee Name" FORMAT A30;
SELECT UPPER(emp_last_name) || ', ' || emp_first_name || ' '
    || emp_middle_name "Employee Name"
FROM employee
WHERE INSTR(emp_last_name||emp_first_name,'oy') != 0
ORDER BY emp_last_name, emp_first_name;

Employee Name
---------------
BORDOLOI, Bijoy
JOYNER, Suzanne A
```

5.
```
SELECT SUBSTR(emp_last_name,1,4) "Name",
    SUBSTR(emp_ssn,6,4) "SSN"
FROM employee
ORDER BY emp_last_name;

Name    SSN
----    ----
Amin    2222
Bock    1111
Bord    6666
8 rows selected.
```

7.
```
SELECT emp_last_name "Last Name",
    NVL(emp_superssn,'Top Supervisor') "Supervisor SSN"
FROM employee
ORDER BY emp_last_name;

Last Name       Supervisor SSN
--------        -------------
Amin            999555555
Bock            999444444
Bordoloi        Top Supervisor
8 rows selected.
```

9.
```
SELECT emp_last_name "Last Name", work_pro_number "Project",
    ROUND(work_hours,0) "Hours"
FROM assignment a, employee e
WHERE e.emp_ssn = a.work_emp_ssn AND
    work_pro_number IN (2,10)
ORDER BY work_pro_number, emp_last_name;

Last Name       Project     Hours
--------        ------      -----
Bock                2           9
Prescott            2          22
Zhu                 2          12
6 rows selected.
```

11.
```
COLUMN "Gender" Format A6;
COLUMN "Dep Name" FORMAT A15;
```

```
SELECT dep_name "Dep Name", dep_gender "Gender",
    RTRIM(TO_CHAR(dep_date_of_birth, 'MONTH'))||' '||
    TO_CHAR(dep_date_of_birth, 'DD, YYYY') "Birth Date"
FROM dependent;

Dep Name      Gender      Birth Date
-------       ------      --------------
Jo Ellen      F           APRIL 05, 1996
Andrew        M           OCTOBER 25, 1998
Susan         F           MAY 03, 1975
7 rows selected.
```

13.
```
SELECT TO_CHAR(SYSDATE, 'DAY') "Day"
FROM dual;

Day
------
TUESDAY
```

Note: The day listed will vary depending on the date the query executes.

CHAPTER 11

1.
```
SELECT * from department;
```

3.
```
adoDepartment.RecordSource = strSQL
adoDepartment.Refresh
```

5.
```
EXEC SQL
    DECLARE DEPT_LOC TABLE
        (DPT_NO                    NUMBER(2),
        DPT_LOCATION               CHAR(20) )
END-EXEC.
```

CHAPTER 12—SQL CODING EXERCISES AND QUESTIONS

1.
```
CREATE USER bob IDENTIFIED BY wonderful;
CREATE USER matilda IDENTIFIED BY bootcamp;
CREATE USER makita IDENTIFIED BY swordfish;
```

3.
```
CREATE USER sally IDENTIFIED BY exciting
DEFAULT TABLESPACE users
    TEMPORARY TABLESPACE temp
    QUOTA 15M ON users
    QUOTA UNLIMITED ON temp
    PASSWORD EXPIRE;

GRANT create session TO sally;
```

5.
```
CONNECT sally/exciting;
ALTER USER sally IDENTIFIED BY metalmusic;
```

7.
```
GRANT unlimited tablespace TO bob;
```

9.
```
CONNECT bob/wonderful;
CREATE TABLE books (
    Book_Id     CHAR(6),
    Book_Title  VARCHAR(50),
    ISBN        CHAR(15),
    Book_Price  NUMBER(6,2) );
```

None. Bob has the privilege to create an index on any table that he has created as the owner of the table.

11. `GRANT select ON bob.books TO PUBLIC;`

13. `REVOKE ALL ON bob.books FROM sally;`

No, Sally can still query the books table because bob granted SELECT to PUB-LIC.

15. `GRANT books_mgr TO sally, makita;`

17. `DROP ROLE books_mgr;`

END-OF-BOOK EXERCISE SOLUTIONS FOR APPENDIX C EXERCISES

CHAPTER 1

1. The relationship between the *patient* and *patient_note* tables is one-to-many, meaning each patient can have many different patient_note rows in the *patient_note* table.

3.  ```
    SELECT *
    FROM patient
    WHERE pat_id = '100306';
    ```

    ```
    PAT_ID     PAT_SSN       PAT_LAST_NAME
    ------     --------      -----------
    PAT_FIRST_NAME
    -------------
    PAT_MIDDLE_NAME
    -------------
    PAT_STREET_ADDRESS
    ----------------
    PAT_CITY                              PA    PAT_ZIP     PAT_DATE_
    -------                               --    ------      --------
    PAT_TELEPH    BED_NUMBER    DATE_LAST
    ---------     ---------     --------
    100306     222333306     Santiago
    Samuel
    Sampson
    Southwest Drive #22
    Edwardsville                          IL    62025       07-JUN-84
    1005551039           36     17-FEB-02
    ```

5.  ```
    SELECT *
    FROM bed_type;
    ```

    ```
    BE     BED_DESCRIPTION            DATE_LAST
    --     ---------------------      --------
    R1     Regular Ward-Fixed         17-FEB-02
    R2     Regular Ward-Adjustable    17-FEB-02
    ER     Emergency Room-Rollaround  17-FEB-02
    10 rows selected.
    ```

7.  ```
    SELECT ward_id, ward_dept_name
    FROM ward_dept;
    ```
    ```

```
WARD_     WARD_DEPT_NAME
-----     --------------------
MEDS1     Medical Surgical Ward 1
MEDS2     Medical Surgical Ward 2
RADI1     Radiology Dept
18 rows selected.
```

9.
```
SELECT staff_id, specialty_code
FROM staff_medspec
WHERE specialty_code = 'RN1';

STAFF     SPE
-----     ---
67555     RN1
66444     RN1
```

11. The relationship is named *treatment*. Information is stored in four tables: *patient, staff, service,* and *treatment*.

13. The table is named *prescription*. The other tables with relationships are named *patient, staff,* and *medicine*.

15.
```
SQL> INPUT
REM Displays staff information
COLUMN "Last Name" FORMAT A20;
COLUMN "First Name" FORMAT A20;
COLUMN Title FORMAT A5;
SELECT staff_id, staff_last_name "Last Name",
    staff_first_name "First Name", date_hired,
    hospital_title "Title"
FROM staff
WHERE hospital_title = 'M.D.'

SQL> SAVE Staff-Info.sql
Created file Staff-Info.sql
Start Staff-Info.sql

STAFF     Last Name     First Name     DATE_HIRE     Title
-----     ---------     ----------     ---------     -----
23232     Eakin         Maxwell        06-JAN-98     M.D.
23244     Webber        Eugene         16-FEB-95     M.D.
10044     Sumner        Elizabeth      16-FEB-01     M.D.
13 rows selected.
```

CHAPTER 2

1.
```
REM Table patient_archive
CREATE TABLE patient_archive (
    pat_id          CHAR(6) CONSTRAINT pk_patient_archive PRIMARY KEY,
    pat_ssn         CHAR(9) CONSTRAINT nn_pat_ssn_archive NOT NULL,
    pat_last_name   VARCHAR2(50) CONSTRAINT nn_pat_last_name_archive NOT NULL,
    pat_first_name  VARCHAR2(50) CONSTRAINT nn_pat_first_name_archive NOT NULL,
    pat_middle_name VARCHAR2(50),
    pat_street_address VARCHAR2(50),
    pat_city        VARCHAR2(50),
    pat_state       CHAR(2),
    pat_zip         CHAR(9),
    pat_date_of_birth    DATE,
```

```
    pat_telephone_number CHAR(10),
    date_last_updated DATE );
```

Students will insert a test row describing information about themselves.

3. `SELECT * FROM patient_archive;`

Information displayed will vary from student to student.

5.
```
REM Table ward_dept
CREATE TABLE ward_dept (
    ward_id             CHAR(5) CONSTRAINT pk_ward_dept PRIMARY KEY,
    ward_dept_name      VARCHAR2(50) CONSTRAINT nn_ward_dept_name NOT NULL,
    office_location     VARCHAR2(25) CONSTRAINT nn_ward_dept_location NOT NULL,
    telephone_number    CHAR(10),
    date_last_updated DATE );
```

7. `DESC ward_dept;`

Name	Null?	Type
WARD_ID	NOT NULL	CHAR(5)
WARD_DEPT_NAME	NOT NULL	VARCHAR2(50)
OFFICE_LOCATION	NOT NULL	VARCHAR2(25)
TELEPHONE_NUMBER		CHAR(10)
DATE_LAST_UPDATED		DATE

9.
```
REM Table staff2
CREATE TABLE staff2 (
    staff_id            CHAR(5)  CONSTRAINT pk_staff2 PRIMARY KEY,
    staff_ssn           CHAR(9)  CONSTRAINT nn_staff2_ssn NOT NULL,
    staff_last_name     VARCHAR2(50) CONSTRAINT nn_staff2_last_name NOT NULL,
    staff_first_name    VARCHAR2(50) nn_staff2_first_name NOT NULL,
    staff_middle_name   VARCHAR2(50),
    ward_dept_assigned  CHAR(5) CONSTRAINT fk_staff2_ward_dept
        REFERENCES ward_dept(ward_id),
    office_location     VARCHAR2(50),
    date_hired          DATE DEFAULT NULL,
    hospital_title      VARCHAR2(50) CONSTRAINT nn_staff2_title NOT NULL,
    work_phone          CHAR(10),
    phone_extension     VARCHAR2(4),
    license_number      VARCHAR2(20),
    salary              NUMBER,
    wage_rate           NUMBER(5,2),
    date_last_updated   DATE );
```

11.
```
SELECT staff_id, staff_ssn, staff_last_name
FROM staff2;
```

The output should be 4 rows of information.

13.
```
UPDATE staff2
SET office_location = 'SW4000'
WHERE staff_last_name = 'Webber';
```

```
STAFF_LAST_NAME
-------------
OFFICE_LOCATION
-------------
Webber
SW4000
```

15. `ALTER TABLE medicine ADD (med_unit_cost NUMBER(7,2));`

CHAPTER 3

1. COLUMN room_id FORMAT A7;
   SELECT *
   FROM room;

   ```
   ROOM_ID     ROOM_DESCRIPTION          DATE_LAST
   ------      --------------------      --------
   SW1001      General MedSurg, Single   03-JAN-01
   SW1002      General MedSurg, Single   03-JAN-01
   SW1003      General MedSurg, Single   03-JAN-01
   61 rows selected.
   ```

3. COLUMN service_id FORMAT A10;
   COLUMN service_description FORMAT A30;
   SELECT service_id, service_description, service_charge
   FROM service;

   ```
   SERVICE_ID    SERVICE_DESCRIPTION     SERVICE_CHARGE
   ---------     -----------------       -------------
   36415         Blood Draw              35.55
   82947         Blood Glucose           20.4
   85018         Hemoglobin              25
   105 rows selected.
   ```

5. COLUMN staff_last_name FORMAT A15;
   COLUMN staff_first_name FORMAT A15;
   SELECT staff_last_name, staff_first_name, date_hired, license_number
   FROM staff
   ORDER BY staff_last_name;

   ```
   STAFF_LAST_NAME      STAFF_FIRST_NAM     DATE_HIRE    LICENSE_NUMBER
   -------------        -------------       --------     ------------
   Adams                Adam                29-JAN-85
   Barlow               William             16-MAY-01    MO9873346
   Becker               Robert              14-DEC-82    IL2398457
   24 rows selected.
   ```

7. SELECT staff_first_name, staff_middle_name, staff_last_name,
          date_hired, license_number
   FROM staff
   ORDER BY staff_last_name, staff_first_name;

   ```
   STAFF_FIRST_    S     STAFF_LAST_N     DATE_HIRE    LICENSE_NUMBER
   -----------     -     -----------      --------     ------------
   Adam            A     Adams            29-JAN-85
   William         A     Barlow           16-MAY-01    MO9873346
   Robert          B     Becker           14-DEC-82    IL2398457
   24 rows selected.
   ```

9. SELECT medicine_code, doseage_prescribed
   FROM prescription
   ORDER by medicine_code;

   ```
   MEDICIN     DOSEAGE_PRESCRIBED
   -------     --------------------
   9999001     200 Mg. 4 times/day.
   9999001     50 Mg. IV every 4 hours.
   9999001     50 Mg. IV every 4 hours.
   25 rows selected.
   ```

11.
```
COLUMN staff_id FORMAT A8;
COLUMN specialty_code FORMAT A14;
COLUMN date_awarded FORMAT A12;
SELECT staff_id, specialty_code, date_awarded
FROM staff_medspec
WHERE specialty_code = 'RN1'
ORDER BY staff_id;
STAFF_ID     SPECIALTY_CODE      DATE_AWARDED
-------      --------------      -----------
66444        RN1                 08-MAR-88
67555        RN1                 04-FEB-92
```

CHAPTER 4

1.
```
COLUMN "Last Name" FORMAT A15;
COLUMN "First Name" FORMAT A15;
COLUMN "City" FORMAT A15;
COLUMN "State" FORMAT A5;
COLUMN "Zip Code" FORMAT A10;
SELECT pat_last_name "Last Name", pat_first_name "First Name",
    pat_city "City", pat_state "State", pat_zip "Zip Code"
FROM patient
WHERE pat_zip = '62025';

Last Name      First Name     City            State    Zip Code
--------       ---------      -----------     -----    -------
Earnhardt      Earnest        Edwardsville    IL       62025
Franken        Frank          Edwardsville    IL       62025
Monday         Mandy          Edwardsville    IL       62025
25 rows selected.
```

3.
```
COLUMN "Last Name" FORMAT A15;
COLUMN "First Name" FORMAT A15;
COLUMN Title FORMAT A5;
COLUMN "Ward-Dept" FORMAT A10;
SELECT staff_last_name "Last Name", staff_first_name "First Name",
    hospital_title "Title", ward_dept_assigned "Ward-Dept"
FROM staff
WHERE (ward_dept_assigned = 'ONCOL' OR ward_dept_assigned = 'MEDS1')
    AND hospital_title = 'M.D.';

Last Name      First Name     Title     Ward-Dept
--------       ---------      -----     --------
Eakin          Maxwell        M.D.      MEDS1
Bock           Douglas        M.D.      MEDS1
Klepper        Robert         M.D.      ONCOL
```

5.
```
COLUMN "Last Name" FORMAT A15;
COLUMN "First Name" FORMAT A15;
COLUMN Title FORMAT A5;
COLUMN "Ward-Dept" FORMAT A10;
SELECT staff_last_name "Last Name", staff_first_name "First Name",
    hospital_title "Title", ward_dept_assigned "Ward-Dept"
FROM staff
WHERE ward_dept_assigned NOT IN ('ONCOL', 'MEDS1', 'CARD1', 'RADI1')
    AND hospital_title = 'M.D.'
ORDER BY ward_dept_assigned;
```

```
Last Name       First Name      Title       Ward-Dept
--------        ---------       -----       --------
Sumner          Elizabeth       M.D.        EMER1
Schultheis      Robert          M.D.        OUTP1
Becker          Robert          M.D.        SURG1
7 rows selected.
```

7. COLUMN "Med Code" FORMAT A8;
    COLUMN "Medicine Name" FORMAT A25;
    COLUMN "Quantity" FORMAT 99999999;
    SELECT medicine_code "Med Code", med_name_common "Medicine Name",
    quantity_stock "Quantity"
    FROM medicine
    WHERE quantity_stock NOT BETWEEN 500 AND 25000;

```
Med Code      Medicine Name       Quantity
-------       -----------         -------
9999003       Valium                36000
9999005       PenVK                 34365
9999015       Nystatin           45000000
5 rows selected.
```

9. COLUMN "Last Name" FORMAT A15;
    COLUMN "First Name" FORMAT A15;
    COLUMN Title FORMAT A5;
    SELECT staff_last_name "Last Name", staff_first_name "First Name",
        hospital_title "Title"
    FROM staff
    WHERE staff_last_name LIKE '%o%' AND hospital_title = 'M.D.'
    ORDER BY staff_last_name, staff_first_name;

```
Last Name     First Name      Title
--------      ---------       -----
Barlow        William         M.D.
Bock          Douglas         M.D.
Bordoloi      Bijoy           M.D.
5 rows selected.
```

11. COLUMN "Last Name" FORMAT A15;
    COLUMN "Bed" FORMAT 9999;
    SELECT pat_last_name "Last Name", bed_number "Bed"
    FROM patient
    WHERE bed_number IS NULL;

```
Last Name     Bed
--------      ---
Howard
Mullins
North
Overstreet
```

CHAPTER 5

1. SELECT COUNT(*) "Number of Staff Members"
    FROM staff;

```
Number of Staff Members
-----------------------
                     24
```

3.  ```
    SELECT MAX(date_hired) "Newest Staff Member"
    FROM staff;

    Newest St
    ---------
    15-OCT-01
    ```

5.  ```
    COLUMN "Average Wage" FORMAT $999,999;
    COLUMN "Total Wage" FORMAT $999,999;
    SELECT AVG(wage_rate) "Average Wage", SUM(wage_rate) "Total Wage"
    FROM staff;

    Average Wage    Total Wage
    -----------     ---------
             $8           $16
    ```

7.  ```
    COLUMN "Bed Type" FORMAT A18;
    SELECT bed_type_id "Bed Type", COUNT(bed_type_id) "Number Counted"
    FROM bed
    GROUP BY bed_type_id;

    Bed Type    Number Counted
    -------     ------------
    E2                       4
    E3                       2
    ER                       4
    10 rows selected.
    ```

9.  ```
    COLUMN "Service Category" FORMAT A16;
    SELECT service_cat_id "Service Category",
        COUNT(service_cat_id) "Number of Services"
    FROM service
    WHERE service_cat_id NOT IN ('LAB','INJ')
    GROUP BY service_cat_id;

    Service Category    Number of Services
    ---------------     ----------------
    CAR                                  1
    OLA                                 18
    PRO                                  9
    5 rows selected.
    ```

11. ```
    COLUMN "Staff Member ID" FORMAT A15;
    SELECT staff_id "Staff Member ID",
        COUNT(service_id) "Treatment Count"
    FROM treatment
    GROUP BY staff_id;

    Staff Member ID    Treatment Count
    -------------      -------------
    01885                           14
    10044                            8
    23100                            8
    16 rows selected.
    ```

13. ```
    COLUMN "Staff Member ID" FORMAT A15;
    SELECT staff_id "Staff Member ID",
        COUNT(service_id) "Treatment Count"
    FROM treatment
    WHERE staff_id NOT IN ('66432', '66444')
    ```

```
GROUP BY staff_id
HAVING COUNT(service_id) >= 10;

Staff Member ID      Treatment Count
-------------        -------------
01885                           14
23232                           13
66427                           12
```
5 rows selected.

15.
```
COLUMN "Average Charge" FORMAT $9,999.99;
COLUMN "Service" FORMAT A7;
SELECT service_id "Service",
    AVG(actual_charge) "Average Charge"
FROM treatment
GROUP BY service_id
HAVING AVG(actual_charge) >= 1000
ORDER BY AVG(actual_charge);

Service    Average Charge
------     ------------
12010          $1,480.00
12001          $3,325.00
12002          $6,500.00
```
6 rows selected.

CHAPTER 6

1.
```
COLUMN p.pat_id FORMAT A6;
COLUMN pat_last_name FORMAT A15;
COLUMN note_comment FORMAT A45;
SELECT p.pat_id, pat_last_name, note_comment
FROM patient p, patient_note pn
WHERE p.pat_id = pn.pat_id;

PAT_ID    PAT_LAST_NAME    NOTE_COMMENT
------    -------------    -------------------------------------
100001    Able             Patient admitted from surgery at 1715 hours
100001    Able             Abdominal dressing dry and intact following
                           liver surgery. Biliary drainage tube with
                           moderate amount (50cc) of dark greenish
                           drainage noted this shift.
100002    Benton           Patient admitted from surgery at 0810 hours
```
174 rows selected.

3.
```
COLUMN "Staff Member" FORMAT A25;
COLUMN "Ward or Dept" FORMAT A36;
SELECT staff_last_name || ', ' || staff_first_name "Staff Member",
    ward_dept_name "Ward or Dept"
FROM ward_dept wd, staff s
WHERE wd.ward_id = s.ward_dept_assigned
ORDER BY ward_dept_name, staff_last_name, staff_first_name;

Staff Member         Ward or Dept
-----------------    --------------------------------
Adams, Adam          Administrative Processing Department
Boudreaux, Beverly   Administrative Processing Department
Clinton, William     Administrative Processing Department
```
24 rows selected.

5. COLUMN "Category" FORMAT A8;
   COLUMN "Category Description" FORMAT A25;
   COLUMN "Service" FORMAT A7;
   COLUMN "Service Description" FORMAT A25;
   SELECT sc.service_cat_id "Category", service_cat_desc "Category Description",
       service_id "Service", service_description "Service Description"
   FROM service_cat sc, service s
   WHERE sc.service_cat_id = s.service_cat_id AND
       sc.service_cat_id IN ('CAR','LAB')
   ORDER BY sc.service_cat_id, service_id;

```
Category     Category Description     Service   Service Description
-------      ------------------       ------    ------------------
CAR          Cardiology               93000     EKG/Interp
LAB          Laboratory-General       80048     Basic Metabolic
LAB          Laboratory-General       80050     General Panel
18 rows selected.
```

7. COLUMN "Patient" FORMAT A25;
   COLUMN "Bed" FORMAT 9999;
   COLUMN "Bed Desc" FORMAT A27;
   SELECT pat_last_name || ', ' || pat_first_name "Patient",
       p.bed_number "Bed", bed_description "Bed Desc"
   FROM patient p, bed b, bed_type bt
   WHERE p.bed_number = b.bed_number AND
     b.bed_type_id = bt.bed_type_id
   ORDER BY p.bed_number;

```
Patient           Bed    Bed Desc
------------       ---    ----------------
Benton, Barbara     1     Regular Ward-Fixed
Chen, Rue           4     Regular Ward-Fixed
Davis, David        6     Regular Ward-Fixed
56 rows selected.
```

9. COLUMN "Patient" FORMAT A25;
   COLUMN "Bed" FORMAT 9999;
   SELECT pat_last_name || ', ' || pat_first_name "Patient",
       p.bed_number "Bed"
   FROM patient p, bed b
   WHERE p.bed_number = b.bed_number(+) AND
       p.bed_number IS NULL
   ORDER BY pat_last_name, pat_first_name;

```
Patient            Bed
-----------------  ---
Howard, Ronald
Mullins, Mildred
North, Norbert
Overstreet, Orville
```

11. COLUMN "Patient" FORMAT A20;
    COLUMN "Prescription" FORMAT A20;
    COLUMN "Staff Member" FORMAT A20;
    SELECT pat_last_name || ', ' || pat_first_name "Patient",
        m.med_name_common "Prescription",
        staff_last_name || ', ' || staff_first_name "Staff Member"
    FROM patient p, medicine m, staff st, prescription pr

```
WHERE p.pat_id = pr.pat_id AND
    m.medicine_code = pr.medicine_code AND
    st.staff_id = pr.staff_id
ORDER BY pat_last_name, pat_first_name;
```

```
Patient                 Prescription        Staff Member
-------------           -----------         -----------------
Algebra, Albert         Rocephin            Sumner, Elizabeth
Ashcroft, Arthur        Lanoxin             Brockwell, Mary Elle
Boudreaux, Billy        Lanoxin             Bock, Douglas
25 rows selected.
```

13.
```
COLUMN "Patient" FORMAT A20;
COLUMN "Prescription" FORMAT A20;
COLUMN "Staff Member" FORMAT A20;
SELECT pat_last_name || ', ' || pat_first_name "Patient",
    m.med_name_common "Prescription",
    staff_last_name || ', ' || staff_first_name "Staff Member"
FROM patient p, medicine m, staff st, prescription pr
WHERE p.pat_id = pr.pat_id AND
    m.medicine_code = pr.medicine_code AND
    st.staff_id = pr.staff_id AND
    st.staff_id = '66425'
ORDER BY pat_last_name, pat_first_name;
```

```
Patient                 Prescription        Staff Member
-------------           -----------         -----------------
Chang, Charlie          Lanoxin             Quattromani, Toni
Chang, Charlie          Alupent             Quattromani, Toni
Pauley, Paul            Alupent             Quattromani, Toni
5 rows selected.
```

CHAPTER 7

1.
```
COLUMN "Last Name" FORMAT A15;
COLUMN "First Name" FORMAT A15;
SELECT pat_last_name "Last Name", pat_first_name "First Name"
FROM patient
WHERE pat_id IN
    (SELECT pat_id
     FROM treatment
     WHERE service_id IN ('82947', '90788'));
```

```
Last Name       First Name
--------        ---------
Davis           David
Quentin         Quincy
Mousseau        Mickey
13 rows selected.
```

3.
```
SELECT pat_last_name "Last Name", pat_first_name "First Name"
FROM patient
WHERE pat_id IN
    (SELECT pat_id
     FROM treatment
     WHERE service_id NOT IN ('82947', '90788'))
ORDER BY pat_last_name, pat_first_name;
```

```
Last Name       First Name
--------        ---------
Able            Andrew
Algebra         Albert
Ashcroft        Arthur
54 rows selected.
```

5.  ```
    SELECT pat_last_name "Last Name", pat_first_name "First Name"
    FROM patient
    WHERE pat_id IN
        (SELECT pat_id
         FROM prescription
         WHERE medicine_code IN ('9999003', '9999008'))
    ORDER BY pat_last_name, pat_first_name;
    ```

    ```
    Last Name       First Name
    --------        ---------
    Ridgeway        Ricardo
    Youngman        Yvonne
    Zebulon         Zeb
    ```

7.  ```
    COLUMN hospital_title FORMAT A20;
    COLUMN staff_last_name FORMAT A15;
    COLUMN staff_first_name FORMAT A15;
    SELECT staff_last_name, staff_first_name, hospital_title, date_hired
    FROM staff
    WHERE date_hired <
        (SELECT Min(date_hired)
         FROM staff
         WHERE hospital_title = 'R.N.');
    ```

    ```
    STAFF_LAST_NAME   STAFF_FIRST_NAM   HOSPITAL_TITLE   DATE_HIRE
    -------------     -------------     -------------    --------
    Webber            Eugene            M.D.             16-FEB-95
    Bock              Douglas           M.D.             11-AUG-87
    Quattromani       Toni              M.D.             10-NOV-89
    9 rows selected.
    ```

9.  ```
    COLUMN "Service ID" FORMAT A10;
    COLUMN "Description" FORMAT A40;
    SELECT s.service_id "Service ID", s.service_description "Description"
    FROM service s
    WHERE service_id IN
        (SELECT s.service_id
         from service s, treatment t
         WHERE s.service_id = t.service_id AND service_charge - actual_charge >
            (SELECT AVG(service_charge - actual_charge)
             FROM service s, treatment t
             WHERE s.service_id = t.service_id AND service_cat_id = 'SUR'));
    ```

    ```
    Service ID   Description
    ---------    ------------------------
    12001        Thoracic-General Exploratory
    12007        Cranial
    12010        Spinal-Exploratory
    ```

11. ```
    COLUMN "Last Name" FORMAT A15;
    COLUMN "First Name" FORMAT A15;
    ```

```
COLUMN "Ward-Dept" FORMAT A20;
COLUMN salary FORMAT $9,999,999;
SELECT staff_last_name "Last Name",
    staff_first_name "First Name", ward_dept_assigned "Ward-Dept", salary
FROM staff s1
WHERE salary =
    (SELECT MIN(salary)
     FROM staff s2
     WHERE s1.ward_dept_assigned = s2.ward_dept_assigned AND
     hospital_title = 'M.D.')
ORDER BY ward_dept_assigned;
```

```
Last Name       First Name      Ward-Dept       SALARY
----------      ----------      ---------       -------
Quattromani     Toni            CARD1           $225,325
Sumner          Elizabeth       EMER1           $165,000
Eakin           Maxwell         MEDS1           $150,000
7 rows selected.
```

13.
```
COLUMN "Last Name" FORMAT A15;
COLUMN "First Name" FORMAT A15;
COLUMN "Ward-Dept" FORMAT A9;
COLUMN salary FORMAT $9,999,999;
SELECT staff_last_name "Last Name", staff_first_name "First Name",
    ward_dept_assigned "Ward-Dept", salary "Salary",
    date_hired "Date Hired"
FROM staff s1
WHERE date_hired =
    (SELECT MAX(date_hired)
     FROM staff s2
     WHERE s1.ward_dept_assigned = s2.ward_dept_assigned AND
         salary IS NOT NULL)
ORDER BY ward_dept_assigned;
```

```
Last Name       First Name      Ward-Dept       Salary      Date Hire
----------      ----------      ---------       -------     --------
Boudreaux       Betty           ADMI2           $32,895     05-NOV-00
Boudreaux       Beverly         ADMIN           $37,520     15-OCT-01
Quattromani     Toni            CARD1           $225,325    10-NOV-89
12 rows selected.
```

CHAPTER 8

1.
```
CREATE OR REPLACE VIEW medicine_view (med_code, common_name,
    scientific_name, quantity, units) AS
SELECT medicine_code, med_name_common, med_name_sci, quantity_stock,
    unit_measure
FROM medicine;

COLUMN common_name FORMAT A18;
COLUMN scientific_name FORMAT A16;
COLUMN units FORMAT A20;
SELECT *
FROM medicine_view
WHERE quantity <= 1000;
```

MED_COD	COMMON_NAME	SCIENTIFIC_NAME	QUANTITY	UNITS
9999004	Dalmane	Flurazepam	855	Milligram
9999007	Atarax	Hydroxyzine	855	M.Gram/C.Centimeter
9999018	Bactroban Ung. Ointment	Mupirocin	367	Tube

3.
```
CREATE OR REPLACE VIEW patient_view AS
SELECT *
FROM patient WITH READ ONLY CONSTRAINT vw_patient_view_read_only;

DESC patient_view
```

Name	Null?	Type
PAT_ID	NOT NULL	CHAR(6)
PAT_SSN	NOT NULL	CHAR(9)
PAT_LAST_NAME	NOT NULL	VARCHAR2(50)
PAT_FIRST_NAME	NOT NULL	VARCHAR2(50)
PAT_MIDDLE_NAME		VARCHAR2(50)
PAT_STREET_ADDRESS		VARCHAR2(50)
PAT_CITY		VARCHAR2(50)
PAT_STATE		CHAR(2)
PAT_ZIP		VARCHAR2(9)
PAT_DATE_OF_BIRTH		DATE
PAT_TELEPHONE_NUMBER		CHAR(10)
BED_NUMBER		NUMBER(4)
DATE_LAST_UPDATED		DATE

5.
```
CREATE OR REPLACE VIEW prescription_view (prescription, pre_date,
    dosage, directions, medicine, patient, staff_id, staff) AS
SELECT pr.pre_number, pr.pre_date, pr.dosage_prescribed,
    pr.dosage_directions, m.med_name_common,
    pa.pat_last_name || ', ' || pa.pat_first_name,
    pr.staff_id, s.staff_last_name
FROM prescription pr, patient pa, staff s, medicine m
WHERE pr.pat_id = pa.pat_id AND
    pr.staff_id = s.staff_id AND
    pr.medicine_code = m.medicine_code;

SQL> SELECT *
  2  FROM prescription_view
  3  WHERE prescription = '755444020';
More . . .
```

PRESCRIPT	PRE_DATE	DOSAGE	DIRECTIONS	MEDICINE	PATIENT
755444020	12-JUL-02	2 G.	daily in IV.	Rocephin	Algebra, Albert

STAFF_ID	STAFF
10044	Sumner

7.
```
CREATE OR REPLACE VIEW staff_location_view (staff_member, staff_id,
    ward_dept_id, ward_department, telephone, exten) AS
SELECT s.staff_last_name || ', ' || s.staff_first_name,
    s.staff_id, w.ward_id, w.ward_dept_name, s.work_phone,
    s.phone_extension
FROM staff s, ward_dept w
WHERE w.ward_id = s.ward_dept_assigned;
```

```
COLUMN staff_member FORMAT A20;
SELECT *
FROM staff_location_view
WHERE ward_dept_id = 'MEDS1';
```

```
STAFF_MEMBER              STAFF     WARD_
------------              -----     -----
WARD_DEPARTMENT                               TELEPHONE     EXTE
---------------------                         ---------     ----
Eakin, Maxwell            23232     MEDS1
Medical Surgical Ward 1                       1005559268    0001

Bock, Douglas             01885     MEDS1
Medical Surgical Ward 1                       1005559268    0011
```

9.
```
DROP VIEW staff_location_view;
DROP VIEW treatment_view;
```

11.
```
CREATE SYNONYM wd FOR ward_dept;
```

13.
```
CREATE SEQUENCE patient_number_sequence
INCREMENT BY 1 START WITH 700000 CACHE 10;
```
Sequence created.

15.
```
INSERT INTO patient (pat_id, pat_ssn, pat_last_name, pat_first_name)
    VALUES (patient_number_sequence.nextval,'900000002','Zucker','Zumwalt');
INSERT INTO patient_note VALUES
    (patient_number_sequence.currval,SYSDATE,
    'Patient admitted from surgery at 0815 hours',SYSDATE);
```

```
SELECT p.pat_ssn, p.pat_last_name, p.pat_first_name,
    p.pat_id, pn.pat_id, note_date, note_comment
FROM patient p, patient_note pn
WHERE p.pat_id = pn.pat_id AND pat_ssn='900000002';
```

```
PAT_SSN     PAT_LAST_NAME   PAT_FIRST_NAME   PAT_ID   PAT_ID   NOTE_DATE
--------    -------------   --------------   ------   ------   --------
NOTE_COMMENT
------------------------------------------------------------------
900000002   Zucker          Zumwalt          700002   700002   12-JUL-02
Patient admitted from surgery at 0815 hours
```

CHAPTER 9

1.
```
REM Program: c9-1.sql
REM Programmer: dbock; 7-14-2003
REM Description: A patient report - solution to SQL Exercise C.9.1.

TTITLE 'Patient Information'
BTITLE SKIP 1 CENTER 'Not for external dissemination.'

SET LINESIZE 60
SET PAGESIZE 24
SET NEWPAGE 1

SET NUMWIDTH 4;
COLUMN "Pat ID" FORMAT A6;
COLUMN "Last Name" FORMAT A14;
COLUMN "First Name" FORMAT A14;
COLUMN "Date Birth" FORMAT A10;
```

```
COLUMN "Bed" FORMAT 9999;
SELECT pat_id "Pat ID", pat_last_name "Last Name",
    pat_first_name "First Name", pat_date_of_birth "Date Birth",
    bed_number "Bed"
FROM patient
ORDER BY pat_id;
```

3.
```
REM Program: c9-3.sql
REM Programmer: dbock; 7-14-2003
REM Description: A room and bed control break
REM   report - solution to SQL Exercise C.9.3.

TTITLE 'Room-Bed Information'
BTITLE SKIP 1 CENTER 'Not for external dissemination.'

SET LINESIZE 60
SET PAGESIZE 24
SET NEWPAGE 1

SET NUMWIDTH 4;
COLUMN "Room ID" FORMAT A10;
COLUMN "Bed '' FORMAT 999999;
COLUMN "Type" FORMAT A8;
COLUMN "Available" FORMAT A10;

CLEAR BREAKS
BREAK ON "Room ID" SKIP 1 ON REPORT
COMPUTE COUNT OF "Room ID" ON REPORT

SELECT room_id "Room ID", bed_number "Bed '', bed_type_id "Type",
    bed_availability "Available"
FROM bed
ORDER BY room_id, bed_number;
```

5.
```
REM Program: c9-5.sql
REM Programmer: dbock; 7-14-2002
REM Description: A master-detail patient and patient note report -
REM solution to SQL Exercise C.9.5.

SET LINESIZE 60
SET PAGESIZE 24
SET NEWPAGE 1

CREATE OR REPLACE VIEW patient_view (pat_id, name,
    note_date, comments) AS
SELECT p.pat_id, p.pat_last_name||', '||p.pat_first_name,
    pn.note_date, pn.note_comment
FROM patient p, patient_note pn
WHERE p.pat_id = pn.pat_id
ORDER BY p.pat_id;

COLUMN today NEW_VALUE date_var
SELECT TO_CHAR(SYSDATE, 'MM/DD/YY') today
FROM dual;

COLUMN name NEW_VALUE patient_name_var NOPRINT
COLUMN pat_id FORMAT A9
COLUMN name FORMAT A15
COLUMN comments FORMAT A37

TTITLE LEFT date_var RIGHT 'Page: ' FORMAT 999 sql.pno -
    CENTER 'Patient Name: ' patient_name_var SKIP 2
```

```
BTITLE SKIP 1 CENTER 'Not for external dissemination.'

CLEAR BREAKS
CLEAR COMPUTES
BREAK ON pat_id SKIP PAGE
COMPUTE COUNT LABEL 'No. Notes' OF "comments" ON pat_id

SELECT pat_id, name, note_date, comments
FROM patient_view;
```

7.
```
REM Program: b9-7.sql
REM Programmer: dbock; 7-14-2002
REM Description: A master-detail patient and patient note report -
REM solution to SQL Exercise C.9.7.

SET LINESIZE 60
SET PAGESIZE 24
SET NEWPAGE 1

COLUMN today NEW_VALUE date_var
SELECT TO_CHAR(SYSDATE, 'MM/DD/YY') today
FROM dual;

COLUMN name NEW_VALUE patient_name_var NOPRINT
COLUMN pat_id NEW_VALUE pat_id_var
COLUMN pat_id FORMAT A9
COLUMN name FORMAT A15
COLUMN comments FORMAT A37

ACCEPT pat_id_var PROMPT 'Enter a patient identifier: '
PAUSE Press the Enter key to continue.

TTITLE LEFT date_var RIGHT 'Page: ' FORMAT 999 sql.pno SKIP 1 -
       CENTER 'Patient Name: ' patient_name_var SKIP 2
BTITLE SKIP 1 CENTER 'Not for external dissemination.'

CLEAR BREAKS
CLEAR COMPUTES
BREAK ON pat_id SKIP PAGE
COMPUTE COUNT LABEL 'No. Notes' OF "comments" ON pat_id

SELECT p.pat_id, p.pat_last_name||', '||p.pat_first_name "name",
    pn.note_date, pn.note_comment "comments"
FROM patient p, patient_note pn
WHERE p.pat_id = pn.pat_id AND p.pat_id = '&pat_id_var'
ORDER BY p.pat_id;
```

CHAPTER 10

1.
```
COLUMN "Staff Name" FORMAT A30;
SELECT UPPER(staff_last_name) || ', ' || staff_first_name || ' '
    || staff_middle_name "Staff Name"
FROM staff
ORDER BY staff_last_name, staff_first_name, staff_middle_name;

Staff Name
------------------
ADAMS, Adam Allen
BARLOW, William Allen
BECKER, Robert B
24 rows selected.
```

3.
```
COLUMN "Staff Name" FORMAT A30;
SELECT UPPER(staff_last_name) || ', ' || staff_first_name || ' '
    || staff_middle_name "Staff Name"
FROM staff
WHERE INSTR(staff_last_name||staff_first_name||staff_middle_name,'dr') != 0
ORDER BY staff_last_name, staff_first_name, staff_middle_name;


Staff Name
----------------
BOUDREAUX, Betty
BOUDREAUX, Beverly
```

5.
```
COLUMN "Staff Name" FORMAT A30;
SELECT UPPER(staff_last_name) || ', ' || staff_first_name || ' '
    || staff_middle_name "Staff Name"
FROM staff
WHERE INSTR(UPPER(staff_last_name||staff_first_name||staff_middle_name),'OR')
!= 0 OR
    INSTR(UPPER(staff_last_name||staff_first_name||staff_middle_name),'RO') !=
0
ORDER BY staff_last_name, staff_first_name, staff_middle_name;


Staff Name
---------------
BECKER, Robert B
BECKER, Roberta G
BORDOLOI, Bijoy
8 rows selected.
```

7.
```
SELECT SUBSTR(staff_last_name,1,4) "Name",
    SUBSTR(staff_ssn,6,4) "SSN"
FROM staff
ORDER BY staff_last_name;


Name    SSN
----    ----
Adam    3287
Barl    9002
Beck    9991
24 rows selected.
```

9.
```
COLUMN "Service" FORMAT A7;
COLUMN "Service Charge" FORMAT $999,999;
COLUMN "Actual Charge" FORMAT $999,999;
COLUMN "Difference" FORMAT $999,999;
SELECT s.service_id "Service", s.service_charge "Service Charge",
    t.actual_charge "Actual Charge",
    ABS(s.service_charge - t.actual_charge) "Difference"
FROM service s, treatment t
WHERE s.service_id = t.service_id AND
    ABS(s.service_charge - t.actual_charge) > 50;
```

Service	Service Charge	Actual Charge	Difference
12010	$3,500	$1,480	$2,020
12007	$10,000	$8,500	$1,500
99058	$155	$435	$280
12001	$6,200	$450	$5,750

11. COLUMN "Service" FORMAT A7;
     COLUMN "Rounded Charge" FORMAT $999,999.99;
     SELECT service_id "Service", ROUND(service_charge,-1) "Rounded Charge"
     FROM service
     ORDER BY service_id;

     ```
     Service    Rounded Charge
     ------     ------------
     10060           $260.00
     10061           $320.00
     10120           $230.00
     105 rows selected.
     ```

13. COLUMN "Hospital Title" Format A20;
     COLUMN "Staff Name" FORMAT A30;
     SELECT staff_last_name||', '||staff_first_name "Staff Name",
         hospital_title "Hospital Title",
         RTRIM(TO_CHAR(date_hired, 'MONTH')) || ' ' ||
         TO_CHAR(date_hired, 'DD, YYYY') "Date Hired"
     FROM staff
     ORDER BY date_hired;

     ```
     Staff Name             Hospital Title    Date Hired
     ---------------        -------------     ---------------
     Schultheis, Robert     M.D.              DECEMBER 14, 1979
     Becker, Robert         M.D.              DECEMBER 14, 1982
     Becker, Roberta        M.D.              DECEMBER 14, 1982
     24 rows selected.
     ```

15. COLUMN "Patient Name" Format A25;
     COLUMN "60th Birthday" FORMAT A15;
     SELECT pat_last_name||', '||pat_first_name "Patient Name",
         TO_CHAR(pat_date_of_birth, 'DD-MON-YYYY') "Date Hired",
         TO_CHAR(ADD_MONTHS(pat_date_of_birth, 720), 'DD-MON-YYYY')
         "60th Birthday"
     FROM patient
     ORDER BY pat_date_of_birth;

     ```
     Patient Name     Date Hired    60th Birthday
     -------------    ----------    -----------
     Grant, Gregory   05-DEC-1951   05-DEC-2011
     Monday, Mandy    21-MAY-1952   21-MAY-2012
     North, Norbert   15-JAN-1956   15-JAN-2016
     63 rows selected.
     ```

17. COLUMN "Room #" FORMAT A8;
     COLUMN "Bed" FORMAT 9999;
     COLUMN "Bed Description" FORMAT A35;
     COLUMN "Bed Availability" FORMAT A16;
     SELECT b.room_id "Room #", b.bed_number "Bed", bt.bed_description "Bed
     Description",
         DECODE(b.bed_availability,'Y','Occupied','Available') "Bed Availability"
     FROM bed b, bed_type bt
     WHERE bt.bed_type_id = b.bed_type_id
     ORDER BY b.room_id, b.bed_number;

```
Room #        Bed       Bed Description            Bed Availability
------        ---       ----------------------     ---------------
ER0001        50        Emergency Room-Rollaround   Occupied
ER0001        51        Emergency Room-Rollaround   Available
ER0001        52        Emergency Room-Fixed        Occupied
98 rows selected.
```

CHAPTER 11

1. `SELECT * from medical_specialty;`

3. `adoMedSpec.RecordSource = strSQL`
   `adoMedSpec.Refresh`

5.
```
EXEC SQL
    DECLARE ROOM_DATA TABLE
       (ROOM_ID                 CHAR(6),
        ROOM_DESCRIPTION         CHAR(25),
        DATE_LAST_UPDATED        CHAR(10) )
END-EXEC.
```

CHAPTER 12

1. `CREATE USER jim IDENTIFIED BY superuser;`
   `CREATE USER henrietta IDENTIFIED BY hogwarts;`
   `CREATE USER chen IDENTIFIED BY li;`

3.
```
CREATE USER mita IDENTIFIED BY bordoloi
    DEFAULT TABLESPACE users TEMPORARY TABLESPACE temp
    QUOTA 4M ON users QUOTA UNLIMITED ON temp PASSWORD EXPIRE;
GRANT create session TO mita;
```

5. `CONNECT mita/bordoloi;`
   `ALTER USER mita IDENTIFIED BY castle;`

7. `GRANT unlimited tablespace TO jim;`

9.
```
CONNECT jim/superuser;
 CREATE TABLE autos (
      Auto_Id                    CHAR(22),
      Auto_Description           VARCHAR(50),
      Auto_Price                 NUMBER(7,2) );
```

   None. Jim has the privilege to create an index on any table that he has created as the owner of the table.

11. `GRANT select on jim.autos TO PUBLIC;`

13. `REVOKE ALL on jim.autos FROM mita;`

15. `GRANT auto_sales_mgr TO mita, chen;`

17. `DROP ROLE auto_sales_mgr;`

INDEX

A

Absolute value (ABS) function as value of magnitude, 215–16
ACCEPT command and interactive report writing, 195–96
Accounts, basic/Oracle database administration and creating/altering/dropping user, 248, 251–53
Active X Data Objects (ADO) and embedding SQL in Visual Basic 6.0, 229–32
Active X Data Objects (ADO.NET) and embedding SQL in Visual Basic.NET, 234–35
Aggregate functions:
  GROUP BY clause
    expressions, use with, 97–98
    HAVING clause, 101–5
    limitations, 97
    nesting average (AVG) function in maximum (MAX) function, 98–99
    NULL value, 99–100
    ORDER BY clause, 101
    overview, 96
    WHERE clause, 100
  implementing
    ALL keyword, 91–92
    average (AVG) function, 92–93
    COUNT function, 95
    DISTINCT keyword, 91–92
    maximum (MAX) function, 94–95
    minimum (MIN) function, 94–95
    rules to understand/follow, 92
    SUM function, 93–94
  objectives, learning, 90–91
  report writing, basics of interactive, 198
  review exercises/questions, 106–8, 315–17
  subqueries, 141
  summary/conclusions, 105
ALL keyword:
  aggregate functions, 91–92
  dictionary view, data, 250
  subqueries, 142–43
ALTER TABLE command, 31
American National Standards Institute (ANSI), 5

B

BETWEEN operator and WHERE clause, 75–78
BREAK command and interactive report writing, 183–85, 187–88, 190, 193

C

CACHE clause and sequences, 168
Cartesian product of the tables, 111–12
Character (CHAR) function and interactive report writing, 195
  See also character (string) functions *under* Functions, selected subset of Oracle
Character data, 22–23
Character matching (LIKE and NOT LIKE operators), 78–81
CHECK option:
  integrity, data, 28–29
  views, 156
Ch9-5.sql program and interactive report writing, 195
Classes and embedding SQL in Visual Basic.NET, 234
CLEAR command and interactive report writing, 198
COBOL, embedding SQL in, 237–39
Codd, E. F., and the relational model, 2–3
Coding exercises, end-of-book SQL, 289–309, 326–44
  See also review exercises/questions *under individual subject headings*
COLUMN command:
  formatting output, 50–52
  report writing, basics of interactive, 195, 198–200
Columns and fundamental relational operations, 7
  See also individual subject headings

AND operator and WHERE clause, 67–68, 70–72
ANY keyword and subqueries, 143–45
Ascending (ASC) options and ORDER BY clause, 61
Assignment table, 270–71
Average (AVG) function, aggregate functions and, 92–93, 98–99

Commands:
  column commands to format output, 50–52
  errors, single table query basics and common, 53
  Visual Basic.NET, 235–37
  See also commands *under* SQL*Plus; Report writing, basics of interactive; SELECT statement; Tables; *individual subject headings*
Commas, errors in placing, 54
COMMIT command confirming operations to the database on the server, 38
Company database schema:
  overview, 12–13, 263–64
  table definitions
    assignment table, 270–71
    constraints, additional table, 272–73
    create tables and indexes, 273–77
    department table, 264–65
    dependent table, 271–72
    dept_locations table, 265–66
    employee table, 266–69
    projects table, 269–70
Comparison operators, 58–59
  See also under Subqueries
Composite index, 40–41
Composite primary keys and multiple foreign keys, 34–36
COMPUTE command and interactive report writing, 185–86, 188, 198
Concatenated index, 40–41
CONSTRAINT option and views, 156
  See also constraints, data integrity and table *under* Tables
Control break reports. *See under* Report writing, basics of interactive
Copying techniques, 14
Correlated subqueries. *See* correlated *under* Subqueries
COUNT keyword, aggregate functions and, 95

D

Database administration, basic and Oracle:
  accounts, creating/altering/dropping user, 248, 251–53

A NOTE TO PARENTS

STEM CHALLENGES FOR MINECRAFTERS IS JUST WHAT YOU AND YOUR CHILD HAVE BEEN WAITING FOR, an educational workbook that doesn't feel like an educational workbook. This colorfully illustrated, video game-themed learning tool is focused on four critical domains for young, twenty-first-century learners: **SCIENCE, TECHNOLOGY, ENGINEERING,** and **MATH**. These content areas can be taught in isolation, but teaching them together (using diamond swords, zombies, creepers, and redstone traps for added fun) allows for deeper understanding and authentic connections to the world where kids live (and play.)

Children won't need to be nagged to dive headfirst into this collection of over thirty STEM challenges. Each lesson invites gamers to use the same kinds of creativity, critical thinking, and problem-solving skills they enjoy using in their favorite video game. Stand back as they go beyond rote learning and enjoy having the freedom to take risks, form theories, and pose unique solutions to complex real-world problems.

Whether they're learning about algorithms, physics, animal adaptations, or architectural design, they're **FINDING NEW INTERESTS AND BUILDING CONFIDENCE IN THE CLASSROOM** and beyond. *GET READY FOR A BRAIN-BUILDING STEM ADVENTURE!*

THE PHYSICS OF FORCE

To smash a block, a Minecrafter must apply a *force* to the block. You apply a force to the pedals when you ride a bike. You apply a force to the ground when you walk. You apply a force to a ball when you throw or kick it.

DRAW AN ARROW SHOWING THE DIRECTION THAT STEVE WILL SWING THE PICKAXE AND APPLY FORCE TO THIS BLOCK.

UNOFFICIAL
STEM CHALLENGES FOR
MINECRAFTERS
GRADES 3–4

BY JEN FUNK WEBER

SKY PONY PRESS
NEW YORK

Visit our website at www.skyponypress.com.

Authors, books, and more at SkyPonyPressBlog.com.

10 9 8 7 6 5 4 3 2 1

Library of Congress Cataloging-in-Publication Data
is available on file.

Cover design by Brian Peterson

Interior design by Kevin Baier

Cover and interior art by Amanda Brack or used by permission
from Shutterstock.com.

Print ISBN: 978-1-5107-3758-7

Printed in China

Now draw your own diagram showing an example of forces at work in the game of Minecraft. Use arrows to show the direction of the forces.

You view Minecraft on a flat, two-dimensional screen, but the mobs, blocks, and world in Minecraft are three-dimensional. Understanding and visualizing this requires some imagination your part.

TWO-DIMENSIONAL, or **2D,** shapes have two dimensions. We usually call these length and width. 2D shapes are flat. This is a 2D chest.

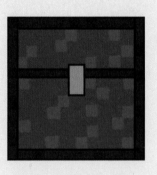

THREE-DIMENSIONAL, or **3D,** shapes have three dimensions. We usually call these length, width, and height. 3D shapes are solid. This is a 3D chest.

Shape Sifter

Find and circle the five 3D shapes listed below.

CIRCLE	SQUARE	CYLINDER	RECTANGLE
PENTAGON	SQUARE-BASED PYRAMID	OCTAGON	SPHERE
CUBE	TRIANGLE	TRIANGULAR PRISM	HEXAGON

MINERAL HARDNESS

In Minecraft, some minerals are harder than others. The same is true in the real world. A *hardness scale*, where 1 is the softest and 10 is the hardest, is based on ten minerals. Geologists and mineralogists use this scale to classify the 3,800+ known minerals.

Hard, Harder, Hardest

The first (softest) mineral on the hardness scale is talc. It's where we get talcum powder. The last (hardest) mineral on the hardness scale is diamond.

Complete the puzzle challenge on the next page to put the other 8 minerals of this scale in order of hardness. Here are the rules: **BEGIN AT THE DOT BELOW EACH MINERAL NAME AND WORK YOUR WAY DOWN TO FIGURE OUT WHERE IN THE SCALE IT BELONGS.** *Every time you hit a horizontal line (one that goes across), you must follow it across to the next vertical line.*

Can you write the name of each mineral in its proper place on the scale?

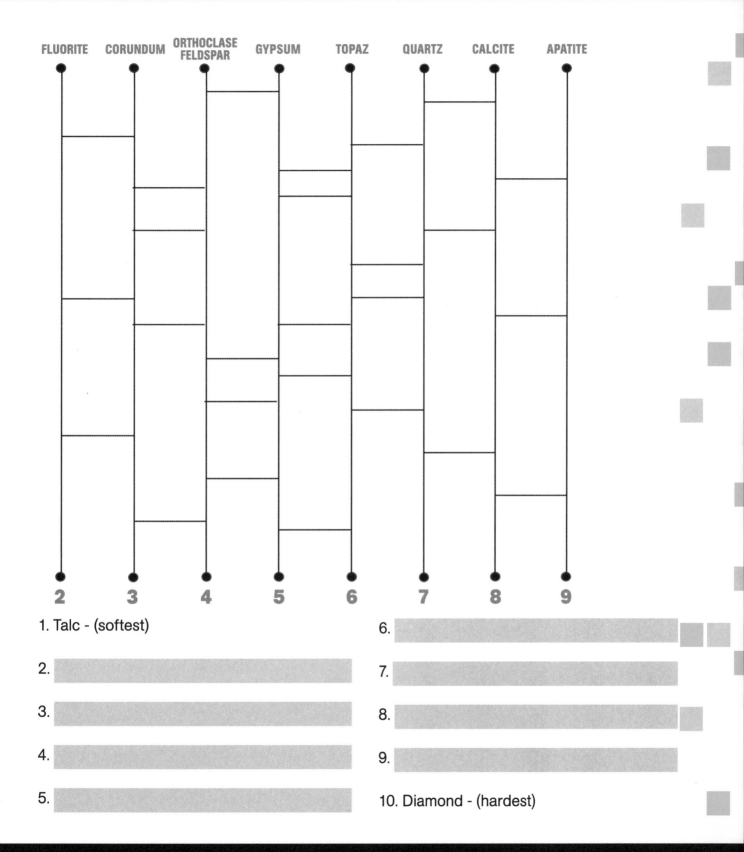

FLUORITE   CORUNDUM   ORTHOCLASE FELDSPAR   GYPSUM   TOPAZ   QUARTZ   CALCITE   APATITE

2   3   4   5   6   7   8   9

1. Talc - (softest)

2.

3.

4.

5.

6.

7.

8.

9.

10. Diamond - (hardest)

Video game designers use **STORYBOARDS** to plan how a game will flow. Each box contains a sketch of what will happen at each stage of the game. The boxes can be moved around, and new ones can be added to alter the game. Check out this storyboard for a trip to the Nether.

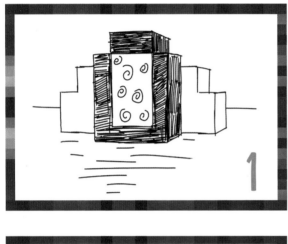

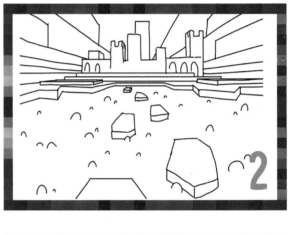

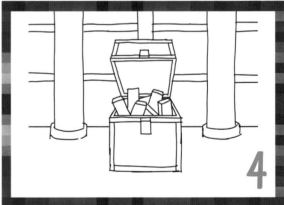

You Be the Designer!

Sketch a storyboard for an interactive Minecraft experience.

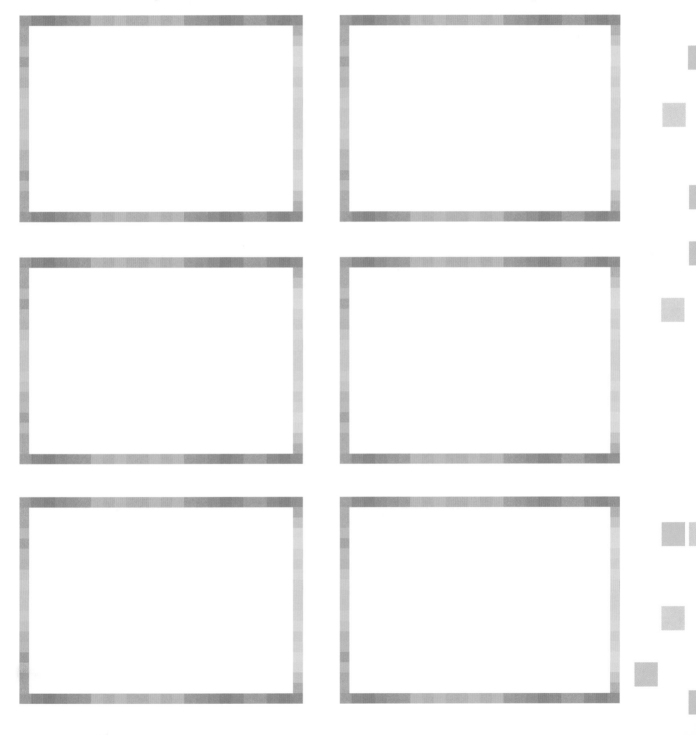

Lightning that strikes a house can do a lot of damage, ruining electronics or starting a fire. A metal pole, or lightning rod, placed on top of a building can conduct the energy from a strike to the ground, where it dissipates (spreads out and gradually disappears). **A LIGHTNING ROD IS A TOOL DESIGNED TO REDUCE DAMAGE FROM STORMS.**

Zombie Pigman Prevention

In Minecraft, a pig struck by lightning turns into a zombie pigman. In this puzzle, a lightning rod will protect every pig within 2 blocks horizontally, vertically, and diagonally. For example, every pig (shown as a red dot) is safe, protected by the lightning rod (shown as a yellow dot):

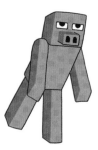

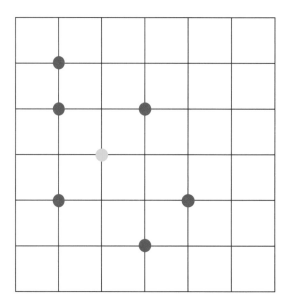

PLACE THREE YELLOW LIGHTNING RODS (YELLOW DOTS) ON THE GRID BELOW.

Place them in such a way that they keep all the pigs safe during the next lightning storm. Remember that for a pig to be protected, it must be within 2 blocks of the rod.

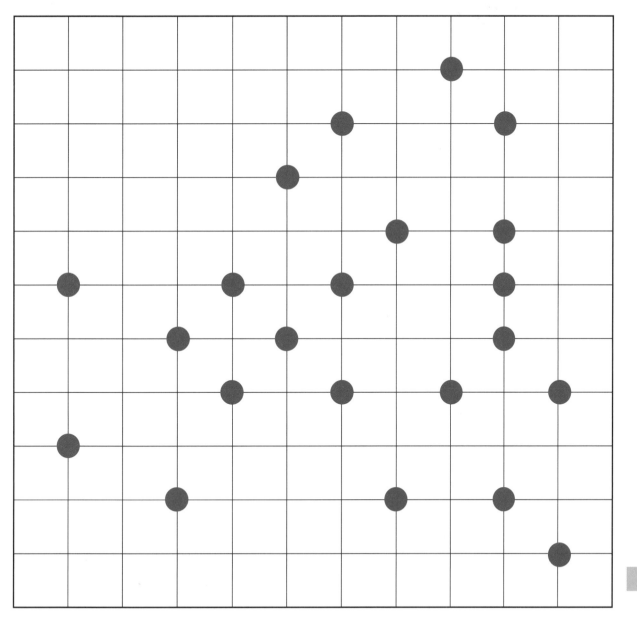

PREDICTING PATTERNS

Minecraft mobs are programmed to move and behave in certain ways. By observing how different mobs move, you discover patterns that help you predict how the mobs will move in the future.

Predicting a Mob's Moves

Meet Bat, whose movements in the game are programmed to follow these rules:

1) Bat will move as many as three squares at a time horizontally or vertically (not diagonally) in the direction he's facing.

2) If Bat runs into a **DOOR**, he's dead. Game over.

3) If Bat comes to a **WINDOW** (W), he opens it and keeps going in that direction until he meets another object.

4) If Bat meets with a **POTION** (P), he must turn right and can go another 3 squares.

5) If Bat runs into a **SPIDER** (S), he eats it and refuels. He can go another 3 squares in the same direction.

6) If Bat comes to a **CAVE**, he goes to sleep for the rest of the game. Zzzzz.

S	Bat ➡		P
P	S	Cave	S
	Door		
P	S	W	P

USING WHAT YOU KNOW OF BAT'S MOVEMENTS, DRAW A LINE ON THE GRID ABOVE TO TRACE HIS PATH IN THE GAME. How does Bat's journey end?

Try this one! How does Bat's journey end?

	Door		P		S		P
S			W		Door		
		S				S	
W			P		← Bat		W
	W				S		S
Door			Cave		P		
	P			S			P
S			S			Door	

Observing Mob Patterns

Consider the movements of an *Enderman* in the game. How does it act when you stare at it? How far can it teleport? What does it do when it encounters water? **CHOOSE A MOB AND DESCRIBE ITS MOVEMENTS HERE AS YOU PLAY.**

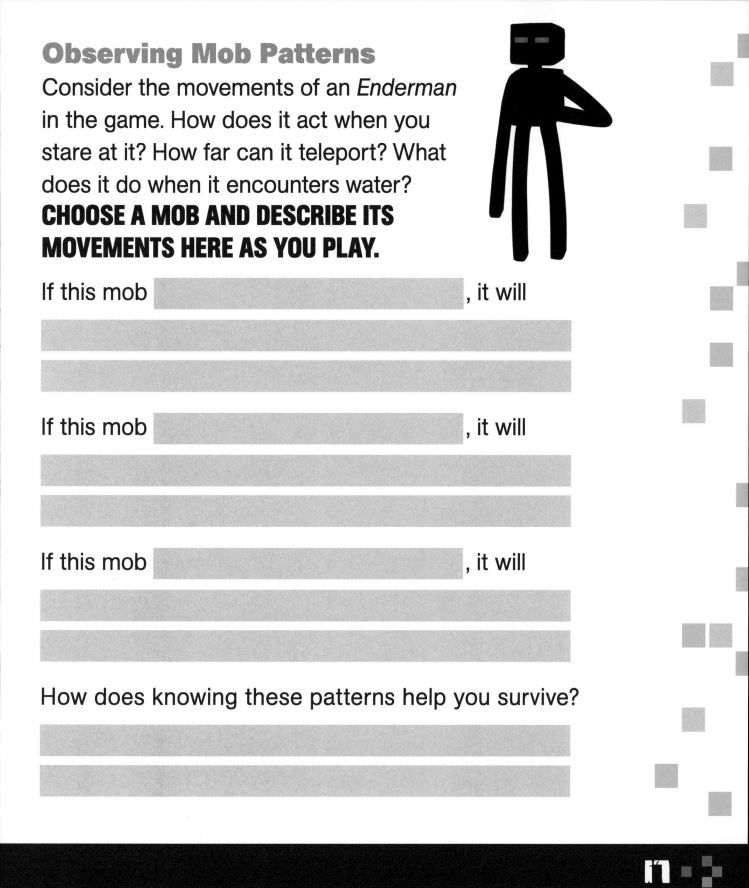

If this mob _____, it will

_____

_____

If this mob _____, it will

_____

_____

If this mob _____, it will

_____

_____

How does knowing these patterns help you survive?

_____

_____

In the real world, we measure time by minutes, hours, days, years, etc. A day/night cycle lasts 24 hours.

In Minecraft, time is measured in ticks. An in-game day/night cycle lasts 24,000 ticks, which equals 20 real-world minutes.

Screen Time Dilemma
SOLVE THIS WORD PROBLEM ABOUT TIME.

If Keaton gets his homework and chores done before bedtime at 9:00, he can use his free time to play Minecraft.

He gets home from school at 3:30 and walks his dog for a half hour. He leaves at 4:00 for fencing practice and gets home 2 hours later. Dinner is at 6:00.

Keaton figures he needs an hour to do homework. Eating dinner takes half an hour, and it's his night to do dishes, so that's another half hour. He's got his shower down to twenty minutes before bed.

Will Keaton have time to play Minecraft?
If so, how many in-game day/night cycles
will he get to play?

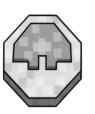

Write your own Minecrafting word
problem below. Challenge a friend or
family member to solve it!

ARCHITECTURE: DRAWING TO SCALE

If a picture is drawn *to scale* or a model is built *to scale*, it means the drawing or model has the **SAME PROPORTIONS AS THE REAL-WORLD OBJECT, BUT IT'S SMALLER OR LARGER.** In math, art, construction, and elsewhere, the term *scale* represents the relationship between a measurement on a drawing or model and the corresponding measurement on a real-world object.

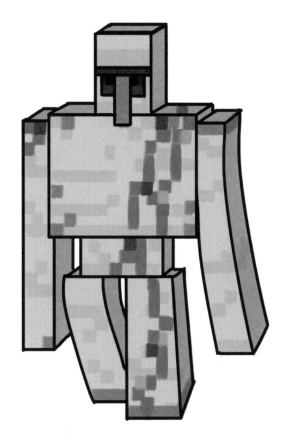

For example, 1 inch on a construction blueprint might represent 10 feet on a real-world house. One centimeter on a map might represent 18 real-world kilometers.

Supersize That Golem

Use the grid to copy the picture. Examine the lines in each small square in the smaller grid. Transfer those lines to the corresponding square in the large grid. Changing the size of the grid is one way to one way to increase scale and enlarge a drawing.

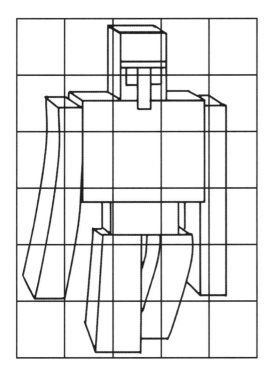

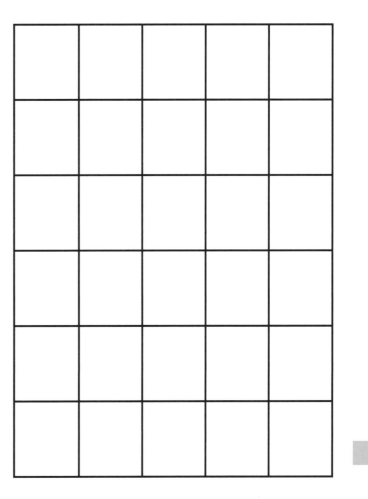

An **ALGORITHM** is a set of steps to accomplish a task. If you give a friend directions to get from her house to yours, you create an algorithm. In computer science, an algorithm is **A SEQUENCE OF STEPS THE COMPUTER FOLLOWS TO SOLVE A PROBLEM OR BUILD A WORLD OR DO ANY OTHER TASK.** Learning to create algorithms will help you write computer programs.

WRITE AN ALGORITHM TO TELL A FRIEND HOW TO SOLVE A PROBLEM OR MAKE SOMETHING IN MINECRAFT.

How to

1.

2.

3.

A Plant cocoa beans on jungle logs.

B Eat cookies.

C Combine wheat and cocoa beans on craft bench to make cookies.

D Enter the jungle.

E Find and collect cocoa beans.

F Add bonemeal to cocoa beans.

Order Up!

These scenes showing Minecraft activities are an algorithm for making cookies in Minecraft, but they are all mixed up. Can you put them in logical order from what happens first to what happens last?

Write the correct order of these scenes here:

___ ___ ___ ___ ___ ___

RUBE GOLDBERG MACHINES

Reuben Lucius "Rube" Goldberg (1883–1970) was an American cartoonist with a degree in engineering. He drew, invented, and built **WILDLY COMPLICATED MACHINES THAT DID SIMPLE TASKS.** His contraptions used common household objects connected in silly but logical ways.

Now, his work inspires artists, engineers, inventors, and many others.

Chain Reactions

Setting up a string of chain reactions is a way to build a Rube Goldberg Machine in Minecraft. Let's say the goal is to get a pig to drop a cooked pork chop. The process starts when you shoot an arrow at a wooden button. The process ends with a lava bucket setting a pig on fire and arrows firing from a dispenser, destroying the pig.

DESIGN YOUR OWN RUBE GOLDBERG MACHINE OF CAUSE AND EFFECT IN THE SPACE BELOW. Take it online and build, test, and improve your machine.

RUBE GOLDBERG MACHINES

What's the Point?

Solve this two-part puzzle. First, name the icons and figure out where each word goes in the crossword. The first word has been added for you. Second, transfer the numbered letters from the crossword to the numbered spaces at the bottom to reveal the purpose of a Rube Goldberg machine.

WATCH OUT SKELETON!

CH OUT
LETON!

E V O K E R

| 6 | 9 | 2 | 12 | 6 | 7 | 6 | | 1 | 13 | 13 | 5 | 11 | 3 | | 13 | 5 | 11 |

| 6 | 12 | 8 | 12 | 6 | 9 | 10 | | 11 | 1 | 4 | 7 | 10 | 3 | 4 |

SIMPLE AND COMPLEX MACHINES

In science, **"WORK"** means using energy to apply a force to an object and move it some distance. A **SIMPLE MACHINE** is a device that makes work easier by changing the direction of or increasing the force. A **"SIMPLE MACHINE"** helps a person do the same amount of work with less effort.

Laugh Machine

The letters in the word **MACHINE** have been mixed in with the names of the six simple machines. Cross out the letters M-A-C-H-I-N-E in each row of letters, then write the remaining letters on the spaces. Finally, write the letters from the numbered boxes on the spaces with the same numbers to spell the answer to the joke.

What simple machine can cut the Minecraft ocean biome in half?

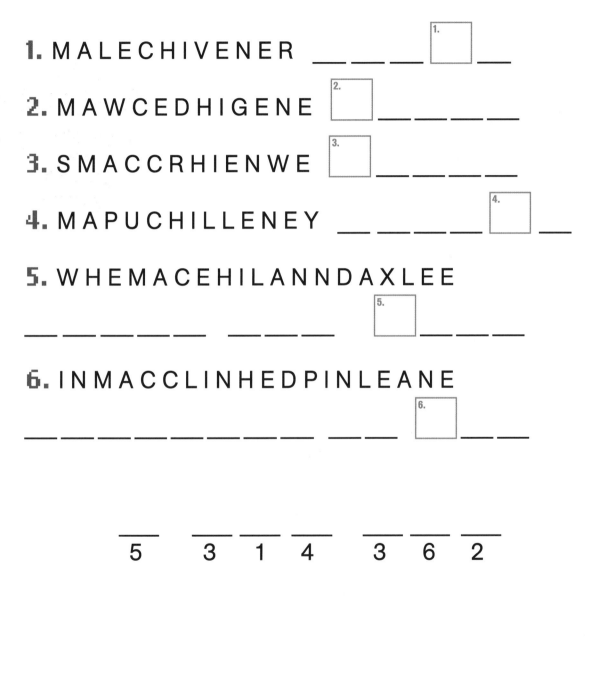

1. M A L E C H I V E N E R ___ ___ ___ [1.] ___

2. M A W C E D H I G E N E [2.] ___ ___ ___ ___ ___

3. S M A C C R H I E N W E [3.] ___ ___ ___ ___ ___

4. M A P U C H I L L E N E Y ___ ___ ___ ___ [4.] ___

5. W H E M A C E H I L A N N D A X L E E

___ ___ ___ ___ ___ ___   ___ ___ ___ [5.] ___ ___ ___ ___

6. I N M A C C L I N H E D P I N L E A N E

___ ___ ___ ___ ___ ___ ___ ___ ___   ___ ___ [6.] ___ ___

___   ___ ___ ___   ___ ___ ___
5   3 1 4   3 6 2

WEATHER AND CLIMATE

Weather and climate are not the same things. **WEATHER** is what you have on any given day. **CLIMATE** is the weather of a region on Earth averaged over a long period of time.

Wither's Weather Words

Help the wither match the correct word to each clue and write the word in the boxes, as in a crossword.

ANEMOMETER	PRECIPITATION	TEMPERATE CLIMATE
BAROMETER	RAIN GAUGE	THERMOMETER
HYGROMETER	SATELLITE	WIND VANE

1. Water (in various forms) that falls to the ground

2. A tool in space that monitors weather and climate on Earth

3. A tool that measures wind speed

4. A tool that measures wind direction

5. A tool that measures atmospheric pressure (the force pushing on objects from the weight of the air above them)

6. A tool that collects and measures rainfall

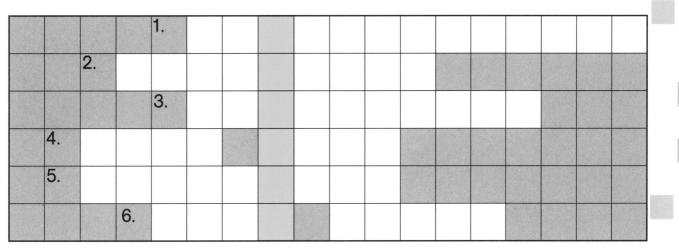

If you and the wither place the words correctly, the letters in the yellow column will spell the answer to this question:

What is the brightest light level you can enjoy in the game without worrying about snow and ice layers melting?

REAL BIOMES

Many Minecraft biomes are based on real-world climates.

BENEATH EACH ILLUSTRATION, WRITE THE LETTER PAIR FROM THE CLIMATE DESCRIPTION THAT BEST FITS THE BIOME PICTURED.

jungle	ice plains	desert	extreme hills

Descriptions

ES *Mountain climate:* Temperatures decrease with altitude, and high peaks are covered with snow.

AN *Temperate climate:* Warm and cold temperatures, no extremes, and rain through the year.

EC *Polar climate:* Cold temperatures all year and little precipitation.

IC *Tropical climate:* Warm temperatures all year and lots of rain.

OR *Desert climate:* Dry, very little rain, and extreme temperatures.

If you've matched the correct description to each picture, the letters will spell the answer to the question below. Can you separate the letters into the two-word answer?

WHAT DO SCIENTISTS STUDY IN ORDER TO LEARN WHAT THE EARTH WAS LIKE LONG AGO?

(Hint: They come from Antarctica.)

__ __ __   __ __ __ __ __

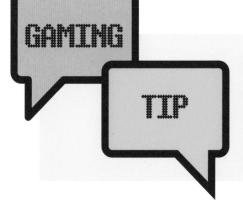

Check out the weather mods available for Minecraft online. You can add more dramatic storms, like hurricanes, to the game.

ADAPTATIONS are physical and behavioral traits that help animals survive. Having fur that matches an animal's environment is a common real-world adaptation. It provides **CAMOUFLAGE**, helping the animal blend with its surroundings. Prey animals with this adaptation can hide from predators, and predators can sneak up on prey without being noticed.

Minecraft rabbits usually have one of six different skins. ("Skins" are the textures used on the mobs.) What skin a rabbit has is determined by the biome where it spawns. For instance, 80% of rabbits in snowy biomes will be white, and 100% of rabbits in desert biomes will be gold.

Create a Creature

Invent an animal or mob and give it adaptations that allow it to thrive in one of the Minecraft biomes. What unique features help it find food and defend itself? Draw your creature below.

Adapt to Match

Many animals are adapted to match their environments. You need to adapt to reading backward to match the eight animals with one of their adaptations. Write the letter of the adaptation under the correct animal.

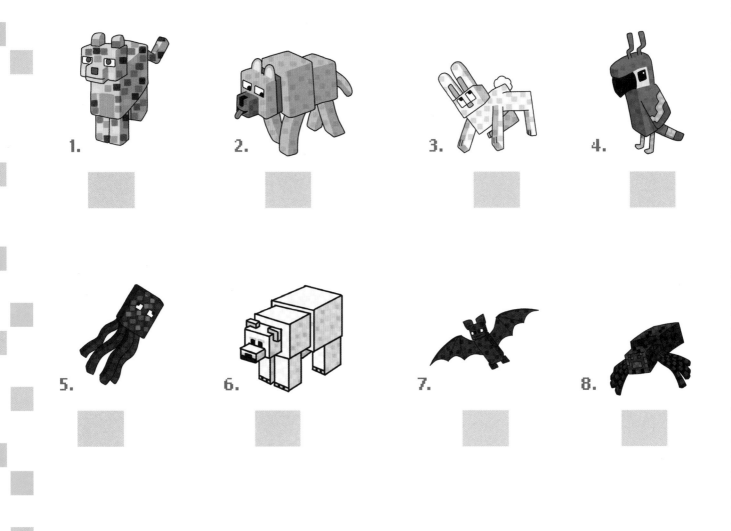

1.

2.

3.

4.

5.

6.

7.

8.

K. Yerp egral llik ot kcap a ni tnuh yeht.

F. Tnuh ot sbew dliub slamina eseht fo ynam.

I. Doof dnif ot dna yaw sti dnif ot noitacolohce sesu lamina siht.

H. Retaw gnidnuorrus duolc ot kni toohs nac lamina siht.

S. Mraw lamina citcra siht peek spleh taf fo reyal a.

E. Lamina siht looc pleh ecafrus eht ot esolc slessev doolb htiw srae gnol.

N. Senob ffo taem naelc lammam siht spleh repapdnas ekil eugnot a.

T. Sdees dna stun tae ti spleh lamina siht no kaeb devruc eht.

Use the letters you added to the grey boxes to fill in the answer to the riddle below!

Why is a giraffe's neck so long?

___ ___ ___   ___ ___ ___ ___   ___ ___ ___ ___ ___
7   4   6   8   3   3   4   6   4   7   1   2

Some plants grow where it's hard to get food and sunlight and where they might be eaten by animals. **PLANTS ADAPT TO THEIR ENVIRONMENTS IN ORDER TO SURVIVE.** Some plants grow large, brightly colored, or scented flowers to attract pollinators. Some plants grow thorns so animals won't eat them. How do carnivorous, or meat-eating, plants survive? **RESEARCH THE VENUS FLYTRAP PLANT ONLINE AND WRITE ONE OR MORE FACTS ABOUT IT BELOW.**

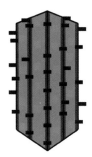

Meat-Eating Plant Mob
INVENT A CARNIVOROUS (MEAT-EATING) PLANT FOR MINECRAFT. Where will it spawn naturally? What animals will it eat? How will it trap its prey? How has it adapted to its environment? Draw and describe your plant here.

A Biome Like Mine

Minecraft has many biomes and creatures that inhabit them, just like in the real world. Consider the landscape and features of the town or area where you live. **INVENT A NEW MINECRAFT BIOME USING YOUR OWN SURROUNDINGS FOR INSPIRATION.**

Name of my biome:

1. What kind of terrain does your biome have?

2. What is the climate of your biome?

3. What resources are available?

4. What plants grow?

5. What animals do you encounter most?

6. How have the plants and animals adapted to this environment?

Draw and color a portion of your biome here. Include plants and animals.

RESOURCE MANAGEMENT

The real world has a limited supply of many natural resources, like fresh water, clean air, coal, and oil. **HUMANS ALL OVER THE PLANET ARE WORKING TO CONSERVE, OR SAVE, AVAILABLE RESOURCES AND FIND RENEWABLE RESOURCES**—like sun and wind power, fast-growing wood alternatives, and more—to replace the limited ones. Answer the questions below. Ask your parents for help if needed.

What are some ways you and your family conserve water?

What are some ways you and your family conserve energy?

Collecting Resources

It's harvest season; time to bring in the wheat. You want to be efficient and gather as much as possible. **DRAW A LINE FROM START TO STOP THAT PASSES THROUGH EVERY WHEAT ONCE AND ONLY ONCE.** Your line can go up, down, left, or right, but not diagonally. Ready, set, harvest!

START ⬇

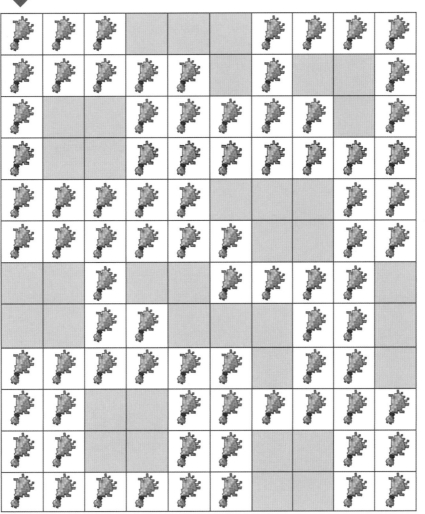

⬇ **STOP**

Conditionals are if-then statements written into computer code that tell a program to do something only under certain conditions.

You make if-then decisions every day. If it's raining, you might wear a raincoat. If you finish your homework, you might get to play video games.

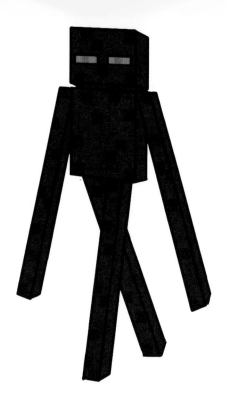

FINISH THESE CONDITIONAL STATEMENTS USING WHAT YOU KNOW ABOUT MINECRAFTING:

1. **IF** a player stares at an Enderman, **THEN** the Enderman will

.

2. **IF** a player sleeps in a bed, **THEN** their spawn point is

.

3. **IF** a creeper comes within three blocks of a player, **THEN** it will eventually   .

Only When If-Then

NEED SOMETHING FUN TO DO? TRY THIS MINECRAFTING CONDITIONALS GAME WITH TWO OR MORE PLAYERS.

1. If you've ever been killed by a skeleton in Minecraft, then yodel for 10 seconds.

2. If your shoes have laces, then tie the laces from the left shoe to the laces on the right shoe and proceed carefully to the closest door.

3. If you've ever worn a pumpkin on your head in Minecraft, then say the name of a pumpkin dessert in an Enderman voice.

4. If you've never built a redstone contraption, then do an impression of a creeper exploding.

5. If you have a first name that starts with a consonant, then spell Ender Dragon backward in a singing voice.

SPIDER WEBS

Spiders secrete silky threads used to engineer webs that trap prey. Spider threads are light, flexible, and surprisingly strong. They are comparable to steel and Kevlar (the stuff bulletproof vests are made of).

Web Challenge

HELP THE SPIDER NAVIGATE ITS WAY TO THE CENTER OF ITS STRONG WEB TO EAT ITS PREY.

Connecting Threads

Scientists use spider silk as a model to design medical devices and products that need to be flexible, light, strong, water-resistant, or sticky. Some of the items they've come up with so far are artificial tendons and ligaments, thread for stitches, adhesives, and bandages.

How would you use a lightweight, flexible, super-strong, water-resistant, sticky thread? **WHAT INVENTIONS COULD YOU MAKE WITH SPIDER SILK, AND WHAT EVERYDAY PROBLEMS COULD YOU SOLVE?** Write your ideas here.

GENETICS

INHERITED TRAITS ARE CHARACTERISTICS PASSED FROM PARENTS TO OFFSPRING. ALL ORGANISMS INHERIT TRAITS FROM THEIR PARENTS. Some characteristics to look for in animals are body structure, skin texture, fur color, and shapes of eyes, ears, noses, and faces. Family members share many traits, which is why they often look similar.

An *animal never gets a trait from just one parent*. Rather, every trait gets input from both parents. So even though a piglet has a crooked tail like her father, she got genetic input for her tail from both her mother and father.

Mob Babies

Below are sets of mob parents with different characteristics that their baby can inherit. **DRAW THEIR BABY IN THE BOXES PROVIDED USING TRAITS AND GENETIC INPUT FROM BOTH PARENTS.** For example, choose your baby zombie's eye color based on its parents' eye colors.

BONES

Minecraft skeletons drop bones. Thankfully, your skeleton does not!

Bones are part of the skeletal system. **ANIMALS THAT HAVE BONES, INCLUDING HUMANS, ARE CALLED VERTEBRATES.** Bones serve many functions. Some protect soft, fragile parts of the body. For example, your skull protects your brain. Other bones help you move, like the bones in your arms and legs, which support muscle.

Know Your Bones

Your body has over 200 bones, but only 10 have been dropped here. **CAN YOU CIRCLE ALL 10 BONE NAMES IN THE CHART BELOW?**

Cranium	Mandible	Vertebrae	Clavicle	Navel
Sternum	Ribs	Pelvis	Cartilage	Teeth
Liver	Femur	Nostril	Tibia	Fibula

No Bones About It

THESE 10 STATEMENTS ARE EITHER TRUE OR FALSE. YOU DECIDE. If you think a statement is true, circle the letter in the T column. If you think it's false, circle the letter in the F column.

1.	T	F	Most people have 12 ribs, but a few (very few) have 13.
2.	T	F	The biggest joint in your body is your shoulder.
3.	T	F	Your body has 206 bones.
4.	T	F	More than half your bones are in your hands and feet.
5.	T	F	Bone marrow, in the middle of most bones, is stiff and hard as steel.
6.	T	F	The smallest bone in your body is the stapes in the ear.
7.	T	F	The largest bone in your body is the humerus in your upper arm.
8.	T	F	Only about 10% of Earth's animals have bones.
9.	T	F	Human babies are born with twice as many bones as you have.
10.	T	F	Broken bones repair themselves.

MAGNETISM is a force all around you. You can't see it, but you can see what it does. Magnets exert a force, attracting certain metals, particularly iron, nickel, and cobalt.

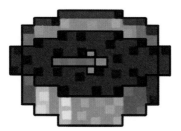

MAGNETS come in different shapes, such as bars, horseshoes, and rings. Each has two poles, called **NORTH** and **SOUTH.** North and south poles (opposite poles) are attracted to each other, while two north poles or two south poles (like poles) repel each other.

Magnet Magic Trick

Magnets are so fun and fascinating that they're used in many magic tricks. Here's one you can try. **IMPRESS YOUR FRIENDS BY MAKING ONE PAPERCLIP MAGICALLY (OR MAGNETICALLY) STICK TO ANOTHER.** You need two metal paperclips and a small (but strong enough) magnet you can hide behind a finger or two.

1. Hold one curved end of a paperclip between your thumb and one or two fingers of one hand. Also hold the magnet between these same fingers, pressed against the paperclip. Keeping the magnet hidden can be tricky. You'll need to practice.

2. With your other hand, place the second paperclip so it's barely touching the exposed end of the first one. The force of the magnet will attract the second paperclip to the first and hold it there. Impressive!

Now challenge your friends to do the same—but don't give them the magnet!

Stuck!

This iron golem is magnetized. As he wanders around the village path he's on, magnetic objects stick to him. **CIRCLE THE ITEMS THAT ARE MOST LIKELY TO STICK TO HIM.** Remember, a magnetic force works over a distance, so he doesn't have to be touching an item to have it attract and stick.

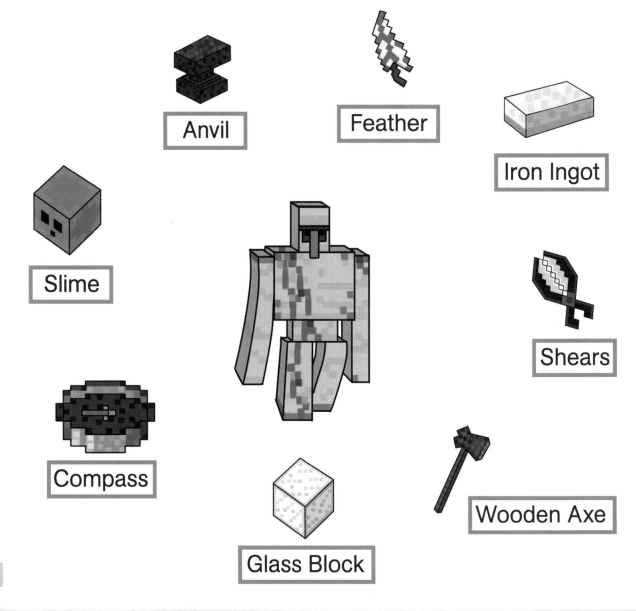

Anvil

Feather

Iron Ingot

Slime

Shears

Compass

Glass Block

Wooden Axe

SOUND

Sound is a vibration that travels through air, water, or solid matter and can be heard.

WHEN AN OBJECT VIBRATES, IT MOVES THE AIR AROUND IT, MAKING PARTICLES IN THE AIR VIBRATE, TOO. The vibrating particles close to the object cause the particles next to them to vibrate, and on and on, farther away from the original vibrating object. This flow of the vibration away from the object is called a wave.

THINK OUTSIDE THE BOOK

Try this experiment to see the effects of sound waves. Stretch plastic wrap tightly over a bowl and secure it with a rubber band. Sprinkle pepper on top of the plastic. With permission and care, bang a metal pot loudly with a metal spoon near the bowl. Watch the pepper closely. What happens? Why do you think it happens?

Sound Words

A piston hits each of the letter strings below from the left-hand side, causing a chain reaction, like a wave. When the piston hits the first letter, it changes the letter to the one that follows it in the alphabet. The change in the first letter causes a change in the letter next to it, and on and on. The wave travels through the whole word, changing each of the letters in turn.

CAN YOU IDENTIFY THE SOUND WORDS THAT THE PISTON CHANGED? (Note: The letter Z changes to an A when it's hit by a wave.)

U N K T L D = ___ ___ ___ ___ ___ ___

O H S B G = ___ ___ ___ ___ ___

D B G N = ___ ___ ___ ___

D Z Q C Q T L = ___ ___ ___ ___ ___ ___ ___

U N B Z K   B G N Q C R = ___ ___ ___ ___ ___

___ ___ ___ ___ ___ ___

WATCH OUT! An evoker rolled the letters below from the ones that come before them in the alphabet. The correct letters spell the answer to this joke. **DECODE THE ANSWER.**

What did the skeleton say when the bat squeaked in her ear?

P V D I !   U I B U   N F H B I F S U A !

__ __ __ __! __ __ __ __

__ __ __ __ __ __ __ __ __ __ __!

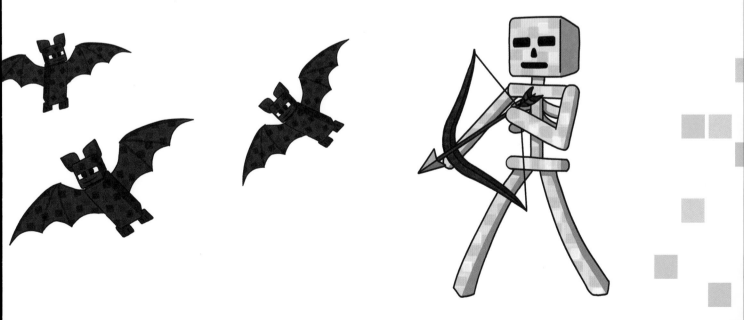

MAKING WAVES

SLAM!

Facts about Minecraft's sounds are coming at you on the waves below. **READ EVERY OTHER LETTER ON THE WAVE TO DECIPHER THE MESSAGES.**

Minecraft's music and sound-effect producer is

D W A R N O I N E G L O R T O R S Y E A N G F A E I L N D

— — — — — — — — — — — — —

DANIEL ROSENFELD

Originally, he wanted to be

A O S M T S U S N O T B C O A R R E D H R R I E V P E U R S

— —————— ——— ———————

A STUNT CAR DRIVER

His Minecraft skin is the default skin with this one change:

A R J A U T K O E E B L O A X M H A E L A L D

— ————————— —————

A JUKEBOX HEAD

Ghast sounds are made by

D D A L N R I O E W L D S L C I A U T

————————— , ————

DANIEL'S CAT

FOSSILS

Remains of ancient life are preserved in rocks as fossils. **THESE FOSSILS PROVIDE INFORMATION ABOUT THE ORGANISMS AND ENVIRONMENTAL CONDITIONS FROM MILLIONS AND BILLIONS OF YEARS AGO.** They are also evidence of evolution.

Conditions have to be just right for fossils to form, so very few organisms become fossilized. It happens when an animal is buried by sediment (mud, volcanic ash, sand, etc.) soon after it dies. Layer upon layer of sediment builds up. The animal's soft tissues decompose quickly, but the bones remain. Gradually, the bones are replaced by rock minerals, which are the fossils you see in museums. **AS EARTH'S TECTONIC PLATES SHIFT, LAYERS OF ROCK THAT ENCASE FOSSILS ARE PUSHED TO THE SURFACE.**

DID YOU KNOW?

Erosion from wind, rain, and rivers can expose fossils near the surface, as can people who dig and look for them.

Fossil Match

FOSSILS TELL US A LOT ABOUT A CREATURE'S BONE STRUCTURE, and every kind of animal has a unique bone structure. Match each forearm to the correct animal. Write the number in the blank line.

1. Bird

2. Lion

3. Human

4. Frog

5. Horse

6. Whale

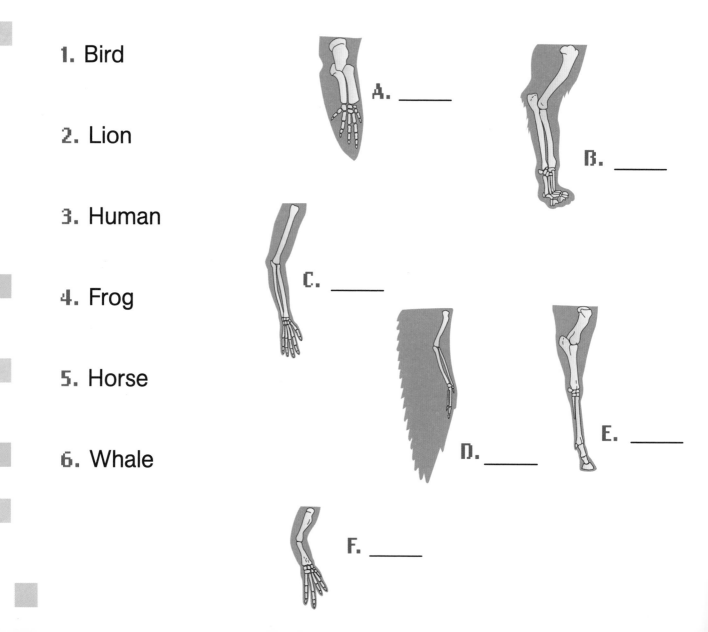

A. _____

B. _____

C. _____

D. _____

E. _____

F. _____

THINK OF YOUR FAVORITE MONSTER OR MOB IN MINECRAFT. WHAT WOULD ITS FOSSIL LOOK LIKE? DRAW IT HERE:

ANSWERS

THE PHYSICS OF FORCE

SHAPE SIFTER

CIRCLE	SQUARE	CYLINDER	RECTANGLE
PENTAGON	SQUARE-BASED PYRAMID	OCTAGON	SPHERE
CUBE	TRIANGLE	TRIANGULAR PRISM	HEXAGON

MINERAL HARDNESS
Hard, Harder, Hardest
1. Talc
2. Gypsum
3. Calcite
4. Fluorite
5. Apatite
6. Orthoclase Feldspar
7. Quartz
8. Topaz
9. Corundum
10. Diamond

VIDEO GAME DESIGN
Answers may vary.

LIGHTNING ROD MATH

PREDICTING PATTERNS
Predicting a Mob's Moves
Bat ends his journey asleep in the cave

1.
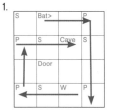

Bat dies when he runs into the door.
Game over!

2.
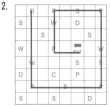

Observing Mob Patterns
Answers may vary.

MATH GETS REAL
Screen Time Dilemma
Keaton has 5½ hours (330 minutes) from the time he gets home from school to the time he goes to bed. He walks his dog for 30 minutes, spends 2 hours (120 minutes) at fencing practice, ½ hour (30 minutes) eating dinner, ½ hour (30 minutes) doing dishes, 1 hour doing homework (60 minutes), and 20 minutes showering. That's 4 hours and 50 minutes (290 minutes) used for chores and activities. Yes, Keaton does have time to play Minecraft. Keaton has 40 minutes to play Minecraft, for 2 in-game day/night cycles.

ALGORITHMS
Order Up!
D, E, A, F, C, B

Write an Algorithm
Answers may vary.

RUBE GOLDBERG MACHINES
What's the Point?
Maximum effort for minimal results

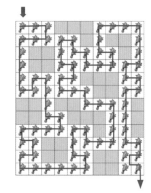

SIMPLE AND COMPLEX MACHINES
Laugh Machine
Lever, Wedge, Screw, Pulley, Wheel and Axle, Inclined Plane
What simple machine can cut a Minecraft ocean biome in half?
A See Saw (a sea saw, get it?)

WEATHER AND CLIMATE
Wither's Weather Words
1. Precipitation
2. Satellite
3. Anemometer
4. Wind Vane
5. Barometer
6. Rain Gauge
Eleven is the highest light level you can enjoy without snow and ice layers melting.

REAL BIOMES
What do scientists study in order to learn what the earth was like long ago? (Hint: They come from Antarctica.) ICE CORES

Ice cores are cylinders drilled out of the Antarctic ice. It's like the tube of slush you get when you stick a straw into a slushy drink, put your finger on the top of the straw, and then pull the straw out. Scientists have drilled ice cores from two miles below the surface where the ice was formed a long time ago. By studying the old ice, we can learn what the climate was like when that ice formed.

ANIMAL ADAPTATIONS
Adapt to Match
1. N, 2. K, 3. E, 4. T, 5. H, 6. S, 7. I, 8. F
Why is a giraffe's neck so long?
Its feet stink

PLANT ADAPTATIONS
Answers may vary.

WORLDS WITHIN WORLDS
A Biome Like Mine
Answers will vary.

RESOURCE MANAGEMENT
Answer may vary. Some answers may include:
What are some ways that you and your family conserve water?
Turning off the water while you brush your teeth.
Taking shorter showers.
Using rain barrels to collect water.

What are some ways that you and your family conserve energy?
Turning off the lights when you're not using them.
Using solar-powered lights or adding solar panels to your home.
Using energy-efficient lightbulbs in your home.

Collection Resources

CONDITIONALS
1. If a player stares at an Enderman, then the Enderman will teleport toward the player and attack it.
2. If a player sleeps in a bed, then their spawn point is set at that location.
3. If a creeper comes within three blocks of a player, then it will eventually explode!

SPIDER WEBS
Web Challenge

CONNECTING THREADS
Answers will vary.

GENETICS
Answers will vary.

BONES
Know Your Bones
Cranium
Mandible
Vertebrae
Clavicle
Sternum
Ribs
Pelvis
Femur
Tibia
Fibula

No Bones About It
1. T, 2. F, 3. T, 4. T, 5. F, 6. T, 7. F, 8. T, 9. F, 10. T

MAGNETS
Stuck
Circle the following items:
Anvil, Iron Ingot, Shears, Compass.

SOUND
Think Outside the Book
Banging the pot creates sound vibrations that cause the pepper to bounce or move.

Sound Words
Volume: how loud or quiet a sound is
Pitch: the lowness or highness of sound
Echo: sound waves that bounce off objects
Eardrum: sound waves cause this membrane in the ear to vibrate
Vocal chords: these vibrate when a person talks or a cat purrs

What did the skeleton say when the bat squeaked in her ear?
Ouch! That megahertz!

A hertz (Hz) measures wave frequency. One hertz is one wave cycle per second. A megahertz (MHz) is 1,000,000 cycles per second. The average human ear detects sounds between 20 and 20,000 Hz. Sound waves around 20 Hz are low-pitched, *bass* frequencies. Sound waves above 5,000 Hz are high-pitched, *treble* frequencies, like Minecraft bat squeaks. Did you notice that people can't hear frequencies above 20,000 Hz? That means you can't hear sound from waves that are 1,000,000 Hz (or 1 MHz.) Radio waves are measured in MHz.

MAKING WAVES
Daniel Rosenfeld
A stunt car driver
A jukebox head
Daniel's cat

FOSSILS
Fossil Match
1. D
2. B
3. C
4. F
5. E
6. A